Saying All That Can Be Said

Harvard-Yenching Institute Monograph Series 134

Saying All That Can Be Said

The Art of Describing Sex in Jin Ping Mei

Keith McMahon

Published by the Harvard University Asia Center
Distributed by Harvard University Press
Cambridge (Massachusetts) and London 2023

Printed in the United States of America

The Harvard University Asia Center publishes a monograph series and, in coordination with the Fairbank Center for Chinese Studies, the Korea Institute, the Reischauer Institute of Japanese Studies, and other faculties and institutes, administers research projects designed to further scholarly understanding of China, Japan, Vietnam, Korea, and other Asian countries. The Center also sponsors projects addressing multidisciplinary and regional issues in Asia.

The Harvard-Yenching Institute, founded in 1928, is an independent foundation dedicated to the advancement of higher education in the humanities and social sciences in Asia. Headquartered on the campus of Harvard University, the Institute provides fellowships for advanced research, training, and graduate studies at Harvard by competitively selected faculty and graduate students from Asia. The Institute also supports a range of academic activities at its fifty partner universities and research institutes across Asia. At Harvard, the Institute promotes East Asian studies through annual contributions to the Harvard-Yenching Library and publication of the *Harvard Journal of Asiatic Studies* and the Harvard-Yenching Institute Monograph Series.

Library of Congress Cataloging-in-Publication Data

Names: McMahon, Keith, author.
Title: Saying all that can be said : the art of describing sex in Jin Ping Mei / Keith McMahon.
Other titles: Harvard-Yenching Institute monograph series ; 134.
Description: Cambridge, Massachusetts : Harvard University Asia Center, 2023. |
Series: Harvard-Yenching Institute monograph series; 134 | Includes bibliographical references and index. |
Identifiers: LCCN 2022035946 | ISBN 9780674291355 (hardcover)
Subjects: LCSH: Xiaoxiaosheng. Jin Ping Mei ci hua. | Erotic literature, Chinese—16th century—History and criticism. | Chinese literature—Ming dynasty, 1368–1644—History and criticism. | Sex in literature—16th century. | Sex and history—China.
Classification: LCC PL2275.E74 M35 2023 | DDC 895.13/46—dc23/eng/20221004
LC record available at https://lccn.loc.gov/2022035946

Index by Mary Mortensen

♾ Printed on acid-free paper

Last figure below indicates year of this printing
30 29 28 27 26 25 24 23

Contents

Illustrations

Preface

After I delivered a talk on the novel *Jin Ping Mei* 金瓶梅 some years ago, someone asked a question that has often been asked: whether or not the novel could be read without the sexually explicit passages. My mission that day was to emphasize the worth of the totality of the novel, so I replied that those passages were essential. But I would no longer so insist on that. No one has to read them, though I nevertheless believe that those passages are so remarkable and unprecedented that they should be taken as seriously as any other part of the novel. But how to examine and talk about them is a perilous question. What words to use to qualify them is a challenge: are they explicit, graphic, obscene, pornographic, erotic, or high erotic? These are some of the words that I use as I go through this process. How to evaluate these passages is another question, which I answer in this book, in the simplest terms, by considering them as aesthetically artful. The explicit renditions of bodies in sexual acts are both linguistically diverse and intricately interwoven with the complex plot. In other words, they are inherent elements of the narrative.

My point is that pornography speaks, though how to define the word "pornography" in terms of *Jin Ping Mei* is another major question. How should that dangerous and sensational word be used? At a recent conference, some people recommended abandoning it when speaking of premodern literature. It is anachronistic and too tainted with Eurocentric bias. But the word has a practical use for the purpose of categorizing and evaluating a range of topics having to do with sexually explicit scenes in both *Jin Ping Mei* and dozens of other fictional works of the Ming and Qing. The word is also useful for the purpose of defining what the phrase "sexually explicit" means. Situating the novel in its own history of sexual culture, describing and evaluating the types and modes of language used in such scenes, addressing the situations and personalities of the characters involved, and considering the context of other sexually explicit fiction in the Ming and Qing are the main areas that I explore in this book under the broad rubric of pornography, though I mainly stay within the realm of Chinese literature of the sixteenth to nineteenth centuries.

The above questions signal the problematic nature of writing about sex.[1] Will you look as though you are reading the novel on the sly, so to speak, and only enjoying its obscenity—as Zhang Zhupo 張竹坡 said long ago?[2] Or are you too reserved and circumspect, too careful to say what is there to be said, too delicate and brittle because you are afraid of missing a key perspective or of offending someone? Another issue has to do with the limits of sexual and erotic vocabulary and the translation and transition between Chinese then and English now. The Chinese repertoire has a long history and does not easily or transparently transition to contemporary English: much glossing is needed.

A reference to the songs that appear in *Jin Ping Mei* helps clarify how I treat the sexually explicit passages in the novel. Many of the songs are a popular form from the late Ming called *qu* 曲, which the author copies copiously from preexisting songbooks and plays as well as from memory, and in some cases he creates them for the novel. As with many of the passages of sexual description, many of the songs can be easily understood by modern readers. But other songs have meanings that modern readers can understand only if they know the songs' historical context, as in the case of four songs in chapter 27 that are from the famous early Ming play *Pipa ji* 琵琶記 (The lute). The songs in *Pipa ji* use delicate language to refer to the sublime lovemaking of the two central characters. When the same songs appear in a scene of sex between Ximen Qing 西門慶 and Pan Jinlian 潘金蓮, they drastically diverge from earlier and later scenes in the same chapter, in which Ximen Qing has rough sex with two of his wives. The title of the play does not appear in the novel; readers would

1. That issue ultimately also includes making films about sex, whether fictional or documentary (as in films about sex workers). See de Villiers, *Sexography*.

2. See Roy, "Chang Chu-p'o on How to Read the *Chin P'ing Mei*."

have understood the irony of the allusion. It is the same in passages of sexual activity in which Ximen Qing is in no instance without his aphrodisiacs and sex tools, which were widely available in the late Ming, which the novel refers to but with only minimal description, and about which readers of the times would be presumed to know. The songs and passages of sexual description share the fact that they are there to show Ximen Qing and his partners engaging in pleasure and entertainment. They can be entertaining in themselves, especially in terms of the novel's sheer linguistic exuberance. But they also have their particular structures of meaning. Kissing and thrusting, for example, are not simply what one might assume based on twenty-first-century expectations. Descriptions of sex differ in terms of mode of language (whether lofty or graphic, for example) or in terms of the status and personalities of the characters. Sex with concubine Pan Jinlian differs from sex with wet nurse Ruyi 如意 or courtesan Zheng 鄭. Some passages quote directly from other works; some words and images appear repeatedly, as if the author was resorting to formulaic ingredients for constructing sexual scenes; and other passages seem entirely unique. These are the types of variables that I consider.

My assumption throughout is that the passages of sexually explicit description are full of thematic meaning and aesthetic purpose. The novel displays an exuberance of pornographic portrayal that it sustains from beginning to end. The same energetic voice devotes itself both to portraying the erotic sublime and to portraying the graphic and explicit plunge into excess, not to mention the deceit, manipulation, and conflict that come before, during, and after. Sometimes it is a matter of describing the pure energy of one sexual body entwining and colliding with another, leaving aside for the moment the complexities of before and after.

During the writing of this book, David Roy's translation of the novel has been a constant aid, supplying me with interpretations of difficult passages, translations that I often adopt, and references to multitudes of sources. Li Ling's work on the art of the bedchamber and other related texts has been of invaluable use, and the conference in honor of his seventieth birthday (held on June 12–13, 2017, at Zhejiang University in Hangzhou, China) gave me a chance to explore one of my earliest topics in this project, of which chapter 2 is a longer and more developed version. The chapter also appeared in earlier form as an article in 2019 under the title "The Art of the Bedchamber and *Jin Ping Mei* 金瓶梅" (in *Nan Nü: Men, Women and Gender in China*, 21.1: 1–37). Two other conferences gave me chances to express and develop ideas in a rich context of scholarly interaction: Comparative Pornographies: Transnational Approaches to Writing Sex, East and West, held on March 9, 2019, at the University of California at Los Angeles; and the symposium in honor of David Roy, *Jin Ping Mei* and the World: Translation and Transculturation, held on December 5, 2019, at Harvard University. A version of chapter 3 appears as "The Language of Sex in *Jin Ping Mei*" in the December 2022 issue of *Harvard Journal of Asiatic Studies.* In addition, a chapter called "Wives, Concubines, Prostitutes, and Other Men's Wives: The Portrayal of Sex in *Plum in the Golden Vase*," appears in the volume *Approaches to Teaching The Plum in the Golden Vase (The Golden Lotus)*, which takes wording and ideas from various parts of this manuscript; and a chapter called "Sexual Portrayal in *Jin Ping Mei*" appears in the volume *Jin Ping Mei, A Wild Horse in Chinese Literature*, published in celebration of the Danish translation of *Jin Ping Mei*, and which takes ideas from various parts of this manuscript.

Many thanks go to the following people who helped with sources and other information, read and commented on parts of the project, or were present at the above events, including: Vincent Durand-Dastès, Li Ling, Li Xiaorong, Liu Yongqiang, Meng Fanzhi, Pan Jianguo, Pan Yue, Qi Lintao, David Rolston, Andy Schonebaum, Simon Schuchat, Mark Stevenson, Giovanni Vitiello, Wang Jian, Wu Cuncun, Paola Zamperini, and the two reader-referees, who provided generous critiques. Others too numerous to name wrote books and articles that have given me great inspiration, Ding Naifei in particular. Vickie Doll of the Watson Library East Asian Collection at the University of Kansas helped countless times with hard-to-find sources. For final production of the book, my gratitude goes to Jeanne Ferris, copyeditor; the two production managers, Kristen Bettcher and Kristen Wanner; and Mary Mortenson of Lawrence, Kansas, who created the index.

My wife, Deborah Peterson, always comes up with the best metaphors, analogies, and examples, as well as just the right word, and always in record time. This book would be better if I had the same brilliance. During its writing I enjoyed the company of Miska in New Haven, Connecticut, my granddaughter, Kaija Ann Staples, in Washington, D.C., who came into the world in 2019, and grandson, Liam Neal Staples, who joined us in 2022.

A Note on Textual Conventions

The translations from *Jin Ping Mei* are mine unless otherwise noted.

For references to Chinese novels, I give chapter (or in some cases *juan* 卷) number followed by page number. For example, JPM 1.20 indicates chapter 1, page 20, of *Jin Ping Mei*, the Chongzhen edition. JPMCH 1.20 refers to chapter 1, page 20, of *Jin Ping Mei cihua*, the *Liren* 里仁 edition. JPMCH, Bu Jian, ed., refers to the edition with interlinear comments by Zhang Zhupo. Roy, 1.1.20 refers to volume 1, chapter 1, page 20, of David Roy's translation *The Plum in the Golden Vase*. If only one number appears, it refers to the chapter.

For quotations in Chinese that appear in the main text or the footnotes, I give pinyin romanization for very short passages only.

CHAPTER I

Saying All That Can Be Said

Creative Obscenity

Jin Ping Mei 金瓶梅, or *The Plum in the Golden Vase*, is one of the most admired novels in Chinese history. Written in the late sixteenth century, it is a cutting social satire, a vivid portrait of Ming 明 dynasty (1368–1644) popular culture, a tour de force of linguistic style, and a penetrating rendition of gender roles. But it is most famous and infamous because of its shameless sexual portrayals, which have led to the book's censorship for most of its existence—including the present. These contents have generated both notoriety and fascination, but also an overall hesitation among scholars to put them to close analysis. How, after all, does the language of sex function in the novel? What does the representation of sexual activity accomplish in terms of its use of language and imagery? What, in short, is *Jin Ping Mei*'s art of describing sex? The novel's sexually explicit portrayals are in fact full of thematic content and loaded with social and aesthetic meaning.[1] Readers cannot but feel that the author is there to say all that can be said about sex in a polygamist's household in a wealthy urban setting of sixteenth-century Ming China. He does not care about how explicit and obscene he needs to be. As Huang Lin 黄霖 says, "It is as if the *Jin Ping Mei* author has soaked in those everyday surroundings

1. "The assumption here is that sex stands for more than sex in *Chin p'ing mei*" (Carlitz, *Rhetoric*, 25, 44).

to such an extent that he doesn't take the obscene as being obscene, but instead simply sees it as an objective part of human existence."[2] It is as if the author is discovering a newly creative and constructive way to write, taking it as far as he can go. The seventeenth-century commentator to the Chongzhen 崇禎 edition of the novel writes: "This book is about exposing all the affairs of the world, no matter how trivial or momentous, no matter what level of intensity. Whatever the world may hold, the author doesn't hesitate to penetrate its depths" (此書只一味打破世情, 故不論事之大小冷熱, 但世情所有, 便一筆刺入).[3] The word "exposes" also translates as "smashes" and "breaks" (*dapuo* 打破), as in smashing the standards of decency. "Penetrate" also translates as "stab" and "pierce" (*ciru* 刺入), as an author does when engaging in satire. Saying all that can be said is my shorthand way of rendering this comment, which comes at a moment when two friends of the rich, polygamous merchant Ximen Qing 西門慶 devour seven bowls of pork and noodles apiece, shortly after which a servant delivers a set of rare delicacies—which one of the men similarly gobbles up, amazed that such things exist. The portrayal of wanton eating appears alongside that of wanton sex, both "affairs of the world" (*shiqing* 世情), though no one is in doubt that sex is the more central of the two. Everything fits together in one complete picture, as told in the vigorous dance of words that describes it.

Jin Ping Mei is far from being the first piece of writing in Chinese history to represent sex in such an open way. The practice of writing explicitly about sex had already existed for nearly two millennia, beginning with the texts of the "art of the bedchamber" (*fangzhong shu* 房中術), which use elegant and euphemistic language to discourse about the art of sex for the sake of nourishing health and longevity. The art of writing elegantly and metaphorically about sex also existed for many centuries in the tradition of sensual, erotic poetry that goes by the name "fragrant and bedazzling" (*xiangyan* 香艷), which saw a resurgence in the late Ming.[4] In addition, a wealth of texts about pleasure apart from the sexual realm

2. Huang Lin, *Huang Lin jiang*, 185.

3. *Jin Ping Mei*, *Xinke xiuxiang piping Jin Ping Mei* 新刻繡像批評金瓶梅, 52.681, the Chongzhen 崇禎 (1628–1644) version (hereafter *JPM*, in contrast to JPMCH, the *cihua* edition, and JPMCH, Bu Jian, ed., the edition containing interlinear comments by Zhang Zhupo 張竹坡).

4. See Li Xiaorong, *Poetics and Politics*.

has existed since ancient times. In spite of changes through history, these texts share a common emphasis on a combination of erudition and refinement in the incorporation of sensual and aesthetic pleasure into daily life.[5] But though *Jin Ping Mei* is an heir of these traditions, its art and aesthetic of describing sex and sexual enjoyment is something new, depicting them not only in the refined way of past times but also in newly vulgar and graphic ways. In so doing, the novel assumes that sexual pleasure is something to be reckoned with and implies that it is neither easily ignored or diminished, nor necessarily easily enjoyed.

The length and extent of this and other Ming novels' sexual portrayals are unprecedented. How this came to be so—that is, the historical context for such an appearance—is not easy to describe. The succession of Ming emperors, officials, and other prominent men notorious for sexual license certainly provides something of a backdrop, though other such men and women have existed since the distant past and are the subject of many writings from ancient times through to the novels and stories of the Ming and Qing.[6] The expansion of urban life is another factor, which allowed for an alternate cultural space that challenged imperial styles of authority. Accompanying such an expansion was a growth in importance of money and commerce, which was further accompanied by the growth in sixteenth-century China of an economy of conspicuous consumption and a value system based on excess and luxury.[7] All such factors help explain the social milieu that *Jin Ping Mei* describes and satirizes, a milieu in which Ximen Qing is the quintessential embodiment of a new kind of man. Having no parents or siblings, and thus shorn of the obligations of belonging to a clan, he is a sharp businessman who devotes himself to two main pursuits: the accumulation and spending of money and the avid enjoyment of sexual pleasure.[8] He has at hand a wide array of aphrodisiacs,

5. See Nylan, *Chinese Pleasure Book*, 17–18, which focuses on pleasure as encompassed by the word *le* 樂, "to take or derive pleasure in."

6. On *Jin Ping Mei* in light of Ming emperors, see Huang Lin, *Huang Lin jiang*, 160–175; Carlitz, *Rhetoric*, 7–17 and 36–40 (on social, political, and intellectual milieus); and Plaks, *Four Masterworks*, 157–180.

7. On luxury consumption in this period, see Dauncey, "Illusions of Grandeur"; Volpp, "Gift of a Python Robe"; and Zurndorfer, "Silver, Piracy, Conspicuous Consumption."

8. See Ge, *Xueyin lusi*, 37 and 44–49.

sex tools, and illustrated erotica, which are part of the same consumer milieu and were widely produced at the time.[9] Women are at the center of this world of promiscuous consumption, both as ones consumed in the market of concubines, prostitutes, maids, and mistresses, and as consumers of jewelry, cosmetics, clothing, food, drink, and furniture.[10] That market had long existed by the late Ming, having begun in the Song dynasty (960–1279) to take the recognizable shape that it would have in the novel.[11] *Jin Ping Mei* appeared during the time of a thriving commercial book market and print culture, which included the publication of erotica such as the novella *Ruyijun zhuan* 如意君傳 (The lord of perfect satisfaction), from which *Jin Ping Mei* occasionally borrows, and other novellas in classical language from a few decades earlier.[12] It was a time when authors and publishers could count on earning profit by means of the production of reading pleasure, and when many of them remained anonymous and were thus freer to write dangerously. In other words, they could engage in writing for profit and pleasure outside the guidelines of state orthodoxy, a trend that also began in the Song dynasty.[13]

What is most central to my reading is the idea of the new space of reading and writing that appeared at this time in which the obscene could exist as if it were constructive to be obscene. The art and aesthetics of sexual description and the messages it carries are the crux of this space. What matters is what *Jin Ping Mei* accomplishes in its writing of sex, which includes both the artful use of language and imagery as well as

9. See Su Yufen, *Mingdai chunyao yanjiu*, 26–34, 49, 53–66, and 79–83 (for their appearance in fiction); and Chen Hsiu-fen, "Nourishing Life."

10. For the link between money and sex, see Roy, "Confucian Interpretation," 58–59; Carlitz, "Puns and Puzzles," 232–233; Plaks, *Four Masterworks*, 154; and Satyendra, "Metaphors of the Body," 94.

11. On the sudden proliferation of the depiction of city life (including sexual life) in this period, see Wu Cuncun, "Plebification of Male-Love," 73–74. See also Ding Naifei, *Obscene Things*, 87–88; Clunas, *Fruitful Sites*; Dauncey, "Illusions of Grandeur"; and Bossler, *Courtesans* (on the market in women in the Song).

12. See Stone, *Fountainhead*; and Richard Wang, *Ming Erotic Novellas*.

13. See Ding, *Obscene Things*, xxx and 50, citing Cherniack, "Book Culture"; Shang Wei, "*Jin Ping Mei* and Late Ming Print Culture" and "Making of the Everyday World"; Lin Chen, "Yanqing xiaoshuo," 47–49; and Ge Fei, *Xueyin lusi*, 156–158. Although *Jin Ping Mei* was not published until years after its composition, it eventually became a product of this same print culture.

the way the author uses sexual descriptions to evaluate and comment on characters, situations, and sexual and psychic states of being.[14] An inherent part of its depiction is the world of consumption, which is evident in the author's keen attention to the spending and investment of money and the consumption of luxury goods, including food, medicine, clothing, art, furniture, and miscellaneous items such as premium incense or precious wood for a coffin. The same milieu harbors an art of pleasure, though not one that the main enjoyers of pleasure in the novel necessarily articulate themselves. These characters are the target of the author's satire, which focuses on the philistine traits of the wealthy upstart merchant, his wives, friends, and bondservants. They are ostentatious owners of luxury goods, as witnessed in a scene in which the flatterer and sponger Ying Bojue 應伯爵 compliments Ximen Qing's new official clothes, which are equipped with a girdle that bears "a decorative plaque of rhinoceros horn" (*xijiao dai* 犀角帶). No one else's outfit can compare, Ying Bojue boasts on his master's behalf, in particular because Ximen Qing's so-called "heaven penetrating rhinoceros horn" (*tongtianxi* 通天犀) is made from the "horn of the water rhinoceros, not the dry-land rhinoceros" (水犀角，不是旱犀角)—which Ying enthusiastically claims can be proven by putting it in water, since only this kind of horn will "divide the water in two" (*fen shui wei liangchu* 分水爲兩處, 31.396).[15] Rhinoceros horn is one of many luxury items imported from abroad that mark this period as one of "material opulence" and "extravagant lifestyles."[16] Here is a case of the lampooning of pretentious connoisseurship, accompanied by satire of the relationship between the philistine man of influence, who has gained an office he does not deserve, and his sponging friend, who is expert in the art of flattery, ever willing to play the role of the toadying clown and doing so intelligently.[17] Satire likewise emerges in the portrayal of sexual pleasure, though as I show below, something additional takes place there that amounts to a kind

14. This point is also made in Huang Lin, *Huang Lin jiang*, 185.

15. See Roy, 2.31.216–217, his translation, and 2.31.528, n. 9 (for earlier references to such properties). Unless I indicate otherwise, all translations are my own.

16. See Zurndorfer, "Silver, Piracy, Conspicuous Consumption," 7 and 10. Both Wu Yueniang 吳月娘 and Ximen Qing wear clothing and apparel that are above their rank. See Dauncey, "Illusions of Grandeur," 48 and 50.

17. For Ying Bojue as clown, see Hanan, "Sources," 55, as cited in the Nongzhu ke 弄珠客 preface to the novel. On his cleverness, see Ge, *Xueyin lusi*, 208–209.

of deference to sexual desire and even a salute to it—even though the author describes characters who ruin themselves in the process of enjoyment.

Dissolute Voice, Moral Voice

In her 2002 study of the novel, *Obscene Things: Sexual Politics in* Jin Ping Mei, Ding Naifei writes of the dominant perspective in *Jin Ping Mei* as coming from and catering to the male seducer's point of view. It is a "deeply misogynist" perspective that is fascinated by the "wanton woman" (*yinfu* 淫婦), her "cunning speech," and her sexual formidability, which it describes in obscenely explicit ways. Ding writes of the resulting "seamlessly double line of discourse," which amounts to "an ultimately moral exposition with obscene undertones," in the shadow of which the presumed male reader "may take (his) pleasure *without having to pay for it* (as Jinlian and the likes of her do, heavily)." The same "double line" or fissure between the critical and satirical voice, on the one hand, and the voice of pleasure, on the other, further emerges in Ding's reference to an argument that the Qing commentator Zhang Zhupo 張竹坡 (1670–1698) makes in justification of the novel's explicit description of the wanton woman. It is only by detailing her in all her guises, only by actually becoming her, Zhang says, that the writer can speak the truth about her. The truth, moreover, is one that he tells to avoid becoming stained by her, which is also a way of claiming moral superiority over her as embodied in the projected ideal reader, who is a proper moral male subject.[18]

The problem that arises here, as Ding continues and as others have also observed, is the difficulty of determining where one voice begins and the other ends. How is one to discern where the dissolute voice ends and the moral lecturer's begins? The moral exertions on the part of the writer or commentator inevitably betray the stains of libidinal interest.[19]

18. See Ding, *Obscene Things*, 119–120, 122, 136, and 231. See also Roy, "Chang Chu-p'o," 233, 236–238, and 241–242. Preface writers and others likewise argue for the proper way to read the novel. See Son, "Reading an Authorless Text," 448–449.

19. See Ding, *Obscene Things*, 117 (on fascination); 153 (cunning speech); 187 (moral exposition); 228 (misogynist); 232–233 (dissolute and stern voices); and 295, n. 17 ("flickerings of a dissident libidinal charge").

In Shang Wei's words, "the recurring theme of hedonism that runs through the entire novel" conflicts with the warnings and comments interspersed elsewhere about the excesses of its characters.[20]

By way of cutting through this dilemma, I would like to extend Ding's reference to the dissolute voice by observing that it is unwieldy to contain it entirely under the umbrella of misogyny or dominant male perspective. Ding implies as much when, while continuing to hold that the novel is deeply misogynist, she says that she cannot "think it so in a total way without any leaks or letups."[21] Taking the first meeting between the illicit lovers Ximen Qing and Pan Jinlian 潘金蓮 as an example, Ding writes that it evokes "a constant shifting of perspective so as to compose a flow of meaning filled to bursting with desire."[22] It is this shifting perspective and its "leaks and letups" that attract my attention as well—that is, the dissolute voice that says it all, even while regularly speaking in authoritative tones and satirizing the characters it depicts. Such shifts are not necessarily or purely a case of being contradictory and/or having it both ways. The same shifting perspective is something that Shang Wei and others have also noted and examined in terms of *Jin Ping Mei*'s "hybrid form of multivocality"—that is, its quoting from and imitation of a wide range of other texts and voices, including popular songs, joke books, drama, fiction, medical texts, and almanacs.[23] As Shang Wei writes, the narrator "apparently experiences no difficulties shuttling between conflicting voices and views as he carries us from one page to the next."[24] Lest we take such conflicting voices as signs of mere carelessness or obfuscation, a reference to Roland Barthes is relevant. He talks of "writerly" enjoyment—that is, of writing that takes place outside the limits of a system of authority and conformity that would reduce the writer either

20. Shang Wei, "*Jin Ping Mei* and Late Ming Print Culture," 196–197. See also Hsia, *Classic Chinese Novel*, 169, 178, and 184–185 (that taking "so many pains to describe the sexual act belies the attitude of moral censure").

21. Ding, *Obscene Things*, 228.

22. Ding, *Obscene Things*, 228.

23. Shang Wei, "*Jin Ping Mei* and Late Ming Print Culture," 189; see also 199.

24. Shang Wei, "Making of the Everyday World," 83. See also Rolston, "Oral Performing Literature," 33, 35, 47, and 51; and Carlitz, *Rhetoric*, 114–127. Such observations go back to Hanan, "Text" and "Sources."

to silence or more respectable proportions, even though in this case he still periodically bows to that authority.[25] It is the risk and liberty that the author takes that I want to examine in the form of his art of describing sex, regardless of, in spite of, and in the midst of dominant or critical or conflicting perspectives. It is especially *Jin Ping Mei*'s use of sexually explicit language and imagery that complicates the notion that the novel and its pornography are inherently misogynistic, a purely negative notion that potentially misses the depths and range of meanings that pornographic language in fact contributes.

The reference above to speaking the truth about the wanton woman brings me to one of Ding's most useful contributions, her attention to what she calls the "situational complexities" of the female characters.[26] Such an attention further qualifies and complicates the issue of the dominance of the male perspective, as undeniable as it may be. The novel's focus on the conditions of the various women and their life trajectories further qualifies and contextualizes the seeming divide between dissolute and moral voices. Such life trajectories are a matter of the positions a woman occupies at particular moments and places—whether, for example, she has gone from bond maid to main wife to concubine, as in Pan Jinlian's case; from prostitute to concubine, as in Li Jiao'er's 李嬌兒; from widow and main wife to concubine, as in Meng Yulou's 孟玉樓; or from bond maid to main wife, as in Pang Chunmei's 龐春梅. The bond maid–turned-concubine is different from the bond maid–turned-prostitute, the prostitute-turned-concubine, or the remarried widow, all of whom differ from the socially valorized woman—whether in the form of the chaste ideal of orthodox morality or in the form of the actual main wife and virgin at marriage, Wu Yueniang (or, as I show below, her main wife alternates, Meng Yulou and Li Ping'er).[27]

The attention to "situational complexities" highlights women's strategies and motivations, however compromised and abject the women

25. Roland Barthes writes that "the writerly text is a perpetual present, upon which no *consequent* language (which would inevitably make it past) can be superimposed," and which takes place before some system would "[reduce] the plurality of entrances, the opening of networks, the infinity of languages" (*S/Z*, 5). See also Ding, *Obscene Things*, 161–162 and 189 (on "semio-philia").

26. Ding, *Obscene Things*, xxi.

27. See Ding, *Obscene Things*, xx–xxiii and 198–199 (on trajectories).

often may be. It also highlights the differences in the descriptions of the sex that Ximen Qing has depending on which woman he is with. Women's speech is particularly important, especially Pan Jinlian's—which is some of the most difficult to understand and translate because it is rich in twists and undertones. She and her fellow wives, as well as maids and other bond servants, compete for access to the man, vying to outdo and, if necessary, destroy each other in the process. They resort to the opportunistic use of power derived from the man as well as their own relative status, a type of power that rises markedly when they have sexual access to him, as the novel repeatedly shows. Such access gives a woman firmer standing among her peers, and bearing a son brings yet higher status. Ding refers to the effects of such a "parasitic mode of power," which "while unable to transform [the] host body . . . almost always succeeds in eventually perverting and eroding it from within and underneath." Zhang Zhupo refers to such a manipulative interception of power using the age-old concept of *quan shu* 權術, "the art of maneuvering power"—which, as Ding writes, "is no mere resistance of power, but an active using of it in the contrary, or reverse, direction. It is a sending it back along the same connecting line whence it came, except in such a way as to make the receiving point accept it *as if it were its own*" (emphasis in the original).[28]

Defining Jin Ping Mei*'s Pornography*

Examining the novel's portrayals of sex cannot ignore another key issue that I have alluded to above, which has to do with the status that the novel has gained because of its obscenity. *Jin Ping Mei* has for long been considered an "obscene" or "salacious book" (as in the term *yinshu* 淫書), which has led to it becoming a "prohibited book" (as in *jinshu* 禁書). In turn, that has meant that since the early Qing, and even today, it has been subject to censorship and condemnation. In practical publishing terms this has to do with the percentage of the text that until now prevents it from being published and distributed in complete form—about 2 percent

28. See Ding, *Obscene Things*, 184 (parasitic), 175 (sending back), and 192 (intercepting "master's sexual power").

of its length, according to one estimate.[29] This is an interesting number because it forces an examination of what those portions do that is excessive and objectionable. Although the Chongzhen edition commentator and others have treated the portions as if they were as constructive parts of the book as any other, the sensitive nature of such scenes has generated either an overall negative view of sex in the book or, as I said above, a tendency to avoid such scenes in close readings of the novel—topics I return to in the conclusion to this chapter.

For my purposes the word "pornography" best labels those portions, though the term needs to be defined and qualified, as well as compared in its use here with its application in early modern Europe. I need the word to characterize a range of descriptions of sexual acts and bodies. It is useful as a phenomenon that, under the definition I adopt, promotes the hyperbolic notion that, under the pornographic eye, no one is exempt from the excesses of sexual desire. The pornographic eye wants to see all it can see of humans in their sexual form. It wants to expose everything about them, leaving nothing out. No one can avoid being drawn in.[30] Saying such things does not mean that pornography is necessarily good, but neither is it necessarily all bad.[31] It is capable of ugliness and beauty, degradation and sublimation (more in a moment on its possible effects as something that can produce harm). Some even say that pornography has the radical potential of promoting a utopian world featuring the free rein of desire, however constructed and fantasized such a world may seem to be. It leads to a pornotopia or fantasy space, in which everyone fulfills their desires.[32] *Jin Ping Mei* does not necessarily conform to a scenario such as the latter, though there are elements of it in the novel and other Ming and Qing fiction, which I periodically bring into the discussion. But

29. Liu Yongqiang estimates that a recent censored edition cut about 19,000 characters from the original 800,000 (*Zhongguo gudai xiaoshuoshi xulun*, 291). For the history of modern editions and difficulty of access to the novel, see Qi Lintao (Rick Qi), *Jin Ping Mei English Translations*, 15–16.

30. "Everyone arouses everyone else's desire" and there is "orgasm all the way around" (Bauer, *How to Do Things*, 10).

31. It is "neither inherently good nor bad, neither necessarily transgressive nor oppressive" (Sullivan and McKee, *Pornography*, 3).

32. See Williams, *Hardcore* and *Porn Studies*; Kipnis, *Bound and Gagged*; Bauer, *How to Do Things*; and Zamperini, "Pornography."

my aim is rather to test what *Jin Ping Mei* is and is not in terms of a definition that I lay out in the following pages. In the simplest terms, the underlying question is how pornographic is *Jin Ping Mei*, and to what ends? That is, what roles do the pornographic, obscene, or salacious contents of the novel play? What do they do and not do, and where do they go?

At the most basic level, I take "pornography" as a convenient label referring to explicit portrayals of sexual acts—whether elegant and suggestive, on the one hand, or vulgar and graphic, on the other. Some passages in *Jin Ping Mei* are so indirect as to leave the realm of what could conventionally or conveniently be thought of as explicit, but I include them in the discussion because they are inherent in the art of describing sex in *Jin Ping Mei* and Chinese fiction in general. Other common assumptions are that pornography both describes and excites sexual arousal and that it must be considered offensive. Some would say that literature is not pornographic but only erotic, until it becomes grotesque and offensive. It has to have something forbidden and transgressive about it, and it is something to be secret about because of that forbidden, outrageous, and/or shameful quality.[33] The term "high erotic" helps make such distinctions, a term I define as referring to elegant and suggestive description. Another notion is that pornographic literature is intended for the titillation of and consumption by an audience of potentially great numbers of readers, as in the case of *Jin Ping Mei* via its publication and marketing as a printed text. The novel became a sensation and was even "hung on city gates to advertise it," as was the custom in Ming times.[34] Thus, pornography brings commercial gain to those who produce it.

According to these definitions, *Jin Ping Mei* is intermittently or occasionally pornographic. It is dedicated (even relentless at times) in its pornographic descriptions, but pornography is by no means its all-encompassing purpose. Nevertheless, as relatively small a percentage of the novel as these descriptions make up, if *Jin Ping Mei* were filmed today, it would have to include full and regularly occurring portrayals of nudity, arousal, and sexual acts (both same-sex and different-sex, and both abusive and passionate), and its use of obscene language would be abundant.

33. See Zamperini, "Pornography," 488.

34. Shang Wei, "*Jin Ping Mei* and Late Ming Print Culture," 188. See also Sullivan and McKee, *Pornography*, 4; and Mudge, *The Whore's Story*, 27–28.

Filmmakers would doubtless decide not to go as far as the original novel to create a product that would sell more broadly and be less offensive and more suited to contemporary tastes—as hard as it would be to find actors capable of appreciating and representing the unique qualities of the original.

A reference to pornography in Europe helps deepen this rough and porous definition, for which I also begin to generalize about the wider body of pornographic literature in Ming and Qing China. The first level of commonality is the one just referred to: the explicit description of sexual bodies, pleasure, and acts when such description violates social norms. The ease with which characters meet and have sex is inherent in this level and is a matter of the erasure of conditions that normally apply in terms of what is likely or permissible. A man longs for sex with a woman he does not know, and she is automatically receptive; a desiring woman chances upon a naked man (not her husband) and invites him to have sex.[35] In both cases, the male writer and reader imagine a woman to be easily open to sexual encounters, especially if she is a widow or married to a man who fails to please her. Such are the conditions in a great number of lesser-known works of the Ming and Qing, in which the thematic voice, including the voice of moral authority, is minimal and pro forma. The focus is on portraying characters having sex, time after time and couple after couple. They may or may not suffer in the end for their excesses, but their characterization is neither complex nor profound.

Jin Ping Mei is unlike other Chinese works because of its greater attention to, rather than erasure of, credible conditions. When, for example, Ximen Qing encounters the female house servant, Ben Siniang 賁四娘 (Ben the Fourth), suddenly kisses her, and asks for sex, the ease with which she submits might appear to be a case of the pornographic ease (or gratuitousness) of engaging in yet another opportunity to describe sex. But the affair is otherwise credible because of the power Ximen Qing has, the rewards such a servant woman stands to gain, and the disfavor or punishment she might otherwise suffer. Given the nature of social relations in the novel, conditions exist that explain such a woman's agreeing so readily. Such interactions deeply determine the description of sex

35. Stephen Marcus refers to the "elimination of external or social reality" (quoted in Hunt, introduction, 39).

in the novel, which consistently bears characteristics that correspond to the status and personality of the partners involved—for example, in this case Ben the Fourth is a servant and wife of an employee, not Ximen Qing's main wife, concubine, or courtesan. The description in this instance is of a raw and precipitous act, devoid of interludes filled with eating, drinking, and talking, and it is portrayed in graphic language.

A second level of commonality is the obsessive repetition of sexual acts, with endless variations that go to extremes of pleasure. Pornography likes reducing sexual acts to a matter of "repetition and enumeration."[36] It likes lists and scores. It likes to compare and rank sexual organs and their capacities. People possess gargantuan sexual appetites, having sex for hours and days at a time. Penises are huge—though they can also be pathetically small or, in the Chinese case, retracted, only to appear at a sudden moment, as in stories of adept monks who disguise themselves as women and infiltrate harems and nunneries.[37] Vaginas are wide or tight; they flow copiously; and women are sexually ravenous. Pornography is about the relentless and obsessive attempt to portray sex in all its forms and even to go beyond what is humanly possible to create supernormal fantasies. It wants to break all boundaries of decency and be as offensive, grotesque, and bizarre as possible.[38]

Jin Ping Mei partially fits this definition, although, again, in comparison with other Ming and Qing works it hardly counts as obsessive or reductive. In tone and volume, the eighteenth-century *Guwangyan* 姑妄言 (Capricious words), for example, is far more extreme and representative—obsessive, repetitive, hyperbolic, derisive, and fond of the supernormal.[39] Nevertheless, Ximen Qing and his partners enjoy forms of repetition and combination and like to bend the limits of human capacity. The novel sometimes ventures into the supernormal, especially after Ximen

36. DeJean, "The Politics of Pornography," 114.

37. See Martin Huang, *Desire*, 133–134.

38. See Hunt, introduction, 39 ("endless . . . variation and combination"); Norberg, "The Libertine Whore," 239 (drenching); Weil, "Sometimes a Scepter Is Only a Scepter," 131 (size) and 148 (insatiableness); and Zamperini, "Canonizing Pornography," 277 ("repetition").

39. See Martin Huang, *Desire*, 251–270; McMahon, "Pornographic Doctrine"; Stevenson, "*Guwangyan*"; and Vitiello, *The Libertine's Friend*, 134–138 and 146–153. Thanks to Mark Stevenson for this translation of the title.

Qing acquires the monk's aphrodisiac. And it likes the graphic, bizarre, and grotesque, though again not as greedily and provocatively as other works do. Portrayals of the fluids and sounds of sex are recurrent, which are both graphic and grotesque. Some descriptions might seem bizarre and degrading to modern readers, but presumably they appealed to the late Ming male reader's taste and his fascination with female arousal. A comment by the Chongzhen commentator illustrates this in the following example, which I examine more fully in chapter 5. It is a scene that represents a kind of fantasy that pornographic works in general share: the woman's all too ready arousal. After tying Pan Jinlian up, Ximen Qing teases her vagina with his toe, "causing her wanton essence to flood forth like a snail secreting its slime" (挑的淫精流出，如蜗之吐涎, 27.355)—words copied from the earlier novel *Ruyijun zhuan*.[40] In the same scene, their sex makes a sound "like a school of loaches plunging through the mud" (如數鰍行泥淖中相似, 27.355), words also copied from *Ruyijun zhuan*.[41] The Chongzhen commentator calls this a "good description" (*hao moxie* 好摹寫, 27.355). Similar descriptions appear elsewhere when Ximen Qing is with his most wanton women, as I define them below.

The graphic grotesque in such instances betrays a mixture of tones. In its reference to women's sexual fluids, the novel uses animal imagery to evoke the intensity of arousal. The woman's arousal is awesome and uncanny, and though the words carry a note of delight, at the same time they render her grotesque. The implication is that only a wanton woman reacts in such a way, since she is considered to be innately prone to such behavior. This is especially the case with a woman such as Pan Jinlian (main wife Wu Yueniang would not be described in this way).[42] The male writer or reader looks on with a possible leer, which appears unmistakably in other works—*Guwangyan*, in particular. *Jin Ping Mei*, as I have been

40. I am using Roy's translation for "snail secreting its slime" (2.27.144). See Xu Changling 徐昌齡, *Ruyijun zhuan* 如意君傳, in *Siwuxie huibao* (hereafter, SWXHB), vol. 24, 44. For the first reference to a fictional work, I give the author, but afterward I give the title only. The same words occur two more times, both with Wang Liu'er 王六兒 (38.494 and 79.1140). See Stone, *Fountainhead*, 121–122.

41. Roy, 2.27.145, his translation. See *Ruyijun zhuan*, 45, which has "bulls" (*niu* 牛) instead of "loaches." The same description occurs again in a scene with Ximen Qing and Lady Lin 林太太 (*JPMCH*, 78.2456).

42. See Ding, *Obscene Things*, xx and 137.

saying, tends to mute or suppress the leer, though animal imagery and metaphor are never absent for long. Neither are satire and comedy. When Ximen Qing fails to visit Pan Jinlian for too long a time, she is resentful and desirous and dares to seduce the young servant boy, Qintong 琴童, who "spills his glob of donkey spunk" in her "jadelike body" (一滴驢精髓; 傾在金蓮玉體中, 12.146).[43] The wanton, ravenous, and ravishing Pan Jinlian, abandoned by the unfaithful Ximen Qing, will not tolerate his absence. However, she will for now make do with this handsome young servant, whom she dominates and manipulates for her own ends. In the jarring contrast between donkey and jadelike body, the quality of the comically inferior beast ostensibly belongs to the man but clings to her as well, wanton woman that she is.

The depiction of the woman's pleasure is in fact key to the discussion of *Jin Ping Mei*'s pornography, a point to which I often return below. For now, suffice it to say that the image of the woman's sexual pleasure is best taken not as a realistic or naturalistic representation (though there are elements of that) but as a "pastiche or collage"—that is, a collection of vocabulary and images, often recycled, recombined, and elaborated upon by the male writer.[44]

A third level of commonality has to do with the association between pornography and social and political criticism. In both China and Europe, "sexual events . . . explain political events."[45] In Europe in particular, pornography has been linked with "attacks on absolutist political authority," in Lynn Hunt's words, and the push for democratic values and revolutionary change. It is in fact taken for granted among many scholars of pornography in the United States that the rise of pornography significantly coincided with the rise of modern democracy.[46] Pornography coincided with—and was used for—the promotion of personal liberty as opposed to the oppressions of religion and the state. The goal was to challenge and transform political and cultural institutions. If such statements belong to hard-and-fast definitions of pornography, then the

43. Roy, 1.12.233, his translation.

44. See Ding, *Obscene Things*, 162; see also 192.

45. Weil, "Sometimes a Scepter Is Only a Scepter," 140.

46. Hunt, introduction, 11. See also Hunt, "Pornography and the French Revolution," 303; DeJean, "The Politics of Pornography," 117–118; and Ferguson, *Pornography, the Theory*, xii (on pornography and democracy).

term cannot be used in China until the very late Qing and early republic, when a new vocabulary and discourse of sex and individual desire emerged. It was in the late 1910s and early 1920s that the word *xing* 性, for example, first acquired its meaning as "sex," superseding older terms such as *yin* 淫 (wanton, salacious) and *yu* 慾 (desire) and becoming part of a discourse that advocated sex as an inherent and healthy part of "human nature" (the classic meaning of *xing*). The agenda was to promote liberation from the repressions of the past, especially in the form of limits to individual liberty and desire.[47] The new discourse called forth a new desiring subject, quintessentially represented by the desiring woman, who was now supposedly legitimized and released from the yoke of the past—in particular, the yokes of the Confucian chastity regime and of polygamy and concubinage. Facets of that woman can be found in *Jin Ping Mei* and other novels of the Ming and Qing, as I sometimes show below. But whatever facets there may be, none are in terms of anything like the overthrow of the chastity regime or the system of polygamous marriage. The "Confucian structure of feeling," as Haiyan Lee writes, still prevails.[48]

However, I would like to avoid such a narrow definition of pornography and deny exclusive ownership of the word by European languages, even if this means redefining it. Pornography in both China and Europe is inherently subversive and transgressive in nature. I mainly speak in terms of the fact that *Jin Ping Mei*'s pornography is loaded with political and social meaning, conforming to the broader generalization just mentioned: that sexual events explain political events, including sexually political ones (as in "situational complexities"). A common idea is that "sexual disorder [is] a sign of a breakdown in public order."[49] A bad ruler is a debauched one, even though in seventeenth- and eighteenth-century Europe, the bad ruler is in particular a tyrant opposed to democratic values. In *Jin Ping Mei*, the debauchery is concentrated in the wealthy merchant rather than the ruler, though the novel frames the

47. See Rocha, "*Xing*," 608, 615, and 617; and Haiyan Lee, *Revolution of the Heart*. The production and marketing of pornography was transformed as well, but that is beyond the scope of this study.

48. See Haiyan Lee, *Revolution of the Heart*, 25–69.

49. Hunt, "Pornography and the French Revolution," 309. See also Carlitz, *Rhetoric*, 50.

emperor as the source of corruption that allows Ximen Qing to advance his interests with impunity.[50] Other pornographic fiction of the Ming and Qing depicts debauched rulers and other figures of authority—though these works are not all necessarily as complex in theme and portrayal as *Jin Ping Mei.* Some engage in pornography chiefly for entertainment, titillation, and shock. Pornographic satire, in contrast, is about figures who abuse privilege and authority, such as the high officials in the Song capital and Ximen Qing at the local level in *Qinghe* 清河 County. Readers of the novel no doubt also had in mind the cases of the Jiajing 嘉靖 (1507–1567), Longqing 隆慶 (1537–1572), and Wanli 萬曆 (1563–1620) emperors, whose behavior Ximen Qing's distantly echoes.[51]

So far I have been talking about what pornography conveys in terms of its contents, themes, and ideological implications. Pornography also serves as a vehicle of provocation. It is a kind of political act, not only when critical of some specific target but simply by the nature of its utterance. As Robert Darnton has written, pornographic books censored by the ancien régime in France threatened the state not merely because of their offensiveness, but also because their publication constituted a denial of the state's control over their contents.[52] In *Jin Ping Mei*, characters enjoy sex to an extreme degree, as seen in the many passages describing unbridled sexual pleasure. The publication of this and other works with pornographic contents challenged the state's desire to guarantee synchrony between its moral and political agendas, on the one hand, and the contents of literature and other writings, on the other hand. In such a context, pornography bears an intensity of message, as if to drive home some raw form of truth and meaning. It is a drive in itself, which words such as "subversive" or "transgressive" only describe in a pale way.

Such challenge and provocation also have to do with pornography's alleged reality effect, as seen, for example, in the charge that it has a negative effect on society. In the latter sense, pornography allegedly incites the kind of behavior that it illustrates. Addressing such a notion, Ming

50. See Ding, *Obscene Things*, 203 (his "will to imperial sexual power").

51. See Huang Lin, *Huang Lin jiang*, 166–175; Carlitz, *Rhetoric*, 36–44; and Plaks, *Four Masterworks*, 161–165.

52. See Darnton, *Forbidden Best-Sellers*.

and Qing writers and readers commonly referred to a Buddhist idea to account for the use of licentious language, an idea referred to above in reference to Zhang Zhupo. To make his teaching convincing, the argument went, a Buddhist preacher speaks in the language of the object of the moral lesson—in this case, the licentious woman. Authors claim that their use of licentious language was a way of leading people to enlightenment, as in the saying "using the licentious to preach the dharma" (*jie yin shuo fa* 借淫說法). Zhang refers to such knowledge derived from experience using another Buddhist expression: "the art of knowledge through direct experience" (*xian shen shuofa* 現身說法), through which one "becomes" the licentious woman to understand and distance oneself from her.[53] Those who disagree with such assertions point out the impossibility of preventing people from reading only the lewd parts of a book, deriving lewd satisfaction from them, and disregarding the message of enlightenment. Works like *Jin Ping Mei*, in other words, degrade public morals and enforce licentious behavior.

Similar debates occurred in the twentieth-century United States. Most famously, antiporn feminists have argued that pornography plays an integral role in the social degradation and exploitation of women and thus that it helps in "creating and maintaining a system of civil inequality." As a stereotypically gendered discourse, pornography's sexual subordination of women both produces and enforces misogynistic beliefs.[54] The language and images of pornography, whether in modern society or the Ming of *Jin Ping Mei*, not only degrade the human objects of desire but also reinforce ways in which culture and society force them into such roles by ranking them as subordinate beings. Such an antiporn stance has been criticized for its narrow, purely negative definition of pornography, a definition that the opposing viewpoint says exaggerates the capacity of pornography to do what the antiporn stance says it can. The more important question should be about whether and how pornography can in

53. See Ding, *Obscene Things*, 137 and 229–234.

54. Brennan, review of Ferguson, 155–156. See also Ferguson, *Pornography, The Theory*, xiv-xv; and Williams, "Porn Studies," 11. The most famous of the antiporn feminists, Catherine MacKinnon and Andrea Dworkin, belong to an earlier phase grounded in the assumption that "pornography expressed the power and the pleasure of heterosexual men" (Williams, "Porn Studies," 7; see also Ferguson, *Pornography, The Theory*, 34–56).

itself be invested with such power and authority.[55] In short, it is precisely the grounding in culture and its social constructions that is at stake, and for this we still need more accurate language and expertise, including cross-cultural expertise. As Paola Zamperini says, the need is to continue "creat[ing] such a language precisely, . . . through the relentless practice of contextualizing and grounding [our] explorations in a deep understanding of the cultures that [produce]" such texts.[56]

In *Jin Ping Mei*'s pornography, as well as that of numerous other works of Ming and Qing fiction, it is a matter of the portrayal of the sexually powerful and wealthy polygamist, who assumes easy access not only to his wives, concubines, and courtesans but also to subservient women such as household servants and his son's wet nurse. It goes without saying that in Ming society, in which polygamy is normal and legal, women and lower-status individuals in general are deeply beholden to polygamist, philandering masters. They give themselves to such men because of the benefits they can gain and for fear of the harms they might suffer if they refuse. The novel enunciates such truths by referring to the impossibility for any one woman to bind Ximen Qing's heart, as in the narrative aside that warns, "Don't any human be a woman, for your every joy and sorrow will be at the will of someone else" (爲人莫做婦人身，百年苦樂由他人, 12.149).[57] Elsewhere Yueniang says that Ximen Qing can buy all the women he wants, and no number is too many: "We're like wives serving in an army, merely taking up space and nothing more" (俺們都是老婆當軍，充數兒罷了, 40.521).[58] In short, *Jin Ping Mei* conducts its own critique of the sexual and hierarchical values of its times, though again as I have said above not with any notion of overthrowing those values or forecasting new ones.

A final aspect of pornography's so-called reality effect relates to the way in which it is taken as an object of desire and a form of sex in itself, to be consumed as such. It is an inherently "interactive" discourse.[59] It

55. Bauer says: "for since pornography is not formally invested with whatever illocutionary power it has, we need to think about exactly how it might possess the authority to subordinate or silence women" (*How to Do Things*, 76; see also 56–57, 62–63, and 78–80).

56. Zamperini, "Pornography," 490.

57. Roy, 1.12.239, his translation (slightly modified).

58. Roy, 3.40.446, his translation (slightly modified).

59. Ullén, "Pornography and Its Critical Reception." See also Ferguson, *Pornography, The Theory*, 7–8.

implicitly tries to persuade the reader that it presents a reality—or that somewhere there is such a reality—that the reader can experience and consume, then and there, divorced from external considerations and conditions of possibility. This explains the obsessive repetition of scenes with nearly identical and only slightly varied elements in works such as *Guwangyan*, as if in an attempt to arrive at a scene of not only complete satisfaction but also complete rendition of that satisfaction—that is, the perfect portrait that captures the state of sexual ecstasy. In spite of its satire and the undercutting of its characters, at times *Jin Ping Mei* likewise gestures in such a direction. This is especially so in its poetic passages, both long and short, which extol the pleasures of sex. Recall the notion of pornographic utopia. Sheer repetition belongs to the same scheme, as in counting (thrusts) and switching (positions or partners). So, by counterexample, do portrayals of the failure to arrive at a state of fulfillment. A space and time emerge that evoke a sheer sense of presence, freed from social relations and critical considerations about those relations—though it is obviously the case that not all readers feel this way and that such a sense of suspension still involves systems of value and ranking that stretch in multiple directions.[60]

Some would say that applying the word "pornography" to *Jin Ping Mei* is anachronistic, the term not having appeared until the mid-nineteenth century in Europe. They might also say that the word is too contaminated with Eurocentric bias or that it is simply dangerous to use because of the contentions surrounding it. Even talking about pornography makes a person notorious. A translation of this study into Chinese would have to settle on a Chinese term for "pornography," probably *seqing wenxue* 色情文學—which itself would have to undergo an examination of its history and applications.[61] That term is also a later invention that did not exist at the time of the novel. But in spite of such misgivings, and even though pornographic description takes up only a small portion of the text, I prefer the word precisely because of its strong connotations. To instead call *Jin Ping Mei* an "erotic novel," as is sometimes done, is convenient, but "erotic" is too kind and innocent a word. *Jin Ping*

60. For the sense of presence, see Ullén, "Pornography and Its Critical Reception."

61. For a discussion of such terms, including *seqing*, *yinhui* 淫穢 (obscene), *xiaxie* 狎褻 (indecent), and *yanqing* 艷情 (erotic), see Lin Chen, "Yanqing xiaoshuo," 31–32.

Mei is a brazen and unruly book, and its pornographic passages are a key sign of that. Furthermore, the word "pornography" is simply useful as a label for the features that I have listed above and that I repeat and elaborate upon below. Also useful in my consideration of the word is the opportunity to define it in the comparative context of *Jin Ping Mei* and other more dedicatedly pornographic works of the Ming and Qing, the body of which is so large that it demands recognition and examination. The relevance of these works necessarily arises because of their shared vocabulary and imagery, character types, plots, and motifs. The rest of this chapter returns to the world of *Jin Ping Mei* and the examination of its art of describing sex both in light of its thematic platform (which can be called its pornographic morality) and in terms of its modes of portrayal (that is, the modes and types of language it uses).

For my reading, I refer to both of the novel's main versions, the *Jin Ping Mei cihua* edition (金瓶梅詞話), and the Chongzhen/*xiuxiang* edition (the *Xinke xiuxiang piping Jin Ping Mei* 新刻繡像批評金瓶梅).[62] As Tian Xiaofei summarizes, the Chongzhen edition is in general less didactic, tending to let actions and words speak for themselves and leaving meaning between the lines, rather than adding judgmental asides. It is more concise and polished, cutting out or shortening most of the popular songs and song suites, and it eliminates many of the errors and inconsistencies that appear in the *cihua* version.[63] The Chongzhen edition is further notable for its more sympathetic portrayal of Pan Jinlian compared to both the *Shuihu zhuan* (水滸傳 *Water Margin*) and *cihua*, a portrayal that turns her into a more "complicated character."[64] The *cihua* edition is nevertheless essential, especially in its complete translation by David Roy, as are the variations between the *cihua* and Chongzhen editions, to

62. On differences between the editions, see Hanan, "Text"; Tian Xiaofei, *Qiushui tang* and "A Preliminary Comparison."

63. See Tian Xiaofei, *Qiushui tang*, 7, 25, 82, 98, 158, 159, 182, and 250, and "A Preliminary Comparison," 348 and 351; Hanan, "Text," 21 and 24; Plaks, "The Chongzhen Commentary" and *Four Masterworks*, 68 (for "polished"); Rolston, *Traditional Chinese Fiction*, 65–66, 237–38, and 241 (on its streamlining effects); Ge, *Xueyin lusi*, 195, 197, and 293 (on its superiority and antididactic qualities); and Qi Lintao, *Jin Ping Mei English Translations*, 24–27. For views that favor the *cihua* edition, see Roy, Introduction; Carlitz, *Rhetoric*; and Rolston, "Oral Performing Literature," 46–52, 47 (on cuts).

64. Tian Xiaofei, "A Preliminary Comparison," 371.

which I refer when they are meaningful. The point is not to debate which text might be more authoritative. Instead, it is to indicate a preference for one reading over another, but also at times to underscore the value of considering more than one version of a particular passage. As I have noted above, *Jin Ping Mei*—especially the *cihua* edition—is full of "contrasting, if not conflicting, messages." It has a "multiplicity of voices, styles, and languages," a summation that applies to its descriptions of sex as well.[65] Such a mixture and variety are features that the book shares with other publications of the times that offered multiple attractions in a printed format, such as almanacs, literary miscellanies, and daily-life encyclopedias.[66] In terms of the book's pornography, this means that although it is deeply thematic in nature, it is also there for the sake of indulging its own linguistic exuberance.[67] The *cihua* edition, again, tends more in this direction than the Chongzhen version, as I occasionally demonstrate below.

Conclusion: A Disruptive Text

Jin Ping Mei is an unruly, disruptive, and transgressive text. It is so not only because of its explicit and well-crafted descriptions of sex, but also because of its exuberant portrayals of wanton and dissolute men and women. These characters are wanton and dissolute and they come to disastrous ends, but the author portrays them in all their sexual intensity, though not without notes of humor and satire. In undertaking such portrayals, the novel defines what I label as its pornography as follows.

65. Shang Wei, "*Jin Ping Mei* and Late Ming Print Culture," 196 ("contrasting . . . messages"), and 204 ("multiplicity of voices"); see also 97, 202, 204, and 213; Hanan, "Sources," 59 and 60; C. T. Hsia, *Classic Chinese Novel*, 166 and 176; and Rolston, "Oral Performing Literature," 35.

66. See Wang, *Ming Erotic Novellas*, 28; and Shang Wei, "Making of the Everyday World," 70, 77–78, and 81–82. The daily-life encyclopedias contain topics reflecting the social world of the novel, such as game-playing, sexual arts, and norms of brothel behavior.

67. Shang Wei notes that "the robust appetites of his [the author's] characters become manifest in his own narrative" ("Making of the Everyday World," 91; see also 83).

Pornography is the realm of graphic sexual description, vulgar slang, and grotesque obscenity. It is the world of oral, genital, and anal sex; playing with, manipulating, and at times abusing sexual parts of the body; and partners who banter with and tease each other. It is about trying different positions in sex and doing anything possible to intensify and prolong the stimulations of sex, such as using sexual aids or aphrodisiacs. It likes to portray others being drawn in, whether by watching sex secretly, imitating it in their own behavior, or being compelled to participate. The partners have at their disposal illustrated manuals of other people having sex. In other works, though not in *Jin Ping Mei*, they read pornographic stories to learn about sex and whet their interest. A common plot in Ming and Qing pornography (as I discuss in chapter 7) is about a male libertine who has one sexual adventure after another with the virgins, widows, married women, maids, and prostitutes who eventually join his polygamous household. *Jin Ping Mei*'s polygamy never works so well, though the novel has a central point in common with other Ming and Qing fiction: it is likewise chiefly about the sex of the polygamous, philandering man, for whom women are easily available. It is not about sublime love between two people who love each other exclusively. In other words, the sex of monogamous lovers such as Zhang Junrui 張俊瑞 and Cui Yingying 崔鶯鶯 from the *Xixiang ji* (西廂記 "Story of the Western Wing") is not a focus of portrayal in *Jin Ping Mei* or other Ming and Qing pornographic novels. Their sex is so sublime that no words can portray it, except in the most rarefied and indirect way. Nevertheless, *Jin Ping Mei* has its own sublime, which I call its high erotic, and which it employs as a significant subset of its sexual portrayals that lean toward the evocation of sublime love but still stay within the realm of the complicatedly polygamous man and his female partners. The high erotic avoids vulgar and graphic description; uses elegant, allusive, and elliptical language; and ultimately veers toward no portrayal at all, as if implying that to portray such a thing as the finest sexual love, even in elegant language, were to degrade and profane it. *Jin Ping Mei*'s high erotic mode inevitably carries an ironic tone in that no couple in the novel, even if described in such a way, actually conforms to the fantasy of sublime lovers.

Let me say two more final words about *Jin Ping Mei*'s pornography. First, it pays to situate oneself within the long line of readings of the novel that have appeared since its first arrival, including the readings from the past century or so of scholarship about it. To address this point, below I summarize the perspective presented by Ding Naifei, who I think has done the most enlightening analysis of *Jin Ping Mei* research in the twentieth century, and who takes into account readings since the late Ming. Ding writes that "twentieth-century readings in Chinese of the representations of sex and women (*nüse*) in *JPM* have remained within the paradigmatic readings set up in the early 1920s by Lu Xun [魯迅] and Hu Shi [胡適]."[68] The latter two can be summed up by Hu Shi's characterization of the novel's sexually explicit passages as portraying nothing but "bestial desire."[69] Similar views, though presented in less blunt terms, can be seen in the 1980s and 1990s in the United States.[70] The question behind such a characterization—and, moreover, the question that haunts "almost all twentieth-century interpretations of *Jin Ping Mei*" (again, such interpretations are inherited from the Ming and Qing) is whether or not it is "an obscene book (*yinshu*)."[71] Such a question assumes that one must decide between a good obscene and a bad one—that is, in short, between an obscene that is loaded with thematic meaning (proper for serious reading and academic research) and an obscene that is about bad sex or the kind of sex that people looking for titillation like to read about. The problem with readings such as these, as Ding continues, is their failure "to account for the representation of sex and women in a contextualized and contextualizing manner."[72] What we should instead be reaching for is

68. Ding, *Obscene Things*, 6; see also xxv (for "socially framed" ways in which the novel has been read).

69. Hu Shi's words (*shouxing de rouyu* 獸性的肉慾) are quoted in Ding, *Obscene Things*, 18; see also 3. In a similar appraisal from about the same period, Zheng Binyu 鄭賓于 describes sex in *Jin Ping Mei* as a case of "animal lust" (*shouyu* 獸慾) ("Lun yinshu," 148).

70. For example, Plaks writes that "the number of scenes depicting erotic experience in sympathetic terms are no more than a handful" (*Four Masterworks*, 138) and nothing in the novel could "be taken as a glorification of the sex act" (138; see also 139, 142, and 151). Roy says that "it was never any part of the author's intent to celebrate the pleasure of sex" (introduction, xxxvii). See also Carlitz, *Rhetoric*, 48–52; and Zhang Guoxing, *Zhongguo gudai xiaoshuozhongde xing miaoxie*. In a more optimistic appraisal, Ge Fei describes the novel as "by no means antipathetic to sexual desire" (*Xueyin lusi*, 160). See also Wang Rumei, *Wang Rumei jiedu Jin Ping Mei*, 33.

71. Ding, *Obscene Things*, 4. Ding recalls Zhang Zhupo's strenuous denial that *Jin Ping Mei* is an obscene book.

72. Ding, *Obscene Things*, 6.

twofold. First is a reading of sexual representation that escapes the forced decision between whether or not the representation is of pleasurable or approvable sex. Second is an ability to read the novel's female characters according to what I have cited from the beginning: their situational circumstances. In other words, we need to be able to read these characters and their modes of behavior according to such variables as their social position, personal talents, and dispositions, which for women such as Pan Jinlian include sex and sexuality, "their primary and perhaps only weapon of choice."[73]

Such interpretations have in fact already taken place.[74] But though others have occasionally examined passages of explicit sexual description, they have hardly done so in sustained fashion. What I try to show in this regard, in brief, is that the novel's descriptions of sex have an art to them. *Jin Ping Mei* contains a full range of such portrayals, though it avoids the bizarre and sensational extremes found in shorter works from the same period and later. It contains the extreme rarefication found in the high erotic literature of the "fragrant and bedazzling" mode, though rarely without notes of irony. *Jin Ping Mei*'s descriptions of sex have method in terms of what they describe and how they describe it. The portrayals are thematic in that they convey meaning having to do with particular characters in particular situations. The novel presents sex satirically and humorously, but also in a way that lavishly depicts sexual pleasure and excess. In doing so, it portrays sexual pleasure as something that involves intense, even "intolerable levels of excitation."[75] It likes to portray sex as a form of sheer expenditure, inherently veering to excess—even deadly excess. This explains the endings of many works, including *Jin Ping Mei*, in which characters suffer death or punishment or else withdraw in a form of religious awakening. Nevertheless, the novel is not there to condemn

73. Ding, *Obscene Things*, 44. See also Ning Zongyi and Luo Derong, *Jin Ping Mei dui xiaoshuo meixue de gongxian*, 285–291.

74. See, for example, Ning Zongyi and Luo Derong, *Jin Ping Mei dui xiaoshuo meixue de gongxian*; Tian Xiaofei, *Qiushui tang*; Ge Fei, *Xueyin lusi*; and Yang Zhishui, *Wu se*.

75. O'Hara, *Visions of Global America*, 114. I am thinking of the Lacanian concept of *jouissance*, in which pleasure overwhelms the coherent sense of self. Sex in this mode belongs to that "sphere of non-utilitarian behavior in which the self not only abandons the self, but takes the risk of wasting itself, of being hurt" (Illouz, *Why Love Hurts*, 189).

something such as pleasure in sex but instead to show that things go on in that realm that a *xiaoshuo* 小說 writer cannot afford to ignore.

My second final word for this chapter places the novel in a larger historical context. Stories of sexual profligacy existed for centuries before Ming and Qing authors took to converting them into sexually explicit narratives. I am referring to the accounts passed down in much less explicit ways of notorious figures of the ancient past, especially royal figures such as the Zhou 周 dynasty's Xia Ji 夏姬 (seventh century BCE) and the multiple men she consorted with; the Qin 秦 dynasty's queen dowager, Zhao Ji 趙姬 (died 228 BCE), and her affair with Lao Ai 嫪毐, who had such a large penis that he could balance a wooden wheel on it; the Han 漢 dynasty's Empress Zhao Feiyan 趙飛燕 (45–1 BCE) and her reputed orgies with men smuggled into the palace; and the Tang 唐 dynasty's Empress Wu Zetian 武則天 (624–705), whom historical accounts report as having paramours while she was ruler. The many stories of sexual profligacy among men include those about the imperial grandson Liu Jian 劉建 (died 121 BCE), who committed incest with his sisters and forced palace women to have sex with animals; Sui Yangdi 隋煬帝 (569–618) and his sexual labyrinth, into which he forced thousands of virgins; and the Jin 金 dynasty's Prince Hailing (Hailing Wang 海陵王, 1122–1161), who liked to steal other men's wives, with whom he indulged in sexual antics in the palace.[76] The original versions of these stories appeared in minimal terms in texts such as the *Zuo zhuan* 左傳, dynastic histories, or miscellaneous histories and collections of tales.[77] We can say that *Jin Ping Mei* and other Ming and Qing works "pornographized" the material their authors found in older sources, which can in turn be thought of as examples of pornography before it actually appeared. Although *Jin Ping Mei* is not about a historical figure such as Zhao Feiyan or Prince Hailing, the novel can nevertheless be read as an implicit political allegory about Ming rulers, as many others have noted already. Similar to other works of its period, it takes the lurid but minimal hearsay

76. For accounts of Liu Jian, see Ban Gu 班固, *Hanshu* 漢書, 53.2414–16; and Sima Qian 司馬遷, *Shiji* 史記, 59.2096. See also Goldin, *Culture of Sex*, 88–92 (on bestiality found nowhere else in ancient texts) and "Copulating," 60.

77. Xia Ji and Zhao Feiyan appear in chapter 7. On Hailing, see Feng Menglong 馮夢龍, *Xingshi hengyan* 醒世恆言, story 23 ("Jin Hailing zong yu wang shen" [金海陵縱欲亡身]); and McMahon, *Celestial Women*, 45–53.

about dissolute men and women and churns up an entire narrative that is intermittently pornographic, exploiting and intensifying the libidinal charge that already existed in those previous works. The novel produces a steady flow of critical commentary that darkens most of its characters. But its descriptions leave a remainder that produces an alternative flow of meaning beyond the voice of critical commentary, a flow that overwhelms that voice. In other words, it can be said that while leaning on that same voice of authority, the novel tests and pushes the boundaries established by that voice, both in portraying characters who violate such boundaries and in its own riotous dance of words.

CHAPTER 2

Jin Ping Mei *and the Art of the Bedchamber*

Commonalities between Jin Ping Mei *and the Art of the Bedchamber*

The Chinese texts of the art of the bedchamber consist of instructional manuals for men on how to master sex with women. The earliest sources date from the Mawangdui 馬王堆 tombs of the third century BCE and the latest are from the Ming and Qing and include illustrated albums. Offshoots of the bedchamber texts extend to modern times.[1] They occupy a key place in premodern Chinese sexual culture that they share with the even larger body of texts consisting of the sexually explicit novels and stories of the Ming and Qing dynasties, in particular *Jin Ping Mei*. The two genres possess key commonalities, even if they differ vastly in theme and content. What appears as the art of the bedchamber in Ming and Qing fiction drastically departs from the spirit and emphasis of the classic tradition that appeared by early in the Han dynasty (206 BCE–220 CE). I use "classic" to refer to the series of bedchamber texts from the Mawangdui tombs, the ones from the Six Dynasties (220–589 CE) and the Tang dynasty (618–907 CE) preserved in Japan, and Ming texts such as the sixteenth-century *Sunü miaolun* 素女妙論 (Wondrous discourse of the plain woman)—which, as late as it is, is highly consistent with the

1. Examples include Jolan Chang, *The Tao of Love and Sex*; Reid, *The Tao of Health, Sex, and Longevity*; and Wang Qiang, *Les secrets de la puissance sexuelle*.

earlier texts, and which I cite frequently below.[2] The purpose of sex in this literature is to harmonize *yin* 陰 and *yang* 陽 for the sake of nourishing health and longevity. Although passionate frenzy is at times part of the picture, the overall premise is that sex should be measured and temperate, not rushed or violent. A person should not strain the body or "act wildly and wantonly" (*kuangwang renyi* 狂妄任意).[3] As it appears in Ming and Qing fiction, the art of sex instead focuses on ways in which characters make themselves sexually powerful by using potent drugs and mastering occult techniques. Like many of their counterparts in other works, the characters of *Jin Ping Mei* indulge their desires with little restraint.

The differences between the art of the bedchamber and the novel are not surprising, with the most basic and obvious difference lying at the level of genre. The classic art of the bedchamber focuses on instruction and elucidation. Its texts are a cross between practical manuals and discourses on the wisdom of sex. Achieving harmonious interaction and harnessing pleasure for the sake of "physical cultivation," the art strives for thorough awareness of the sexual body, both the man's and the woman's.[4] It divides intercourse into stages and treats each in detail. It elucidates the parts of the woman's body, including the structure of the vagina from shallow to deep, the signs and stages of the woman's arousal, ways to anticipate and ensure the woman's stimulation, and techniques and styles of thrusting. It advises the reader about harms and excesses to avoid, methods to improve health and longevity, aphrodisiacs for increased arousal, and cures for dysfunction.

The status of pleasure is key in contrasting the art of the bedchamber with *Jin Ping Mei*. In the art of the bedchamber, physical and spiritual well-being are equally if not more important than pleasure. When carried out properly, sex is fundamentally healthy. It both strengthens and harmonizes the body, with climax commonly taking place for the woman

2. The text of *Sunü miaolun* can be found in Li Ling 李零, *Zhongguo fangshu gaiguan*, 190–203. See also Li Ling and McMahon, "Contents and Terminology"; and for translations of Mawangdui texts, Harper, *Early Chinese Medical Literature*; and Wile, *Art of the Bedchamber* (which includes texts up to the Ming). References to *Sunü miaolun* and other texts of the art of the bedchamber will be from Li Ling, *Zhongguo fangshu gaiguan*.

3. *Sunü miaolun*, in Li Ling, *Zhongguo fangshu gaiguan*, 201; see also 199.

4. Harper, "Sexual Arts of Ancient China," 581; see also Umekawa, "*Tiandi yinyang jiaohuan dalefu*," 254.

as expressed by the single word *kuai* 快 (meaning joy, delight, and satisfaction) but ideally—that is, for optimum health—less often for the man. For him, ejaculation (*xie* 瀉) is but a "temporary pleasure" (*zankuai* 暫快), too much of which leads to illness and even death.[5] In some passages, the act of sex is purely for the sake of healing dysfunction, as in the regime that has the man repeat a thrusting routine a number of times a day for a recommended period, after with the malady should be cured. Maladies include weakness of *jing* (essence, 精) and irregularity of menses.[6] In general, the art of the bedchamber helps solve problems and promotes successful, harmonious sex. Social contradictions are absent, and lust and passion are not part of the picture. The focus is on the aesthetics and techniques of sex, treating intercourse as a healthful activity and—as also seen in the Indian *Kamasutra*—discouraging the tendency to turn it into a rash, unchecked act.[7]

Such behavior hardly appears in *Jin Ping Mei*. In some portrayals, sex can be beautiful and sublime, but in others it is rough, raw, and ferocious and takes place in a context, as I have said, that pays enormous attention to life complexities both within and beyond the acts of sex. Vulgar and grotesque imagery is common, whether referring to sensual pleasure or a sexual part of the body or as an obscene joke. The novel is about characters who meet but should not meet, people who cheat and deceive each other, argue and fight, plot against rivals and innocent victims, and in the end die of excess. Women, Pan Jinlian in particular, use sex opportunistically to bargain for gifts, favors, and other types of advancement. Ximen Qing resorts to a mysterious aphrodisiac that gives him superhuman power and finally causes his death. For him, having sex inevitably means having too much sex and suffering because of it, though the novel portrays him and other characters experiencing plenty of pleasure along the way.

But as differently oriented as the classic art of the bedchamber and the novel may be, broad commonalities exist that encourage situating the

5. Pfister, "Gendering Sexual Pleasures," 52 (*zankuai*). See also Li Ling, *Zhongguo fangshu gaiguan*, 118 (from *Yufang mijue* 玉房秘決), and 199 and 201 (from *Sunü miaolun*).

6. See the regime called the "eight benefits" (*ba yi* 八益), in Li Ling, *Zhongguo fangshu gaiguan*, 116 (from *Yufang mijue*).

7. See Doniger and Kakar, trans., *Vatsyayana Mallanaga*, xl and xli (shielding it "from the ferocity of unchecked desire").

two in dialogue. Before discussing these commonalities, I need to make two qualifications. One is the fact that I am taking the classic art of the bedchamber as a generic whole and comparing it with the practice of sex in the anonymous novel, *Jin Ping Mei*, written sometime in the latter half of the sixteenth century. In fact, the art of the bedchamber includes a range of texts and practices over a long span of time, with varying tones and emphases, and only the latest texts in it could have been known to the *Jin Ping Mei* author. Other works of Ming and Qing fiction use the term "art of the bedchamber" (*fangzhong shu* 房中術) or near equivalents, but they mold the contents and principles of the classic texts to their own creative purposes. A modified form of the term appears only once in *Jin Ping Mei*, when Ximen Qing refers to the aphrodisiac that he is about to receive as "the drug for the art of the bedchamber" (*fangshu yao* 房術藥, 49.638). Nevertheless, the classic bedchamber texts make up a consistent tradition in that they share a basic purpose: to treat sexual intercourse as a body of knowledge. By this I mean a body of justifiable knowledge—that is, a subject that is worth treating in a serious and respectable fashion. The texts create an entire discourse about sexual intercourse that, as Charlotte Furth says, lends "spiritual dignity to the sex act" and that comes with a common core set of principles, concepts, terms, and concerns, and furthermore they teach a set of technical practices referred to as *shu* 術, which amount to a curriculum of methods for the exercise of sexual intercourse.[8]

Most importantly, treating sex this way means that, as sensual as it is, sex is not simply a lustful act, carried out blindly and mindlessly. To repeat Donald Harper's words, intercourse in the art of the bedchamber is "for the sake of physical cultivation rather than as a consequence of passion."[9] What these words leave unsaid and understated is the role and definition of pleasure. The Mawangdui text *He yin yang* 合陰陽 (Joining *yin* and *yang*) at one point refers to bodies experiencing "pleasurable excitation" (*leyang* 樂養 [癢]), but it immediately continues, "[a]lthough

8. Furth, "Rethinking van Gulik," 127. See also Schipper, *The Taoist Body*, 144–155, especially 147 and 150.

9. Harper, "Sexual Arts of Ancient China," 581; see also *Early Chinese Medical Literature*, 415.

desirous, do not act" (*sui yu wu wei* 雖欲勿爲).[10] This is a good example of how the body of knowledge known as the art of the bedchamber treats pleasure: as something to know and control. As Rodo Pfister says, the man engages in "controlled action" and remains in a state of "intermediate" and "prolonged" stimulation.[11] Of central importance is the notion of prolongation, which is a core precept of the classic ancient views of pleasure in the broadest sense: not merely sexual pleasure but also pleasure in such things as music and friendship, food and wine, and the enjoyment of beautiful scenery. As Michael Nylan notes, in their philosophies of pleasure, thinkers from the Warring States period (475–222 BCE) on generally valued "moderation and refinement" in pleasure, eschewed "precarious or fleeting pleasures," and instead preferred sustained forms of pleasure "that could support, rather than deplete or corrupt, the polity, the family, or the body."[12]

Depletion is likewise anathema in the art of the bedchamber, whose principle is that if pleasure turns into lust (*se* 色), then it is harmful and wasteful. In some branches of the art of the bedchamber, pleasure is deemed too dangerous to be worthy of playing any role. In a late imperial practice of Daoist internal alchemy called "duo-cultivation" (*shuangxiu* 雙修), the couple has intercourse for the sake of spiritual refinement, expelling all lascivious thoughts.[13] Texts of women's internal alchemy that appear in the Qing call for treasuring and enhancing *jing* and *qi* 氣 and eschewing sexual interaction altogether.[14] The well-known practice for men, called "returning *jing* to nourish the brain" (*huan jing bu nao* 還精補腦), encourages them to prevent loss by channeling *qi* and *jing* internally, whether by preventing their emission, absorbing them from the woman, or by channeling them internally by means of solo practice.

10. *He yin yang*, in Li Ling, *Zhongguo fangshu gaiguan*, 37. The text of *He yin yang* can be found in Li Ling, *Zhongguo fangshu gaiguan*, 36–38.

11. Pfister, "Gendering Sexual Pleasures," 52–53; see also 59.

12. Nylan, *The Chinese Pleasure Book*, 33, 34–35, and 51.

13. See Despeux and Kohn, *Women in Daoism*, 211–215; Liu Xun, "Numinous Father and Holy Mother," 121, 128, and 129; Raz, "The Way of the Yellow and the Red," 86 (for similar practices of ritualized intercourse in sixth-century Celestial Master Daoism); Li Ling, *Zhongguo fangshu xukao*, 368–386; and Goldin, *Culture of Sex*, 118–119.

14. See Valussi, "Men and Women" and "Female Alchemy"; Wile, *Art of the Bedchamber*, 192–219; and Despeux and Kohn, *Women in Daoism*.

Common to all these practices is the notion that sexual arousal is beneficial for activating *jing* and *qi* but it should be harnessed for physical and spiritual refinement. The practitioner, once aroused, must channel the aroused energy wisely and not lose it in dissipating lust. The texts of the art of the bedchamber leave no doubt about the deep pleasures of sex and describe it as a passionately experienced act, but they likewise leave no doubt about its dangers.

My second qualification is that it does not even matter whether the *Jin Ping Mei* author had read a work such as *Sunü miaolun* or referred to concepts from internal alchemy. The art of the bedchamber and related teachings traveled in various forms, such as what passed haphazardly or as a sort of common knowledge and in the form of objects such as sex tools. Self-proclaimed specialists existed, who sold and promoted sex tools, drugs, and associated expertise. The tools included the silver clasp and dildos, the latter of which existed for both male and female use from the Han to the Ming and Qing dynasties. They appear frequently in *Jin Ping Mei* and were widely available for purchase at the time the novel was written.[15] In the Ming elaborate and expensive albums existed that illustrated positions of intercourse, and these albums appear three times in *Jin Ping Mei*, though the novel reveals no details about their contents. Although key bedchamber texts seem to have disappeared around the Tang dynasty (though they had found their way to Japan by the tenth century in the *Yixin fang*, or Ishinpō, 醫心方), their contents appeared elsewhere in both written and oral form, including *Sunü miaolun*.[16] In short, it is safe to assume that the author and readers of *Jin Ping Mei* shared a knowledge of the art of the bedchamber and the related fields of nourishing life and internal alchemy (which I discuss below), however indirect or intermittent their influences may have been. The novel is, so to speak, free to take what it wants, whether it does so faithfully, twistedly, or haphazardly or whether it reinvents or creates its own art of sex. *Jin Ping Mei* can even be taken as an implicit critique of the art of the bedchamber,

15. For a brief history of dildos, see Li Ling, *Zhongguo fangshu kao*, 409–424. For an updated version, see Li Ling, *Wanbian*, 405–425. I also discuss these objects below.

16. The *Yixing fang* is a compendium of texts of the art of the bedchamber and can be found in Li Ling, *Zhongguo fangshu gaiguan*, 100–143. With the exception of the Mawangdui texts, *Sunü miaolun*, and *Xiu zhen yanyi* 修眞演義, all other bedchamber texts that I cite appear discontinuously in *Yixin fang*.

as if to say that a truer understanding of sexual desire can come only with an exploration of the vicissitudes of lust beyond the scope of sexual physiology and technique.

The first commonality between *Jin Ping Mei* and the classic art of the bedchamber is the governing assumption of the woman's sexual formidability, a motif that occurs across Ming and Qing fiction.[17] Her desires are strong and even overwhelming, which means, as the art of the bedchamber insists, that the man's duty is to please her in sex, for which he must be masterful and well prepared. A corollary to this theme is that pleasing the woman sexually will lead to her happiness and well-being. In sharing these basic notions, the bedchamber texts pointedly contrast the man's fragility with the woman's potency. As for *Jin Ping Mei*, it takes the woman's capacity for pleasure for granted, which eliminates any need to explain it, and creates a man who is already expert, with a never failing penis, but who always relies on both tools and drugs to succeed in sex. Another facet of the presumption of the woman's sexual capacity is that intercourse with her takes time and attention. According to the art of the bedchamber, sex must begin with mutual understanding and proceed with appropriate timing, being neither too hasty nor too slow. The man must attune himself to the woman's state of mind and body. In general, he observes the woman and responds to her; in contrast, she acts spontaneously, her delight ensured by his attentive efforts. He regulates his breathing and movements, and above all he controls himself. He should remain in a sustained state of pleasure, in which he prolongs sensations while avoiding taking pleasure to the fullest extent—for if he did, that would mean ejaculating, after which he would no longer be able to enjoy pleasure, nor could he continue to stimulate the woman.[18] Ximen Qing does not regulate his movements in the manner of the art of the bedchamber, nor does he practice conservation of *jing*. But in his own manner he achieves states of prolonged stimulation both for himself and the woman and (as the man does in the art of the bedchamber) avoids ejaculating too soon or only for his own pleasure. Sex takes place preceded by and interwoven with moments of diversion, whether in the form

17. Such fiction includes fox lore, in which it is common to find "exhaustible men dealing with inexhaustible women" (Huntington, *Alien Kind*, 179).

18. See Pfister, "Gendering Sexual Pleasures," 44–45, 52–53, 56, and 59.

of conversation, eating, drinking, or playing games. The partners play with different sexual positions and use sex tools and drugs to extend their pleasure and excitement.

Second, both the ancient art of the bedchamber and *Jin Ping Mei* share the underlying premise that the sexual act is a contest and field of struggle.[19] The texts of the art of the bedchamber confine this notion to the matching of sexual energies, while the novel extends it to the entire realm of sexual and social interaction. The *Yufang zhiyao* 玉房指要 (Essentials of the jade chamber) refers to the woman as "enemy" and tells the man that "when encountering the enemy, he should view her as if she were no more than tile or stone, but himself as if gold or jade" (御敵，當視敵如瓦石，自視如金玉).[20] At stake is whether or not the man can win—that is, stay erect and lead the woman to sexual delight. Or will he fail miserably even after resorting to aphrodisiacs and sex tools, as does the doctor whom Li Ping'er 李瓶兒 briefly marries in *Jin Ping Mei*? Poetic passages describing sex as mock battle appear in *Jin Ping Mei*, in which man and woman fight metaphorically as if to defeat and kill each other. Both end satisfied and well spent. But as I just said, battle also makes up the core of *Jin Ping Mei*'s narrative, in the form of women's alliances and enmities and their attempts both during and after sex to win favors from Ximen Qing. Struggles such as these do not appear in the art of the bedchamber, which exists as if innocent of the realities of social and domestic interaction.

Third, both the novel and the art of the bedchamber center around the man's relations with multiple women. In addition to his wife, concubines, and maids, Ximen Qing seeks other men's wives and courtesans, as well as occasional male lovers. The art of the bedchamber is less specific, merely emphasizing the idea that the sexually masterful man not only can but should have sex with multiple partners. The *Yufang zhiyao* says that he should emulate the ancient Yellow Emperor (Huangdi 黄帝), who "rode" (*yu* 御) twelve hundred women and was thereby able to attain immortality. According to the *Yufang mijue* 玉房秘诀 (Secrets of the jade chamber): "If a man wants to follow the way of nourishing life,

19. Doniger argues that an "agonistic view of sex is the essence" of the *Kamasutra* (*Redeeming the Kamasutra*, 66). I deal with sex as battle in chapter 4.

20. *Yufang zhiyao*, in Li Ling, *Zhongguo fangshu gaiguan*, 102.

gathering *qi*, and circulating *yin* and *yang*, he cannot do it with just one woman. He must take three, nine, eleven, the more the better!" (欲行陰陽取氣養生之道，不可以一女爲之，得三若九若十一，多多益善), adding that "ten or more women in one night will yield the best results" (一夕易十人以上尤佳).[21] In all cases, he can do such things only if he has trained himself to protect his vital energies, while also drawing nourishment from the woman.[22] As in the case of sex as battle, the art of the bedchamber omits the realities of the situation of one man and many women, while the novel narrates at great length the complications of the polygamous family.

The fourth commonality may seem too obvious to mention, but it is crucial in characterizing what the classic art of the bedchamber and the novel do and do not share. This commonality is the openness in describing sex—that is, the lengthy, explicit, and dedicated description of naked bodies and sexual acts—for which both have a particularly developed vocabulary, though one that overlaps only partially. The novel includes both refined and vulgar extremes, which I examine at length in the next three chapters. The art of the bedchamber strictly adheres to the level of the elegant and refined, preferring veiled, euphemistic terms and always avoiding the vulgar. For addressing such topics, both have experienced rejection by mainstream orthodox culture, though both in their own ways appeal to the orthodox voice for self-justification. The art of the bedchamber was for centuries a marginal (even suppressed and condemned) tradition, passed on secretly, ignored, and periodically lost. *Jin Ping Mei* was soon banned for obscenity and still occupies a problematic status, though many consider it one of the best Chinese novels ever written.

The Art of the Bedchamber and Ming and Qing Fiction

Before going into more specific traces of the art of the bedchamber in *Jin Ping Mei*, I need to give a fuller explanation of the way Ming and Qing fiction other than *Jin Ping Mei* refers to and interprets the art of the

21. *Yufang zhiyao* and *Yufang mijue*, in Li Ling, *Zhongguo fangshu gaiguan*, 102 and 104, respectively.

22. See Pfister, "Gendering Sexual Pleasures," 55–56; and Goldin, *Culture of Sex*, 47.

bedchamber. This is for two reasons. First, *Jin Ping Mei* is unusual because of its lack of direct mention of the terms for the art of the bedchamber (except in the partial instance mentioned above). The latter's influence is nevertheless apparent because, besides the commonalities already mentioned, the novel includes elements that clearly belong to that tradition in the form of things such as drugs and sex tools and positions of intercourse, including the latter's appearance in the erotic albums. In contrast, the words "art of the bedchamber" (*fangzhong shu*) or alternative terms do occur prominently in other fiction. Second, when other fiction refers to the "art of the bedchamber," it does so primarily in terms of the methods and terminology of Daoist internal (or inner) alchemy, which it typically represents in a way that portrays characters taking pleasure to extremes and, as I said above, trying to overpower and exploit one another by means of drugs or occult techniques. My overall point is that whatever commonalities the art of the bedchamber and *Jin Ping Mei* have or do not have, knowledge of the art of the bedchamber (however direct or indirect) was widespread in the Ming and is therefore something that, we must assume, informs the portrayal of sex in the novel. The evidence of other works of Ming and Qing fiction helps prove this point.

To understand the way in which Ming and Qing fiction represents the art of the bedchamber, it is necessary to explain the art of the bedchamber in relation to the long-established practices of health and longevity that appear under various rubrics such as the art of nourishing life (*yang sheng* 養生), Daoist internal alchemy (*neidan* 內丹), and the exercises of *daoyin* 導引, known as "guiding and pulling"—versions of which appear in the form of today's exercises known as *qigong* 氣功 ("*qi* work," sometimes called Chinese yoga).[23] The art of the bedchamber, in other words, should be seen as a branch of such practices, even though it has commonly been shunned and excluded. Basic to all such practices is the channeling and transfer of *qi* and *jing*, which can happen in both healthy and unhealthy ways. As taught in the art of the bedchamber, sexual intercourse elevates the circulation of *qi* and fills the entire body with its healthy flow.[24] At the same time, since *jing* and *qi* can be transferred from

23. See Lo, *How to Do the Gibbon Walk*; Kohn, *Chinese Healing Exercises* ("healing exercise" is Kohn's translation of *daoyin*); and Kohn and Wang, *Internal Alchemy.*

24. See Schipper, *The Taoist Body*, 147 and 150; and Wile, *Art of the Bedchamber*, 6–7, 10–12, and 41–42.

one person to another, partners may increase their levels of both during the act of sex but also risk depletion. This notion is basic to all literature about sex in China, including *Jin Ping Mei*—though in its case the notion is mainly articulated in medical terms, not those of the art of the bedchamber or Daoist sexual alchemy. A brief reference to the woman's "stealing essence and sucking marrow" (*duo jing xi sui* 奪精吸髓) occurs in a scene of sexual battle, in which it amounts to a rhetorical flourish rather than a true dramatization of such a process.[25] Otherwise all that the reader finds are passing mentions of, for example, the term *daoyin* (which only appears in the *cihua* edition), when Ximen Qing receives a *daoyin* massage from his barber that makes "his entire body feel relaxed and relieved" (*nongde hunshen tongtai*, 弄的渾身通泰, 52.677). The author needs to provide no explanation. Readers would know that the barber is "guiding and pulling" *qi* around Ximen Qing's body for the sake of his health and comfort. The assumption is that Ximen Qing, like anyone else, risks suffering injury to his *qi* and *jing* and periodically needs remedy and repair. In fact, his death will be due to such an injury.[26]

As I have said, the term "art of the bedchamber" or alternative forms of it commonly appear in other Ming and Qing works—though never in a way that reverently adheres to the spirit of the classic bedchamber arts.[27] For example, the Ming novel *Xiuta yeshi* 繡榻野史 (The history of the embroidered couch, ca. 1597), which appeared not long after *Jin Ping Mei*, refers to the "methods by which Daoist immortals cultivate and

25. This reference only occurs in the *cihua* edition, JPMCH, 78.2458. For other possible allusions to sexual alchemy, see chapter 4.

26. Another such brief reference is to the ancient "Yellow Court" (*Huangting* 黄庭) classics about nourishing life (also only in the *cihua* edition). The same chapter contains what some say is a veiled allusion to a Daoist practice of the internal circulation of *qi*. Ximen Qing chases Chunmei, who runs to the top of a hill in the garden and then back down to the "waist" (*yao* 腰) of the hill, and then asks if the gate is locked. Her run up and down the hill and his asking about the gate suggest the process of the internal circulation of *qi*. Satyendra refers to the notion that "the gate between the Middle and Lower Cinnabar Fields . . . must be solidly closed towards the end of this breathing technique" ("Metaphors of the Body," 91). See also 27.706 and 720–21; JPM, 27.355–356; Roy, 2.27.131 (and 505, n. 20), and 2.27.145 (and 509, n. 62); and Stone, *Fountainhead*, 37. For "Yellow Court," see Shanghai shi *Honglong meng* xuehui, *Jin Ping Mei jianshang cidian*, 326.

27. Pan Jianguo ("Daojiao fangzhong wenhua") and Wan Jingchuan ("Lun fangzhongshu") agree that fiction's primary focus is on methods and terminology from sexual alchemy.

nourish themselves through cinnabar refinement" (仙家修養煉丹的法) and the practices of "internal alchemy" and "the art of refining cinnabar" (*neidan, lian dan shu* 煉丹術).[28] In this case as elsewhere, the methods consist not of exercise techniques but of an aphrodisiac that the man applies to the surface of his penis to make it "stay hard and firm all night without fail" (長大堅硬，通宵不跌倒, 1.136–137). Another drug goes in the vagina to stimulate the flow of "*yin* essence" (*yinjing* 陰精), giving the woman "indescribable pleasure" (快樂不可勝言, 1.136). The drugs come with instructions for use that the narrative presents in detail, echoing the arcane tone that typically surrounds such practices. Similar drugs with similar effects appear in *Jin Ping Mei*, but without the detail and terminology found here and elsewhere that would have been widely known at the time.

Other works refer to the mastery of exercises that stir and channel the flow of *qi* and enhance sexual performance. The resort to such techniques contrasts with the mere reliance on a drug, though the results are similar in terms of what practitioners become capable of doing. A story in the late Ming collection *Sengni niehai* 僧尼孽海 (Monks and nuns in a sea of sin) tells of monk specialists who gain the favor of a Yuan 元 dynasty (1271–1368) emperor by teaching him the "art of circulating *qi*" (*yun qi shu* 運氣術).[29] The story is unique in that, using the term *fangzhong shu*, it directly cites the *Sunü miaolun*'s nine sexual positions, which the monk persuades the emperor to use with women recruited into the palace. This is a rare case of nearly verbatim lifting from a text of the classic art of the bedchamber.[30] However, as loyal as the story is to the wording of the *Sunü miaolun*, the image of the decadent emperor, egged on by a fawning monk, hardly conforms to the spirit of the classic art of the bedchamber.

A more detailed portrayal of methods appears in the mid-Qing novel *Zhulin yeshi* 株林野史 (The scandalous story of the Zhulin Grove), which refers to the bedchamber arts in terms of Daoist internal alchemy and uses the expression "methods of the battle of absorption" (*cai zhan zhi fa* 採戰之法), which readers would know refers to the absorption of *jing*

28. Lü Tiancheng 呂天成, *Xiuta yeshi*, in SWXHB, vol. 2, 2.205. See also Wong, "Anatomy of Eroticism."

29. Tang Bohu 唐伯虎, *Sengni niehai*, in SWXHB, vol. 24, 7.81–82.

30. The text lifts only about half of what is in *Sunü miaolun* and modifies it somewhat. For this reference, I am indebted to Xue Yingjie, "Wenren shenfen," 114.

by one partner from the other. A man with such skills can "go all night without ejaculating" (*yiye ye buxie* 一夜也不洩) and "can mount ten women in one night" (*yiye neng yu shinü* 一夜能御十女), language that is typical of the art of the bedchamber.[31] But although ejaculation control appears in the art of the bedchamber, when the latter uses battle metaphors it does not encourage the kind of aggression that takes place in *Zhulin yeshi*, in which the man tries mercilessly to tantalize the woman. She decides that he is being "cheeky" (*taoqi* 淘氣), "churns up her *qi*" (*yunqi qi lai* 運起氣來), and drains him of essence. When he desperately tries to pull himself out, she "clamps herself so firmly" on his penis that he can no longer move (一夾箝的, 挺結實, 7.48). Whereas the *Sengni niehai* story merely refers to "circulating" or "churning *qi*," *Zhulin yeshi* provides an illustration of someone resorting to such methods, which the woman has mastered.[32] Ximen Qing can likewise "go all night without ejaculating," but he does so only by resorting to a drug, which allows more automatic results than the training that he would need to master such a skill as the channeling of *qi*. The words *neidan* and *lian dan shu* do not occur in *Jin Ping Mei*.

A final example of the fictional adoption of technical vocabulary appears in the Kangxi 康熙 era (1661–1722) novel, *Xinghua tian* 杏花天 (Heaven of apricot flowers). Not unusual is the mention of a "bedchamber art" (*fangshu* 房術) in the form of a pill that allows a man to "last all night without slack" (*tongxiao budai* 通宵不怠).[33] More interesting is the appearance of the image of the penis taking the form of a head with a mouth that can move to stimulate the woman. A Daoist adept teaches the protagonist a "method of riding women" (*yu nü zhi fa* 御女之法) called

31. Chidao ren 痴道人, *Zhulin yeshi*, in SWXHB, vol. 20, 2.10, 13.95, and 14.103. It also refers to the art of the bedchamber as "the bedchamber arts of Pengzu" (*Pengzu fang zhi shu* 彭祖房之術, 8.54) or, more simply, "methods and arts" (or "occult techniques," *fashu* 法術; 8.54 and 16.116). *Fashu* appears once in *Jin Ping Mei*. It is the term Wu Yueniang uses to refer to Ximen Qing's aphrodisiac, and it only occurs in the *cihua* edition, JPMCH, 53.1485.

32. See also the anonymous Ming novel *Yinglie zhuan* 英烈傳, 1.6 (*fangzhong yun qi zhi shu* 房中運氣之術, "the bedchamber art of circulating *qi*"); and the anonymous Qing novel, *Wutong ying* 梧桐影, in SWXHB, vol. 16, 4.45 (which refers to *suo yang* 縮陽, "retracting the *yang*"; *cai zhan* 彩戰, "the battle of absorption"; and *yang gui hu yang* 養龜護陽, "nourishing the turtle and protecting the *yang*").

33. Tianfang daoren 天放道人, *Xinghua tian*, in SWXHB, vol. 17, 2.56.

the "*bijia* exercise" (*bijia gongfu* 比甲功夫, 2.65–66). In internal alchemy, *bijia* refers to a type of duo-cultivation, mentioned briefly above, in which partners eschew lustful thoughts and refrain from resorting to varieties of sexual positions or thrusting techniques.[34] *Bijia* means "other," and in this case it refers to the reciprocal borrowing of energy from the "other." But *Xinghua tian* interprets the exercise in its own way, which involves the art of "absorbing and supplementing" (*cai bu* 採補) to "solidify essence" (*gu jing* 固精)—that is, to halt emission (2.67–68). Instead of reciprocity, it has the man "circulating *qi*" to make his penis move on its own, with a mouth that can "bite and nibble" (*ken yao* 啃咬) at the woman's "flower heart" (*huaxin* 花心, 2.68 and 4.82–83)—that is, stimulate the sensitive areas around the entrance to the vagina (explained further below). Mastering such an art allows *Xinghua tian*'s protagonist to please women as never before, to the extent that the first woman he practices with dies of overstimulation. "Absorption," "solidification," "circulation," and "other" are all terms found in texts of sexual alchemy. But the image of the penis moving like a mouth, "biting and nibbling," takes the battle of sex to a new level of male mastery. Such an image appears elsewhere in Ming and Qing fiction, in which it finds its female match in portrayals of the vagina that can clamp on the penis, as seen above in *Zhulin yeshi*. Both the image of the penis moving on its own and the woman's ability to clamp appear only marginally in *Jin Ping Mei*, but those appearances would be easily missed without knowledge of the above passages in *Xinghua tian* and other novels. I return to the two images more fully in chapter 4, on sex as battle.

Such references to the art of the bedchamber and internal alchemy represent a sensationalizing reduction of those practices that is common across Ming and Qing fiction.[35] Fundamental notions such as the

34. *Bijia* 比甲 is probably an alternative (perhaps incorrect) writing of *bijia* 比家. *Xinghua tian* provides no elucidation, but see Liu Xun, "Numinous Father and Holy Mother," 121, 128, and 129; and for *bijia*, see Cao Heng 曹珩 (fl. 1630s), *Daoyuan yiqi* 道元一氣. See also Despeux and Kohn, *Women in Daoism*, 211–15 (on "twosome cultivation"); and Valussi, "Female Alchemy," 143.

35. See also chapter 5 of *Taohua ying* 桃花影, in which a monk transmits occult skills; chapter 7 of *Chundeng mishi* 春燈迷史, in which a man takes an aphrodisiac pill and puts one in the woman's vagina; and chapter 2 of *Wushan yanshi* 巫山艷史, in which both the stop method and the use of aphrodisiac pills appear.

guarding or "solidifying" of essence lose their spiritually transformative qualities and become part of a repertoire of methods and skills to ensure sexual mastery. Partners use the practices to push pleasure to its extremes, meanwhile stealing vital forces from each other and in some cases causing or suffering harmful, even mortal, consequences.

I want to make a final point before returning to *Jin Ping Mei* and its correspondences with the art of the bedchamber. This involves the sense of "classic" that I have used to label the ancient bedchamber texts. The same sense applies to "classic" texts of medical literature as practiced by the medical men called "master physician" (*taiyi* 太醫) or "medical official" (*yiguan* 醫官) in *Jin Ping Mei* and other fiction. "Classic" in this shared sense contrasts with a range of beliefs and practices that would be considered unorthodox, including the use of the monk's aphrodisiac, or the performance of spirit possession by Old Woman Liu (Liu Pozi 劉婆子) during Ximen Qing's final illness (79.1151). The science of the classic medical practitioner informs many of the novel's descriptions of illness, which mainly have to do with sexual or reproductive matters.[36] One of the doctors (He 何) twice refers to Ximen Qing's swelling and blockage during his final illness using the term *biandu* 便毒 (79.1149–1150), a common medical expression in the Ming for "poison in the region of relief." Another doctor (Ren 任) characterizes Ximen Qing's illness as a case of "*yang* collapse" (*tuo yang* 脱陽, 79.1147–1148), another common medical term.[37] In the medical thought of the time, the cause of such illnesses was generally ascribed to sexual excess, which led to disease through depletion and which was a major focus of concern in the late Ming. Although the *Jin Ping Mei* author was conversant with classic Chinese medicine, he was not so conversant—or chose not to be openly so—with the classic art of the bedchamber or Daoist sexual alchemy. Nevertheless, the concepts of sexual excess and its moral and physical effects are common to traditions of the art of the bedchamber, *daoyin* exercises,

36. Old Woman Liu's ritual is called *tiao shen* 跳神. See Cullen, "Patients and Healers," 103, 108, and 109–115.

37. Both medical men are referred to as "literate healers," *yiguan* being Doctor Ren's 任 title (as seen in the title of JPM, chapter 54). See Cullen, "Patients and Healers," 108–109. On *biandu*, see Schonebaum, *Novel Medicine*, 122–125 and 129–130 (on *biandu* possibly standing for syphilis). For both *biandu* and *tuo yang*, see Xu Yuanzhen, *Zhongyi cishi*, 522 and 633 (under *hengxuan* 横痃); and Roy, 4.79.647–648 and 650.

and internal alchemy. The same concepts inform the progress toward Ximen Qing's death.

Elements of the Art of the Bedchamber in Jin Ping Mei

To get back to *Jin Ping Mei*, besides the commonalities listed above, the most specific and obvious traces of the contents of the classic art of the bedchamber appear, first, in *Jin Ping Mei*'s references to positions of intercourse, though the names have changed, and second, in the novel's use of sexual devices, chemicals, and aphrodisiacs, which by the time the novel was written had become more widespread, varied, and potent than in pre-Ming times. I discuss these obvious cases below. Here I begin with elements that have a more minimal or nebulous presence but that deserve attention nevertheless—namely, references to the structure of the vagina, the art of thrusting, and the practices of kissing and absorbing saliva.

In the art of the bedchamber, including the Ming *Sunü miaolun*, the vagina has as many as eight levels of depth beyond the clitoris, which is called "red pearl" (*chizhu* 赤朱), or "red ball" (*hongqiu* 紅毬), while the levels have names such as "zither strings" (*qinxian* 琴弦), at one "inch" (*cun* 寸), and "uneven teeth" (*maichi* 麥齿), at two inches. An important piece of knowledge transmitted in the art of the bedchamber is that thrusting beyond a particular point—"grain seed" (*gushi* 穀實), at five inches—is too deep and therefore harmful, as harm for the woman occurs at a shallower depth than for the man. Harmony best takes place between zither strings and uneven teeth. Shallow thrusts allow *qi* to accumulate, but if thrusts go too deep, the *qi* disperses and the inner organs suffer harm.[38]

Jin Ping Mei ignores such knowledge. Some of the technical terms for parts of the vagina appear in *Sengni niehai*, mentioned above—namely,

38. *Sunü miaolun*, in Li Ling, *Zhongguo fangshu gaiguan*, 195–196. See also Li Ling and McMahon, "Contents and Terminology," 165–166, citing *Yufang mijue* and *Sunü miaolun*. An "inch" corresponds to about a finger's breadth. See Li Ling and McMahon, "Contents and Terminology," 164.

"zither strings," "grain seed," "uneven teeth," and "baby rat" (*yingshu* 嬰鼠), which the Ming *Sunü miaolun* lists.[39] Strangely, the term "zither strings" appears in *Jin Ping Mei*, but in reference to a part of the penis (74.1025–1026). The author may have heard the term somewhere but misapplied it (intentionally or not). None of the other terms appears in the novel, which once refers to the interior of the vagina as the "vagina chamber" (*pinwu* 牝屋), as I describe below, and has several different terms for the clitoris and the vagina, as I also show below.

As for the art of thrusting, *Jin Ping Mei* and other works of Ming and Qing fiction use the same word for "thrust" as the art of the bedchamber does: *chousong* 抽送 (that is, "pull out"), *chou*, and *song* ("send in"). In addition, all differentiate between "deep" (*shen* 深) and "shallow" (*qian* 淺) thrusts. But the art of the bedchamber describes specific numerical sequences of deep and shallow thrusts, such as "nine shallow and one deep" (*jiu qian yi shen* 九淺一深), and when and why to apply them. In *Jin Ping Mei* and other Ming and Qing works, thrusts are typically precipitous and exaggerated, going into the hundreds and thousands—as in *Xiuta yeshi*'s 10,000 thrusts (2.202)—without any attempt to apply a particular method or sequence. Some works mention the best-known sequence of "nine shallow and one deep" and other combinations, thus showing a token knowledge of the methods, though without the rationales supplied in the texts of the art of the bedchamber.[40]

Nevertheless, *Jin Ping Mei* roughly reflects the distinction between shallow and deep in the scene at the grape arbor, in which Ximen Qing goads Pan Jinlian by using his toe to stimulate her "flower's heart" (*huaxin* 花心), causing her "lascivious essences to flow" (*yinjing liuchu* 淫精流出, 27.355). The term "flower's heart" may mean clitoris, as Roy translates it, but it may refer generally to the sensitive areas near the entrance to the vagina. Later Ximen Qing puts on himself both the silver clasp and the "sulfur-dipped ring" (*liuhuang quan* 硫黄圈) and, "refusing to enter deeply [*shen ru*]," dallies "only at the mouth of her vagina, knocking and

39. *Sengni niehai*, in SWXHB, vol. 24, 1.50 and 7.81–82. "Baby rat" seems to be a collapsing of *yingnü* 嬰女, "baby girl," and *choushu* 臭鼠, "stinking rat."

40. For references to these methods in *Yiqing zhen* 怡情陣, *Zaihua chuan* 載花船, *Chundeng mishi*, *Xinghua tian*, and *Taowu xianping* 梼杌閑評, see Pan Jianguo, "Daojiao fangzhong wenhua," 67. The expression for "nine shallow and one deep" occurs, for example, in *Yiqing zhen* (Jiangxi yeren 江西野人, *Yiqing zhen*, in SWXHB, vol. 22, 2.23).

thumping himself against her" (不肯深入，只在牝口子來回擂晃，27.356) and purposely bringing her to an extreme of excitation. The sulfur-dipped ring acts something like a dildo, other types of which he also possesses. Likewise with Wang Liu'er 王六兒，Ximen Qing "dallies deliberately" at the "mouth of her vagina, titillating her flower's heart, refusing to go more deeply [*shen ru*], . . . so exciting her that her lascivious waters rush forth" (故作逗留；牝口子；挑弄其花心，不肯深入，急的婦人淫津流出，79.1140). Titillating the "flower's heart" and dallying at the entrance constitute stimulation of the "shallow" parts of the woman's genitals. A man following the art of the bedchamber would do so after first engaging in foreplay by caressing her body and genitals with his hands and mouth, only proceeding to use his penis to stimulate the "shallow" erectile areas of her vulva after observing that she was ready.[41] He would finally enter—that is, thrust deeply—only after observing that she was ready. Readiness is key in the art of the bedchamber. The man attends to the woman's signs and never proceeds to the next stage unless she is ready. Ximen Qing instead goads and tantalizes the two women, exploiting their sensitivity to render them helpless with arousal.

Another scene describes deep penetration, as Ximen Qing achieves utmost pleasure with Pan Jinlian while entering the "vagina chamber" (*pinwu* 牝屋). The passage is copied in part from an earlier novel, *Ruyijun zhuan*, to which the *Jin Ping Mei* narrator adds a brief aside, explaining that *pinwu* is a woman's deepest spot and that getting there gives a man utmost pleasure. The underscored words are from *Ruyijun zhuan*: "His organ penetrated all the way to her cervix. The cervix is the innermost recess of the vaginal chamber and contains a fleshy growth like the budding pistil of a flower. When the head of his penis penetrates to this point, the man will feel a melting sensation the pleasure of which is indescribable" (那話攮進去了，直抵牝屋之上. 牝屋者，乃婦人牝中深極處，有屋如含苞花蕋，到此處，男子莖首，覺翕然暢美不可言，27.357).[42]

41. For more on such terms, see chapter 4. For such references in the Chinese art of the bedchamber and the Indian *Kamasutra* in light of the science of sexual medicine, see Korda, Goldstein, and Sommer, "History of Female Ejaculation." Also see Levin, "Clitoral Activation Paradox"; and Pfister, "Sexual Body Techniques." Yao Lingxi 姚靈犀 wrongly identifies *huaxin* as the womb (*Pingwai zhiyan* 瓶外卮言，174).

42. See also *Ruyijun zhuan*, 42; and Roy, 2.27.148, his translation (slightly modified). A later passage similarly refers to a deep and marvelous spot, JPM.52.676.

Ximen Qing's move hurts Pan Jinlian, who suddenly jerks upward. This causes the sulfur-dipped ring to break inside her, after which she goes limp, "feels dizzy, and loses her senses" (頭目森森然, 莫知所之, 27.357).[43] The informative aside about the nature of the *pinwu* is unique in *Jin Ping Mei*, which suddenly takes on an explanatory tone like an instructional manual. Though the term *pinwu* does not appear in the texts of the art of the bedchamber, the novel's tone is characteristic of these texts: one of the sharing of confidential knowledge between men needing to learn the art of sex with women.

The act of kissing offers another example of the novel's commonality with the art of the bedchamber. The first scene of sex between Ximen Qing and Pan Jinlian describes her mouth flowing with "sweet spittle," as she smiles and proffers the "tip of her tongue" (*tiantuo* 甜唾, *shejian* 舌尖, 4.57). Another scene describes Ximen Qing and Song Huilian 宋蕙蓮 "kissing and sucking each other's tongues" (*qin zui za she* 親嘴咂舌, 23.294–95).[44] Finally, in the first passionate scene between Chen Jingji 陳敬濟 and Pan Jinlian after Ximen Qing's death, "they kiss and smack for quite a while, truly a case in which the sweet rouge of her lips fills his mouth, as he swallows in vain the juices of her tongue. Her sweet spittle transfuses his heart, as it floods through his vitals" (兩個咂了一回. 正是: 得多少脂香滿口涎空嚥, 甜唾融心溢肺肝, 80.1165).[45]

The swallowing of saliva in this passage may seem strange to twenty-first-century readers, unless they know about its long history in *daoyin* practices and inner alchemy. As a common part of scenes of sexual description in *Jin Ping Mei*, kissing shares features with the classic art of the bedchamber (however partial the link may be), and as such can be divided into two aspects. First is the act of kissing and sucking from each other's mouths, and second is the ingesting of saliva during lovemaking and the belief in the healthful benefits of doing so. Swallowing one's own

43. This phrase also comes from *Ruyijun zhuan*, 45 (in which the Empress Wu 武 speaks of herself).

44. "Sweet spittle" and "sucking . . . tongues" come from Roy, 1.4.85 and 2.23.49.

45. See also JPMCH, 80.2504; and Roy, 4.80.675, modifying his translation by taking *kong* 空 to mean that Chen Jingji kisses "in vain," unable to follow through with intercourse. The Chongzhen edition has *yong* 顒 (solemn, large) instead of the *cihua* edition's *rong* 融 (melt, blend, fuse), which I prefer. My interpretation of *kong* benefited from the help of Wu Cuncun of Hong Kong University.

saliva has long been part of *daoyin* exercises and longevity techniques that do not involve the art of the bedchamber.[46] A late Ming text, for example, writes that saliva abounds at the tip of the tongue, and if it is frequently swallowed into the "cinnabar field" (*dantian* 丹田), it gives "pleasure" (*changmei* 暢美) and dispels stagnation.[47] The Tang dynasty bedchamber text *Dongxuanzi* (洞玄子, The master of the dark cave) describes the act of kissing in which man and woman gently suck (*shun* 吮) and nibble on each other's lips and tongue and "drink each other's saliva" (*ru qi jinye* 茹其津液).[48] The Six Dynasties text *Sunü jing* (素女經, Classic of the plain woman) has the man "kissing her mouth and sucking [*shun*] her tongue" (*xian qikou, shun qishe* 銜其口, 吮其舌).[49] These two passages most resemble the scene with Ximen Qing and Song Huilian, which like many others in the novel simply describes the act of kissing.

But the two other passages from *Jin Ping Mei*, especially the one about Chen Jingji and Pan Jinlian, sound distantly like the art of the bedchamber's reference to the stimulating and healthful effects of kissing and swallowing saliva. The *Yufang zhiyao* says that the man should drink generously of the woman's oral secretions, which will bring a flash of refreshment and make him look like a virgin maiden.[50] The Ming *Sunü miaolun* writes that kissing allows the man "to absorb her [the woman's] *yin jing* and replenish his *yang qi*, while drawing in the *qi* of her nostrils in order to fill his spine marrow. In swallowing her saliva he will nourish the cinnabar field, thereby causing the hot *qi* to penetrate to the *niwan* point and spread through the four limbs. The overflow will benefit the *qi* and the blood, halt the aging of the face, and increase longevity" (吸陰精

46. See the Mawangdui text *Shiwen* 十問 in Li Ling, *Zhongguo fangshu gaiguan*, 31; and Harper, "Sexual Arts of Ancient China," 550–552 and 586 (which refers to "blue-gem spring" as the "reservoir of saliva under the tongue"). See also Harper, *Early Chinese Medical Literature*, 128 and 394, n. 3 (for a translation of *Shiwen* 十問); and Kohn, *Chinese Healing Exercises*, 88, 141, and 143.

47. See Chen Hsiu-fen, "Visual Representation," 158, n. 41, citing from Gao Lian's 高濂 *Zun sheng bajian* (遵生八箋), the latter of which is further cited below.

48. *Dongxuanzi*, in Li Ling, *Zhongguo fangshu gaiguan*, 106.

49. *Sunü jing*, in Li Ling, *Zhongguo fangshu gaiguan*, 108. See also Wile, *Art of the Bedchamber*, 87.

50. *Yufang zhiyao*, in Li Ling, *Zhongguo fangshu gaiguan*, 105; and Wile, *Art of the Bedchamber*, 101.

而補陽氣，引鼻氣以填脊髓，含津液以養丹田，令泥丸熱氣透徹，貫通四支，溢益氣血，駐顏不老).[51]

Besides "saliva" (*tuo* 唾), the only words that the novel shares with the art of the bedchamber are *yi* 溢, meaning flood or overflow, and *shun* 吮, meaning suck. Nevertheless, the reference to "sweet spittle" and the fact that it "transfuses his heart, as it floods through his vitals" distantly echoes the art of the bedchamber. Given the long tradition of the invigorating effects of the fluids of the mouth upon the internal organs, whether through swallowing one's own or one's partner's fluid, it is not difficult to imagine this knowledge becoming part of the received concept of kissing—though it would be going too far to say that Chen Jingji and Pan Jinlian are practicing the art of the bedchamber in the spirit of the passages quoted above.[52]

POSITIONS OF INTERCOURSE

An unmistakable reflection of the classic art of the bedchamber lies in *Jin Ping Mei*'s reference to positions of intercourse, which as a category of practices have existed since ancient times and which appear throughout Ming and Qing fiction. The fact that this aspect is more prominent in fiction than other contents of the classic art of the bedchamber coincides with a point that Wendy Doniger makes about the Indian *Kamasutra*. In the latter's modern revival, a mistaken impression has been that positions are what the book is mainly about, and they occupy its "best thumbed" pages, as she writes.[53] The bias is similar in Ming and Qing fiction, including *Jin Ping Mei*, in which the practice of a variety of sexual positions becomes in effect the defining practice of the art of sex, though positions capture only a fraction of what the classic texts are about.

51. *Sunü miaolun*, in Li Ling, *Zhongguo fangshu gaiguan*, 203; and Wile, *Art of the Bedchamber*, 41–42, his translation (with slight modification), and 133. See also Li Ling, *Zhongguo fangshu kao*, 398 (on *niwan*, "mud pellet," a point inside the head behind and between the eyes).

52. The expression *feigan*, meaning "lungs and liver" ("vitals" in the above translation), differs from the language of the art of the bedchamber, which uses *wuzang* to refer to "the five internal organs." *Feigan* instead is a common metaphor for the inner self or true feelings, not the actual organs.

53. Doniger, *Redeeming the Kamasutra*, 19–20.

Nevertheless, that fraction is relevant in terms of the way in which *Jin Ping Mei* reflects the spirit of what the practice of sexual positions represents: playfulness in the act of sex. In other words, the art of the bedchamber is not only about mastering techniques and improving health. Partners may also enjoy themselves in using varieties of postures and movements, as do the characters in *Jin Ping Mei*. Instead of (or in addition to) losing themselves in passionate frenzy, they coordinate with each other in playfully alternating between various positions. Ximen Qing shows Pan Jinlian an erotic album that Li Ping'er gave him, which illustrates twenty-four positions that he and Pan imitate that night, though the novel gives no names for the positions and supplies no description of any of the moves. Knowing that he and Li Ping'er have already performed them, Pan Jinlian is eager to match, if not outdo, her rival. Later Chen Jingji and Pan Jinlian use the same album, with Pan Jinlian adding a move that she did not use with Ximen Qing by asking the maid Chunmei 春梅 to help push Chen from behind in case he gets tired (83.1201). In doing so, they are following the model of erotic albums that likewise employ a third person.[54]

The positions and their names are highly consistent from the earliest texts of the art of the bedchamber to the *Sunü miaolun* in the Ming. But different names appear in *Jin Ping Mei* and other works of Ming and Qing fiction, with a few exceptions. Three positions are broadly consistent, even if their names are not: the man entering from the rear, the woman reclining or lying on her back with the man facing her, and the woman in the superior position. The ones in the classic art of the bedchamber resemble the moves of *qigong* exercises in using the names of insects and animals. An example of the first position is the art of the bedchamber's "attached cicada" (*chan fu* 蟬附), in which the woman lies on her stomach as the man enters from behind.[55] In variations of the position, the woman can also be on all fours as the man enters from behind (a variation

54. A third reference to the albums and positions occurs when Ximen Qing is with Lady Lin (78.1116). The albums are related to (if not the same as) the ones reproduced in Robert van Gulik's *Erotic Colour Prints of the Ming Period*. See also Cahill, "Introduction to R. H. van Gulik."

55. It is called this in the Mawangdui and the texts of the art of the bedchamber preserved in the *Yixin fang*, and *chan fu shi* 蟬附勢 in the Ming *Sunü miaolun*, which uses the word *shi* for position.

called "the tiger's play" [*hu you* 虎游]),[56] or she can be straddling the man and facing his feet (a variation called "the rabbit fleeing" [*tu wu* 兔騖]).[57] In *Jin Ping Mei* and other works, however, the position of the man entering from the rear goes by the label "taking fire from the other side of the mountain" (*ge shan qu huo* 隔山取火), abandoning the elegance of insect or animal names and instead using a racier metaphor.

For the second position, the Mawangdui texts have the "monkey latches on" (*yuan ju* 猨據), with different names for variants that depend on how the man holds the woman's legs and feet. For example, in Ming erotic albums he can be supporting himself on his knees and wrists while his abdomen rests against the back of her uplifted thighs, as in *Jin Ping Mei* and elsewhere—where the position is called "rowing the boat at night" (*diao ye xing chuan* 掉夜行船).[58] In the third position, called the "sucking fish" (*yu zuo* 魚嘬) in the art of the bedchamber, the woman faces and straddles the man, who is lying on his back.[59] For the second and third positions, *Jin Ping Mei* describes Ximen Qing and Pan Jinlian in a long session in which they change from one position to another: "now she is on top dousing the red candle, in the next instant they switch to rowing the boat at night" (纔去倒澆紅蠟燭, 忽然又掉夜行船).[60] Though *Jin Ping Mei* does not describe "rowing the boat at night" in detail, we can base our understanding of it on an illustration in a Ming album,

56. It is called this in the Mawangdui and *Yixin fang* texts and "the tiger's stance" (*hu bu shi* 虎步勢) in *Sunü miaolun*.

57. Thus called in the Mawangdui and *Yixin fang* texts, and "the rabbit licking," *tu shun shi* 兔吮勢, in *Sunü miaolun*.

58. Alternatively, he can have her sitting in a chair and take her legs over his shoulders or around his waist, which appears in both the erotic albums and *Jin Ping Mei*.

59. See Li Ling and McMahon, "Contents and Terminology," 170; Li Ling, *Zhongguo fangshu gaiguan*, 193–194; and Wile, *Art of the Bedchamber*, 124–126. The *Sunü miaolun* has the "monkey pounces" (*yuan bo shi* 猨搏勢), with the woman sitting on the man (perhaps the same as the Mawangdui "latches on"). The position called the "dragon flies" (*long fei shi* 龍飛勢) resembles the stance of the woman on her back with her legs up in the "monkey pounces" of the earlier texts. In addition, *Sunü miaolun* has the "phoenix soars" (*feng xiang shi* 鳳翔勢), in which the woman lies face up, raising her thighs with her hands as the man enters. *Sunü miaolun*'s "fishes nibbling" (*yu sha shi* 魚唼勢; Wile's translation) features two women and a man.

60. JPMCH, 6.148. Instead of "rowing the boat at night," the Chongzhen edition has "stealing fire from the other side of the wall" (偷來火隔墻; 6.81).

where it goes by the same name.[61] Readers of the time can be assumed to need no explanation.

Other positions that the novel names but that do not appear in the art of the bedchamber occur in the scene at the grape arbor, which is another example of the generic divergence between fiction and the texts of the art of the bedchamber. This is the scene referred to above, in which Ximen Qing goads Pan Jinlian by dallying at the mouth of her vagina. The art of the bedchamber uses minimal language to refer to arousing the woman, in one instance describing her as being so excited that she "desperately pleads for mercy" (*qiu si qiu sheng* 求死求生).[62] The actual playing out of such a scene is left to the work of the imagination, which the authors of *Jin Ping Mei* and other narratives gladly carry out—commonly presenting a scene in which the man deliberately tantalizes the woman. Ximen Qing has Pan Jinlian lie on her back with her feet separately suspended on ropes tied to an arbor post above, after which he "assumes the position of 'Inserting the Arrow Upside Down'" (*maile ge dao ru linghua* 賣了個倒入翎花). Here, the word for "assume" (or "deploy," *maile* 賣了) comes from the language of adopting a position in martial arts. He teases her for a while and then takes a nap, after which he tells her that he is "going to perform the position of the 'old monk chiming the bell'" (我要耍個老和尚撞鐘). He then penetrates to the "vagina room," causing the sulfur-dipped ring to break (27.355 and 357).[63] Other novels and stories describe sexual positions more fully, in some cases giving a greater variety of names than I have listed.[64] But regardless of the variations in nomenclature and generic tone, the "assumption of positions" implies a departure from blind frenzy. Stimulation is broken down and extended, just as the art of the bedchamber teaches.

61. For Roy's identification (based on van Gulik), see 1.6.491, n. 24. For an illustration, see van Gulik, *Erotic Colour Prints*, vol. 2, 231.

62. *Dongxuanzi*, in Li Ling, *Zhongguo fangshu gaiguan*, 108.

63. Roy, 2.27.144, his translation of the first of the two positions. See also the passage about Ximen Qing and Wang Liu'er, 79.1140; and Yao Lingxi, *Pingwai zhiyan*, 174 (on chiming the bell).

64. See, for example, Li Yu 李漁, *Rouputuan* 肉蒲團, chapter 3. A monk performing a position called "the foreign monk plays the cymbals" (*fanseng xi nao* 番僧戲鐃), in which he carries the woman in his arms as he inserts himself, appears in Taoyuan zuihua zhuren 桃源醉花主人, *Bie you xiang* 别有香, in SWXHB, vol. 8, 4.38–40. Illustrations of forty-three positions appear in an album by Ye Huasheng 鄴華生, *Su'e pian* 素娥篇.

DRUGS AND DEVICES

The other most obvious overlap between the novel and the art of the bedchamber involves the use of sexual devices, chemicals, and aphrodisiacs, which Ximen Qing is never without. Their effects include increasing stimulation and endurance in the man, stimulation (and sometimes pain) in the woman, and such things as the creation of either wet or dry (or looser or tighter) conditions in the woman. Aphrodisiacs taken by mouth and substances applied to sexual organs and other parts of the body are one thing; devices that fit over the penis to stimulate the woman or insulate the penis, or that are inserted in the vagina to stimulate her, are another—and Ximen Qing owns and uses all of them. In comparison with the classic art of the bedchamber, tools and drugs are more central to the practice of sex in *Jin Ping Mei*, in which they are like weapons that the man uses to arm himself and ensure victory. The weapon-like aspect is yet more pronounced in other Ming and Qing pornography, as I show below.

As far back as they go, the classic sources already show a "wealth of knowledge" about aphrodisiacs and sex devices.[65] As mentioned above, by the Ming such things were widely sold, appearing in both cheap and costly forms that were available to people from all levels of society, including emperors, officials, and urban commoners. Some were made from rare and precious materials, including animals such as seal, otter, and gecko (one of which is consumed by a character in *Xiuta yeshi*).[66] In *Zun sheng ba jian* 遵生八箋 (Eight discourses on respect for life), a sixteenth-century book on nourishing life, Gao Lian 高濂 notes the wide use of drugs and devices, which often caused harm to their consumers. Among other substances and objects, he mentions drugs taken by mouth; fragrances, pills, powders, pastes, and other solutions put in the ears, nose,

65. Harper, "Ancient and Medieval Chinese Recipes," 94–95; see also Li Ling, *Zhongguo fangshu kao*, 421–434.

66. See Su Yufen, *Mingdai chunyao yanjiu*, 26–34 (for the gecko, 30–31), 49, 52–66 (for sale near brothels, along with erotic albums), 79–83 (for appearance of drugs and devices in fiction); and 84–97 (injuries suffered because of their use). Thanks to Chen Hsiu-fen of the National Chengchi University for leading me to this source. For the gecko pill, see *Xiuta yeshi*, 4.284.

or navel (or rubbed on the penis, placed in it, or put in the vagina); and devices tied to the base of the penis, placed in the anus, or worn around the abdomen—many of which appear in some form in *Jin Ping Mei*, though only one with the same name as in Gao Lian's work.[67]

The novel's consistent reference to such things reflects its emphasis on sex as both a literal and a metaphorical battle, in which frequent sex with multiple women requires more than the normal man's capacity. Ximen Qing needs gadgets to impress his partners and ensure that he performs well, though the tools are also used for variety and entertainment. In this light, their use conforms to the notion in the art of the bedchamber of prolonging the sexual act. Ximen Qing, the rich merchant and owner of a wholesale medicine shop, is a likely sort of person to know about and indulge in what the marketplace has to offer in terms of sexual paraphernalia. The novel's readers can likewise be presumed to know about such things, if not themselves to be users.

Ximen Qing's reliance on both drugs and devices can be seen from the first scene of sex to nearly the last, in all of which he "wears at the base of his member a clasp made of silver and saturated with drugs" (根下又帶着銀打就，藥煮成的托子, 4.60). The clasp is a tool that, as the narrator further describes, extends the length and thickness of his organ, though he leaves unsaid the type of drug it is saturated with. More such things appear in the scene at the grape arbor, where he takes out his clasp and sulfur-dipped ring and dallies for a while, as mentioned above, after which he "picks a dab of an ointment called 'Amorous Cries of Boudoir Beauties' and smears it in the opening of his frog's mouth" (捻了些閨艷聲嬌，塗在蛙口內, 27.356–57).[68] As with substances in other stories, this ointment makes his penis grow strong and firm. As for the sulfur-dipped ring, Yao Lingxi 姚靈犀 claims that it is a sheath made of ox tendon (or other animal materials) that goes around the penis, generates heat when

67. See Gao Lian, *Zun sheng ba jian*, 859–861 and 784 (for *liuhuang quan*, also found in *Jin Ping Mei*, as noted below, and Roy, 27.509, n. 66); and Chen Hsiu-fen, "Visual Representation," 159. Part of Gao Lian's book has been translated by John Dudgeon, "Kung-Fu for the Four Seasons," and "The Eight Ornamental Sections," in Berk, ed., *Chinese Healing Arts*, 19–56.

68. Roy, 2.27.146–147, his translation of ointment.

rubbed, and has a surface that is smooth when entering and rough when pulled out.[69]

Nearly the full range of Ximen Qing's sex tools appears a few chapters later in a scene with Wang Liu'er, where in addition to his clasp he takes out his "lovers' sheath, a sulfur-dipped ring, a drug-dipped white satin band, a pendant jade ring, a navel aphrodisiac plaster," and finally his "Burmese bell" (相思套, 硫黄圈, 藥煮的白綾帶子, 懸玉環, 封臍膏, 勉鈴, 38.494).[70] As I have said, the use of such chemicals and devices spans the entire tradition of the art of the bedchamber, beginning in the Mawangdui manuscripts—which, for example, refer to a liquid used to wipe on the penis to strengthen it and increase its size, medicine put in the opening of the penis, a cloth dipped in medicine and used to excite desire, chemicals for tightening the vagina, and supplements and aphrodisiacs taken by mouth.[71] Later texts of the art of the bedchamber continue this tradition, as for instance the *Dongxuanzi*, which writes of sulfur combined with other ingredients to "cure slackness and coldness of the woman's private parts and abruptly shrink them" (療婦人陰寬冷急小).[72] From these older sources, it is possible to speculate that the desired effect of the sulfur-dipped ring is to create tightness and/or dryness in the vagina, supposedly to increase stimulation for the man. Another of the

69. Yao Lingxi, *Pingwai zhiyan*, 193. See also JPMCH, 27.1025; Roy, 2.27.509, nn. 66 and 68 (ring and similar ointment in *Hailing yishi* 海陵佚史). The ring also appears in 52.676. For a powder with a slightly different name (*zhanshengjiao* 顫聲嬌), see 77.1103; and Roy, 4.77.570. Gao Lian also refers to a sulfur-dipped band or hoop (*gu* 箍; *Zun sheng ba jian*, 860).

70. Roy, 2.38.388, his translation of "pendant jade ring" and "navel aphrodisiac plaster." See also Yao Lingxi, *Pingwai zhiyan*, 123 (on the clasp) and 194 (on the navel plaster for "solidifying the *jing*"). Navel creams appear in the Song dynasty and can be found in Ming almanacs. See Su Yufen, *Mingdai chunyao yanjiu*, 40–41.

71. *Yangsheng fang* 養生方 writes: "rub the jade whip with it [the medicine-dipped cloth], and the horse [the vagina] will then be startled" (操以循 (揗) 玉筴 (策), 馬因惊矣), as cited in Li Ling, *Zhongguo fangshu gaiguan*, 10; and Harper, *Early Chinese Medical Literature*, 341–342, his translation. See also Li Ling and McMahon, "Contents and Terminology," 151–153 and 160–161; and Harper, "Ancient and Medieval Chinese Recipes," 94. A similar practice from ancient times is "inside augmentation" (*neijia* 內加), that is, rubbing the body with a medicine-dipped cloth, *Zaliao fang* 雜療方, in Li Ling, *Zhongguo fangshu gaiguan*, 20; and Harper, *Early Chinese Medical Literature*, 363–365, his translation.

72. *Dongxuanzi*, in Li Ling, *Zhongguo fangshu gaiguan*, 138 (on sulfur, also citing *Yufang zhiyao*); and Wile, *Art of the Bedchamber*, 113, his translation (slightly modified).

substances that Ximen Qing uses, "Quavery Voices of Amorous Beauties" (*zhanshengjiao*) is explicitly said to "stem the flow of lascivious waters" (*sezhu yinjin* 澀住淫津, 77.1103), a function that has been part of the art of the bedchamber since ancient times.[73]

Although the novel provides little or no detail about most of its drugs and devices, Yao Lingxi (in the 1930s), Robert van Gulik (in the 1950s and early 1960s), Li Ling 李零 (in the 1990s and 2000s), Su Yufen 蘇玉芬 (in 2011), and others have tried to identify them. According to Yao, the *xiangsi tao* (相思套), "lovers' sheath," goes over the penis, keeps poison out, and stimulates the woman.[74] It is a sort of dildo, the history of which has been studied from excavated artifacts from the Han and Song dynasties and through comparisons with objects found in Ming and Qing fiction.[75] Speculation suggests that the lover's sheath, which goes over the penis, is made of a cow's flesh or pig's bladder and thus is similar to the sulfur-dipped ring in terms of its material. It differs from other dildos that are made of metal or porcelain and are hollow in the middle for fitting over the penis, with holes at the base through which they can be tied around the waist (or, in one model, tied to a woman's foot for her own use).[76] Other varieties exist, including one Ximen Qing is shown using below, but in general they can be divided into soft versus hard, hollow versus solid, and those for use by men versus those for use by women (including double dildos).[77]

The Burmese bell (*mianling* 緬鈴 or 勉鈴, also *mianziling* 勉子鈴) plays a slightly greater role in the novel than the objects just mentioned.

73. Roy, 4.73.385 and 4.77.570, his translation. The substance is also part of what Pan Jinlian puts into the white satin band (73.1011). See Li Ling and McMahon, "Contents and Terminology," 153 and 161–162 (on tightening the vagina, called *yue* 約 in *Zaliao fang*); and Levin, "Wet and Dry Sex," 465–469.

74. Yao Lingxi, *Pingwai zhiyan*, 193.

75. See Li Ling, *Wanbian*, 405–425; and Chen Hai, "G-dian."

76. See Li Ling, *Wanbian*, 415–416. In the Qing novel *Zhulin yeshi* (7.47), a man fits a *xiaoyang quan* 銷陽圈 (ring for spent *yang*) over himself, takes an aphrodisiac pill, and then gives another type of dildo, called a *Guangdong bang* 廣東膀 (Cantonese shoulder), to one woman while he is with another. He tells the first woman to steep the dildo in hot water (which stiffens it), tie it to her foot with its red string at the top, and use it to play with herself.

77. Van Gulik equates the jade-pendant ring with the silver clasp in form and use (*Sexual Life*, 281; see also the picture of a clasp on the facing page).

It appeared in the Ming as a device inserted into the vagina for stimulation, and it shows up in numerous fictional works. Said to be about the size of a longan (a fruit like the lychee but slightly smaller), it is made of concentric layers of thin sheets of gold or copper, connected by an opening in each layer except for the outer one, with the space between the layers filled with mercury. When warmed up or shaken, it vibrates and makes a slight sound.[78] The first time it appears in *Jin Ping Mei*, it falls out of Ximen Qing's sleeve, making a "tinkling sound" (*hualang yisheng* 滑浪一聲) and being "heavy to the touch when Jinlian picks it up and holds it in her hand" (拿在手內沉甸甸的). "What in the world is this?," she asks. "And how come it makes half my arm feel numb?" (是甚麼東西兒?怎的把人半邊胳膊都麻了?). Ximen Qing tells her it is from Burma and that one puts it in the "stove" (*lu* 爐) before intercourse—"stove" or "crucible" being an inner alchemical term for vagina (16.199–200). The presumption is that Ximen Qing got it from Li Ping'er, who in turn got it from her husband's eunuch uncle, who once served in the imperial palace—from which he obtained it and other treasures, including the erotic album. When the Burmese bell appears in the late Ming novella *Xiuta yeshi*, the owner stores it in an exquisite round box that has a seven-layered structure (2.146 and 3.253). The Qing novella *Xinghua tian* portrays a man having sex with one wife while using bells to satisfy each of his other eleven wives (13.254–255).

The silver clasp and white satin band have an overlapping story of their own, with the clasp favored by Ximen Qing and the band favored by the two women, Pan Jinlian and Wang Liu'er. Ximen Qing never discusses the clasp or tells why he uses it, but he insists on using it even when women prefer that he not. He once wears two clasps and a sulfur ring, saying that he wants to do the "flower in the rear courtyard" (*houtinghua* 後庭花) with Jinlian, who has him remove the sulfur ring (which would cause her pain, she says), leaving him with only one of the silver

78. This description is based on Pan Jianguo, "Mianling xinkao," 265–269. See also van Gulik, *Erotic Colour Prints*, vol. 1, 146–148, and *Sexual Life*, 165–166; Roy, 1.521, n. 6; and Wu Xiaoling, "*Jin Ping Mei* 'mianling' shi." Van Gulik cites a nineteenth-century claim that soldiers plundering the imperial palace in Beijing found numerous such balls, "made of thin silver with a loose pellet of brass inside somewhat like a grelot [a small spherical bell]" (*Sexual Life*, n. on 166). It is not impossible that such objects existed in the palace and possibly still exist there.

clasps on (52.676). Showing her pain, she bites down on a handkerchief, but in a case of deal making that commonly accompanies sex in the novel, she gets him to agree to give her a present that she longs for. On a later occasion, in this case hoping to get pregnant, she insists that the clasp not only "knocks against her and hurts" (*gede ren teng* 格的人疼) but also will not let him all the way in. She proposes using a new method, a white satin band (*bailing daizi* 白綾帶子) that she will make for him (72.1003). Ximen Qing uses a clasp in preparation for sex with Meng Yulou, who wants him to take it off immediately and wonders why he must wear it. He refuses to remove it and starts thrusting vigorously until Meng Yulou tells him to slow down because she has been unwell lately (75.1053). To her, the clasp is a piece of nonsense.

As for the white silk band, an illustration appears in a Ming erotic album that, as van Gulik describes, consists of a "flat ring, apparently made of green jade [thus perhaps an illustration of the pendant jade ring], which fits about the base of the member in erection. Below, attached to this ring, are two silk loops. They pass round the scrotum and then run between the man's buttocks; drawn tight, they are wound around his waist and tied on his back"—supposedly, van Gulik continues, to keep the penis erect.[79] These descriptions provide a picture of something like what appears in the novel, as can be seen in the Chongzhen illustration in chapter 73. Pan Jinlian ties the band to the "base of [Ximen Qing's] chowry handle" (*zhubing genxia* 麈柄根下), with "the two ribbons attached to it securely behind his back" (繫在腰間，拴的緊緊的)—the effect of which is to make his member "stretch farther than usual, to over seven inches" (比尋常更舒七寸有余, 73.1022–1023). She exclaims that the band is better than the clasp, allowing him to go deeper, which gives Ximen Qing a "melting sensation the pleasure of which is indescribable" (心中覺翕翕然暢美不可言, 73.1023).[80] Pleasing Ximen Qing to win his heart is only

79. Van Gulik, *Sexual Life*, 281. Van Gulik also refers to a "silk band" (*juandai* 絹帶) mentioned in a Ming text in which a man winds the band tightly around the base of his penis; see *Erotic Colour Prints*, vol. 1, 145–146). See also Li Ling, *Zhongguo fangshu gaiguan*, 213; Yao Lingxi, *Pingwai zhiyan*, 194; and Wile, *Art of the Bedchamber*, 139. An illustration of a strap attached to a clasp appears in van Gulik's *Erotic Colour Prints*, vol. 1, plate XIII, which shows an old man with a young woman.

80. See also JPMCH, 73.2231. "Two ribbons . . . his back" is from Roy, 4.73.416, 417 (illustration), and 418. See also Roy, 3.51.568, n. 27 (on the substance). Pan Jinlian adds the

one of Pan Jinlian's goals. The other more important one at this moment, as noted above, is getting pregnant. The nun Xue 薛 has just brought her a fertility potion and a charm that will guarantee that she has a male baby.

The description of the band that Wang Liu'er makes for Ximen Qing and the scene that follows contain another reference to the use of a dildo that might easily fail to attract the reader's attention. Wang's band is finer than Pan Jinlian's. Since Wang has a less secure hold on Ximen Qing, she needs to please him more. Her goal is to keep him coming to her house and, through their affair, to support her and her husband for as long as possible. The detail appears after he ties the band to himself using a circlet made of her hair, this being part of what makes Wang's band finer. He then places over the tip of his penis a sheath called a *jingdong renshi* (景東人事), a "Yunnanese tickler," which is another kind of dildo. As the passage describes it, he takes the circlet of hair, "wraps it around the base of his turtle, then ties around his waist the two brocade straps that are attached to the circlet; and caps his turtle head with a 'Yunnanese tickler'" (套在龜身下, 兩根錦帶兒, 扎在腰間, 龜頭又帶着景東人事). Nothing tells the reader what the "tickler" looks like, how big it is, how it is attached, or how he acquired it. For example, does it have holes in it to string straps through, as with other dildos? What is it made of—metal, ivory, tree gum, or animal flesh (materials known to be used in other types of dildos)? Is it open at the tip, leaving his glans exposed? *Jingdong* refers to a part of Yunnan Province, and *renshi* (literally, "the human affair") is a term for sex. Yunnan, like Burma, is an exotic place. Similarly, another kind of dildo is called the *Guangdong renshi* 廣東人事, the "Cantonese tickler," with Guangdong being exotic because it is a port for trade with foreign lands.[81]

But the Yunnanese tickler appears only in passing, because at this point Ximen Qing takes the monk's aphrodisiac pill—after which Wang Liu'er manipulates his penis and makes it swell so that it becomes "purple like the color of liver" (*se ruo zigan* 色若紫肝, 79.1140). The focus thus turns to the monstrosity of his penis, *se ruo zigan* being the same

aphrodisiac powder mentioned above to the inside of her silk band to stem vaginal secretions (73.1011). The powder is also used with Ben the Fourth, 77.1103.

81. JPMCH, 79.2511. The "Yunnanese tickler" does not appear in the Chongzhen edition (79.1139–1140). See also Roy, 4.79.633–635, his translation; Yao Lingxi, *Pingwai zhiyan*, 160; and Li Ling, *Wanbian*, 413–414 and 405–425 (on *jingdong renshi*, including materials dildos were made of).

four characters used to describe the penis-like head of the monk who supplies Ximen Qing with the aphrodisiac (49.635). Leaving the dildo yet further behind, the next sentence turns to Wang Liu'er's strap, which proves to be better than both the silver clasp and white satin band. Ximen Qing and Wang continue for hours, "passing wine to each other's mouths, kissing, playing, and eating until lamplighting time" (兩個一遞一口飲酒, 咂舌頭頑笑, 吃至掌燈, 79.1140). The reader can only imagine how Ximen Qing in this case and at other times used the various types of dildos to help stimulate the woman or protect himself from excess stimulation: neither the narrative nor the commentators address the technical use of these objects. Whatever the case may be, dildos are a key part of Ximen Qing's repertoire of tools. As a sexual connoisseur, Ximen Qing has an impressive collection of such things, the exact use of each of which is perhaps irrelevant to the author except to signal Ximen Qing's steady reliance on them.

THE MONK AND THE APHRODISIAC

Of all Ximen Qing's tools or drugs, none compares to the aphrodisiac that he acquires from the foreign monk (*huseng* 胡僧) at the halfway point of the novel. It is a fantasy drug with fantasy effects, made in the laboratory of the god Laozi 老子 from a recipe transmitted by the goddess Xiwangmu 西王母. Nevertheless, there is some reality in it, as can be inferred from the wide availability of such drugs in the period of the novel. Ming sources warned about the drugs' ill effects, from which even the emperor suffered. According to one report, the Longqing emperor (reigned 1567–1572) experienced a case of priapism, which presumably resulted from the use of drugs and prevented him from presiding at court.[82] Ximen Qing's drug has a similar effect. When the *Sunü miaolun* addresses the use of such drugs, it warns that some of them only cause "the true *yang* to dry up and be depleted" (*zhenyang he ke* 眞陽涸渴). Instead of depending on them to improve performance, the text continues, it is better to save one's energy by "spending a night alone" (*du su yixiao* 獨宿一宵).[83] Still, in the beginning the monk's aphrodisiac launches

82. See Shen Defu 沈德符, *Wanli yehuo bian* 萬曆野獲編, 21.547.

83. *Sunü miaolun*, in Li Ling, *Zhongguo fangshu gaiguan*, 200. See also Gao Lian, *Zun sheng ba jian*, 860.

Ximen Qing to a radically new level of sexual endurance. Both it and the "pink cream" (*fenhong gao* 粉紅膏) that he gets from the monk, which goes in the opening of the penis, have immediately powerful effects that he experiences time after time.[84]

The monk represents a character type that appears throughout Ming and Qing fiction: a master of sexual practices that are typically predatory in nature, whose appearance illustrates the direction fiction commonly takes in what it represents as the sexual arts. Such characters are typically "dark" (*hei* 黑), "foreign" (*hu* 胡, or *fan* 番, 梵), and from the west—in *Jin Ping Mei*, "India" (*tianzhu guo* 天竺國). In the novel, he is a comic allegorical figure and object of satire, "having descended to the mundane world from Cold Shivers Temple, which is located beneath Navel Waist Peak, in the Dense Sperm Forest" (密松林齊腰峰寒庭寺下來的). The author portrays him as looking like an engorged penis, the skin of his head "purple like the color of liver" (*se ruo zigan*), and he wears a "long flesh-colored gown" (穿一領肉紅直裰). When Ximen Qing first sees him, "a flow of jade-white mucous trickles out of his nose" (鼻口中流下玉筯來, 49.635). Here, this is a farcical sign of concentrated energy, not poor hygiene, as if *jing* were flowing from his penis-like head. He has extraordinary power, as shown in the fact that he covers the distance from the temple to Ximen Qing's home in no time, arriving without a drop of sweat, while Dai'an (玳安) arrives separately and much later, sweating profusely and out of breath (49.636).[85] When characters such as the monk appear elsewhere in Ming and Qing fiction, they kidnap and rape women whom they force to serve them. Although *Jin Ping Mei* does not present any of these situations, the monk's appearance, the references to Laozi and Xiwangmu, and the centuries of lore about foreign monks, Tantrism, and sexual alchemy, combine to suggest such a picture. He is an alien presence who possesses occult powers.[86]

84. See JPM, 49.638–639, 50.645, and 51.665.

85. Roy, 3.49.193, 195 ("flesh-colored gown," "jade-white mucous," and the monk's place of origin come from Roy, the latter slightly modified). See also JPMCH, 49.1345. On the figure of the foreign monk, see Xue Yingjie, "Wenren shenfen," 108–121; and in fiction, *Yinglie zhuan,* 1.6, *Sengni niehai*, 7.81–85, and *Shenlou zhi* 蜃樓志 (to be discussed in chapter 8).

86. As Durand-Dastès writes, the "Tantric, obscene, and orgiastic" monk commonly stands in contrast to a chaste and dignified China ("Rencontres hérétiques," 44).

Besides the monk and the behavior he can be presumed to represent, the next nearest trace of influence of the lore associated with him consists of the novel's two references to the cinnabar field (*dantian* 丹田), one of the key centers of energy storage and circulation in Daoist internal alchemy. The first reference is in the monk's initial instruction about the aphrodisiac's use and effects, when he says that the drug will make "your cinnabar field . . . glow in the dark" (丹田夜有光, 49.638).[87] Before looking at the second reference, let us briefly identify the cinnabar field in its Daoist context. It would be known to all practitioners of physical and spiritual *daoyin* exercises and internal alchemy. Located in the lower abdomen, it is a place to which the practitioner can direct concentration and where he or she can experience a sense of centeredness, as vital energy rises from there to the head, after which it sinks down and pervades the entire body (to simplify one type of practice among others). In the sexual arts, the practitioner absorbs vital essence from his or her partner into the cinnabar field and from there up the spine to the *niwan* point in the brain. For example, the Ming text *Xiu zhen yanyi* (修眞演義, Exposition of cultivating the true essence) speaks of the so-called "three peaks" (*sanfeng* 三峰), from which the man may gather "medicine" (*yao* 藥) from the woman to replenish and strengthen himself via the corresponding three cinnabar fields. The upper peak is in the mouth, from which the man absorbs "the *jing* of saliva" (*tuo zhi jing* 唾之精). The middle peak produces "medicine" from between the breasts, while the lower peak does so from the secretions of the vagina.[88]

Ximen Qing never pretends to know about any of the techniques of "drinking" (*he* 喝), "eating" (*shi* 食), or "inhaling" (*xi* 吸) "medicine" through the mouth or penis. But the scene in which the second reference to the cinnabar field appears contains a likely—though hazy—allusion to the man's absorption of essence from the woman. Ximen Qing has just swallowed the new aphrodisiac, after which he feels "unaffected" (*you ru wu wu* 猶如無物), as if he has no sensation in his organ. He brings Pan Jinlian to a "height of passion" (*qingji* 情極) as "his word plunges deeply into

87. Roy, 3.49.200, his translation.

88. *Xiu zhen yanyi*, in Li Ling, *Zhongguo fangshu gaiguan*, 215. See also Kohn, *Chinese Healing Exercises*, 15; Li Ling, *Zhongguo fangshu kao*, 354–355 (on *neidan*); Wile, *Art of the Bedchamber*, 37–38 and 140–41 (on *dantian* and *Xiu zhen yanyi*, respectively).

her vagina, intently grinding back and forth" (那話直抵牝中, 只顧揉搓, 51.665). She pleads with him, saying, "I am finished, Dada, you have fucked me to death" (親達達, 罷了, 五兒合死了). "Her tongue becomes cold, and she gives way to a climax, after which Ximen Qing feels a sense of heat from her vagina that penetrates to his cinnabar field, which gives him a feeling of utter, indescribable bliss" (舌尖冰冷. 泄訖一度, 西門慶覺牝中一股熱氣直透丹田, 心中翕翕然， 美快不可言, 51.666).[89] Compare this passage with the one noted above in the *Sunü miaolun*: "In swallowing her saliva he will nourish the cinnabar field, thereby causing the hot *qi* to penetrate to the *niwan* point and spread through the four limbs." Given that the secretions of the vagina constitute medicine that comes from the lower peak, the words in this passage conceivably reflect the flow of essence from her lower peak to his cinnabar field.

As I have said, the art of absorbing and directing *qi* and *jing* had long existed by the time the novel was written, while the three peaks appear in other Ming and Qing works of fiction.[90] But it is also the case that the use of the term *dantian* here might be little more than a rhetorical flourish, an instance of using a rarefied, specialized term to color the picture of Ximen Qing's ecstasy. He experiences a similar flow of heat as found in the *Sunü miaolun*. It is as if the pill gives him the ability not only to attain the desensitized state of control necessary to please the woman, but also to cause essence to flow to his cinnabar field for him, without the need for the training and focus required in the techniques of internal alchemy.

Conclusion: Describing Pleasure

By way of conclusion, we may ask: who is Ximen Qing in light of the art of the bedchamber? As I have said, the art of the bedchamber and *Jin*

89. Also see JPMCH, 51.1407; and Roy, 3.51.239–240 ("unaffected"). I have adopted the wording in the Chongzhen edition (五兒合死了) rather than the *cihua* edition's 五兒的死了, "Your little Fivey is dying."

90. See Pan Jianguo, "Daojiao fangzhong wenhua," 65 (referring to *Zaihua chuan*, *Feijian ji* 飛劍記); and *Yiqing zhen*, 3.40–43 (referring to the three peaks and quoting a passage from *Xiu zhen yanyi*).

Ping Mei belong to two separate genres with different, even incompatible, impulses. One is about a man achieving perfect control over the self in sex, turning the act into one whose goal is harmony and health and that belongs to a continuum of practices that, if fully undertaken, result in physical and spiritual transformation. The other is about a man who relies on tools and drugs for sexual endurance and about people for whom sex involves extremes of pleasure and pain and for whom intercourse is always complicated by lust, jealousy, and self-interest.

The difference between the two lies especially in their treatment of pleasure, which the novel describes in a contradictory way that it never resolves. *Jin Ping Mei* persistently portrays the experience of sexual pleasure, especially in its poetic passages. Ximen Qing enjoys time after time with his partners, not to mention hours of entertainment—in the form of music and other performances, playing games, and eating—with wives, courtesans, servants, and friends. Just as persistently, the author detracts from such scenes by injecting the chaotic and conflicting elements that I have referred to as the complexities of social life, which take place both within and beyond the activity of the bedchamber. Ximen Qing's moments of pleasure give way to what the novel portrays as the situation of a person who does not deserve such pleasure. He is the local merchant and boss, who gains power because of his influence and money—the spending of which he says can even buy the favor of the gods, as he once brags to Wu Yueniang (57.746–747). Ximen Qing exudes "the air of the marketplace" (*shijing qi* 市井氣, 60.794), a phrase the author uses satirically to denote his shallow taste and love of flashy clothing, furniture, and sexual gadgets. He loves to show off his upstart prowess and wealth. The men and women around him try as much as possible to gain what they can from him—that is, to eat off his plate, both literally and figuratively.[91] They are his subjects, and they include his wives, other lovers, sworn brothers, and servants (who immediately switch masters once he is no longer there). His use of the monk's aphrodisiac quintessentially summarizes his character and modus vivendi. Just as the drug represents a fraudulent appropriation of power, so do Ximen Qing's commercial activities, which generate the same kind of behavior in the people who surround him.

91. I have summarized this theme from Ding, *Obscene Things*.

The art of the bedchamber uses far fewer words to describe pleasure and, as I have said, locates it mostly in the woman. The man experiences a measured form of pleasure and a sense of lightness and well-being, not the intense form of pleasure that the novel describes.[92] The bedchamber texts would accuse Ximen Qing of being an aberrant practitioner of the art of the bedchamber, someone who ignores its key principle that enjoying sexual pleasure means learning how to control and guide it. He also ignores the fact that the art of the bedchamber is just one branch of a repertoire of practices intended for physical and spiritual well-being. In using the monk's drug, he resembles the figures in fiction and popular lore who take short cuts to immortality, such as Monkey in *Xiyou ji* 西游記 (Journey to the west) when he erases his name from the registry of life and death or when he steals immortality pills from Laozi or peaches from Xiwangmu 西王母, the Queen Mother of the West. Monkey yearns to be forever young, but dismisses the goal of spiritual transformation that should accompany that pursuit. In the didactic framework of *Jin Ping Mei* and *Xiyou ji*, such behavior amounts to the fraudulent appropriation of power.

As different as the novel and the art of the bedchamber are, as I have said, they share a small world in which each believes in talking explicitly about the pleasures and acts of sex. Both evoke moments of mutual understanding and satisfaction between sexual partners, as when *Sunü miaolun* says: "When man and woman meet in mutual delight, there is no need for words. They already know what each other wants" (男女好逑. 未發言語而知其情).[93] *Jin Ping Mei* portrays similar moments of mutual harmony, especially in its poetry. But in contrast to the language of the novel, that of the art of the bedchamber is as denuded as possible of sensationalism and excitement, as naked as the bodies it describes may be. It excludes references to bizarre excess, which its and *Jin Ping Mei*'s readers would have known about from famous legendary and historical cases. The art of the bedchamber addresses the problem of excess by creating an entire discourse about nonexcessive sex, one that affirms the act by treating it as a legitimate body of knowledge with, as I have said, a carefully articulated set of principles, terms, and concerns. Such a body of knowledge

92. See Pfister, "Gendering Sexual Pleasures," 45 and 52–53.
93. *Sunü miaolun*, in Li Ling, *Zhongguo fangshu gaiguan*, 202.

argues for the positive effects of sexual pleasure, though it also anticipates the dangers and imbalances that can occur.

As for *Jin Ping Mei*, the following chapters provide a more complete account of its descriptions of sexual pleasure. Suffice it to say for now that it goes for noise and excitement, combines the elegant and the obscene, and luxuriates in the lurid and explicit. It fears nothing that can be said about sex. Other Ming and Qing works follow the same path, though some exceptions occur that affirm sexual pleasure as something that can be experienced without the danger of excess.[94] *Jin Ping Mei*'s greatest contrast with the art of the bedchamber is its insistence upon portraying the tumultuous relations of the polygamous family, in which even if a woman is at times a welcoming companion, she is also a defiant, cunning, and resistant one who aims to keep the man in a state in which he must constantly rely on his wits, not to mention tools, drugs, and money, no matter how skilled he is in sex.

94. See, for example, the Qing novel *Shenlou zhi* (discussed in chapter 8) and the sixteenth-century erotic novellas *Sanmiao zhuan* (三妙傳) and *Tianyuan qiyu* (天緣奇遇), discussed in Wang, *Ming Erotic Novellas*, 146–147.

CHAPTER 3

The Language of Sex in Jin Ping Mei

A Borderline Text

Ding Naifei refers to *Jin Ping Mei* as a "borderline text between the high literary and pornographic."[1] What does this borderline quality mean in terms of the novel's language of sex—in other words, the language the novel uses and how that language works in terms of its aesthetics, meaning, and function? What is the art of the high literary portrayal, on the one hand, and what is the art of the pornographic, on the other hand? Such questions have to do with both the artful use of language and the way the novel's author uses description to evaluate and comment on characters, situations, and sexual and psychic states of being. Scholars of *Jin Ping Mei* have long spoken of its multiple voices and its complex layers of intertextual reference.[2] The same qualities apply to the language of sex in the novel, of which there has so far been no sustained, critical analysis.[3] That language must be examined in terms of its various modes and

1. Ding, *Obscene Things*, xix. Mark Stevenson and Paola Zamperini generously commented on earlier versions of this chapter.

2. See Hanan, "Sources"; Carlitz, *Rhetoric*, 95–113 and 114–127; Roy, introduction; Rolston, "Oral Performing Literature," 14–36; Shang Wei, "*Jin Ping Mei* and Late Ming Print Culture," 188–189 and 202, and "Making of the Everyday World"; and Tian Xiaofei, *Qiushui tang*.

3. For forays into that topic, see Carlitz, *Rhetoric*, 44–52; Keulemans, "*Jin Ping Mei* chongtan"; Tian Bing'e, "*Jin Ping Mei* xing miaoxie sibian"; and especially Qi, *Jin Ping*

ranges of use, its historical and literary contexts, and also what I have referred to above as the situational circumstances of Ximen Qing and the women he consorts with—all of whom occupy particular positions in particular moments and places. In short, the book invites readings according both to the ways in which its language both describes and evokes pleasure, and to the moral and thematic purposes to which the book puts the language of sex and to which readers have put it ever since its appearance in the late Ming.

For convenience of analysis, I echo Ding's characterization by referring to two basic poles. However, instead of the term "high literary" I use "high erotic," and instead of "pornographic" I use simply "graphic." Similarly, Patrick Hanan long ago wrote of figurative and allusive, versus plain and direct, language.[4] The one pole favors elegant and elliptical description, and the other focuses on raw sights and sounds. In the one mode, the author exalts the act, aiming it toward the level of the sublime; and, in the other, he describes it in a series of discrete actions in plain and direct language, sometimes crude and vulgar. *Jin Ping Mei* inherits the high erotic from the ancient past, both borrowing from others and creating its own versions (including parodies and pastiches). The graphic mode is something that comes to fruition in the novel's own era and to which *Jin Ping Mei* contributes immensely. The art and aesthetics of the description of sex, whichever the mode, begin with linguistic practices—that is, the types of language that the author uses and has the characters use. What words does he use to portray the acts of sex—in other words, what is the vocabulary for such things as parts of the body or the actions of intercourse? Moreover, what is the art of sex that the characters practice and speak about—that is, the ways in which they have and talk about sex? How does the description vary depending on the situation and the people involved?

Before proceeding, I must first qualify the words that I often use to refer to *Jin Ping Mei*'s sexually explicit contents. The word "explicit" is necessary but troublesome, unless it is clear that sometimes it means that a particular passage leaves no doubt that it is talking about sexual acts

---

Mei English Translations. Also see Wong, "Anatomy of Eroticism," though that work is not about *Jin Ping Mei.*

4. Hanan, "The Erotic Novel."

(whether in an elegant or allusive way or in a direct and graphic way) and, moreover, that in so doing the novel is committing the type of offense that has long led to its censorship and condemnation. But sometimes I use "explicit" to distinguish between the (relatively) nonexplicit, adumbrative nature of the high erotic from the raw and explicit qualities of the graphic. This latter distinction—between adumbrative and explicit—can also be considered a matter of curtailed versus uncurtailed description, or reticent versus nonreticent.

Another qualification about the notion of explicit is that it does not automatically or necessarily mean realistic or naturalistic. Although such description exists in *Jin Ping Mei* and other Ming and Qing novels, it is important to view the language of sex in the novel more as if it is linguistically performative than realistically descriptive.[5] The depiction of sex is full of figurative meaning: it is verbally playful; and it is full of sexually political content, in this latter sense especially in terms of the situational complexities of the novel's female characters. In other words, if the word "graphic" seems to connote realistic or naturalistic language, then (though that may sometimes be the case), I also insist that the graphic is just as artful and full of thematic meaning as the high erotic.

Moreover, neither mode is a pure or rigid category, nor do the two alone necessarily capture all the possible modes or registers of the language of sex. Other distinctions can be made, as in language in the mode of sex as mock battle (which I treat as an alternative mode of the high erotic in chapter 4), the mode of the dirty joke, that of the art of the bedchamber, or (especially in other novels) the language of Daoist inner alchemy.[6] One could also distinguish between passages in prose or a variety of poetic forms, such as regulated verse (*lüshi* 律詩), *ci*-lyrics (*ci* 詞), or popular songs or operatic arias (*qu* 曲). The author commonly mixes modes and creates a range of expression, even going abruptly from one mode to another. A flowery sentence may suddenly contain a vulgar word. An elegant passage may be deeply ironic, especially when it depicts characters who are anything but the exalted lovers that the high erotic mode

5. See Keulemans, "*Jin Ping Mei* chongtan"; and Ding, *Obscene Things*, 187–189 (on the novel's "semio-philia," which is not to be mistaken for "realism").

6. See Pan Jianguo, "Daojiao fangzhong"; and Lin Chen, "Yanqing xiaoshuo," 50 (on modes of portrayal).

might otherwise imply. The language may be poetic, but in the tone of the comic ditty or doggerel. A dirty joke may be allusive but still crude and insulting. Whatever the mode or shade of portrayal, the author conveys a tinge of sensation, excitement, and even awe. In other words, it is clear that sexual pleasure is what he is unabashedly talking about, and that he "relishes" describing it, as many readers have noted.[7] Descriptions commonly stand alone as references to sheer sexual ecstasy, even if the surrounding narrative leaves no doubt that the characters who are enjoying themselves are venal and corrupt.[8] Again, all such passages are laden with socially complex meaning, not to mention ironic counternotes or elements of humor and satire—as in scenes of passionate frenzy, when the author resorts to comic exaggeration or inserts incongruous interludes.[9] Sex with the concubine who was a former bond maid is different from sex with the concubine who was previously a wealthy man's main wife. The language that describes each of these characters and situations differs accordingly.

Jin Ping Mei*'s Art of Describing Sex*

My focus in this chapter is on the high erotic, but two passages of graphic description are my first examples. After beginning his secret affair with Ben the Fourth, servant and the wife of one of his employees, Ximen Qing goes back to see her and, in contrast to the common scene in which partners take their time before having sex, they begin "without wasting a word": they enter an inner room, she takes off her clothes and lies down on her back, and they "go right to it" (無閒話；就幹起來). "As it happens," the passage continues, "the woman likes keeping her legs together while doing it. Her secretions flow out in a hot flood, completely soaking the mat. . . . . She opens her eyes wide and keeps calling out, 'dear papa'" (原來老婆好並着腿幹. 那浪水熱熱一陣流出來，把床褥皆濕. . . . 婦人瞪目，口中只叫親爹). Ximen Qing asks her for her childhood name, which she

7. See, for example, Carlitz, *Rhetoric*, 50.
8. See Ding, *Obscene Things*, xxv; and Hsia, *Classic Chinese Novel*, 184–185.
9. See Carlitz, *Rhetoric*, 44, 95–113, and 114–127.

tells him—adding that she was the fifth child in her family, which excites him as he "moans and mutters and keeps calling out, 'Ye Fivey'" (口中喃喃吶吶，就叫葉五兒不絶, Ye being her premarital surname). There is nothing the woman does not know about sex, the narrator adds, so it is not surprising that when they finish and he goes to wipe his penis, she stops him so that she can lick it clean for him. As always, Ximen Qing is generous to his partners. Before they separate, he gives her a few pieces of silver, saying that he does not give her clothing because he is afraid her husband would notice that, which "would be embarrassing" (*bu hao yisi* 不好意思, 78.1111–1112).[10]

In such passages, one concrete, sensational detail comes after another in a relatively straightforward way (not poetic, euphemistic, or metaphorical), as in their going right to it, her keeping her legs together, the reference to his "moans and muttering," and her licking him clean. Such is the manner of the graphic mode, whose favorite images are the raw sights and sounds of sex, its ferocity and precipitousness, and the sheer copiousness of sensual effects.[11] It is especially the set of nonverbal syllables, "*nan'nan'na'na,*" that clinches the scene—syllables that occur at least nine other times in the novel, including in cases of people "muttering" angry or drunken words or, barely awake, "moaning" sleepily.[12] The syllables also appear when Ximen Qing "murmurs" to another of his illicit partners, the servant Song Huilian, to whom he says that he will give her jewelry and clothing if she will sleep with him. His affair with her likewise begins abruptly: he runs into her when no one else is present and "with one hand pulls her to him by the neck, kisses her, then murmurs" his proposal (便一手摟過脖子來，就親了個嘴，口中喃喃吶吶説道; 22.285). With other women, he engages in lengthy preludes, including conversation, eating, and drinking. With Ben the Fourth, he sinks immediately into sexual passion. His brief asking about her childhood name is his way, one presumes, of pretending that she is now his woman, not another man's. Theirs is a pornographic scene full of lurid details about a master of the house who, with the help of his head servant Dai'an secretly trysts with

10. I have chosen the Chongzhen edition's version of the passage, which makes more sense than the *cihua* version. See JPMCH, 78.2445–2446.

11. On the sounds of sex, see Keulemans, "*Jin Ping Mei* chongtan," 396–397.

12. Ximen Qing semiconsciously murmurs *nan'nan'na'na* just before Pan Jinlian gives him the overdose of the aphrodisiac (79.1141).

another man's wife who gladly and hotly gives herself to him, though not without receiving a handsome reward. The few taels he gives her amount to the price of buying a regular housemaid. The reader also learns that, unbeknownst to Ximen Qing, Dai'an has already been having an affair with her.

The scene is an example of how description varies depending on the situation and the partner. High erotic language does not appear in Ximen Qing's affairs with Song Huilian and Ben the Fourth, nor with two other servant women, Ruyi 如意 and Huiyuan 惠元. His affairs with these women are the rawest and most graphic in the novel. With Ben the Fourth, Ximen Qing is enjoying a secret affair with a servant's wife. "Keeping her legs together" and "opening her eyes wide" are details that signal the affair's particular temporality. It is hasty and illicit, and it is with a less elegant, less highly placed woman than his usual partners (his main wife, concubines, and prostitutes), who do not lose themselves and "open their eyes wide."[13] Licking him clean shows that she is eager to do anything for him, a kind of behavior that is unbecoming, if not superfluous, in a high erotic setting.

Before continuing I need to make two points: first, to remark upon the appearance of the woman's arousal in this scene, and second, to distinguish between high erotic language (or diction) and what I refer to as high erotic setting. First, the flow of the woman's secretions is a ubiquitous detail in *Jin Ping Mei* and another example of how such depictions cannot be read as purely realistic or naturalistic.[14] It is better to say that the flow of secretions is a formulaic feature of scenes of sexual arousal in Ming and Qing fiction, a feature that goes back to the ancient art of the bedchamber. It is true that the depiction can in part be read as realistic, but it is better to keep in mind that featuring such details is part of how Ming and Qing writers depicted sex. It is part of the assumption of the woman's powerful sexual nature—a core assumption in the novel and in Ming and Qing fiction in general, as well as in the ancient art of the bedchamber. The woman's formidability is such that naturally, so to speak,

13. Wet nurse Ruyi similarly "falls into a stare" (*dengmu* 瞪目; 78.1121). The Ming bedchamber text *Xiu zhen yanyi* describes such a reaction as common in the heat of passion, in Li Ling, *Zhongguo fangshu gaiguan*, 212.

14. Ding writes about the "unreadable" nature of such scenes (*Obscene Things*, 192).

it includes the richness of her arousal. Second, high erotic language has to do with the level of diction the author chooses to use. In contrast, high erotic setting refers to atmosphere and environment, as well as the character and behavior of the people involved. Diction and setting do not necessarily line up with each other. A high setting may suddenly contain raw diction, and a session of raw and frenzied sex may be written with elevated diction.

To return to Ben the Fourth and Ximen Qing, the setting in this case conforms to the expectations of Ximen Qing's practice of the art of sex, which build on the fundamental notion that the wealthy man such as he can and should enjoy sex not only with his main wife, concubines, and prostitutes but also with handsome boy servants and other men's wives—though, it is implied, not the wives of his superiors, unless they are widows (like Lady Lin). In Ximen Qing's life, such partners are expected to know and associate with each other. They can even become allies, as in the case of Pan Jinlian and her maid, Chunmei; or Pan Jinlian and her co-wife Meng Yulou. Two of the prostitutes, Li Guijie 李桂姐 and Wu Yin'er 吳銀兒, become adopted daughters, the first of the wife Wu Yueniang, and the second of the concubine Li Ping'er. The affair with an adulterous lover such as Ben the Fourth is an exciting and secret side adventure, as sometimes are the affairs with prostitutes. In affairs with a maid or prostitute, the man's secrecy risks angering his openly established partners, though if he wishes, he may take his secret lovers into the open and incorporate them into his household—as Ximen Qing does with the prostitute Li Jiao'er, the adulterers Pan Jinlian and Li Ping'er, and almost does in the cases of the servant Song Huilian and the wet nurse Ruyi.

Ximen Qing's art of sex necessarily implies an art of living that includes wearing good clothing, eating well, and drinking high-quality alcohol, tea, and other beverages—although the novel makes his tastes appear to be philistine.[15] He and his wives live in a lavishly accoutered home, with specially designed rooms, furniture, and gardens. They own art works and antiques and use fine utensils for eating and drinking. The same conditions apply in the brothel and the homes of the secret lovers, Wang Liu'er and Lady Lin. Ximen Qing employs loyal and intelligent

15. See Huang Lin, *Huang Lin jiang*, 186–200, especially 199 on philistine [*shijing* 市井] taste and for a comparison with *Honglou meng*).

male and female servants, some of whom also serve as sexual partners, and some of whom may be present while the master and a partner have sex (for example, Chunmei is present when he has sex with Pan Jinlian). The best servant knows how to read a master's or mistress's wishes and helps them in their arrangements for sessions of sex with both open and secret partners. The well-lived life includes playing games (dominoes, backgammon, and chess), guessing riddles, telling jokes, listening to and playing music (especially love songs), watching opera and other entertainment, and going on outings. All such activities belong to what the literati culture of the late Ming would cultivate and condone, though ideally without the venality and corruption of the characters in *Jin Ping Mei*.[16]

As for the art of sex itself, the beginning and end of sex is not defined by the literal beginning and end of intercourse. In its most artful form, it is unlike Ximen Qing's hasty and furtive affair with Ben the Fourth and should instead begin leisurely and in a pleasant environment. Before the partners take their clothes off, they first enjoy food and drink, which they may trade in sips and bites from each other's mouths. They listen to music, which the woman sometimes plays for the man. They engage in amusing conversation and play games. When the sexual act is finally to take place, a maid prepares the bed; the woman washes her privates; and the partners unclothe, get in bed (or onto a chair or other surface), and begin. Besides having its prologues, intercourse also has its interludes, during which the couple chats, rests, or eats. Food, drink, and sex overlap, with the partners going from one to the other—after all of which they may go to sleep or part to return to other activities.[17]

As *Jin Ping Mei*'s characters practice it, the art of sex is about not only the actions of intercourse but also talking about it, negotiating it, and joking about it. This is where *Jin Ping Mei* explores what no other work of fiction had quite yet explored, as the Chongzhen commentator repeatedly exclaims. A second example of the author's art of description illustrates what I mean, especially in the way it shows characters

16. On the pleasures of literati culture in the late Ming, see Chen Hsiu-fen, "Nourishing Life"; and Cahill, introduction.

17. See Mote, "Yuan and Ming," 248 (on the intertwining of food and sex); and Huang Lin, *Huang Lin jiang*, 192–193.

incorporating humorous banter into their sexual play. A man is not afraid of making fun of his member, nor of his concubine teasing it, and the narrator commonly injects satirical or grotesque descriptions of the aroused or flaccid penis and the aroused vagina. Ximen Qing and Pan Jinlian have just had a thunderous session of sex in the notorious scene in the grape arbor (27.356–357). That chapter soon ends, and the next one begins with Pan Jinlian toying with Ximen Qing's "word" (*nahua* 那話)—which is also translatable as "thing" or "unmentionable," the euphemism used throughout the book for saying what words need not name—which still wears its silver clasp (*yintuozi* 銀托子), the circular ring that Ximen Qing fixes at its base. After its recent exertions, his organ "hangs limp, dinky, and soft, in a ponderous and baggy lump" (軟叮噹毛都魯的壘垂偉長), another example of direct, graphic description. "You're still going to toy with it?," he asks. "It is all dumbstruck now all because of the way you terrorized it!" Otherwise, he continues, "How would it have become so paralyzed and overheated that it can't even manage to get itself up again?" (你還弄他哩，都是你頭裡誂出他風病來了，如何這軟癱熱化，起不來了).[18] "Plead with it a bit" (央及他央及), he tells Pan Jinlian, as she squats down, "giving him a naughty-boy look" (笑瞅了他一眼) and taking a piece of string to tie around his penis and hold in her hand. She addresses it: "You little rascal! A little while ago you were all mean and ferocious, making a person lose her mind. So how do you get so dumbstruck all of a sudden and pretend to play dead!?" (你這廝！頭裡那等頭睜睜, 股睜睜, 把人奈何昏昏的, 這咱你推風病裝佯死兒). She explores his penis with her mouth until it grows again, after which, "that night, the two of them engaged in wanton pleasure, holding nothing back" (是夜, 二人淫樂爲之無度, 28.359–360). The expression "engaged in wanton pleasure, holding nothing back" is the author's common way of indicating that he need not provide further details. It is also his way of reiterating that all such description is for a purpose, and that for the time being there is no more purpose except to give the impression that they are having unbridled sex.

The language that *Jin Ping Mei* uses challenges every translator, as well as the limits of the language the translator is working in. The era of translation and identity of the translator are also factors. For instance, Clement Egerton's language in 1939 is more elegant and allusive than

18. "Dumbstruck" and "overheated" are from Roy, 2.28.151.

David Roy's between 1993 and 2013.[19] The English of an earlier period—say, that of the eighteenth-century pornographic novel *Fanny Hill*—might have been better equipped to translate the novel. Though often varying from his choice of words, I follow Roy's model of translating more or less directly, even if the sound in English is at times unnatural or inelegant. Terms for penis, for example, have the following range of expression: "Word" (*nahua*) is a floating signifier that the *Jin Ping Mei* and other authors frequently use to refer to penis. It is a euphemism that gives hardly a hint of what it refers to, being something "unmentionable" or "that which we will not name." In contrast, words that more directly suggest the penis include the elegant "jade stalk" (*yujing* 玉莖), which appears in the ancient texts of the art of the bedchamber. There are also the plain but fundamentally masculine "*yang* thing" (*yangwu* 陽物), the metaphoric and slightly comic "chowry handle" (*zhubing* 麈柄; chowry being a kind of bushy whisk or flyswatter), and the potent and reptilian "turtle's head" (glans, *guitou* 龜頭). "Word" is a neutral term that carries a bit of a laugh and that can also be used to refer to the vagina, as I show below. "Jade stalk" is an ancient and dignified euphemism, in elegance above "turtle head" and far above "chicken tail" (*jiba* 髻髱), which corresponds to the English "dick" or "cock."[20] While "jade stalk" occurs in the art of the bedchamber, "cock" and its equivalents never do. "*Yang* thing" is likewise a euphemism, not as elegant as "jade stalk" but containing the hallowed word "*yang*" that stands for the masculine principle, paralleling the euphemisms for vagina such as "*yin* door" (or "*yin* gate," *yinhu* 陰户), which contains the word *yin* for the feminine principle. "Chowry handle" is a satirical euphemism, but one that avoids vulgarity. "Turtle head" is slightly grotesque, but likewise above "cock" and denser in meaning in that it connotes potency in the way that turtles and other reptilian creatures such as snakes and dragons do.

Contemporary standard English is fatally determined to use the clinical-sounding and artless "penis" or the dull-sounding "male organ," the archaic but still usable "member," or the vulgar "dick" and "cock"

19. See Qi, *Jin Ping Mei English Translations*, 113–114, 194–195, and 200.

20. Another term at the same level and with the same meaning as *jiba* in Ming and Qing fiction is *liaozi* 膫子.

(among others).[21] The same issue exists for vagina, which I discuss below. Descriptions of the limp or aroused penis pervade the novel, as above when the author refers to it being "limp and dinky," where he follows *ruan* 軟, "soft," with an onomatopoeic phrase, *dingdang* 叮噹, like the dinging of a dangling little bell. Translating such imagery is easier than translating the names for the sexual organs, which are richer in variety in premodern Chinese than in English. Another colloquial descriptive phrase follows: *mao dulu* 毛都魯, which refers to baggy limpness. *Dingdang* and *dulu* are semantically meaningless, both giving the sense of the inert "hangingness" of the postcoital organ after undergoing its drastic change from something to nothing. *Ruan dingdang* already appears several chapters before, when Pan Jinlian pulls Ximen Qing's pants open to expose his limp penis (with the silver clasp still affixed to it) after she discovers him returning from a secret visit to Li Ping'er. She says, "Look at how after one bout with her it's as soft as snot and ruddy as soy, as if paralyzed from a stroke" (一遭就弄的他恁軟如鼻涕濃如醬，却如風癱了一般的, 13.168). When she calls his penis a little rascal, its limpness is rather an endearing feature, or at least she pretends that it is the case. But her reaction to his return from Li Ping'er is one of jealous scorn. Someone else has enjoyed his penis and made it this way. Pan Jinlian uses her most vivid and caustic words, which also means the most vulgar and filthy ones—such language being characteristic of her verbal and emotional energy.

At the point where Pan Jinlian hovers over Ximen Qing's member, the Chongzhen commentator makes a key statement about the novel's portrayal of sex: "Baldly filthy words. But when reading it, one only sees splendor [*fengsao* 風騷], not filth. It is truly a case of the rotten and stinking transformed into the divine and marvelous" (分明穢語，閱來但見其風騷，不見其穢，可谓腐臭化为神奇, 28.359–360). The commentator's focus is on the tension between the obscene and filthy words and the splendid effect that he implies they produce. The suggestion is that readers should shed their repulsed, dismissive, or perhaps merely titillated or tittering reactions and admire the "*fengsao*" of such a scene—that is, the sublime

21. For metaphorical terms for organs, see Qi, *Jin Ping Mei English Translations*, 204–206. In *Fanny Hill*, penis can be "mighty machine" or "plenipotentiary instrument," while vagina is "sweet intersection," "luscious mouth of nature," "cloven spot," or "tender opening."

pleasure that it supposedly evokes. In contemporary Chinese, "*fengsao*" has a negative connotation, referring to loose and seductive behavior (for example, in a coquettish woman). But the Chongzhen commentator uses it in a positive light, in which it refers to sublime and untrammeled behavior.[22] It refers to a person of heightened sensibility, someone who is spirited, unrestrained, and capable of grand romantic and sexual passion—though the commentator might not go so far as to imply that Pan Jinlian achieves such splendor. Instead of her, it is the author whom he is praising and who makes it possible for the so-called "rotten and stinking" (*fuchou* 腐臭) to sheds its rottenness and, as a mark of the novel's marvelous art, become glorious and divine.

Fellatio is central to the novel's presentation of the art of sex, taking place with Ximen Qing's most wanton women—that is, prostitutes, concubines, and extramarital lovers such as Wang Liu'er and Ben the Fourth. A man giving oral sex to a woman does not occur in *Jin Ping Mei*, though it does in other works and in Ming and Qing illustrations.[23] In *Jin Ping Mei* and other fiction, a main wife does not engage in such an act, which goes by the name of "playing the flute" (or "toying with the flute," *pin xiao* 品簫), or sometimes simply "toying" or "tasting" (*pin, pinpin*). Sometimes fellatio is all that takes place, as in an earlier scene in which, "well knowing that playing the flute is her specialty" (明知婦人第一好品簫), Ximen Qing has Pan Jinlian do it instead of "the clouds and rain" (*yunyu* 雲雨), the ancient euphemism for intercourse, and enjoys himself as "he lowers his head to watch the marvel of it going in and out" (垂首翫其出入之妙, 10.125).[24] A similar moment takes place when Ximen Qing visits Li Ping'er next door, while she is still married to her husband. After the maid readies the bed, "they sit shoulder to shoulder, thigh over thigh, drinking and amusing themselves in conversation. Soon, yearning spreads across their faces and lust begins to ripple through their bodies" (並肩疊股, 飲酒調笑. 良久, 春色横眉, 淫心蕩漾). They do the "clouds and rain" for a while, after which they stop and he has her lie across the mat

22. *Feng* comes from the "Winds" section of the *Classic of Poetry* (*Guofeng* 國風, *Shijing* 詩經) and *sao* from the "Poem on Encountering Sorrow" (*Lisao* 離騷).

23. See Du Sansheng 杜三升, *Mixitu daguan* 秘戲圖大觀.

24. Words similar to *chu ru zhi miao* (出入之妙) occur in *Ruyijun zhuan*, in SWXHB, vol. 24, 44 and 51. For the latter's influence on *Jin Ping Mei*, see Hanan, "Sources," 43–47; and Stone, *Fountainhead*, 121–122.

to play the flute for him, a scene that includes a poem with these lines: "The sounds are like neither flute, zither, nor stone; the carnal notes resonate in a way like no other. The curtains of the bed swish and sweep, back and forth; you can't quite tell the note, is it do, re, mi, or fa . . . ?" (不竹不絲不石, 肉音别自唔咿. 流蘇瑟瑟碧紗垂, 變不出宮商角徵, 17.208).[25]

Two things stand out in the two scenes: Ximen Qing's watching himself during the act and the imagery that describes playing the flute. Watching himself signals a taste for savoring special moments of sex.[26] Other such moments recur in the novel with similar wording. They evoke a distancing and relishing of pleasure, being in the midst of it and away from it at the same time. Such is the manner of the supposed connoisseur, who distinguishes himself from the brute who indulges in raw sex—although the connoisseur will occasionally enjoy that as well. In both scenes, playing the flute is something that occurs in place of or besides genital sex and that, in the very wording of "playing the flute," metaphorically takes the participants somewhere else. The sound of it is like music, but not quite the familiar notes. Instead, the notes arrive from some other faintly heavenly and ineffable realm. As the Chongzhen commentator says, filth turns into the divinely sublime.

The description of playing the flute is further meaningful because it leads Ximen Qing to ask whether Li Ping'er does it with her husband. Never, she replies: she never touches him, and they sleep in separate beds. Ximen Qing and Li Ping'er are still in the phase of adulterous love, in which fellatio is central to the type of sex he has with such a woman. Again, he has different types of sex with different types of women at different times and in different circumstances. Oral sex belongs to a special inner circle. After Li Ping'er has her son, descriptions of sex with her

25. The poem in the *cihua* edition makes no mention of "carnal notes" but otherwise ends with the same "I never knew the magic rhinoceros horn could feel so good" (不覺靈犀味美; JPMCH, 17.417). On "rhinoceros horn" as a euphemism for penis, see Roy, 1.13.514, n. 13.

26. Such a moment also takes place in the late Tang *Dale fu* (Rhapsody on the grand pleasure, 大樂賦), whose full title is *Tiandi yinyang jiaohuan dale fu* 天地陰陽交歡大樂賦 (Rhapsody on the grand pleasure of the sexual union of heaven and earth and yin and yang), in Li Ling, *Zhongguo fangshu gaiguan*, 95, *kan chu kan ru*, 看出看入, "watching it go in and then out").

decrease, and playing the flute is no longer a part of it.[27] She has become like a main wife. Until then, the author describes them elegantly, as in the couplet, "Her mouth was like a tiny cherry coming open, her delicate fingers moving back and forth" (一點櫻桃欲綻，纖纖十指頻移, 17.208). The imagery is well-worn, especially the cliché of the cherry-like mouth.[28] But clichés aside, passages such as this have a spirited, laudatory, and eulogistic tone, though they can also be mock-eulogistic. They appear throughout the novel as accompaniments to the straightforward description of sex in prose. In their avoidance of vulgarity and their use of poetic language, they stand apart not only generically as verse versus prose, but also in the printed book as indented portions of the text.

Two other practices besides fellatio stand out as prime examples of the novel's portrayal of the art of sex: the adoption of sexual positions and the use of sex tools and aphrodisiacs. When the joyous act finally takes place after preliminaries, Ximen Qing and his partners reflect the long tradition in the art of the bedchamber of engaging in varieties of positions. They thus demonstrate that the methods of sex are something they are knowledgeable about: they are connoisseurs. Sex is an amusement, like a game, of which pleasure plays a key part, but as I said in chapter 2, sexual pleasure is not achieved in an all-consuming, frenzied way. Partners keep their heads, though in the male perspective of both the Chinese pornographic novel and the art of the bedchamber, the convention is for the man to keep his head, while he tantalizes the woman and makes her lose hers.[29]

Sex tools and aphrodisiacs add to the adventure of sex, giving the man an air of gallantry, as if he is an armed sexual soldier, but also lending him confidence in his contest with the woman, who is a formidable adversary. Although the novel never says so directly, the implication is that Ximen Qing could not satisfy his partners without his tools and drugs. Most devices work to his advantage, ensuring his sexual strength and endurance, though one of them (the silk bands discussed in chapter 2) is something that women make for him for their own advantage. Pan Jinlian

27. See Tian Xiaofei, *Qiushui tang*, 87.

28. The *cihua* edition has: "Her tiny mouth as pretty as a cherry; her fingers gentler than tender shoots" (一點櫻桃小口，兩隻手賽柔荑). See JPMCH, 17.419.

29. See Xue Yingjie, "Wenren shenfen," 77–78.

prefers the band to the clasp, which knocks against her and hurts. The drugs are for either external or internal use, whether as stimulants or irritants applied to the flesh or openings of the genitals or ingested in the form of the aphrodisiac pills Ximen Qing obtains from the foreign monk. They cause eruptions of pain and excitement, whether in the form of the moxa that Ximen Qing burns on women's genitals and the excitement that their pain gives him or in the form of the stimulation from his aphrodisiacs.[30] Moreover, such instances of excitement amount to climaxes of their own in addition to or in place of the climax of orgasm—which, according to ancient wisdom, the man should rarely allow himself. Such is the assumption transmitted in Chinese fiction in general, which echoes the advice of the art of the bedchamber. As for the monk's new drug, once Ximen Qing begins taking it, he moves into a categorically new phase in which he can go for lengthy periods without ejaculating and feels pleasure as never before.

The Uses of the High Erotic

A more thorough account of the high erotic mode begins by again summarizing what it consists of: the use of nonvulgar, nonexplicit, poetic, metaphoric, and euphemistic language. In general, it portrays sexual acts as if they had grand and sublime, even divine, qualities. Sex appears in an idealized form between idealized lovers. Passages describing such sex commonly occur in poetic form, in which they function as interludes to action and dialogue—somewhat like operatic arias. Like the poetic interlude, the aria stylizes and aestheticizes actions and feelings, expands upon moments and images, and lingers over them. It contrasts with the plainness and directness of spoken dialogue or the straightforward narration of action. A well-known example of the high erotic mode comes from Tang Xianzu's 湯顯祖 (1550–1616) opera *Mudan ting* (*Peony*

30. Ding, writes of "his enthrallment to the very smell of burned flesh, waste-bodies" (*Obscene Things*, 219). The scenes of burning moxa on the other's body were influenced by *Ruyijun zhuan*. See Stone, *Fountainhead*, 122.

Pavilion, 牡丹亭), which describes the grand moment of sex that the male and female protagonists have in a dream:

> Behold, the turbid male force steams and roils, stirs and wriggles, and fans love's passions.
> And her tender soul trembles delicately, like a green shoot bursting into bloom.
> It is all but shadows' conjunction, desires brought to completion, effects that appear inside karmic causes.
> (單則是 混陽蒸變, 看他似蟲兒般蠢動把風情搧. 一般兒嬌癡翠綻魂兒顫. 這是景上緣, 想内成, 因中見).[31]

The high erotic characteristically occurs in poetic form, though it also appears in prose. It can be lengthy, as in a passage in *Jin Ping Mei* describing a prostitute's elegant chamber. Sometimes it occupies a single couplet, as in the lines that appear three times in the novel: "As spring enlivens the peach tree's blossoms, their red buds split open. As the breeze teases the willows, their green waists bend" (春點桃花紅綻蕊, 風欺楊柳綠翻腰, 10.126, 59.778, 97.1379). These lines describe the first time a man sleeps with a woman new to sex. In such a context, "split open" and "bend" connote what more explicit prose would relate more straightforwardly. The red of the peach blossoms may allude to the color of the vagina, which the graphic mode would describe more directly (as in the scene discussed below between Ximen Qing and Ruyi, 78.1121). The character for "bud," *rui* (蕊) includes three hearts, perhaps suggesting the vagina's multiple folds—but only perhaps, because the point of such language is to be suggestive and allusive. The waist (*yao* 腰) is near the vagina, which "turns" or "bends" (*fan* 翻) during the act of sex.

The genteel and elegant language of the high erotic may also be put to ironical and satirical use. *Jin Ping Mei* does this characteristically, in some cases by mere juxtaposition. An example occurs in chapter 27, when songs from a famous Ming opera about deep and loyal love appear

31. Tang Xianzu, *Mudan ting*, 10.45. "Shadows' conjunction" is from Owen, *Anthology*, 888; "inside karmic causes" is from Birch, *Peony Pavilion*, 49. Another famous passage of this sort appears in Wang Shifu 王實甫, *Xixiang ji* 西廂記, 137. For translations, see Xu Yuanchong and Frank Xu, trans., *Romance of the Western Bower*, 146; and West and Idema, trans., *The Moon and the Zither*, 333–334.

during scenes of Ximen Qing's raw sex with first one wife and then another. Readers would know that the songs come from *Pipa ji* (*The Lute* 琵琶記), in which the hero, who placed first in the imperial exams, voices his inner conflict about having been compelled to marry the daughter of the prime minister, whom he dares not refuse—though he is already married to a woman he loves back home.[32] The ironic contrast is between not only the tones of the play and the novel but also the different contexts of a man and two wives. The songs, which make delicate reference to lovemaking, appear just after Ximen Qing has forced himself on the pregnant Li Ping'er, who asks that he be gentler, and just before one of the most unbridled scenes of sex with Pan Jinlian. Ximen Qing is newly infatuated with Li Ping'er, and his affair with her has made Pan Jinlian, with whom he had been infatuated, mad with jealousy.

The songs from *Mudan ting* and *Pipa ji* are examples of the high erotic in terms of both the style of language and the quality of character of the lovemakers. But high erotic language can also be elegantly ribald, as in the famous passage that draws a figurative comparison between Pan Jinlian's playing the flute and mosquitoes' biting tender flesh. On a hot evening, Ximen Qing returns home drunk and immediately falls asleep, after which Pan Jinlian, who has been awaiting him, rids their mosquito net of the last remaining mosquitoes. The description begins in plain prose. Seeing "his word lying between his thighs, still wearing its clasp, still tumid and long, she suddenly feels an eruption of desire." She begins to "fondle it with her delicate fingers" before finally "putting it in her mouth to suck" (其腰間那話, 帶着托子, 壘垂偉長, 不覺淫心輒起; 用纖手捫弄; 用口吮之). Ximen Qing awakens and sits up to enjoy the sight, at which point the narrator interjects a lyrical double entendre (*shuangguan* 雙關) on the subject of the mosquito:

> I love its body's graceful lightness, its exquisite dancer's waist, and its hum that vibrates with symphonic harmony.
> At dusk when someone fails to close the red doors, it stealthily penetrates the gauze net.
> It hovers delicately by the fragrant flesh, gently enamored of the jade-like body.
> Wherever it touches with its mouth, it leaves a dash of rouge.

32. See Carlitz, *Rhetoric*, 106–109 (on *The Lute*); and Swatek, "Popular Songs."

It buzzes next to the ears, with hundreds of kinds of sounds—deep into the night, letting no one sleep.
(我愛他身體輕盈, 楚腰膩細. 行行一派笙歌沸. 黄昏人未掩朱扉, 潛身撞入紗厨内. 款傍香肌，輕憐玉體. 嘴到處，胭脂記. 耳邊廂造就百般聲，夜深不肯教人睡).[33]

The prose that follows returns to a graphic description, as Ximen Qing summons maid Chunmei to pour wine for them and, with her in attendance, has Jinlian "get down on all fours facing away from him, and slipping his word into her vagina, he takes the fire from the other side of the mountain, letting her move as she likes while he drinks and enjoys himself from above" (教婦人馬爬在他面前，那話隔山取火，托入牝中，令其自動，在上飲酒取樂, 18.228).

Here the trope of the mosquito serves as a satirical aside, turning the woman into a succubus sucking the blood out of the male victim. Pan Jinlian's hovering over the prone Ximen Qing is a recurrent image, appearing for the last time when she causes his death from an overdose of aphrodisiac.[34] The Chongzhen commentator reacts to the scene by saying: "Of what goes on in the privacy of the bedchamber, what is there not to be found? It is simply that no one dares to expose it" (閨閫之私, 何所不有? 但不堪說破耳, 18.227–228). From the high erotic the narrative switches to a brief but realistic description of a set of moves in plain language: the two getting into position, their movements, and the man's drinking and enjoying himself from above. In short, he enjoys two things at once (the more the better), imbibing wine while the sex takes place "on its own" (*zidong* 自動) below.

It is common for such passages to be interrupted or followed by a drastic transition. The elegant interlude ends and the vulgar world begins.[35] Pan Jinlian objects to Ximen Qing's having Chunmei there, a presence that interferes with the hierarchical privilege Jinlian would like

33. *Jin Ping Mei*'s lyric may have been influenced by a popular song of the times, but the latter does not have a satirical tone or use the image of the blood-sucking mosquito and is about the woman's pleasure. See Wu Cuncun, "'It Was I Who Lured the Boy,'" 330–331.

34. On the figural recurrence of Pan Jinlian over the prone Ximen Qing, see Plaks, *Four Masterworks*, 142–145.

35. On the novel's "predilection for . . . incorporating the languages of incongruous styles, contents, and sources," see Shang Wei, "*Jin Ping Mei* and Late Ming Print Culture," 199.

to claim for herself alone: "What a crafty knave you are! Where does this new trick come from, of all things letting the maid watch? What kind of a put on is this?" (好個刁鑽的強盜! 從幾時新興出來的例兒, 怪辣辣教丫頭看答着, 甚麼張致!). Ximen Qing says that he has already been doing this with "your sister Ping" (*ni Ping yi* 你瓶姨—that is, Li Ping'er), and that they "had quite a good time" (*dao hao shuazi* 到好耍子). "What fucking Sister Ping?!" (*shemma Ping diao yi* 甚麼瓶鳥姨, 18.228), Pan Jinlian replies, and proceeds to curse Li Ping'er for having suddenly married the doctor—an event for which Jinlian suffered twice a few days before. First, Ximen Qing had returned home just after hearing the news of Li Ping'er's unexpected marriage to the doctor and vented his anger by kicking Jinlian. Second, Jinlian received a scolding from Wu Yueniang, who insulted both her and Li Ping'er for violating the ritual taboo of marrying while still in mourning for their deceased husbands. Yueniang's scolding of Jinlian is something that Ximen Qing did not know about, but which the backbiting Jinlian now relates to him. The scene ends after this exchange, which results in creating a rift between him and Yueniang.

The high erotic, as I have said, existed in various forms in China since early times. It is a mode in which lovers enjoy elegant sex and sensual harmony. The texts of the art of the bedchamber supply early examples of its type of language, as does the long tradition of ornate, sensual poetry that I mentioned in chapter 1, which goes by the label *xiangyan* 香艷, "fragrant and bedazzling."[36] While the art of the bedchamber makes direct reference to parts of the body and gives detailed descriptions of sexual moves, *xiangyan* literature generally—though not always—stands at a greater distance, making veiled references to the body, arousal, and sexual movements. The one focuses on knowledge and technique, the other on "pleasure and refinement."[37] Li Xiaorong refers to the *xiangyan* tradition as a poetic realm "depicting sensuality and romantic sentiment in highly aestheticized language," also in "ornate language" (*qiyu* 綺語), which begins with the poetry of Qu Yuan 屈原 (ca. 340–278 BCE) and includes such figures as the Liang 梁 dynasty (502–557) emperor Xiao Gang 蕭綱 (503–551) and the Tang poets Li Shangyin 李商隱 (812?–858)

36. See Li Xiaorong, *Poetics and Politics*.

37. Yao Ping, "Historicizing Great Bliss," 210 (though Yao does not use the term "*xiangyan*").

and Han Wo 韓偓 (844–923).[38] Two texts from the Tang dynasty provide further examples of elegant and tasteful erotica: the *Dale fu* (Rhapsody on the grand pleasure, 大樂賦) and the *Youxian ku* (Journey to the fairy grotto, 遊仙窟), both of which testify to the existence in that period of a social milieu that took sexual pleasure as an inherent part of a life of elite cultural refinement. Both describe sexual acts in polished and euphemistic ways.[39] Moreover, the *Dale fu* does something rare: It cites titles, terms, and techniques from the art of the bedchamber, but not in the spirit of informative discourse and physical cultivation. Instead, it does so squarely to portray the intensity of joy between a man and his wife and concubines, thus predicting a similar phenomenon in Ming and Qing pornography.[40]

Although the two texts were lost for many centuries, only to be rediscovered in the twentieth, something of their style and milieu survives in Ming and Qing literature, including *Jin Ping Mei*.[41] Moreover, as Li Xiaorong has shown, *xiangyan* literature experienced a revival in the late Ming in the sensual poetry of writers including Wang Cihui 王次回 (1593–1642), Zeng Rulu 曾汝魯 (late Ming), and Min Zhengzhong 閔正中 (late Ming).[42] The *xiangyan* type of language and imagery frequently appears in *Jin Ping Mei*, with the author at times writing as a *xiangyan* poet (or at least imitating those poets), as in the lines quoted above: "As spring enlivens the peach tree's blossoms, their red buds split open. As the breeze teases the willows, their green waists bend" (59.778). Compare these lines with a line from a poem by Zeng Rulu titled "Rising Late" ("Yan qi" 晏起):

38. Li Xiaorong, *Poetics and Politics*, 32; see also 1–5 and 35 (on *qiyu*). Han Wo's 韓偓 (844–923) poetry collection, *Xianglian ji* (香奩集), contains in its title another key term of the genre, *xianglian*, "the perfumed cosmetic case" (also used to refer to a woman's chambers).

39. Yao Ping discusses this milieu in its late Tang form ("Historicizing Great Bliss"). See also Levy's translation of the *Youxian ku* (*China's First Novelette*, 10–63).

40. See the text of the *Dale fu*, by Bai Xingjian 白行簡 (776–826), in Li Ling, *Zhongguo fangshu gaiguan*, 93–99, especially 94–96 (on the wife and concubines and reference to the art of the bedchamber). See also van Gulik, *Erotic Colour Prints*, 88–94 (a summary of the contents of the *Dale fu*, especially parts V and VI, 91–92); and Umekawa, "*Tiandi yinyang jiaohuan dale fu*," 273 (on the emphasis on sexual pleasure).

41. This includes the motif of the man enjoying the sight of "entering and leaving" (*kan chu kan ru*, 看出看入), from the *Dale fu* (in Li Ling, *Zhongguo fangshu gaiguan*, 95).

42. See Li Xiaorong, *Poetics and Politics*, 11.

"Having been covered in dew, the crabapple is still fresh in color. Greeting the wind, orchid-musk fragrance still emits from flickering light" (承露海棠犹带色，迎風蘭麝尚浮光).[43] The reference in Zeng's poem is to a night spent making love, which he renders through the image of the woman "covered in dew," where dew is a metaphor for semen. In both *Jin Ping Mei* and Zeng's poem, the image of the wind's effect on flower's blossoms represents the man having sex with the woman. Other commonalities include comparing the sounds of sex to the warbling of birds such as swallows or orioles and the use of *rui* (蕊 bud) to refer to female genitalia.

However, as it appears in *Jin Ping Mei*, what I am calling the high erotic (which includes imitations of *xiangyan*-style poetry) bears an inherently double and ironic meaning, though not always in as self-conscious a way as in the scene of double entendre above.[44] It is so simply by being preceded and followed by narrative that is about anything but harmonious relations between elegantly mannered men and women. The novel resembles *xiangyan* poetry, but it does not stick to that mode in as sustained or dedicated a way as the poetry. At times *Jin Ping Mei*'s high erotic barely emerges from the realm of the erotic ditty, the tone of which is apparent in the "teasing" of the breeze against the willows in the lines above. Under the novel's pornographic eye, sexual activity can never be as rarefied as in the *xiangyan* mode, whose late Ming practitioners self-consciously place themselves in the tradition of great poets such as Li Shangyin and Han Wo. The author of *Jin Ping Mei* has little interest in doing so, which is clearly evident in the transition to the prose and vulgarity that follows high erotic passages—most starkly in Pan Jinlian's curse. The most vulgar language in the novel is usually reserved for cursing, as here, or when men or women refer mockingly or jokingly to the genitals or the act of intercourse. *Diao* (鳥，屌) is a word that men use in *Shuihu zhuan* (*Water Margin* 水滸傳), literally meaning dick or prick. The word's use by a woman is rare, but Pan Jinlian is just the type of woman who would use such a word.[45]

43. Li Xiaorong, *Poetics and Politics*, 123, her translation (slightly modified); see also 124 and 133.

44. In regard to irony, especially in sexual scenes, see Plaks, *Four Masterworks*, 151.

45. Zhang Zhupo makes a comment to this effect, referring to both Pan Jinlian and Wang Liu'er. See Zhang Zhupo, *Jin Ping Mei dufa* (How to read the *Jin Ping Mei*), in Hou Zhongyi and Wang Rumei, eds., *Jin Ping Mei ziliao huibian*, 38.

The Contexts of the High Erotic

Why and in what contexts does the author of *Jin Ping Mei* use elegant language in descriptions of sex? As noted above, such language does not appear in the scenes of Ximen Qing's affairs with Song Huilian or Ben the Fourth.[46] His affairs with these two female servants are side adventures, though the one with Song Huilian could have turned out to be more substantial. In his affair with Pan Jinlian, Ximen Qing did not necessarily intend to make her his most important concubine, but he becomes profoundly attached to her, however many other men and women they also consort with. The first scene of sex in the entire novel is between the two and is in the high erotic, thus in effect announcing the significance of their relationship. The same is true for the first such scene between Ximen Qing and Li Ping'er, as if to predict his special affection for her. The only two descriptions of intercourse between him and his main wife, Wu Yueniang, are also in the high erotic, thus conforming to the pattern in Chinese fiction of portraying more refined and restrained love with the main wife and more wanton love with concubines and prostitutes. Scenes of sex with the prostitute Zheng Aiyue 鄭愛月 and the widow Lady Lin likewise feature sublime qualities, thereby accentuating the special effects of his relationships with the high-class courtesan, on the one hand, and the high-class widow, on the other hand, and lending these affairs correspondingly elevated qualities. Finally, a scene near the end of the novel with Chen Jingji and Pan Jinlian is in the high erotic, as if to signal their passion and success in getting together after so long desiring each other, though at the same time the scene evokes intense irony in the discord between the elevated language of their portrayal and their status as incestuous adulterers.

The first sex between Ximen Qing and Pan Jinlian comes as the climax of a lengthy seduction. It begins:

> The mandarin ducks play in the water, clinging in tight embrace; their heads nestling together, they are like phoenixes flying through the flowers.
>
> How joyous their delight, as if they were joined as one branch!

46. For Song, see 23.297 and 26.335. For Ben, see 78.1111–1112.

How sweet their pleasure, as if their hearts were bound by a single thread!
The one kisses her tightly with his pearly lips; the other presses up against him with her powdered face.
(交頸鴛鴦戲水，並頭鸞鳳穿花. 喜孜孜連理枝生，美甘甘同心帶結.一個將珠唇緊貼，一個將粉臉斜偎. 4.57).[47]

The euphemistic phrases about "the mandarin ducks play[ing] in the water" and "the phoenixes flying through the flowers" refer to the elegant and harmonious love of a monogamous couple, as mandarin ducks supposedly mate for life. However, the image is ironic in that Ximen Qing is a polygamist and both he and Pan Jinlian are adulterers now and will continue to be so throughout the novel. These are centuries-old images, though their cliché quality does not bother the Chongzhen commentator, who exclaims: "A marvelous picture of erotic love!" (*juemiao chuntu* 絶妙春圖, 4.57)—thus emphasizing how scenes such as this stand apart as independent portraits of sexual passion.[48] What comes before and after temporarily falls aside. Or, again, is it the case that we must interpret such passages—and the Chongzhen commentator's reading—as always at least faintly comical and ironic, given the characters involved and the quality of the stock images?

A quatrain from the third scene of Ximen Qing and Pan Jinlian in bed resorts to a common feature of Chinese poetry since ancient times, in which one line alternates with another in parallel counterpoint, as in the scene just cited. But *Jin Ping Mei*'s parallelism has a comic effect in the way that the counterpoint of the lines coincides with the partners synchronizing each other's motions: "Now she is on top dousing the red candle, then suddenly he is stealing fire from the other side of the wall" (方才枕上澆紅燭, 忽又偷來火隔墻, 6.81). In the next couplet, "the butterfly nibbles at the flower's calyx, which quivers in response" (粉蝶探香花萼顫), while "the dragonfly plays over the water, madly dashing back and forth" (蜻蜓戲水往來狂, 6.81–82). Such are the euphemistic double entendres that describe the motions of Ximen Qing's teasing and thrusting.

47. "How joyous their delight" and "how sweet their pleasure" are from Roy, 1.4.83–85.

48. Qi notes that such passages are "independent of the realistic presentation of the scene" (*Jin Ping Mei English Translations*, 190). Also see Hsia, *Classic Chinese Novel*, 184–186; and Shang Wei, "*Jin Ping Mei* and Late Ming Print Culture," 196–197.

The quatrain closes with an image of a grandiose ejaculation, which appears in the *cihua* edition only: "Passion and joy play at their extremes, as the divine turtle sprays forth its clear stream" (樂極情濃無限度，靈龜口內吐清泉)—"divine turtle," as noted above, being another euphemism for the potent penis.[49]

Similar parallelism is featured in Ximen Qing and Li Ping'er's first tryst, which the novel likewise describes in verse—in this case adopting the common motif of comparing them to famous lovers of previous times. The passage is also a case of parallel counterpoint:

> By the glow of the lamplight, inside the mermaid curtains,
> One lover cradles the other in his arms, the other raises high her lotus feet; one warbles like an oriole, the other twitters like a swallow.
> It is like Junrui's rendezvous with Cui Yingying, or Song Yu's tryst with the Goddess of Mount Shaman.
> They make promises as solid as the mountains and deep as the seas, which they murmur into each other's ears.
> The butterfly is amorous, the bee is unchecked, they cannot get enough.
> Behold: The coverlet roils like a sea of crimson waves, as the magic of the rhinoceros horn suffuses her silken breasts.
> Inside the bed curtains hung by silver clasps, her brow's painted arches grace her jade-white face.
> (燈光影裏，鮫綃帳中，一個玉臂忙搖，一個金蓮高舉．一個鶯聲嚦嚦，一個燕語喃喃．好似君瑞遇鶯娘，猶若宋玉偷神女．山盟海誓，依稀耳中，蝶戀蜂恣，未能即罷．正是：被翻紅浪，靈犀一點透酥胸；帳挽銀鈎，眉黛兩灣垂玉臉，13.165).[50]

Once again, the elegantly portrayed scene stands grandly on its own, apart from what is about to follow. Ximen Qing and Li Ping'er suddenly appear alongside legendary lovers (Zhang Junrui and Cui Yingying, and Song Yu and the shaman goddess). But when the author returns to prose,

49. JPMCH, 6.148, using slightly different wording, has "dousing the red candle" followed by "rowing the boat at night" (*diao ye xing chuan* 掉夜行船). "Divine turtle" comes from Roy, 1.6.123–124; see also 1.491, n. 26.

50. I used the Chongzhen version. "Warbles," "twitters," "mermaid curtains," and "painted eyebrows" come from Roy, 1.13.264–266. The "magic rhinoceros horn" is an allusion to a Li Shangyin poem and is an object that supposedly has within it a "single white strand that ran through it from root to tip" (Roy, 1.514–515, n. 13).

he shifts from the sublime to the mundane by signaling the presence of Li Ping'er's maid, "who is already quite familiar with such matters" (*po zhi shiti* 頗知事體, 13.165). She has been quietly watching them all along, to "her great delight" (*bu yi le hu* 不亦樂乎). The last phrase is a cliché from the opening of the Confucian *Analects* that is here put to comic use to refer to the voyeur's excited reaction to what she sees. The contrast between impassioned lovers and the voyeur's eye is a recurrent motif of erotic literature and illustration, summed up in two contrasting expressions from a poetic passage that appears early in the novel, the "infatuation" (*chixin* 癡心) of the lovers versus the "cold eye" (*lengyan* 冷眼, 5.65) of the observer, who in this case is the curious maid secretly observing them—a maid whom Li Ping'er soon offers to Ximen Qing. The cold eye also includes the dispassionate, satirical, or judgmental eye, as embodied in both explicit and implicit comments by the narrator as well as in the implied reader.

Ximen Qing and Li Ping'er's second high erotic scene occurs after they reconcile, a scene that exemplifies the avoidance of reference to bodily sexuality altogether. "After drinking and talking until the middle of the night, they finally spread the kingfisher coverlet, arrange the mandarin duck pillows, get into bed, and prepare to sleep" (飲酒說話到半夜，方才被伸翡翠，枕設鴛鴦，上床就寢). Then follows a brief lyric (*ci*) exaltation: "Under the flickering lamplight, they are like a pair of phoenixes singing a duet in a mirror; Floating in the mist of incense, they are like butterflies dancing ballet among the flowers" (燈光掩映，不啻鏡中鸞鳳和鳴；香氣薰籠，好似花間蝴蝶對舞, 20.251).[51] Such a description could nearly describe the idealized couple of a late Ming *xiangyan* poem, though the language of the poetry in *Jin Ping Mei* does not compare in literary quality. Now finally reconciled and sexually fulfilled, the two sleep until noon the next day.

Passages such as this hardly refer to what might qualify as sexually explicit. Feet rising high is as close as it gets. A butterfly nibbling at calyx, ruby lips, a rhinoceros horn, silken breasts, and bouncing bed covers are next. The idea is not to be explicit but instead to refer only tangentially, figuratively, and by association. That is the tradition in general of Chinese love poetry, as exemplified in the work of poets such as Li Shangyin. Though the texts of Tang erotica mentioned above and some Ming

51. "Under the flickering lamplight" is from Roy, 1.20.406.

and Qing *xiangyan* poetry are more explicit, they are always elegantly so. *Jin Ping Mei* follows the above passage with favored stock images in the form of birds and butterflies, as well as references to famous earlier lovers. "Promises as solid as the mountains and deep as the seas" (*shan meng hai shi* 山盟海誓) is another commonly used expression, which the more literary late Ming poets just mentioned would consider a cliché. The formulaic expression "the butterfly is amorous, the bee is unchecked" (*die lian feng zi* 蝶戀蜂恣) also occurs as "the oriole is unchecked, while the butterfly teases" (*ying zi die cai* 鶯恣蝶採, 80.1164).[52] The words "they cannot get enough" (*wei neng ji ba* 未能即罷) can also appear as "they felt they could never finish" (*wei ken ji xiu* 未肯即休, 21.267–268). Stock images and phrases like these are formulas to be combined and recombined. They appear in scenes of amorous pleasure in dances of words that, in spite of their relative shallowness, retain a level of dignity that stays above the ribald comic ditty. When the interlude is over, the narrative returns to the complex world of social relations, which typically consists of some sort of deal making. This explains the scene after awakening the next day, when Li Ping'er asks Ximen Qing to refashion a piece of precious jewelry for her.

The scene of Ximen Qing with Wu Yueniang is distinctive because it reflects the refined form of sex that the man should have with his main wife, his relationship with whom is the most solid and legitimate. *Jin Ping Mei* and other Ming and Qing works generally adhere to this rule when portraying such partners. A subtle sign of this distinction appears when Ximen Qing tries to have Yueniang call him by the lustful term *dada* 達達 ("daddy"), but she instead calls out *qinqin* 親親 ("dearest"), as if knowing that only his wanton partners utter the word *dada*.[53] It is also the case that, as with Li Ping'er, the scene of his union with Yueniang marks a reconciliation after a period of misunderstanding. The passage begins in plain prose with direct description, in which "With no further delay, Ximen Qing took Yueniang's creamy white thighs, placed them on his shoulders, and inserted his word into her vagina" (西門慶不繇分說，把月娘兩隻白生生腿扛在肩膊上，那話插入牝中). This is followed by a poetic passage that echoes the ones above but is in a slightly recombined

52. Similar words appear in *Xixiang ji*: "the butterfly collects at will" (*ci die cai* 恣蝶採), 137; West and Idema, trans., *The Moon and the Zither*, 334.

53. On the use of *dada*, see Keulemans, "*Jin Ping Mei* chongtan," 401–403.

form, beginning: "He gave free rein to the oriole's abandon and the butterfly's pursuit. Entranced by the clouds and intoxicated by the rain, they felt they could never finish" (一任其鶯恣蝶採，殢雨尤雲，未肯即休).[54] Each of these three four-word expressions occurs numerous times in the novel. As the lovers reach "supreme pleasure" (*meiai wujia* 美愛無加), Ximen Qing asks Yueniang to show more passion, at which point the author lifts lines from an often cited ancient poem (the underscored lines): "Yueniang responds softly, <u>inside the lowered curtains</u>, <u>with pillows pushed together</u>, calling him 'dearest' over and over, <u>as beautiful as any woman could be</u>" (月娘亦低聲，<u>睥幃暱枕</u>，<u>態有餘妍</u>，口呼親親不絶). They finish and "fall asleep cuddled together" for the rest of the night (並頭交頸而睡, 21.267–268).

The copied words are from a fifth-century poem in *xiangyan* style. "Inside the lowered curtains, with pillows pushed together," originally occurs in the "Xuefu" ("Rhapsody on snow," 雪賦), by Xie Huilian 謝惠連 (397–433) of the Liu Song (劉宋, 420–479) dynasty. He writes of a scene in which the man and woman "lower the curtains and push their pillows together" (*di wei yi ni zhen* 低帷以昵枕).[55] A closer version of the same lines in *Jin Ping Mei* appears in the Tang story by Jiang Fang 蔣防 (early ninth century), "The Story of Huo Xiaoyu" ("Huo Xiaoyu zhuan" 霍小玉傳), about a love affair between a courtesan and a man who later betrays her. In their first time in bed, "as she removed her gauze robe, <u>she was as beautiful as anyone could be</u> [*tai you yu yan* 態有餘妍]. <u>They lowered the bed curtains and drew their pillows together</u> [*di wei ni zhen* 低幃暱枕], enjoying the height of ecstasy" (解羅衣之際，態有餘妍，低幃暱枕，極其歡愛).[56] In reaction to these words, the Chongzhen commentator exclaims: "these eight characters make me swoon!" (*bazi hun xiao* 八字魂銷, 21.268).[57]

At its adumbrative extreme, the high erotic mode reduces descriptions to just a few words, as in "and they spent a night of pleasure together" or "no words suffice to describe their passion and affection under

54. From "oriole's abandon" to "intoxicated by the rain" comes from Roy, 2.21.7.

55. Xie Huilian, "Xuefu," in *Zhaoming wenxuan yizhu* 昭明文選譯注, 710.

56. Jiang Fang, "Huo Xiaoyu zhuan," in Zhang Youhe, *Tang Song chuanqi xuan*, 46.

57. The eight characters are *tai you yu yan*, *di wei ni zhen*, of which the novel replaces *di* 低 with *bi* 睥. The words appear commonly elsewhere, as in Tang Xianzu's *Zi chai ji* 紫釵記, in Qian Nanyang, ed., *Tang Xianzu xiqu ji*, 59.

the covers," which refer to the second night Ximen Qing spends with Wu Yueniang, when she has taken the nun's fertility potion (暢美的睡了一夜；被中繾綣，言不可盡).[58] If the author has no reason to narrate further, then such words suffice—which returns us to the question asked above: Why and in what context does the author use the high erotic, which relates to the more basic question of why and in what context is there any description of sex at all? Sex with the main wife after a period of rancor or sex that results in conception are deemed worthy of description. Other nights take place in passing and do not merit narrative display. The second scene of Ximen Qing's sex with Yueniang takes place after a previous night when she pushes him away. It is not yet the right numerological day for her to conceive, so she sends him to Pan Jinlian instead. As it happens, Jinlian has just had hurried and passionate sex with Chen Jingji. Ximen Qing arrives in her room, immediately feels her crotch, and notices its wetness. "Who have you been missing, that your word is so wet?" (你想着誰來，兀那話濕搭搭的) he asks, in this rare case using "word" for the female genitals. "She feels as though she has been found out" (*zi jue xinxu* 自覺心虛), but she manages to ward off suspicion and goes to wash herself, after which the scene closes with the common abbreviation: "Of that evening's sport in the clouds and rain with Ximen Qing, there is no need to go into detail" (當晚與西門慶雲情雨意, 不消說得, 53.697–98).[59]

HIGH EROTIC ARTIFICE: SEX WITH COURTESAN ZHENG

Although the portrayals of Ximen Qing's affairs with Pan Jinlian and Li Ping'er begin with grand and elegant display, they later turn more graphic, with only occasional uses of high erotic language. It is a different story with the two descriptions of Ximen Qing and Wu Yueniang, which are minimally graphic and have no follow-up except passing

58. The first quote is from JPMCH, 53.1485 (describing Ximen Qing's enormity after applying the aphrodisiac cream). The second is from JPM, 53.699 (which contains no reference to size or cream).

59. For a third instance of Ximen Qing's having sex with Wu Yueniang, "it was like sweet rain after a long drought, like old friends meeting in a distant place. Needless to say, they experienced the pure joy of love" (兩個是久旱逢甘雨, 他鄉遇故知, 懽愛之情, 俱不必說, 55.725). For another, again with no details, see 58.762.

references to his spending the night with her.[60] Yueniang's goal in having sex with him is to bear a son, and she has little affection for him; descriptions of their sex are rarer than of his sex with others. In two other cases, one between Ximen Qing and Zheng Aiyue and the other between Chen Jingji and Pan Jinlian, sex begins awkwardly and, in the first case, painfully. But later portrayals rise to more elevated tones in combinations of elegant prose and poetry, though they differ from each other in a major way. The sex between Ximen Qing and Zheng Aiyue has an artificial, formal quality that reflects the tenor of a man's relations with an expensive prostitute. In contrast, the sex between Chen Jingji and Pan Jinlian is adulterous, taking place furtively, hastily, and opportunistically. It is passionate from beginning to end, one of the prime examples of such sex in the novel.

Visiting a longed-for prostitute in an expensive brothel has momentous meaning, which *Jin Ping Mei* evokes in a lofty tone that is specific to the brothel's theatricality. Before discussing that, however, let us first briefly note the unerotic way in which Zheng Aiyue is introduced, which frames and qualifies the high erotic language that the author later uses in scenes depicting her and Ximen Qing. Her name first appears when three prostitutes visiting Wu Yueniang briefly mention that Zheng has just been deflowered (32.413). A key aspect of brothel culture emerges in this scene: the behavior of prostitutes when no men are around. They talk among themselves using slang that Yueniang cannot understand. Referring to an unruly client whom Zheng refuses to see, they say that he has recently been consorting with another prostitute, Dong the Cat (Dong Mao'er 董貓兒), and that "because he twice burned moxa on her tiger's mouth, he stayed doing nails and holes with her for quite a while, but lately he's finally gone away" (因把貓兒的虎口內火燒了兩醮，和他丁八着好一向子，這日才散走了, 32.413). Yueniang does not understand the term "tiger's mouth," nor does she know anything about burning moxa on a woman's vagina, something Ximen Qing would not do with her. Furthermore, she has never heard the expression "nails and holes" (*dingba* 丁八), which some interpret as prostitute's slang for having sex, the character for *ding* resembling the male genital and the character for *ba* resembling

60. See the previous note.

the female.[61] In talking about their work here and elsewhere, the women mention such things as clothing, shoes, jewelry, and hair; episodes in their daily life; and the kinds of things they must do to entertain their customers. Their term for having sex conveys the sense of the working act that sex is for them. As we know from other sources, moxa was just one of many profitable substances sold as aphrodisiacs at the time, and it was commonly available in markets near brothels.[62]

Several features of brothel culture explain its theatricality. First is the company of male clients and their followers, who achieve status by gathering there, seeing each other, and being seen—especially the one who gains the privilege of deflowering a new prostitute. Second is the aura that the brothel and its women try to produce to make the client feel as if he is receiving the best treatment possible. The brothel must be finely furnished and the women well dressed and coiffed, and they must be masters of a range of skills besides the practice of sex, such as drinking, dining, talking, playing games, singing, and playing music. Only after a well-orchestrated combination of such activities do they and their clients finally disrobe and get into bed. A third feature, the most important of all, has to do with the fact that the prostitute must remain independent of her patron. She cannot let emotions take over (famous stories have them doing so, but that is a variant genre). She must be the one in charge, which means making the client feel as if he has gotten what he wants. Ideally, as Sanjay Gautam writes in the Indian context, she both directs the scenes of their encounters and acts in them.[63] The treatment of the client, including the sex that the prostitute has with him, must make him feel divine, but achieving such a goal relies on the control that the woman exerts over both herself and the client. Losing herself in the passion of sex can only be simulated, which explains the artificial and formal quality

61. Though not all scholars agree on this interpretation (some saying it means to argue), I follow Huang Lin and others on *dingba* 丁八. See Huang, *Huang Lin jiang*, 154; Zhang Huiying, *Jin Ping Mei lisu nanci jie*, 155; and Shanghai shi *Honglong meng* xuehui, *Jin Ping Mei jianshang cidian*, 561. Roy translates *dingba* as to "terminate" (2.32.249 and 32.538, n. 12). For another difficult case of brothel argot from the same passage, see Roy, 2.32.539, n. 15.

62. See Su Yufen, *Mingdai chunyao yanjiu*, 52–54.

63. Gautam writes that the prostitute "must always be able to walk away" and that she is the "playwright, director, and actor" (*Foucault and the Kamasutra*, 105 and 108).

of sex in the brothel. Zheng's skills are not up to par in the first scene below, but they are by the second.[64]

When Ximen Qing first visits Zheng, he is a man approaching someone he has heard about who has "just become a woman" (*cai chengren* 才成人, 58.755), a situation that stimulates peak attention in the client. She is a new star at the brothel theater, and being her first client is a singular prize. Ximen Qing visits her one day on a whim, setting out in his fancy "summer sedan chair" (*liangjiao* 涼轎) with its "speckled bamboo shades" (*banzhu lian* 斑竹簾, 59.775). No one knows where he is going except the servants who attend him. When he arrives, he is greeted by another prostitute, Zheng Aixiang 鄭愛香 (Aiyue's sister), conforming to the formula by which the desired woman at first remains out of sight. When Zheng Aiyue finally appears, she is stunning: "If it weren't a portrait of Guanyin by court painter Wu, it would be a beauty drawn by palace painter Mao" (若非道子觀音畫, 定然延壽美人圖, 59.776; both references are to famous past masters).[65] The appearance of the heavenly woman to the lone waiting man is an ancient motif, in which the woman emerges from a distance, like a goddess alighting. The sensation "so strikes [Ximen Qing's] eyes and sways his heart that he could hardly control himself" (不覺心搖目蕩, 不能禁止, 59.776). The comedy of the scene is already apparent, and the Chongzhen commentator affirms it, pointing out what he labels as "the deeper Zheng Aiyue, but the shallower Ximen Qing" (此鄭月兒深處, 西門慶淺人): "Being a person of deep feeling, Zheng is unwilling to greet him with a fullness of erotic welcome. As for Ximen Qing, he is concerned that he not lose the appearance of official dignity. Thus at first seeing each other, they keep a certain loose distance" (鄭月兒深情人, 不肯便滿面春風, 西門慶又恐失官體, 所以乍見時疏疏落落, 59.776–777).[66]

64. Contemporary Taiwanese sex workers report that it is their goal to manage their own bodies and be in control of the sexual acts that take place. See Ho, "Self-Empowerment," 288.

65. See Roy 3.59.459 and 3.59.623, nn. 15 and 16.

66. For the way in which Zheng's character offsets the boorishness of Ximen Qing, see also comments by Zhang Zhupo, *Jin Ping Mei dufa*, in Hou Zhongyi and Wang Rumei, eds., *Jin Ping Mei ziliao huibian*, 29. On Zheng Aiyue's intelligence and difference from other courtesans, and on her and her sister, see Ge, *Xueyin lusi*, 276–279; and on her skill at riddles, see Kelly, "Riddles in *Jin Ping Mei*," 348–349.

Another grand moment takes place when the sisters invite him into Aiyue's room, the description of which qualifies as erotic even though it makes no reference to a sexual act. The fact that the description is of a courtesan's bedroom is sufficient. The *cihua* edition celebrates the occasion with a long poem describing the room's exquisite qualities and ending with the only part of the passage that appears in the Chongzhen edition: "An exotic aroma carried him away. Immaculate and elegant, it was like entering a goddess's den in a sacred grotto, which no human had ever yet reached" (異香襲人，極其清雅. 真所謂神仙洞府，人跡不可到者也，59.777).[67] The scene continues with a series of pleasurable activities, as the two sisters serve Ximen Qing wine and delicacies, the three play a game of dominoes, the sisters serve more food and play music—after which Aixiang finally leaves, thus signaling the transition to the sexual phase of the visit. Ximen Qing takes out his pillbox, which Aiyue thinks is a box of sweet lozenges, only to learn that it is his "supplement" (*buyao* 補藥), which he has never been without since obtaining it from the monk. She is the eighth woman he tries it with. He takes her onto his lap, they kiss, and he toys with her breasts, which under her clothes are "firm to the touch, and creamy as sesame-filled dumplings" (緊緊就就，賽麻團滑膩) and, when he exposes them, "fragrant and white, as lustrous as gleaming jade" (白馥馥猶如瑩玉一般，59.777–778).[68] The prostitute by definition is a woman whom Ximen Qing will use not only for physical stimulation but also to enjoy in an aesthetically sensual way, which the novel represents with none of the satire that will otherwise prevail in the scene.

Although sex in the high-caliber brothel must go smoothly, the next phase of the scene introduces an enormous dissonance, which nevertheless passes by with the professional grace (as well as the frankness) characteristic of the brothel. Suddenly feeling the rise of his erection, Ximen Qing has her hold it in her hand. But Aiyue takes fright at its size, saying, "Dear lover, we've just met today. Be easy with me and just put it in part way, won't you? If you put it all the way in I will simply die!" (我的親親，你今日初會，將就我. 只放半截兒罷! 若都放進去，我就死了). He

67. See Roy 3.59.624, nn. 23–26, for other occurrences of these words, such as *yixiang xi ren* 異香襲人, in Tang Xianzu, *Mudan ting*, 171.

68. Ximen Qing plays with the breasts of only two other women, Pan Jinlian (19.237; as Chen Jingji once does, 53.313), and wet nurse Ruyi, whose breast milk he mixes with a drug to take during his final illness (74.1026, 75.1039, and 79.1137).

must have taken a drug to make it so big, she continues, "otherwise how on its own could it have become so strange looking, all red and purple and monstrous!? It is awful to look at!" (如何天生恁怪剌剌兒的，紅赤赤，紫漒漒，好砢磣人子). Ximen Qing takes no offense, just laughs and asks her to "try and take it in her mouth" (*pinpin* 品品). He is proud of his new size. "What is the hurry?," she asks (*huang zende* 慌怎的), as she tries to divert him once more with an offer of wine, but he only wants to "do the joyous act" (*jiaohuan* 交歡). At that point she has the maid take the wine table away and remove Ximen Qing's shoes, and then she goes to the rear to change clothes and rinse herself.

The focus on the beauty of Aiyue's naked body continues as the text moves into what begins as a session of elegant and alluring sex but derails as Ximen Qing's penetration becomes difficult and painful: "They were a pair of mallards in conjugal repose, two married swans wrapped in their bedding. Ximen Qing saw how fine the painted face's skin was, her vagina immaculate and hairless like a white steamed cake, soft and tender and delightful to behold" (兩個枕上鴛鴦, 被中鸂鶒. 西門慶見粉頭肌膚纖細, 牝淨無毛, 猶如白麵蒸餅一般, 柔嫩可愛, 59.778).

The unblemished description of conjugal birds and woman delightful to behold reflects the tone that Aiyue must uphold and explains her effort to maintain her composure, even when she feels pain:

> He took her tender white legs, gleaming like silver bullion, and wrapped them around his waist, then slipped the clasp on his word and plunged himself into the heart of the flower. But his turtle head was so enormous that he had to moisten and wiggle it for quite a while before he could even get the knob to go in. Wincing and gripping the pillow with her hands, Zheng Aiyue kept her pain to herself but could barely take it, and, half-closing her starry eyes, said softly, 'Can you spare your Zheng Yue'er today please?' But hearing such words only excited Ximen Qing the more, as he began to thrust more vigorously, with ever deepening pleasure. (于是把他兩隻白生生銀條般嫩腿兒夾在兩邊腰眼間，那話上使了托子，向花心裡頂入. 龜頭昂大，濡攪半晌, 方才沒稜. 那鄭月兒把眉頭縐在一處，兩手攀閣在枕上，隱忍難挨. 朦朧着星眼，低聲説道: "今日你饒了鄭月兒罷." 西門慶聽了，愈覺銷魂，肆行抽送，不勝歡娛, 59.778).

Both the *cihua* and Chongzhen editions follow this dissonance with the flowery couplet that appears three times in the novel, with slight variations (a longer poem appears in the *cihua*): "As spring enlivens the peach tree's blossoms, their red buds split open. As the breeze teases the willows, their green waists bend" (59.778).[69] It is a double entendre in which spring and breeze suggest the actions of the man, while peach tree buds splitting open and willow waists bending suggest movement on the part of the woman. The clash between "mallards in conjugal repose" or "white steamed cake" and the actions of "wincing and gripping" could not be more violent. The scene wraps up in one sentence, which reports that they continue until late in the night, when Ximen Qing finally goes home. His session with her culminates a series of bouts in which he tries his new drug with one woman after another, experiencing greater pleasure than ever but causing them both pain and fright.[70]

The next scene between Ximen Qing and Aiyue shows her having now mastered the art of sex with her powerful client. The prose is direct but genteel. She performs smoothly and skillfully, with no apparent pain or hesitation, and she makes sure to remind him how she helped him meet the widow Lady Lin. Her reference to this favor is another mark of how brothel sex functions at a remove from the intimate physical acts that are taking place. Sensual feeling is present, but as something that the woman drives into the man. Aiyue simultaneously engineers not only her own sex with Ximen Qing but also his future sex with Lady Lin, for all of which Aiyue will receive a generous reward. As happened the first time Ximen Qing visited her, a long while goes by in which they talk and eat, after which she finally

> took her slender hand to open Ximen Qing's trousers and expose his word, which she began to play with, making it erupt into a wild gallop as it became all purplish and gleaming. Ximen Qing asked her to take it into her mouth, which she presently did, bending low her powdered neck, gently opening her ruby lips, going back and forth over it, moving it in and out of her mouth, and making a singing, sucking sound. After she had played

69. The first time the couplet appears is when Ximen Qing is with Pan Jinlian (10.126); the second time is when he first has sex with Aiyue; and the third time is when Chen Jingji has sex with his new wife, Ge Cuiping 葛翠屏 (97.1379).

70. In order, the women are Wang Liu'er, Li Ping'er, Pan Jinlian, Li Guijie, Meng Yulou, Wu Yueniang, Sun Xue'e, and Aiyue—all of whom, except for Meng Yulou and Sun Xue'e, express fright or appear to suffer. See chapters 50–53 and 58–59. Wu Yueniang and Aiyue both exclaim about the monstrousness of Ximen Qing's organ in its enhanced state.

with it for a while, the rhinoceros horn became thoroughly engorged, and his desires blazed like fire, which made him ready to do the joyous act. (又用纖手解開西門慶褌帶，露出那話來，替他揑弄. 那話猙獰跳腦，紫漲光鮮. 西門慶令他品之，這粉頭眞個低垂粉頸，輕啓朱唇，半呑半吐，或進或出，嗚咂有聲. 品弄了一回，靈犀已透，淫心似火，便欲交歡, 77.1098).

Taken on their own, such lines would presumably appeal to the literati readers of the late Ming, regardless of the tone of the surrounding narrative. With the preliminaries thus concluded, the episode continues as both partners retreat: she to rinse herself and he to "to take a natural break" (*geng yi* 更衣), during which time he notices that the snow is falling harder, a detail that further enhances the aura of sex in the goddess's grotto. She finally "closes the double-leaved doors and joins him inside the mandarin duck curtains. . . . . There is a poem to illustrate":

In dreams, meetings and partings come and go; when all is over, the remains of the candle glow in red against the gauze curtains.
In true love, as always, spirits join in heavenly union; who says a goddess's abode is out of reach?
(關上雙扉，共入鴛帳 . . . . 有詩爲証: 聚散無憑在夢中，起來殘燭映紗紅，鍾情自古多神合，誰道陽臺路不通, 77.1099).

The poem is a classic, though brief, instance of high erotic hyperbole, utterly parodic in its reference to the "heavenly union" of Ximen Qing and the courtesan-goddess Zheng Aiyue.[71] The preceding prose passage is direct and noneuphemistic (except for "rhinoceros horn"), presenting an erotic scene of full arousal in language that shuns vulgarity but contains a shade of the grotesque ("purplish and gleaming" and the sound of sucking). The passages of prose and poetry differ in that the prose portrays only male arousal, while the poetic lines portray mutual love, as false and incongruous as that may be. Thus takes place a successful sexual event in the elegant brothel, the man feeling as though he has slept with a goddess, who conducts business as coolly as possible with her libertine-rogue of a client.

71. She later sends him delicacies, including melon seeds cracked open with her own mouth (67.903–904). Another visit follows (68.935).

FIGURE 1. "Ximen Qing Treads on the Snow in a Visit to Zheng Aiyue" (西門慶踏雪訪愛月). From chapter 77 of *Jin Ping Mei* 金瓶梅, Lanling xiaoxiao sheng 蘭陵笑笑生, *Xinke xiuxiang piping Jin Ping Mei* 新刻繡像批評金瓶梅 (Hong Kong: Sanlian shudian, 1990).

HIGH EROTIC PASSION: THE AFFAIR BETWEEN PAN JINLIAN AND CHEN JINGJI

The affair between Chen Jingji and Pan Jinlian begins with frenzied trysts, described in graphic language, but ends in portrayals of grandiose exaltation. The affair differs from that between Ximen Qing and Zheng Aiyue in that it is between two lovers who crave each other and take every opportunity to go as far as they can. In the following scene from early in their affair, they exhibit one of the book's most frenzied attempts at sex. The passage comes from a five-chapter section (53–57) by another author (or authors) that contains irregularities and inconsistencies, as readers as far back as Shen Defu 沈德符 (1578–1642) have noted. Scenes in other chapters in which Jingji and Jinlian get together before Ximen Qing dies have the two only going as far as kissing, but the author of the following passage in chapter 53 has the lovers go further. In spite of the anomalies, the fact that the lovers attempt to grab whatever fleshly contact they can is consistent with the overall portrayal of their affair.[72]

They have just begun a frenzied intercourse, but must break off because others arrive to check the baby, Guange 官哥, whom Jinlian is supposed to be watching, but whom she abandons to join Jingji, to the baby's deep fright. Before the others arrive, Jinlian pretends to fend Jingji off, but he keeps pressing himself against her.

> The organ inside his gown felt like a bar of red-hot iron. He kept pushing himself onto her through his clothing, as Jinlian couldn't help but shove herself against him, until she felt his fire-hot penis right next to her, could stand it no more, and taking hold of his gown, pulled it open, and gripped his organ. Jingji in turn pulled feverishly at Jinlian's waistband, suddenly tearing open one of its pleats, [after which] . . . she pulled the waistband down herself, exposed her vagina, and, balancing one leg on the railing, shoved his penis inside her. Because they had been already playing at it for a while, she was flowing wet inside, so Jingji needed only one quick push to plunge himself in. He said, "My darling, standing up like this I can't get it all the way in, can't we do it another way?" Jinlian answered, "Just keep on thrusting for now, we'll manage one way or another."

72. See Hanan, "Text," 12 and 14–39.

(下面單裙子內，卻似火燒的一條硬鐵．隔了衣服只顧挺將進來．那金蓮也不由人，把身子一聳．那話兒都隔了衣服，熱烘烘對着了．金蓮正忍不過，用手掀開經濟裙子，用力捏着陽物．經濟慌不迭的替金蓮扯下褲腰來，劃的一聲，却扯下一個裙裥兒．. . . [金蓮] 就自家扯下褲腰，剛露出牝口．一腿蹺在欄杆上，就把經濟陽物塞進牝口．原來金蓮鬼混了半响，已是濕答答的，被經濟用力一挺，便撲的進去了．經濟道，"我的親親，只是立了不盡根，怎麼處?" 金蓮道，"胡亂抽送抽送，且再擺佈").

At that point, a dog's bark signals Ximen Qing's return, forcing the two to part. It is after this that Ximen Qing goes from Yueniang's room to Jinlian's and discovers her arousal.[73]

As if to signal their final success at consummation, the description of the affair switches to a higher register after Ximen Qing dies. They have finally gotten a measure of freedom to meet more regularly, though they must still avoid being discovered—especially by Wu Yueniang, who has taken charge of the household and has both the authority and the will to expel them both. One day Jinlian signals Jingji to meet her in his room, where "she unties her pants, lies down on the kang, and sends her feet flying to his shoulders, thus allowing Chen Jingji to join her in the pleasure of fornication. Truly, what fear have those whose lustful daring is as high as the sky? They only wish for eternal love in the clouds and rain of their lovers' bed" (解開褲子，仰臥在炕上，雙鳧飛肩，教陳經濟奸耍．正是: 色膽如天怕甚事，鴛幃雲雨百年情). Then follows a rhymed passage in mock high erotic language that could apply to any of the other scenes discussed so far, with only the first two lines making slight reference to the particularity of this affair:

Having met some years before, they take but a moment to couple as one.
For years related as in-laws, they take but an instant to unite in harmony.
The one gently rocks her willowy waist, the other eagerly thrusts his jade stalk.
They pour words of passion into each other's ears, and by their pillows they make promises as solid as the mountains and deep as the seas.

73. JPMCH, 53.1476–1477. "A bar of red-hot iron" is from Roy, 3.53.297–298. The Chongzhen edition differs in that, among other things, Jingji takes out his penis right away and Jinlian is the one to open her waistband, without any rip (JPM, 53.696–697).

The oriole is unchecked, the butterfly teases, arousing the beautiful maiden in thousands of ways.
The rain is relentless, the clouds are blushing, as the enchanting woman flaunts an infinite display.
The one keeps calling for his darling, the other pulls him close crying "my *dada* lover!"
Behold: the willow suddenly turns a fresh new green, while the hue of the flower loses none of its prior red.
(二載相逢, 一朝配偶; 數年姻眷, 一旦和諧. 一個柳腰款擺, 一個玉莖忙舒. 耳邊訴雨意雲情, 枕上説山盟海誓. 鶯恣蝶採, 旖旎搏弄百十般; 狂雨羞雲, 嬌媚施逞千萬態. 一個不住叫親親, 一個摟抱呼達達. 得多少柳色乍翻新樣綠, 花容不減舊時紅, 80.1164).

Only the words *jianshua* 奸耍 jar what is otherwise a description of passionate love. *Jian* has deeply negative connotations, referring to fornication, adultery, and debauchery, while *shua* means "play" or "frolic" (thus the translation "the pleasure of fornication"). Or is it the case that the condemnation usually implied in the word *jian* is the writer's way of emphasizing the no-holds-barred lust of the scene? The rest of the passage conforms to other portrayals in mock high erotic. The lovers Pan Jinlian and Chen Jingji finally enjoy their supposed "eternal love" as they swear their "mountains" and "seas" of loyalty.

A feature of these portrayals not pointed out so far appears in this and other passages, which is common to Chinese writing in general in contrast to English—namely, the frequent lack of pronoun or subject reference, which in this case means the lack of clear reference to whether the subject is the man or the woman. Though interpretations will differ, the gendered color of words and clauses can make up for the lack. The formulaic phrase "the oriole is unchecked, the butterfly teases" (or "collects") implies a masculine subject, while *qini* 旖旎 at the beginning of the next line implies a "gentle and enchanting" woman, who "incites" and "excites" (*bonong* 搏弄) the man in countless ways.[74] *Qini* is like *jiaomei* 嬌媚 in the following line, with *jiaomei* being a trope for a "charming and beguiling" woman. The formulaic phrase "the rain is relentless, the clouds are blushing" has masculine rain in the first half and feminine clouds in the second half, where *xiu* 羞 implies a blushing maiden—

74. *Qini* 旖旎 also occurs as *yini* 旖旎, meaning tender and beguiling.

though that hardly reflects the real Pan Jinlian, again exemplifying the idealizing (but also ironizing) effect of the mock high erotic. Similarly, the passage ends with metaphors that on the surface are unrelated to sexual acts. The line "the willow suddenly turns a fresh new green, while the hue of the flower loses none of its prior red" comes from a poem by the woman poet Zhu Shuzhen 朱淑真 (circa Southern Song; twelfth–thirteenth centuries), here used to signal the freshness and promise of new love—which in Chen's and Pan's case will soon end.[75]

Their passion continues the next day in a passage that also uses the tone of high erotic parody. Jinlian is still in bed as Jingji approaches, peeks through the latticework, and sees "her under the covers, cuddled as if between rosy clouds, her powdered cheeks imprinted with the mark of her jade bracelet" (見婦人被擁紅雲，粉腮印玉).[76] They cannot hold themselves back. While Chunmei is out of the room, Jinlian sticks her tongue through the latticework and the two have a long, deep kiss (80.1165). This point is where the lines I referred to in chapter 2 appear: "her sweet spittle transfuses his heart, as it floods through his vitals." Again, saliva, sweat, and other bodily fluids are nothing strange to the imagery of the *xiangyan* tradition that such lines evoke.[77] The next lines are taken from a song by an anonymous writer about lovers looking back in sadness on their recent consummation:

> The crying of the cuckoo pains us as it penetrates the jeweled blinds, our hearts sewn tight, our feelings sealed fast.
> Her smile now sits in hollowed cheeks, her powdered eyebrows worn with sadness, her delicate fingers thin and wasted.
> (恨杜鵑聲透珠簾，心似針簽，情似膠粘. 我則見笑臉腮窩愁粉黛，瘦損春纖，80.1165).[78]

75. Zhu Shuzhen, "Xin chun" 新春 (New spring), in Zhang Zhang and Huang She, eds., *Zhu Shuzhen ji*, 6–7. The novel changes *caose* 草色 to *liuse* 柳色.

76. This suggests that she slept with her cheek against her bracelet, which left a mark on her face (based on the poetic convention that pictures a sleeping woman with a mark left on her face from a pillow or bracelet). Roy has "her powdered cheeks like fluted jadestone" (4.80.675).

77. See Li Xiaorong, *Poetics and Politics*, 67 and 100–101 (for a line from a poem by Wang Cihui: "Your fragrant and exquisite saliva—I'm waiting for you, my darling," 濃香細唾等卿來).

78. "Hollow[ed] cheeks" and "powdered eyebrows" come from Roy, 4.80.675–676; see also 4.80.851, n. 21 (which refers to an anonymous source of a variant of the poem).

Words such as these give the pair an exalted air, which their circumstances hardly support.[79]

Two key features stamp the affair between Chen Jingji and Pan Jinlian: first, the ways in which its passion exceeds that of Ximen Qing's and Pan Jinlian's affair; and second, Jinlian's dominance over Jingji.[80] When she suspects him of having an affair with Meng Yulou, which could not have happened, he beseechingly pleads innocence. The Chongzhen commentator says this about his manner: "Pan Jinlian had never experienced such kind and gentle treatment. Jingji is as if making up for what Ximen Qing lacked" (金蓮從未受此軟欵溫存, 敬濟似爲西門慶補遺, 82.1192–1193). During a later encounter in her room, she "takes all the love and passion that she experienced with Ximen Qing and gives it to her lover boy in one single night" (婦人把昔日西門慶枕邊風月, 一旦盡付與情郎身上, 83.1196). Jinlian's dominance emerges in the fact that, as handsome and clever as he may be, Jingji is a far less successful man than Ximen Qing. Even considering the polygynous threesome that soon forms between Jinlian, Chunmei, and Jingji, the center of the group is not Jingji but Jinlian. She is the one who has him have sex with Chunmei, thereby ensuring that Chunmei is privy to their affair and will be loyal to them. In their last scene together, Jinlian takes out Ximen Qing's bag of sex tools, both she and Jingji strip, she lies on a reclining chair, and he takes out the erotic album illustrating the twenty-four positions—which they proceed to imitate, one by one (83.1201). As if assuming the role of her former master, Jinlian has Chunmei get behind Jingji and help him push, "for fear he may get tired" (只怕他身子乏了). All three perform the full range of activities that would have taken place if Jingji were Ximen Qing, except that now Jinlian directs the action.

But it is at this moment that the maid Qiuju finally gets her revenge by reporting them to Wu Yueniang. She spies the three of them drunk and naked in a brightly lit room. A poem describes the scene from the eyes of the observer, a point of view that is somewhere between that of Qiuju and a generalized perspective that the author creates and that al-

79. In the *cihua* edition, they sing love songs to each other (see JPMCH, 82.2607–2608; and Roy, 5.82.21). The Chongzhen editor eliminates these, in conformity with his tendency to streamline the text. See Rolston, "Oral Performing Literature," 46–52, especially 47.

80. Hsia notes her dominance in earlier chapters (*Classic Chinese Novel*, 197–198).

ternates between ribaldry and the idyllic tone of the high erotic, furthering the already tour-de-force effect of the parody. In one line, "the one cares not a bit if she is an adulterous widow. The other gives not a jot about who is higher or lower" (一個不顧夫主名分, 一個那管上下尊卑). In the next line, "the one sits back as she gives rein to the passion of clouds and rain, the other leans by her ear promising loyalty as solid as the mountains and deep as the seas" (一個椅上逞雨意雲情, 一個耳畔説山盟海誓). The next line resumes the satirical tone: "The one transforms her widow's chambers into an altar of pleasure. The other, at his mother-in-law's feet, turns the scene into a realm of carnal riot" (一個寡婦房内翻爲快活道場, 一個丈母根前變作汗淫世界). The author closes with a farcically incongruous declaration: "They swear never to part in this life, and vow to continue their joy in the next" (寫成今世不休書, 結下來生歡喜帶, 83.1201–1202). The same expression appears a few chapters later in the affair between Chen Jingji and Chunmei (86.1224).

Lovers swearing eternal loyalty or portrayed as a perfect match appear throughout the novel, even though none of the partners can be imagined as the love-bound monogamists that such words imply. In general, the author refuses to create idealized lovers, instead using such imagery to create an implicit, underlying dissonance that speaks for itself (as in the songs quoted from *Pipa ji*). A scene from a few chapters earlier ends with the same dissonance, though it is more extreme there. Ximen Qing's erection will not go down, but the couplet that ends the scene describes him and Pan Jinlian as if they were a divine couple. At first, Jinlian finds him asleep and feels "his word"—which will not stiffen because, as it happens, he and Chunmei "had been engaging in the bedroom act not long before" (*cai xing fang bujiu* 才行房不久, 73.1022). "Hot with desire" (*yuqing ru huo* 慾情如火), Jinlian wakens and arouses Ximen Qing, after which they exhaust themselves in a long bout, during which he continues relentlessly even after she cries, "Enough! Your little one is dying!" (罷了, 六兒的死了). She has him hold her tight by the waist as "she offers him her nipple to suck" (把妳頭教西門慶咂), until she "faints and goes limp, her wanton waters flooding out and her heart fluttering like a baby fawn's" (不覺一陣昏迷，淫水溢下，婦人心頭小鹿突突的跳). He is "still as hard and stiff as before" (*gangjin rugu* 剛勁如故), but she is too tired for more, so they go to sleep with the sun already rising. The closing lines say, "If you happened to shine on them a silver lamp, you'd find two lovers as if bound by divine decree" (等閒試把銀缸照，一對天生連理人, 73.1023).

The conciseness of this last description captures the idealism inherent in the high erotic in general—in spite of the clash with the detail that cannot go unmissed: Ximen Qing's priapism, a result of the chemicals in the monk's aphrodisiac. The same condition continues the next morning, when "his word still stands as stiff as a stick" (那話還直竪一條棍相似), but when she is too tired for anything except sucking him, which she does furiously, though "his semen will still not come" (*jing hai buguo* 精還不過, 74.1025).[81] The comedy of the scene is already building. Ximen Qing holds Jinlian's head firmly as he thrusts frenetically, causing "her saliva to flow from her mouth and her lipstick rouge to smudge his stalk" (白沫横流，殘脂在莖). In the midst of the frenzy, she suddenly interrupts Ximen Qing to ask him for a fur coat that used to belong to Li Ping'er. He wants to give her a lesser coat, which she resents, and they argue until she goes back to applying her mouth and tongue to stimulate every part of his penis, which the author lists: first "the frog's mouth" (the opening of his penis, *wakou* 蛙口); then his "zither strings," or "frenum" (*qinxian* 琴絃); and next the "knob of his glans" (*guileng* 龜稜).[82] As she finally brings him to a climax, "his rhinoceros horn undergoes the rite of baptism, while his body thrills with the fullness of lust" (靈犀灌頂，滿腔春意透). They achieve the desired result, which she swallows completely (74.1025–1026). The scene is a near-culminating rendition of the entire range of pornographic portrayal, from the image of drooling saliva to that of undergoing the rite of baptism, including the aside in which she tries to make a deal about a fur coat. The undying erection is a premonition of what Ximen Qing will die of a few chapters later: a catastrophic case of priapism caused by the overdose of the monk's pill that Jinlian has him swallow.

81. Here *guo* 過 is the word for "come."

82. I follow Roy's translations of "frenum" and "knob of his glans." As I said in chapter 2, *qinxian* 琴絃 is a term from the art of the bedchamber that refers to a part of the vagina. How it ended up in this context is a mystery, though it may have passed down as part of a hazy batch of art of the bedchamber knowledge, or perhaps the author is creating a deliberately incongruous image. See Li Ling and McMahon, "Contents and Terminology," 164.

Conclusion: Idealized Lovers

Although the *Jin Ping Mei* author refuses to create idealized pairs of divine lovers, he approaches that creation in two cases at the novel's end—in the affair between Chen Jingji and the prostitute Han Aijie 韓愛姐, and in the marriage of Meng Yulou and her new husband, Li Gongbi 李拱璧—for both of which he avoids pornographic details.[83] Han Aijie becomes Jingji's concubine and, after he dies, together with his wife takes on the role of the chaste widow loyally mourning her dead husband. When pressured to remarry, she defaces herself and becomes a nun. The fact that the author portrays the sex between her and Jingji in only the briefest terms accords with the elevated characterization of Han Aijie. He portrays their first intercourse in only five characters—"they conjoined then and there" (*jiaogou zai yichu*, 交姤在一處, 98.1388), where the word "*jiaogou*" ("conjoin") refers to the act in a neutral tone that is neither vulgar nor elegant.[84] The next time they meet, "needless to say, they exchange words of deep love and tender sentiment," after which "they engage in the joyous act [*jiaohuan*], their affection knowing no bounds" (無非說些深情蜜意的話; 交歡之際, 無限恩情, 99.1396).[85] The treatment of the relationship between Meng Yulou and Li Gongbi (who have the happiest match in the novel) is similar, which illustrates a general rule of Ming and Qing fiction: avoid any explicit portrayal of the sex between ideal monogamous partners. On their wedding night, "they exhaust the pleasures of marital harmony, and enjoy the extremes of

83. As is well known, parts of the episode of Chen Jingji and Han Aijie derive from story 3 in Feng Menglong's *Gujin xiaoshuo* 古今小說, "Han the Fifth Sells Love at New Bridge" ("Xinqiao shi Han Wu mai chunqing" 新橋市韓五賣春情). See Hanan, "Sources," 37–40.

84. *Jiaogou* appears three times in the case of Jingji. The first time is with his wife (97.1379), a scene that also uses a variation of the same lines that appeared when Ximen Qing first had sex with both Chunmei and Zheng Aiyue ("As spring enlivens the peach tree's blossoms, their red buds split open. As the breeze teases the willows, their green waists bend," 59.778). The second time is in the passage discussed here, and the third time is with Chunmei just before Jingji is murdered (99.1400). The word also occurs in chapters 8, 37, and 75.

85. "Their affection knowing no bounds" comes from Roy, 5.99.371–373. For the sources of these lines, including a lyric by Liu Yong 柳永, see Roy, 5.99.486, nn. 6 and 14.

conjugal bliss" (極盡魚水之歡，于飛之樂, 91.1295), words that are clichés and metaphoric emblems of the sexual harmony of romantic marriage. Meng Yulou will have such a marriage, becoming the main wife of a husband who will treat her well and even suffer his father's condemnation rather than surrender his love for her.[86]

Placing these two affairs at the end of the novel and avoiding pornographic descriptions of them parallel the portrayal of religious salvation in the cases of both Ximen Qing's son Xiaoge 孝哥 and Han Aijie. In other words, Meng Yulou's marriage to a man who loves her parallels Xiaoge's becoming a monk in the end to atone for his father's excesses. Similarly, Han Aijie abandons prostitution; is a loyal, chaste widow; and in the end becomes a Buddhist nun.[87] The same type of ending appears in the shorter pornographic fiction of the Ming and Qing, including *Rouputuan* 肉蒲團, in which the libertine ultimately realizes the emptiness of sensuality and finds salvation in asceticism.[88] Such endings, as well as the minimal description of both Meng Yulou's wedding night and the sex between Han Aijie and Chen Jingji (98.1388 and 99.1346), can also be said to belong to the cooling down of the latter half of the novel in terms of the play between hot and cold scenes and sections of the narrative that Zhang Zhupo and others describe.[89]

As a rule, *Jin Ping Mei* avoids clumsy and claustrophobic didacticism.[90] It leaves no doubt that Ximen Qing is a shallow and villainous

86. Zhang Zhupo refers to them as having an ideal marriage, *Jin Ping Mei dufa*, in Hou and Wang, eds., *Jin Ping Mei ziliao huibian*, 32.

87. Opinions vary on whether to take the novel as ending on a redemptive note. See Roy, introduction, xxxiv; Carlitz, *Rhetoric*, 128–129 and 132–133, and "Codes and Correspondences"; and Tina Lu, *Accidental Incest*, 195–196 (for the Han Aijie episode "smack[ing] of parody," and Li An 李安 and Han Aijie being "flimsy" cases of moral exemplarity). For a counterargument based on the Chongzhen edition, see Tian Xiaofei, "A Preliminary Comparison," 355 and 388. See also Ge, *Xueyin lusi*, 337–339. Though there is plenty of irony in Han Aijie's portrayal, especially in her devotion to a man such as Chen Jingji, the episode parallels Meng Yulou's transition to monogamous love. I return to the novel's ending in chapter 8.

88. See Vitiello, *The Libertine's Friend*, 98.

89. On hot and cold patterns, see Plaks, "The Chongzhen Commentary," 26, and *Four Masterworks*, 82–85; and Carlitz, *Rhetoric*, 79–82 (the latter two with references to Zhang Zhupo).

90. For this sense of "claustrophobic," see Wu Cuncun, "'It Was I Who Lured the Boy,'" 318.

profligate, but it tends to let the unfolding of the narrative make that point. As for Pan Jinlian, the novel gives the impression that she behaves as she should be expected to behave and that she is the way she is whatever people may think—though this is more the case in the Chongzhen version than in the *cihua* edition and more so in both of those versions than in *Shuihu zhuan.*[91] I say this in particular in spite of Zhang Zhupo's and other critics' readings of Pan Jinlian, which tend to see her as an "arch-*yinfu*," against which the properly moral man—including the proper reader of the novel—must defend and protect himself.[92] I would add that the logic of salvation that appears at the end (when Xiaoge becomes a monk and Han Aijie a nun), as well as other elements of cooling down, are hardly enough to make it seem that all the preceding chapters of obscenity should be soberly dismissed, now that we have learned our lesson—though readers such as Zhang Zhupo might disagree. The Chongzhen editor's comment that I quoted above gets at this sense: "Of what goes on in the privacy of the bedchamber, what is there not to be found? It is simply that no one dares to expose it." In other words, no one dares to engage in such an intensity of portrayal except the author of *Jin Ping Mei.*

In sum, as I said in chapter 1, the novel's descriptions of sex have an art to them. They present an aesthetic of intercourse that is mixed with irony, satire, and comedy and that has technique and method in terms of what the novel describes and how it describes it. The descriptions are thematic in that they convey meaning having to do with particular characters in particular situations. Sex may be beautifully, even reverently, portrayed, but it also appears with ironic undercutting. It may be metaphorically, allusively, and adumbratively described, but also hyperbolically and with elements of fantasy. At times it is presented as if it were the most intense and wonderful act that could be experienced. And in its intensity it may also be raw, grotesque, and extreme. Whatever the case may be, the author revels in the description of sexual pleasure and excess. In doing so, he portrays sexual pleasure as something that involves

91. Tian Xiaofei notes the Chongzhen version's softening of Pan Jinlian's character and its more sympathetic portrayal of her ("A Preliminary Comparison," 371–386, especially 375–376 [on *Shuihu zhuan*]).

92. Ding, *Obscene Things*, xxvii; see also Rolston, *Traditional Chinese Fiction*, 68–69 (on Zhang Zhupo).

intolerable levels of excitation. He likes to portray sex as a form of sheer expenditure that inherently veers to excess, including deadly excess.[93] However, the message is not that we should condemn sex, but simply that it is something that a writer of *xiaoshuo* cannot afford to ignore, that he will use all possible language to represent it, and that he will not refrain from portraying it in the particular form of one of the most stigmatized characters possible: the wanton woman, but whom he will treat as a virtuoso performer who possesses an entire range of talents and formidable characteristics.

93. George Bataille refers to the dissolution of the "self-contained character of the participants," "bordering on death, bordering on murder" (*Eroticism*, 17).

CHAPTER 4

Sex as Battle

An Alternative High Erotic

One of the commonalities that I have mentioned between the art of the bedchamber and the portrayal of sex in *Jin Ping Mei* is the notion of sex as a contest and a field of struggle. Both genres express this by using military terms and imagery to describe the partners in sexual action. In the novel, sex as mock battle appears in three poetic passages, the language and style of which amount to an alternate form of the high erotic. In addition to the use of poetic and densely figurative language, what is high erotic about them is the fact that the action takes place on a grand stage. In contrast to what chapter 3 described as the high erotic portrayal of pleasurable and elegant harmony, the partners in the mode of sexual battle are proud, valiant, and well-matched warriors, who use all their weapons and strength. It is no accident that the three women in these passages are Ximen Qing's most formidable partners: Pan Jinlian, Wang Liu'er, and Lady Lin. He and they are well-matched foes, using all their energy to metaphorically attack and counterattack. They occasionally weaken and retreat, and in the third of the three passages, the partners end bruised and swollen, but in all cases they are satisfied and their energy is well spent. The focus of the portrayal is on the intensity of sexual action, which includes both pleasure and pain, and which for the duration of the scene stands independently from the surrounding narrative. After all such interludes, the novel returns to the complexities of the relations between characters. The elations and exertions of sexual battle disappear from view.

Let me briefly characterize the way in which the classic art of the bedchamber invokes the metaphor of battle, preceding this with a reference to the Indian *Kamasutra*. The latter likewise characterizes sex as a competitive act, adding a dimension not included in the Chinese texts by saying that the art of sex is devoted to "trickery and deception."[1] Women's moans, for example, are not necessarily true signs of pleasure but may be a ploy to excite the man. Similarly, in Ovid's *Ars Amatoria*, the partners try to outwit each other in a quest for their own pleasure; the art of seduction is a constant case of one trying to outmaneuver the other.[2] In the case of the Chinese art of the bedchamber, such matters of deception and maneuver do not appear. Instead, the focus is on how the sexual bodies will interact—in particular, how the sexually fragile man can or cannot please his superior female foe. The texts tell the man that he is not born with natural abilities but must train himself to master sexual knowledge and skill, from the first moments of a sexual encounter to the last. To impress upon him the gravity of these truths, one text compares the sexual superiority of women to "water's ability to put out fire" (猶水之滅火), while another compares a man's sex with a woman to "riding a horse with a rotten rein" (如朽索御奔馬).[3] Yet a third text uses the word "attack" (*gongji* 攻擊) to refer to the man preparing for intercourse. He must be like a "fierce general breaking through a battle formation" (猛將之破陣). The woman is his "enemy" (*diren* 敵人), and he must master methods that he can use against her to ensure his "success in every single battle" (*baizhan bu dai ye*, 百戰不殆也), famous words from the third chapter of Sunzi's *Art of War*.[4] Finally, what is victory? It is a combination of the man's being able to give the woman sexual joy while himself being able to "withdraw while alive" (*shengfan* 生返)—that is, still erect and without having ejaculated, and thereby avoiding an unhealthy loss

1. Doniger, *Redeeming the Kamasutra*, 67–68.

2. See Orrells, *Sex: Antiquity and Its Legacy*, 39, 46, and 48.

3. Quoted in Li Ling, *Zhongguo fangshu gaiguan*, 101 and 102 (from *Yufang mijue* and *Yufang zhiyao*, respectively).

4. Quoted in Li Ling, *Zhongguo fangshu gaiguan*, 108 ("attack," from *Dongxuanzi* 洞玄子), 115 (on the general, from ibid.), and 123 ("enemy" and the line from *Sunzi bingfa* 孫子兵法, from *Yufang mijue*).

of vital essence.[5] *Jin Ping Mei*'s scenes of sex as battle make no direct allusion to the man's fragility, though Ximen Qing's constant reliance on sex tools and drugs makes the same point by implication. Besides her innate capacity, the woman's main weapon is seductive charm, which in *Jin Ping Mei*'s imagery of sexual battle includes her ability to swallow the man whole and drown him in waves of lascivious waters. She is a "painted-face skeleton" and a "gorgeous seductive fox," who fights him with "endless coquettish charm" (*fen kulou, hua huli, baimei qianjiao* 粉骷髅, 花狐狸, 百媚千嬌, 78.1116). Such imagery and language are more plentiful in the *cihua* edition than in the Chongzhen, thus exemplifying the *cihua*'s tendency to greater rhetorical flourishes and leading me to cite more of its variations than usual to give a fuller picture of this motif.

"Fighting to the Death"

The portrayal of sex as battle pervades Ming and Qing fiction, which commonly uses the vocabulary of Daoist sexual alchemy to portray partners' resorting to powerful drugs and occult techniques by way of arming themselves. The most extreme renditions of such contests take the form of brutal combat in which one opponent robs the other of vital essence. Only a minor hint of the motif of absorbing or losing essence appears in *Jin Ping Mei*, and only in the form of a rhetorical flourish rather than a literal portrayal of the deployment of occult techniques. References to *jing* appear in medical terms rather than those involving the dynamics of sexual alchemy. The harm to Ximen Qing's *jing* is not because women steal it from him, but because of his abuse of the aphrodisiac.

If *Jin Ping Mei* were like its contemporary Ming and Qing novels, the women of the three passages might have supernatural sexual power. One late Ming novel has a group of women stripped naked, "blowing a dark swath of *yin* wind, which rises in a black fog" and which weakens and befuddles the male opponent (陰風習習, 黑霧騰騰).[6] The eighteenth-century *Yesou puyan* 野叟曝言 (A country codger's words of exposure)

5. Quoted in Li Ling, *Zhongguo fangshu gaiguan*, 108 (from *Dongxuanzi*).
6. Anonymous, *Yangjiafu yanyi* 楊家府演義, 159.

portrays a female demon baring her naked front in an attempt to kill her male enemy with projectile *yin* force.[7] *Jin Ping Mei* shares the underlying principle of these scenes: women can unleash powerful forces simply by deploying the energy of their inborn sexual strength. But the novel's focus is on the strength and intensity of their sexual energy, to withstand which Ximen Qing must use all his might, wear armor, and deploy weapons (that is, his sexual aids and aphrodisiacs). He and his partners eagerly and hotly join battle, both metaphorically winning and losing in like measure. The first of the three passages is in a scene in which Ximen Qing finds Pan Jinlian sleeping, just having rubbed herself with a special cream to make her skin white like Li Ping'er's. After she wakes, they bathe together until, "inspired by a whim" (*cheng xing* 乘興), Ximen Qing has her get onto a bathing board balanced over the tub, straddles her, and begins a vigorous session of thrusting. The scene is the subject of the chapter illustration in the Chongzhen edition entitled "Pan Jinlian Invites a Guest for a Noon Battle in the Orchid Tub" (潘金蓮蘭湯邀午戰, 29.369; figure 2), which begins by describing the sounds they make, "like crabs mucking around in the mud" (其聲如泥中螃蟹一般). After these few graphic words, the author reverts to poetry, which he prefaces in mock *xiangyan*-style: "she made sounds like swallows and orioles, marvelous beyond what words can describe. And how did this scene of battle look?" (口中燕語鶯聲, 百般難述. 怎見這場交戰?). The Chongzhen edition says:

> The flowery bath roiled and foamed and splashed. The turquoise curtains hung from high, as the autumn clouds darkened with threatening rain.
> The man of genius was roused by desire, ready to display his charms. The gorgeous woman grew joyous, ready to flaunt her skills.
> The waves resounded with noisy clamor, splashing and swashing in one great flood.
> Slipping and slithering, how could they think of stopping? Blocking each other's blows, they could hardly hold their positions.
> The one steered her boat against the current, setting her jade legs into motion.
> The other, like a helmsman gripping the tiller, grasped tight her lotus feet.

7. Xia Jingqu 夏敬渠 (1705–1787), *Yesou puyan*, 80.9b–10a.

FIGURE 2. "Pan Jinlian Invites a Guest for a Noon Battle in the Orchid Tub" (潘金蓮蘭湯午戰). From chapter 29 of *Jin Ping Mei* 金瓶梅, Lanling xiaoxiao sheng 蘭陵笑笑生, *Xinke xiuxiang piping Jin Ping Mei* 新刻繡像批評金瓶梅 (Hong Kong: Sanlian shudian, 1990).

Sloshing through mud and water, the two lovers grew dazed. Drunken with love in their clouds and rain, one could hardly be told from the other.
Of all the bouts that ever took place between phoenixes mating under brocade drapes, none ever matched this battle in the orchid tub!
(華池蕩漾波紋亂, 翠幃高捲秋雲暗. 才郎情動逞風流, 美女心歡顯手段. 矶矶碍碍 弄响聲, 砰砰磞磞 成一片. 滑滑溷溷怎住停, 攔攔濟濟難存站. 一個逆水撐船, 將玉股搖; 一個稍公把舵, 將金蓮擋. 拖泥帶水兩情癡, 殢雨尤雲都不辨. 任他錦帳鳳鸞交, 不似蘭湯魚水戰, 29.381).[8]

The *cihua* edition uses more explicit battle imagery, creating a more vividly warlike atmosphere, though it still centers on the experience of pleasure and excitement. After the second couplet above, the *cihua* edition says:

The one swayed as he deployed his rigid spear, the other swaggered as she wielded her iron sword.

The one defied death as he drove himself inside; the other, drunken with desire, worked her ready skills.

(一個顫顫巍巍挺硬鎗, 一個搖搖擺擺輪鋼劍. 一個捨死忘生往裡鑽, 一個尤雲殢雨將功幹).

The rigid spear is an obvious double entendre. The iron sword evokes the common image of the woman's sexuality as being like a dangerous sword threatening the inherently vulnerable man. The two versions share a few more lines, after which the *cihua* edition expands upon the fury of the battle, extolling their warrior-like pride and valiance, alternating praise for each:

Like a dark stallion galloping wildly about, the man was proud of his prowess. Like a pale-faced witch, the woman took on his charging horses.

The gorgeous beauty was joyous and elated, the eager man bold and strong.
(一個紫騮猖獗逞威風, 一個白面妖嬈遭馬戰. 喜喜歡歡美女情, 雄雄糾糾男兒愿).

8. "Slipping and slithering," "setting her jade legs into motion," and "a helmsman gripping the tiller" are from Roy, 2.29.191–192.

The passage ends with a rousing finale, portraying the two as heroic opponents, with neither one a winner or loser:

> Fighting to the death, neither could call a halt. To win every battle, they attacked with guts and gall.
>
> Shouting, "Kill kill kill," they were brave and full of mettle, their desire never waning. When in history has there ever been a struggle as ferocious as this battle in the tub!
>
> (你死我活更無休，千戰千贏心胆戰．口口聲聲叫殺人，氣氣昂昂情不厭．古古今今廣鬧爭，不似這番水裏戰).[9]

Instead of warbling orioles or twittering swallows, sex as battle portrays splashing, boring, gripping, and charging. Instead of sex as a ballet or duet between elegantly aroused partners, it is a battle of all-out might, with no tenderness or grace. But again that does not mean it is without pleasure, even if some of the pleasure includes pain. Waves splashing and foes "slipping and slithering" evoke bodies rubbing and colliding against each other in furious abandon. The partners are aggressively aroused, hot with desire and fighting with all their "guts and gall."

The image of the pale-faced witch is the only hint in this passage of the motif of the sexually demonic woman, which the Chongzhen edition eliminates in this case but includes in the second and third passages. The second passage features Wang Liu'er, who in contrast to Pan Jinlian complies more easily with Ximen Qing's wishes in life outside the bedroom. But she is a more combative partner when they have sex. In their first tryst, neither knows how the transaction will work. She and her husband (Han Daoguo 韓道國) count on the fact that they will earn considerable income from Ximen Qing by letting her out to him. Her husband conveniently leaves her alone at home, Ximen Qing arrives, and he and Wang Liu'er waste no time in what from the start is a sexual battle, as if the two immediately understand that joining in battle is what they are meant to do. She is a twenty-eight-year-old experienced woman, and she not only gives Ximen Qing what he likes but also directs the act in her own

9. JPMCH, 29.775–776.

assertive ways. They are like grand foes in an epic battle, who push the limits of pleasure by pushing their sexual might as far as it can go:

> A formidable wind bedevils the emerald couch; a deathly air encloses the lovers' quilt.
> On the coral pillow they display their valor; inside the kingfisher curtains they vie in strength.
> The man goes forth roused and impatient, wielding his spear he aims straight for the heart. The female general has not a moment to lose, opening her jaws to swallow her enemy head and all.
> The one deploys a pair of ballistae as he jaunts back and forth attacking the Army of the Crotch. The other brandishes her shields and from all sides clamps down on the Commander from beneath the Navel.
> The one assumes the stance of the "golden rooster standing tall," lifting high her jade-white leg in a burst of energy. The other assumes the pose of "the bare tree with gnarled roots," then "inserts the arrow upside down" and pierces her vagina.
> The battle goes on for hours, as his starry eyes begin to blur; the slightest motion gives him a numbing sensation.[10] The struggle lasts long, her slender waist sways gently; a hundred bouts and a hundred rallies, she can take no more.
> The Mistress of the Hairless Cave retreats along the bridge, sending waves to drown her enemy. The General of Dark Armor feints with his spear, turning back to escape with his life.
> He of the navel aphrodisiac tumbles from his horse, in an instant his flesh is trampled to bits. She that is warm and tight feigns confusion, in another instant she tumbles into the deep ravine.
> He of the heavy armor has lost all sense of focus, he is like a fallen petal beaten by a torrent of rain. She of the brocade hood is at the end of her strength, her muscles working no more; she is like an autumn leaf blown by a violent wind.
> The Sulfur Commandant, helmet askew, armor in pieces, has no more routes of escape. The Silver-Armored General holds fast at camp, still eager for blood.

10. I follow Roy's interpretation here, using different wording (see Roy, 2.37.376). Lévy takes the line as referring to both partners (*Fleur en Fiole d'Or*, 1.27.782 [hereafter I cite Lévy, volume, chapter, and page number only]).

It is just such that: the storm clouds reach the ninth layer of heaven, while below a swath of battered soldiers litter the terrain.

(威風迷翠榻，殺氣瑣鴛衾．珊瑚枕上施雄，翡翠帳中斗勇．男兒氣急，使槍只去扎心窩；女帥心忙，開口要來吞腦袋．一個使雙砲的，往來攻打内襠兵；一個輪傍牌的，上下夾迎臍下將．一個金雞獨立，高蹺玉腿弄精神；一個枯樹盤根，倒入翎花來刺牝．戰良久朦朧星眼，但動些兒麻上來；斗多時款擺纖腰，百戰百回挨不去．散毛洞主倒上橋，放水去淹軍；烏甲將軍虛點槍，側身逃命走．臍膏落馬，須臾蹂踏肉爲泥；溫緊粧呆，頃刻跌翻深澗底．大披掛七零八斷，猶如急雨打殘花；錦套頭力盡觔輸，恰似猛風飄敗葉．硫黃元帥，盔歪甲散走無門; 銀甲將軍, 守住老營還要命. 正是: 愁雲托上九重天，一塊敗兵連地滚 (37.487–88).[11]

The formidable wind and deathly air echo the autumn clouds and threatening rain of the first passage. Scenes from other novels portray similar forms of dark energy, with which one opponent tries to bewitch and confound the other. Threatening clouds, violent wind, and deathly air further the sense of forces joined in cosmic battle. The man is the General of Dark Armor, or Ximen Qing wearing his clasps and sheaths (the next time he visits Wang Liu'er, he brings his entire collection of sexual aids). The enemies assume strategic positions in the form of the woman's "golden rooster standing tall" or the man's "bare tree with gnarled roots" and his "insert[ing] the arrow upside down." The first two come from martial arts, while the third is a sexual position that occurs elsewhere in *Jin Ping Mei* and other novels, in which the man enters the prone woman from above.[12] They resort to chemical weapons, which here appear in the form of the "navel aphrodisiac," which corresponds to Ximen Qing's "navel aphrodisiac plaster" (*feng ji gao* 封臍膏), while "Sulfur Commandant" echoes the "sulfur-dipped ring" (*liuhuang quan* 硫黃圈) or the sulfur that Pan Jinlian applies to the white satin band (73.1011).[13] While the man wears armor, wields a spear, and deploys a pair of ballistae (catapults), the woman

11. The following translations are from Roy, 2.37.375–377: "the one deploys a pair of ballistae," "brandishes," "inserts the arrow upside down," "he of the navel aphrodisiac," "she that is warm and tight feigns confusion," and "he of the heavy armor."

12. For references in other works to "golden rooster standing tall" and "bare tree with gnarled roots" (my translations), see Roy, 2.37.559–560, nn. 29 and 30. For "insert[ing] the arrow upside down," see JPM, 27.355.

13. See 27.356–57, 38.494, and chapter 2.

counters by swallowing her enemy "head and all," using her shields to "clamp" (*jia* 夾) on the man, and—as "Mistress of the Hairless Cave"—drowning him with waves of lascivious waters.[14] The woman's ability to clamp her vagina on the man's penis appears throughout Ming and Qing pornography, as I have mentioned above and discuss below. The drowning of the man recalls the saying in the art of the bedchamber about the woman's sexual superiority as being like the ability of water to put out fire.

The *cihua* edition contains several lines missing in the Chongzhen edition, all alluding to legendary figures, the sum of whom amounts to a figurative whole of the world's supreme erotic lovers:

> In bout after bout, they are like An Lushan meeting the Great Consort. In charge after charge, they are like Zhang Junrui consorting with Maiden Cui.
>
> From all sides they press together, like the Weaving Maiden of the Milky Way trysting with the Herd Boy. Spiraling against each other, they are like the fairy maiden joining with Ruan Zhao. . . .
>
> The one warbles like an oriole, just like Wu Zetian in her affair with Aocao. The other twitters like a swallow, just like Minister Shen when he conjoined with Empress Lü.
>
> (一來一往, 祿山會合太眞妃. 一撞一衝, 君瑞追陪崔氏女. 左右迎湊, 天河織女遇牛郎. 上下盤旋, 仙洞嬌姿逢阮肇 . . . . 一個鶯聲嚦嚦, 猶如武則天遇敖曹. 一個燕喘吁吁, 好似審在逢呂雉).[15]

Passages such as these place the characters on a stage with other grand lovers, both heavenly and earthly, historical and mythical. Empress Wu Zetian 武則天 and Xue Aocao 薛敖曹 (a fictional figure based on the historical palace retainer Xue Huaiyi 薛懷義, d. 694) come from the *Ruyijun zhuan*, on which *Jin Ping Mei* frequently draws. Their affair is one of wild and intense sex, in which pain and pleasure freely overlap. Two other pairs, An Lushan and the Great Consort (Yang Guifei 楊貴妃) and

14. The General of Dark Armor and the Mistress of the Hairless Cave appear in a prosimetric work about sexual combat. See Roy 2.560, n. 32 (his reference to *Fengliu lequ* 風流樂趣, in *Guose tianxiang* 國色天香).

15. JPMCH, 37.1008–1010. Empress Lü and Wu Zetian are rumored to have had illicit lovers after the death of their husband-emperors. See Roy, 2.559, n. 28, referring to Sima Qian, *Shiji*, 97.2702–2703.

Minister Shen and Empress Lü, likewise consist of imperial women and their adulterous lovers, with the two empresses both being widows and thus, by pornographic implication, sexually ravenous. But two other couples, Zhang Junrui and Maiden Cui and the fairy maiden and Ruan Zhao, all lie at the other end of the spectrum of historical romantic figures, that of sublime love—which writers as a rule do not portray pornographically.[16] Similarly, the Weaving Maiden and the Herd Boy are hallowed models of conjugal fidelity, hardly subjects of explicit sexual portrayal. But the composer of these words instead casts a lurid, pornographic eye on all such figures, insisting that no one is exempt from the intensities of sexual desire.

The third scene of sexual battle is the one between Ximen Qing and the widow Lady Lin, and to understand it, readers must be familiar with a variety of traditional weaponry. Ximen Qing has visited Lady Lin once already, when he "exerted all his earthly talent" (*jie pingsheng benshi* 竭平生本事, 69.950) in what is described as an even match between two mutually fulfilling partners. He had just spent the night with Li Jiao'er, which prompts the Chongzhen commentator to say that if he had been with Pan Jinlian, "how could he have cultivated enough energy" to handle Lady Lin (怎得精神培养, 69.947)? Ximen Qing cannot wait for the second visit, for which he has "sharpened his spear and readied his sword" (*mo qiang bei jian* 磨槍備劍) in preparation to "fight the dame to the death" (*ao zhan zhe poniang* 鏖戰這婆娘). As before, they talk, drink, dine, and play games before entering the bedroom. Having brought his bag of tools, Ximen Qing takes his drug, attaches two silver clasps, and then "arches his back to exert all his might, thus beginning a rollicking bout which thunders like the rolling of drums, as the woman lay beneath him letting loose a steady stream of lurid calls" (舉腰展力，一陣掀騰鼓搗，連聲響亮，婦人在下，沒口叫達達如流水). Then follows a passage in verse:

> As the soul-bedeviling formation begins to deploy, the spirit-catching flag commences to unroll.
>
> Out from the soul-bedeviling formation shoots a guardian deity of wine, a demon king of sex, an able warrior long tried in battle. From beneath the

16. In the story of Ruan Zhao, he and a friend live for a while with two female immortals but return to the world only to realize that many generations have lived and died during their absence.

spirit-catching flags emerges a painted-face skeleton, a gorgeous seductive fox, who plies him with endless coquettish charm.

From the one side, drums roar, shaking the earth with the sound of spring thunder. From the other, war cries fill the expanse, billowing clouds of orchid and musk.

On the one side, as waters crash down, the coverlet roils like a sea of crimson waves, he is healthy and invigorated; on the other, swishing and bristling, under curtains hung on silver hooks, she is romantic but shrewd.

The one is impatient to try the range of all twenty-four positions; the other struggles to respond with all eighteen tumbles.

After the long bout, her sweat pours, her hairpins fall askew, and her hair is all a mess; after the lengthy battle, he can't catch his breath, his pillow is knocked aside, and the covers are in disarray.

In no time, their brows swell large and their eyes are blackened; it happened so fast, their flesh splits open and their skin rips apart.

It is truly the case that: As often as he had fought wanton women to the death, no match ever taxed him as much as this!

(迷魂陣擺, 攝魄旗開. 迷魂陣上閃出一員洒金剛, 色魔王能爭貫戰; 攝魄旗下擁一個粉骷髏, 花狐狸百媚千嬌. 這陣上撲鼕鼕, 鼓震春雷; 那陣上鬧挨挨, 麝蘭靉靆. 這陣上復溶溶, 被翻紅浪精神健; 那陣上刷刺刺, 帳控銀鈎情意乖. 這一個急展展, 二十四解任徘徊; 那一個忽剌剌, 一十八滾難掙扎. 鬬良久, 汗浸浸釵橫鬢亂; 戰多時, 喘吁吁枕側衾歪. 頃刻間腫眉臢眼; 霎時下肉綻皮開. 正是: 幾番鏖戰貪淫婦, 不是今番這一遭!, 78.1116).[17]

This is another cosmic battle between demonic forces. Except for the references to pouring sweat, hairpins that are askew, and swollen brows, the entire scene takes place in figurative terms. The same passage in the *cihua* version (which is about ten times longer) is flooded with double entendres and fanciful descriptions of what the opponents wear and the weapons they deploy, drawing on both actual weaponry of the times and

17. "Guardian deity of wine" and "demon king of sex" are from Roy, 4.78.592–594. The last lines could perhaps be read as saying that Ximen Qing alone is the wounded one, which would explain why he had never met a woman like this.

martial arts fiction, as well as creating fictitious objects.[18] On his head the man wears "a flesh-colored helmet" (頭戴肉紅盔), below which "on his torso he dons oily black armor, wears a red cape coated in sharp points and protuberant bands, with a fish-skin belt, and on his feet seamless boots" (錦兜鍪, 身穿烏油甲, 鋒紅袍, 纏觔絛, 魚皮帶, 沒縫靴).[19] These items suggest Ximen Qing's sex tools, especially his dildos and sheaths. "Protuberant bands" (*chanjindiao* 纏觔絛) may allude to the veins of the erect penis. As for weaponry, "he deploys a black-tasseled spear, carries a tiger-eyed whip, a shooting-star noose with a sheath on its head, and hidden-ball arrows" (使一柄黑纓鎗, 帶的是虎眼鞭, 皮薄頭流星槌, 沒毬箭). Black tassels suggest pubic hair, the tiger eye the opening of the penis, and the sheath perhaps the lovers' sheath. "Shooting-star noose" (*liuxing chui* 流星槌) refers to an actual weapon made of a rope with two metal hammer balls at each end—the weapon is also called a meteor hammer or shooting-star mallet. The expression "hidden-ball arrows" uses the slang word for testicles, perhaps suggesting that the erect penis is so large that it hides their presence.[20]

The descriptions of the woman's weapons play with imagery that combines actual weapons and metaphors of seductive energy: "She wields a garrulous-knifed tongue, limitless as the sky, coquettish eyes that shoot like arrows, tears that bedevil the heart, a smiting plaintive pout, a painted-face club, and a silk-curtained cudgel" (使一條隔天邊話絮刀, 不得見, 淚偷垂, 容瘦減, 粉面撾, 羅幃傍). This line is especially difficult to translate, filled with words that act as phonetic alternatives of actual weapons. For example, I have translated *bude jian* 不得見 ("invisible") as "coquettish eyes that shoot like arrows," taking *jian* 見 ("to see") as a play on *jian* 箭 ("arrow"). "Tears that bedevil the heart," *lei tou chui* 淚偷垂, could also be "tears that clobber with deception," taking *chui* 垂 ("hang down" or

18. For the passage in the *cihua* version, see JPMCH, 78.2456–2458.

19. "Flesh-colored helmet," "protuberant bands," "fish-skin belt," and "seamless boots" are from Roy, 4.78.592.

20. For *liuxing chui*, see Lu Xixing, *Zhongguo gudai qiwu dacidian*, 217 (*liuxing* weapons are sometimes categorized as "hidden weapons," or *anqi* 暗器). Roy translates *moqiu jian* as "featherless arrows" (4.78.592) and Lévy as "une flèche sans barbe" ("a beardless arrow," 2.78.779), but I take *qiu* as standing for "balls."

"droop") for *chui* 錘 ("mace" or "bludgeon").[21] Their mounts are similarly described with sexual metaphors and double entendres. The man sits astride a "curly-haired sunken-eyed roan, holding a commander's flag billowing in the clouds and rain" (跨一疋捲毛凹眼渾紅馬, 打一面發雨翻雲大帥旗). The woman "rides a coquettishly charming jade-surfaced cunt, holding a sun-shielding parasol covered with phoenix lovers frolicking in sex" (騎一疋百媚千嬌玉面毬, 打一柄倒鳳顛鸞遮日傘).[22] A weapon found in the novel *Shuihu zhuan* surfaces here in the form of the woman's "red-floss lasso, which sports a mandarin-duck enemy-catching buckle" (紅綿套索鴛鴦扣). The lasso comes with twenty-four hooks and belongs to the female warrior Yizhang Qing 一丈青, who uses it to fell an enemy from his horse. Readers of the time would likely have recognized it.[23] The man opposes the woman using a "double-handled club, with its shooting-star cock-of-a-mallet" (拐子流星雞心搥).[24] In another pairing of weapons, the man's "blazing barrel spear" (火忿忿桶子鎗) opposes the woman's "quivering flesh-armed shield" (顫巍巍肉膀牌), the latter of which Roy interprets as "quivering labia bucklers."[25]

21. For *shourong jian* 容瘦減, Roy has "emaciated mace," inspired by the fact that *jian* 減 plays on *jian* 鐗, a blunt-headed bludgeon (or perhaps *jian* 簡, a kind of whip; 4.78.594). In the case of *fenmian wo* 粉面撾, "painted-face club" (missing in Roy's translation), the word *wo* 撾 refers to a kind of hooked club (one of eighteen mentioned in *Shuihu zhuan*; see Lu Xixing, *Zhongguo gudai qiwu dacidian*, 444). Pronounced as *zhua*, it means to hit, beat, or strike. *Bang* 傍 is a double for *bang* 棒, another kind of club, which Roy translates as scutcheon (a kind of shield). See Shi Nai'an 施耐菴, *Shuihu zhuan* 水滸傳, 2.21.

22. "Curly-haired sunken-eyed roan" and "jade-surfaced" are from Roy, 4.78.594. Although earlier in the same passage *qiu* meant "balls" or "cock," I agree with Roy and take it as "cunt."

23. See *Shuihu zhuan*, 55.649 (on the "twenty-four golden hooks," 二十四個金鈎); and Roy, 4.839, n. 26.

24. *Jixin* 雞心 is a type of date, which explains Roy's translation of *jixin chui* 雞心搥 as "date-shaped mace" (4.78.594). I take it as referring to the penis, based on the facts that *chui* 搥 is a type of cudgel and that *guaizi* 拐子 refers to a weapon shaped like a cane with one or two handles (it is a variation on *liuxing chui* 流星錘, "shooting-star noose"). See Pei Xirong, Han Minghua, and Jiang Songyou, *Zhonghua gujin bingxie tukao*, 207–208, 249–252, 343, and 352. Thanks to Wang Jian of Hunan Normal University for help with this passage.

25. See Roy, 4.78.595.

Nothing of the above is present in the Chongzhen edition. And except for the *cihua* edition's reference to the woman as an "adept at stealing essence and sucking marrow" (能奪精吸髓華), neither edition resorts to the vocabulary of Daoist sexual alchemy. But the reference anyway is devoid of literal meaning in that neither Lady Lin nor the other two women are practitioners of occult sexual arts.

The scene ends after Ximen Qing burns two pellets of moxa, one each on Lady Lin's chest and her vagina. He has won her over, and she is entranced with him. Although each of the three women has a different type of relationship with Ximen Qing, taken as a whole, the three passages are alike in that they condense and stylize the key message of the book about the nature of sexual desire, as I have mentioned above. Sexual desire involves extreme degrees of excitation, it has a fundamental tendency to excess, and it tends toward destruction and death. That is a serious message, however, which the playful tone of the passages virtually erases. The overall effect is to take the dangerous act of sex and render it in fanciful terms, an effect that is inherent in the mode of the high erotic. Recalling the manner of the ancient genre of the *fu* 賦 rhapsody, the author exercises his verbal talent in flourishes of exotic vocabulary and complex metaphors. The portrayal is of sex as mock combat, in which lovers charge one another, alternate in victory and defeat, and emerge exhausted but ecstatically well spent.

"Clamping on Him with a Grip as Tight as a Vice"

The three women in the above passages (Pan Jinlian, Wang Liu'er, and Lady Lin) need to be seen in the larger context of Chinese sexual lore that I have alluded to above in terms of women with supernormal sexual powers. The three ultimately are linked to a long tradition that features a woman with whom sexual intercourse causes a man to become weak and ill, even to the point of death. It is a case of "exhaustible men dealing with inexhaustible women."[26] The woman enjoys intercourse with multiple men, none of whom can keep up with her. She may acquire her

26. Huntington, *Alien Kind*, 179 (speaking of fox lore of the same period).

powers by means of a marvelous drug or through mastery of occult skills and practice, as in the case of Xiwangmu, who strengthens her pure *yin* by intercourse with man after man, who become ill afterward.[27] A late Ming story portrays such a female sexual master, a nun who engages in brutal carnal combat with a Daoist adept of the Complete Perfection (Quanzhen 全眞) school:

> His word rushed into the attack, massive in size, and as hot as a piece of iron heated in the forge. . . . It was as if it had a mouth and tongue that kept biting and sucking. Nun Jia stilled her spirit and held her breath, closed her eyes and grinded her teeth, . . . using her vagina to rub and shake him, and adopting the method of "inhale and exhale, lick and clamp." She tossed him endlessly until finally the adept quivered and trembled and couldn't catch his breath, as a burst of flames shot from his nostrils.
>
> (那話兒奔馳衝突, 長偉異常, 恰似一條火赤煉熱. . . . 宛如有嘴舌的一般, 不住嘖咂. 賈道姑寧神屏息, 閉目咬齒 . . . . 把牝門摩盪畢, 用那吞吐舔夾之法, 連連地顛了百十餘度. 只見那全眞渾身發顫, 氣喘呼呼, 鼻孔中噴出一陣火來).

The adept finally surrenders and ejaculates, allowing the nun to absorb his vital essence.[28]

The nun is a flat representation of such a figure. Stilling one's spirit, holding one's breath, and grinding one's teeth are all well-established practices of Daoist internal alchemy and its meditational techniques, including the exercise of "inhaling and exhaling"—which appears in other passages below that I cite. Pan Jinlian, Wang Liu'er, and Lady Lin obviously are far more than mere prototypes, and none of them uses such techniques. Nevertheless, the reductive, prototypical features of the nun point to key elements of sexual lore that feed the portrayals in *Jin Ping Mei* and other Ming and Qing fiction. In general, sexual intercourse becomes a matter of skill, strength, and competition, the stakes of which are about who (the man or the woman) can avoid defeat. In *Jin Ping Mei*, defeat means final exhausted satisfaction, but in cases of out-

27. See Li Ling, *Zhongguo fangshu gaiguan*, 105 (citing *Yufang mijue*); and Despeux and Kohn, *Women in Daoism*, 39 (on Xiwangmu). On Lady Lin, see chapter 6.

28. Fang Ruhao 方汝浩, *Chan Zhen houshi* 禪眞后史, 53.8b–9a.

right combat, it means radical depletion, which includes illness or even death. The portrayal of battle draws on a repertoire of motifs and images that, at their extreme, come down to two opposing skills: the woman's ability to make her vagina lock onto the man, as in the clamping effect of the nun, and the man's ability to make his penis pulsate, expand, and contract. Although such skills or techniques (*fa* 法) ultimately derive from the lore and practices of Daoist sexual alchemy, pornographic fiction exaggerates them and turns them into something that orthodox Daoism would disown. Such imagery must be assumed as a background that informs the portrayals in *Jin Ping Mei* and other fiction, even if in *Jin Ping Mei* only one of its characters (the foreign monk) is an actual practitioner of occult techniques. Readers of the novel would know of such lore from its appearance in one of the most famous Ming pornographic novels, *Zhaoyang qushi* 昭陽趣史 (The sensational history of Flying Swallow), which is about two of Chinese history's most notorious wanton women: the sisters Zhao Feiyan 趙飛燕 and Zhao Hede 合德.[29] In multiple scenes, the winner of sexual battle is the partner who has superior mastery of what are referred to as "occult arts" (*fashu* 法術) and "methods" or "tricks" (*shouduan* 手段, 1.74). One of the male partners of the sisters in *Zhaoyang qushi* uses the word "system" to refer to his techniques, a word that usually means administrative system or "institution" (*zhidu* 制度, 1.114). Although he exhausts Feiyan, he fails to do so to Hede, who "is undefeatable" (*nong bu dao de* 弄不倒的, 1.115) and whom he calls a true "master" (*gaoshou* 高手), a "woman who knows her methods" (*you shouduande nüzi* 有手段的女子, 1.114).

As for the woman's ability to constrict her vagina, *Jin Ping Mei* contains only a minute reference to it in the poetic passage about Ximen Qing and Wang Liu'er (37.487–488). But it is well-established elsewhere. *Xiuta yeshi*, another well-known Ming pornographic novel, is a few years older

29. Yanyan sheng 艷艷生, *Zhaoyang qushi*, SWXHB, vol. 3. Page references for this work are according to *juan* 卷 (chapter) and page numbers. This novel was the result of several recastings since its first brief version appeared more than a thousand years earlier, in the Han dynasty, and it was often reprinted after its late Ming publication. See below and chapter 7. For brief discussions of this work, see McMahon, *Women Shall Not Rule*, 81–82; Li Mengsheng, *Zhongguo jinhui xiaoshuo baihua*, 108–115; Chen and Wang, introduction, *Zhaoyang qushi*, SWXHB, vol. 3, 15–22; and Milburn, *Empress*, 98–99.

than *Zhaoyang qushi*.[30] It features a woman who has known her "methods" (*shouduan*) since youth. Using them, "she can open and close her vagina, take [the man's] prick, inhale and exhale it, and lock down on him while alternating between fast and slow," and finally make him ejaculate (會開，又會夾，把毯吞進吐出，緊抽緊鎖，慢抽慢鎖, 1.116). In fact, "even if a man were made of iron, she could reduce him to nothing" (便是鐵漢子也弄矮了, 1.123). The same skill appears in *Zhaoyang qushi*, in which another woman who has known her methods since youth can "clamp down tightly" (*jiade jinjinde* 夾得緊緊的1.74), or "lock down" on the man (鎖, 1.106). In this case the term for her skill is "the method of 'churning *qi*' and 'gathering and locking'" (*yun qi shousuo zhi fa* 運氣收鎖之法, 1.74), and it allows her to last all day until a man can endure no longer and finally ejaculates (1.115). "Churning *qi*" has to do with guiding *qi* inside the body, which has long been a part of Daoist internal alchemy and the pursuit of immortality, though here it is put to pornographic use.

Women's locking skills appear in texts as far back as the Han dynasty in brief, though telling, passages. The earliest reference comes from what at first seems an unlikely source: Liu Xiang's 劉向 (77–6 BCE) *Lienü zhuan* 列女傳 (Biographies of exemplary women). However, it is not unlikely if one considers that the reference is in the section about women whom the author labels as "truculent and indulged" (*niebi* 孽嬖). He writes of Xia Ji, whose beauty attracted the attention of multiple men and who, according to one brief sentence, was a master of the "techniques of internal constriction that enabled her to replenish her youth" (內挾技術，蓋老而復壯者).[31] In the slightly later *Liexian zhuan* 列仙傳 (Biographies of immortals), a woman named Nü Wan 女丸 learns sexual skills from an esoteric text that she receives from an immortal, practices them with young men, and likewise retains her youth forever. Clamping is not mentioned but might be assumed to be included in her skills.[32] A different type of locking down occurs in one of the earlier versions of *Zhaoyang qushi*,

30. For discussions of the novel, see Li Mengsheng, *Zhongguo jinhui xiaoshuo baihua*, 80–87; Idema, "'Blasé Literati,'" xxix–lix (for battle imagery, see liv–lv); Wong, "Anatomy of Eroticism"; and Lenny Hu, trans., *The Embroidered Couch*.

31. Liu Xiang, *Lienü zhuan*, 17a. For more on Xia Ji (who also appears in chapters 1 and 7), see also Kinney, *Exemplary Women*, 146 and 269, n. 107.

32. See Liu Xiang, *Liexian zhuan*, 22; and Kaltenmark, trans., *Lie-sien Tchouan*, 180–182.

called *Zhao Feiyan waizhuan* 趙飛燕外傳 (The untold story of Zhao Feiyan), which is probably from the late Tang and, as Olivia Milburn writes, is one of China's earliest extant erotic narratives.[33] The young Zhao Feiyan reads a book called *Pengzu fang* 彭祖方 (Formulas of Pengzu), from which she learns "the art of circulating *qi*" (*xing qi shu* 行氣術), which enables her to block the emperor's penetration as she "closes her eyes and squeezes herself tight" (*ming mu laowo* 瞑目牢握). She is a master of "internal meditation" (*neishi* 內視), by which, like Xia Ji, she can restore virginity after sex and "retain her youth forever."[34]

The same historical figure Xia Ji who appears in the *Lienü zhuan*, which gives only a bare indication of her special skills, becomes the main character of the mid-Qing novel *Zhulin yeshi*, in which these skills play a central role.[35] A feathered immortal teaches her how to "absorb *jing* and guide *qi*" (*xi jing dao qi* 吸精導氣), which allows her to "enjoy her pleasures to the fullest" (*qujin qihuan* 曲盡其歡) and in the process "absorb *yang* to build *yin*" (*cai yang bu yin* 採陽補陰). The terms "absorbing *jing* and guiding *qi*" and "absorbing *yang* to build *yin*" likewise belong to Daoist internal alchemy. The novel further fantasizes this figure by giving her two magic pills: one is for "opening the vagina" (*kai pin wan* 開牝丸) and lubricating it so that she will feel no pain; the other is a "vagina tightening pill" (*jin pin wan* 緊牝丸), which allows her to restore her virginity after intercourse (1.4 and 1.19–20). She uses her skills with a man who, like Ximen Qing, takes a powerful aphrodisiac and encases his "chowry handle" in a sheath (*zhubing* 麈柄). Xia Ji "churns up her *qi*" (*yunqi qi lai* 運起氣來), which makes "her vagina contract and expand on its own" (*pinnei ziqi ziluo* 牝內自起自落). This drains the man, who tries to pull himself out, but she "clamps on him with a grip as tight as a vice" (*yi jia qiande* 一夾箝的, 7.66–68).[36]

33. Milburn, *Empress*, 5 and 37–49 (for a complete translation), and "On *Zhao Feiyan waizhuan*."

34. See Ling Xuan 伶玄, *Zhao Feiyan waizhuan*, SWXHB, *waibian*, vol. 1, 7 and 8. Meditating for three days makes "her flesh become full and solid" (*rouji yingshi* 肉肌盈實, ibid.).

35. See *Zhulin yeshi*, SWXHB, vol. 20, 158.

36. Later, the man tries to "battle her to defeat" (*zhanbai* 戰敗), but she overwhelms him, causing him to go numb, "until before he knew it his semen drained out in wave

No such woman appears in *Jin Ping Mei*, which draws from the same repertoire of images and motifs that appear in other fiction but does not have the images and motifs centrally motivate the plot. A story in the late Ming *Bie you xiang* 別有香 (Of another fragrance) portrays a monk who specializes in the "art of the bedchamber" (*fangzhong zhi shu* 房中之術), which allows him to last all night.[37] A woman who enjoys his performance of his "set of positions" (*taoshu* 套數) with her nevertheless thinks to herself that she is letting him off too easily and must devise a way to make him "lose" (*diu* 丟). In an unwitting moment he reveals to her that one simply has to press upon his navel to make him ejaculate.[38] She takes note and, while later enjoying herself with him, begins "using her *yin* to cut at his stalk, alternating between cutting and clamping" (用陰剪，把莖連剪連夾), and then stealthily presses his navel and makes him ejaculate (4.38–43).[39] In another of the well-known pornographic novels of the late Ming, *Langshi qiguan* 浪史奇觀 (The wonders of the rake), the woman bests the man by tricking him into drinking cold water, which she knows will dispel the effects of the drug he has just taken.[40] The same method appears in *Jin Ping Mei* when the monk gives Ximen Qing the aphrodisiac, telling him that if he wishes to cancel the drug's effects, he can drink a mouthful of cold water, which will cause "the *yang* to return so that the *jing* will suffer no harm" (陽回精不傷; 49.639). Later, when Li Ping'er wishes him to hurry and finish, Ximen Qing drinks cold tea to make himself ejaculate (50.650).

after wave" (不覺洋洋而洩, 16.138). For Xia Ji's ability to stay forever young, see 14.123–124 (where she is "fifty-four" but looks "sixteen or seventeen").

37. *Bie you xiang* is a story collection from some time after 1592, perhaps as late as the 1630s. See *Bie you xiang*, in SWXHB, vol. 8, 4.28–29.

38. In the late Ming novel *Dongyou ji* 東遊記 (Journey to the east, from the collection *Siyou ji* 四遊記, The four journeys, 28.28), a courtesan forces Lü Dongbin 呂洞賓 to ejaculate by suddenly poking him in the ribs. For another version of the same episode, see Schipper, *The Taoist Body*, 163.

39. The navel plays a role in another story in which adepts can "massage their navels to pass *qi*" (*mo ji guo qi* 摩臍過氣). See *Sengni niehai* 僧尼孽海, "Shamen Tan Xian" (沙門曇獻), in SWXHB, vol. 24, 48.See also McMahon, *Women Shall Not Rule*, 169.

40. Fengyue xuan youxuanzi 風月軒又玄子, *Langshi qiguan*, in SWXHB, vol. 4, 21.138–139.

"Bobbing Its Head and Fluttering Its Tongue Like a Snake"

In *Zhaoyang qushi* and *Zhulin yeshi*, the woman sets the terms of sex, both when to have it and whether the man will or will not lose control of himself. In the episodes in which the man prevails, he overpowers her by making his penis pulsate and expand and contract on its own. In short, if the woman can open and close her vagina, the man can turn his penis into an agile homunculus. The two opposing images pervade Ming and Qing fiction, even in the case of the allegorical, nonpornographic early Qing novel *Hou Xiyou ji* 後西遊記 (Sequel to Journey to the West), which features suggestive imagery, but no sexually explicit description. The woman has a vagina-like weapon that can open and close, while her male opponent deploys a cudgel that can expand and contract.[41]

Jin Ping Mei does not take the image of the pulsating penis as far, but something of the agile homunculus appears when Ximen Qing first takes the monk's drug: "His word flew into violent rage. Its edges swelled out, its head leapt up, its sunken eye bulged wide, all its capillaries sprang forth, and it turned purple like the color of liver" (那話暴怒起來, 露稜跳腦, 凹眼圓睜, 橫觔皆見, 色若紫肝, 50.645). A more explicit rendition of the motif appears in *Chipozi zhuan* 癡婆子傳 (Tale of an infatuated woman), another of the renowned works of Ming pornography, written in the same period as *Jin Ping Mei* or somewhat later. The female protagonist tells of a former lover who used to please her: "He was marvelous in his mastery of the art of expanding and contracting. Without moving his body, he made me feel as if there were a shuttle moving across a loom inside me. . . . The mouth of his organ could open and close on its own, enclosing the heart of my flower, making me feel as if my bones were melting away. The ecstasy was so unbearable that it made me swoon" (又美伸縮法, 體不動而內若擲梭 . . . . 物之口能開能合, 而含予之蕊. 即令人百骸欲酥. 樂不能堪, 輒昏暈).[42]

41. Her "Jade-Fire Pincer" (*yuhuoqian* 玉火鉗) "can open and close" (*neng kai neng he* 能開能合). The man defeats her with his cudgel, which "can expand and contract" (*neng da neng xiao* 能大能小; anonymous, *Hou Xiyou ji*, 32.369 and 33.380–81).

42. Furong zhuren 芙蓉主人, *Chipozi zhuan*, 2.63–64. "Heart of my flower" comes from Stevenson and Wu, trans., *A Tale of an Infatuated Woman*, 92 (for *rui* 蕊); see also Zamperini, "Canonizing Pornography," 281; and Vitiello, "Family Affairs."

The Ming sex manual *Sunü miaolun* may have inspired the *Chipozi zhuan* author, or at least serves as evidence that such imagery was present in the sexual lore of the time. In a description of the fifth of nine positions, *Sunü miaolun* writes of the penis "retracting and extending in quick succession, like the head of a turtle" (忽縮忽伸, 如龜頭伸縮), using the same key words for extend (*shen*) and retract (*suo*).[43] A story from *Sengni niehai* (of the same period) describes a monk who is skilled in the method of "extending and retracting, inhaling and exhaling" (*shen suo tun tu* 伸縮吞吐), using the same alchemical terminology—including the practice of "inhaling and exhaling" (*tun tu*)—that women used in two stories mentioned above. Extending and retracting also include the man's ability to withdraw his penis completely into his abdomen, as in the case of the monk in another story from *Sengni niehai*, who could "draw his penis back into his body, as if he were a eunuch, and then extend it to the length of six or seven inches" (縮則有若天閹, 伸則長至六七寸). The phenomenon recurs frequently in Ming and Qing fiction.[44]

More explicit examples of this image appear in two Qing novels, *Xinghua tian* and *Guwangyan*. In the former, the agile penis turns into a little head with a mouth that can open and bite. A Daoist teaches the man how to make his organ "extend and retract on its own, as if it were nibbling and biting at the flower's heart" (自伸自缩, 就如在花心上啃咬一般).[45] The most dramatic rendition of this capacity appears in the mid-eighteenth-century *Guwangyan*, in which a Daoist master has a penis that "alternates between bobbing its head and fluttering its tongue like a snake, and sucking like a baby at the nipple" (那龜頭一時如頑蛇吐信, 一時如小兒咂乳).[46] Later in the same novel, a man of supreme potency has a penis whose opening is "just like a little mouth" that can open and close (17.2026–2027). He drives his wife into helpless ecstasy as his penis

43. *Sunü miaolun*, in Li Ling, *Zhongguo fangshu gaiguan*, 194.

44. For the first story, see *Sengni niehai*, "Magu an ni" (麻姑庵尼), 164. For the second, see *Sengni niehai*, "Shamen Tan Xian," 48. See also *Xinghua tian*, in SWXHB, vol. 17, 9.158, where the penis can "extend and retract on its own" (*zichu zijin* 自出自進); and *Shenlou zhi*, 9.15a, for a monk who has mastered "the magic art of retracting the dragon" (*na long miaofa* 納龍妙法).

45. *Xinghua tian*, 4.82–83. See also the image of the penis "like a mouth that nibbles and bites" (*si ken si yao yiban* 似啃似咬一般). In a later chapter, the penis makes "a sound like geese and ducks gobbling up food," 7.129–130 (若鵝鴨咂食之聲).

46. Cao Qujing 曹去晶, *Guwangyan*, in SWXHB, vol. 36, 1.172; McMahon, "Pornographic Doctrine"; and Vitiello, *The Libertine's Friend*, 134–138 and 146–153.

bites and nibbles inside her and "chomps on her flower's heart like a baby sucking at the breast" (然後一下咬住內中花心，如小孩咂乳一般，17.2031). Here the penis turns into a merciless beast, bound to defeat the ravenously wanton woman. Sexual mastery serves as an allegory for the kind of mastery that men in charge of the government at the end of the Ming should have possessed. If they had been more sexually powerful, the dynasty would not have fallen. As in the case of the woman's locking skill, the penis compared to the baby sucking at the breast has early precedents, though without the political associations of *Guwangyan*. Bedchamber texts from the Six Dynasties and the Tang, as well as the late Tang *Dale fu*, contain the same image of the penis moving "like a child sucking at the breast" (*ru hai'er han ru* 如孩兒含乳), though the effect in this case is gently to stimulate the woman during shallow thrusts.[47] *Guwangyan* instead turns the act into one of perverse manipulation.

An associated skill that men must have at their disposal, which likewise has a long history, is the suppression of ejaculation.[48] The skill is both a matter of lasting a long time to please the woman and a method of preventing the loss of *jing*. *Xiu zhen yanyi* (a late Ming manual of sexual alchemy) calls the technique "locking shut the shrouded gate" (*suobi xuanguan* 鎖閉玄關).[49] The method is central to the art of the bedchamber and sexual alchemy, but it is completely absent in *Jin Ping Mei*. Ximen Qing simply never fails to lose control, though he must rely on drugs and devices. In a story from several decades later by Ling Mengchu 凌濛初 (1580–1644), when a man realizes that he is about to ejaculate, "he immediately stills himself and holds his breath, then proceeds to squeeze his coccyx as if restraining a bowel movement, and thereby succeeds in preventing his ejaculation" (急按住身子，閉著一口氣，將尾閭往上一趟，如忍大便一般，才阻得不來).

47. In order: *Dongxuanzi* ("like a child sucking at the breast," *ru hai'er han ru*); *Xuannü jing* 玄女經 ("like a child sucking at the breast," *ru er han ru* 如兒含乳); and *Dale fu* ("like an infant sucking at the breast," *ru ying'er han ru* 如嬰兒含乳), in Li Ling, *Zhongguo fangshu gaiguan*, 120, 112, and 95, respectively.

48. In terms of classical medicine, the method falls under the rubric of "strengthening *yang* and solidifying essence" (*zhuang yang gu jing* 壯陽固精). *Zhuang yang* refers to methods of supplementing the *yang*, while *gu jing* refers to preventing premature ejaculation and other losses of *jing*. See Xu Yuanzhen, *Zhongyi cishi*, 223 and 343.

49. *Xiu zhen yanyi*, in Li Ling, *Zhongguo fangshu gaiguan*, 214; and Wile, *Art of the Bedchamber*, 136–146 and 140. Wile translates the same technique as "Locking the Mysterious Mechanism."

Unfortunately, he has taken a powerful aphrodisiac that causes his "flesh piece" (*rouju* 肉具) to swell to the size of a melon as it begins to "expand and retract" (*shensuo* 伸縮) on its own, causing him to faint and die.[50] A more detailed representation of the technique appears in a remarkable passage in *Xinghua tian*, in which a Daoist master teaches a man the art of "solidifying essence" (*gu jing* 固精),

> for which there is a marvelous formula, which works in an extraordinary way. While lying down, take the *yin* stalk with the left hand and rub the cinnabar field with the right. Rub yourself several hundred times, beginning gently, then gradually increase the speed. When about to ejaculate, take three fingers and press them on the crotch. Immediately hold yourself in as if holding back urination. Look upward and fix your thoughts on the bright palace. Use a generous amount of bitter wash to wet the penis. Only thus will it become as firm as a sword. . . . Fix your intent and do not stray. Following this method step-by-step will make the turtle grow to nine inches.
>
> (固精有妙訣，作用不尋常. 左手拿住龜，右手摩頂梁. 卧時數數百，前輕後重忙. 但覺微精動，三指谷道藏. 急時小便縮，提起望明堂. 辛酸頻水洗，才得劍劍剛. 一七臨頂奪，誠心不要狂. 尾尾依前法，龜身九寸長).[51]

This is the art of sex in its most methodically instructive mode. The *Xinghua tian* protagonist becomes a master of *qi* flow, which he demonstrates repeatedly as he gathers his twelve wives in a grand polygamous marriage. The battle imagery culminates in the final scene, in which he defeats all of them on one great bed (where defeat means both pleasing and outdoing them), after which "he removes his helmet and armor, dismounts from his warhorse, thrusts his spear into the ground, and stables

50. Ling Mengchu, *Erke pai'an jingqi* 二刻拍案驚奇, "Lin jiansheng lang tun miyao, Chunhua bi wu xie fengqing" (甄監生浪吞秘藥 春花婢誤洩風情), 18.13b–15b. A similar but briefer rendition of the method appears in *Langshi qiguan*, 13.108.

51. *Xinghua tian*, 2.68. In the clause *tiqi wang mingtang* (提起望明堂), *tiqi* (literally, pick up) may refer to lifting the penis (or the head), while *wang mingtang* refers to focusing on the spot between the eyebrows. "Bitter wash" (*xinsuan* 辛酸) refers to a medical solution. The omitted text is "*yi qi lin ding duo*" (一七臨頂奪), for which I do not want to hazard a guess.

his mount" (解胄卸甲, 下了征駒，搠鎗拴馬, 13.257).[52] It is safe to say that the *Jin Ping Mei* author would have known of ejaculation control, since that is a common part of sexual knowledge in China. But Ximen Qing resorts to the exhilaration of the aphrodisiac rather than the wisdom of mastering the art of semen retention.

Conclusion: Ambushing Him from All Sides

As I have discussed sexual battle, it amounts to a physical contest, in which partners use their sexual organs as if they were dueling weapons. In some cases, the sexual battle becomes a competitive game, as in *Zhaoyang qushi* when the sister consorts stage a competition to see how many thrusts a man can execute before ejaculating. They have participants divide into four teams to see whose penis can knock against a drum the loudest, with a naked maid as judge roaming around on a horse. Palace women are divided into four teams to see who emits the most sexual fluids (2.161–165). In Feng Menglong's story, Prince Hailing orders his ministers to expose themselves so that he can rank them according to their penis size.[53] Scenes of sexual contest go back at least to a piece of pseudohistory from the tenth century, which tells how the Tang emperor Xuanzong (玄宗, reigned 685–762) and his favorite consort, Yang Guifei (楊貴妃, 719–756), used to play a game in which she led a team of courtesans against his team of young eunuchs, with the two sides divided into "love formations" (*fengliu zhen* 風流陣) to have a mock battle.[54] A theme that the examples of Zhao Feiyan, Hailing, and Xuanzong share is the decadence of palace life and the boundless extremes of the imperial libido, a theme that *Jin Ping Mei* reproduces except for the fact that it takes place in the household of a wealthy urban merchant. Whatever the context, tools, drugs, occult techniques, and games are part of the activities that diversify the intensity of the drive.

52. See also 4.82–83, 7.129–130, 9.159, and 13.254–257, and a discussion and translation of other parts of the passage in chapter 7.

53. See Feng Menglong, *Xingshi hengyan*, story 23, 49ab.

54. See Wang Renyu 王仁裕 (880–956), *Kaiyuan tianbao yishi* 開元天寶遺事, 75 and 106; and McMahon, *Women Shall Not Rule*, 218. A contest appears in *Guwangyan* that includes evaluating the qualities of women's genitals (14.1657).

The tone of *Jin Ping Mei*'s passages of mock battle is one of elegant ribaldry, with the consequences of the battle going no further than exhaustion. But again, that tone ends once the narrative returns to the complexities of daily life. Likewise, although the scene in Feng Menglong's story may be amusing in itself, its thematic point is the disparagement of the megalomaniac Hailing. In contrast, *Zhaoyang qushi* uses its notorious ancient characters to portray erotic adventure and entertainment. The same contests would be unimaginable in *Jin Ping Mei*. If some form of sexual game were to occur there, it might appear in hearsay about a boorish client in one of the city's brothels, about whom courtesans would gossip in one of their off-duty get-togethers. The dirty games that are germane to *Jin Ping Mei* take the form of the ribald joke and riddle contests that take place among Ximen Qing's drinking companions.[55] There is also the playful sex that characters engage in when they imitate as many sexual positions as they can from the erotic picture albums.

At another extreme, likewise unimaginable in *Jin Ping Mei*, is the kind of battle that takes place in *Bian er chai* 弁而釵 (Hairpins beneath his cap), in which the scene is one of monogamous love between two men in a state of high passion.[56] One man "puts his horse to a gallop and charges the outer gates," at which point the other says: "It has been long since we last fought. Let us wait until our two armies have properly lined up before engaging in battle" (放馬竟闖轅門; "久未經戰, 候兩軍成列, 大戰未晚," 5.174–175). What follows is a session of blissful sex, with no hint of dueling sexual organs or stealing of vital essence.[57] The focus is on a noble and heroic love based on an egalitarian relationship between two men.[58] The imagery of battle replaces any direct description of bodies engaged in sex, which would detract from the aura of sublime love. The characters in *Bian er chai* are both moral and romantic exemplars—a type of figure that, as I showed in chapter 3, appears only at the end of *Jin Ping Mei* in a portrayal that is likewise devoid of explicit description.

55. On riddles in the novel, see Kelly, "Riddles in *Jin Ping Mei*."

56. See Zuixihu xinyue zhuren 醉西湖心月主人, *Bian er chai*, in SWXHB, vol. 6, story 2, chapter 5; and Vitiello, *The Libertine's Friend*, 35 and 73–78.

57. The fourth story of *Bian er chai* says: "Kuang hovers his pestle and enters, while Li lowers his axe and welcomes him in" (匡漂杵而进, 李倒戈相迎, 4.2.286–287).

58. This type of relationship constitutes what Vitiello calls the "paradigmatic model of romantic love" (*The Libertine's Friend*, 66).

CHAPTER 5

Graphic Description in Jin Ping Mei

The Raw Sights and Sounds

In the high erotic portrayal of sex, including sex as battle, a scene takes place at a remove, as if on an alternative, sublimated plane. The partners become like gods and goddesses or, in the variation of sex as battle, like hearty warriors. The writer avoids straightforward, graphic description, and thus sexual pleasure and acts are not described directly. Graphic description may still include metaphors and similes, which are also cases of language at a remove, but the point is not to create a sublime effect. Instead, it is as if to place the portrayal on the same plane as the sex that is supposedly occurring before hypothetical eyes and ears. Its favorite images are the raw sights and sounds of sex, its ferocity and precipitousness, and the copiousness of sensual effects—even in a simple declaration that someone is enjoying the utmost sexual pleasure. Descriptions of this sort typically occur in scenes with Pan Jinlian, Wang Liu'er, Ben the Fourth, Ruyi, and Lady Lin, with whom Ximen Qing has the most unrestrained sex. Raw, graphic sex is thus about unfiltered excess. In morally shaded terms, it is sex at the basest level (more on the quality of baseness below). But even if this is so, the author does not necessarily or unambiguously cast the description in a negative light. As in the other modes, such portrayal foregrounds the all-encompassing energy and fullness of the act, though it also tends to describe its excessive fullness. Pleasure in such scenes is extreme and overwhelming, if not also tinged with pain and aggression and at times described in grotesque detail.

One of the most notable expressions indicating utmost pleasure is one that the author copies from the earlier *Ruyijun zhuan*: "to feel an indescribable rush of pleasure" (*xixiran changmei bukeyan*, 翕翕然暢美不可言).[1] In *Ruyijun zhuan*, this description and its variants describe the ecstasy of both man and woman, but mainly the woman. In *Jin Ping Mei*, in contrast, the words or their variants occur six times: five times for Ximen Qing, and the final time for Pan Jinlian.[2] The word for "pleasure" is *changmei* (暢美), which by itself refers to a physical sense of well-being, in which energy flows freely and without inhibition. It is not unique to sexual acts but can also refer, for example, to the pleasant sensations gained from healing exercises, as in this excerpt from a late Ming text: "Saliva abounds at the tip of the tongue, and if frequently gargled and swallowed into the cinnabar field, it gives pleasure [*changmei*] and dispels stagnation. After one-hundred days of practice, aging will cease" (浸液頻生在舌端，尋常嗽嚥入丹田；於中暢美無凝滯．百日功靈可注顏).[3]

In concise terms, graphic description portrays sexual pleasure and acts plainly and directly, typically though not always without resorting to formal set phrases. One concrete, sensational detail comes after another in a way that is straightforward—that is, nonpoetic, noneuphemistic, and nonmetaphorical. Graphic and high erotic may mingle and alternate, as I have shown above. Sometimes the graphic includes the grotesque and obscene, though the most vulgar words usually occur only when men or women swear or when they refer mockingly or scathingly to the genitals or the act of intercourse. They rarely occur during that act. By "plain" and "direct," I refer to such descriptions as the woman "lying back on the bed" and "taking his word with her hand to put it inside" and "she goes limp and falls back onto the bed, moaning ceaselessly" (仰臥床上；手挐那話往裡放；酥癱于枕上，口內呻吟不止, 50.645). Ximen Qing "takes Yueniang's creamy white thighs and puts them on his shoulders" (把月娘兩隻白生生腿扛在肩膊上, 21.267–268), and or he "takes [Zheng Yue'er's]

1. *Ruyijun zhuan*, 42; alternatively, "to feel a melting sensation the pleasure of which words cannot describe."

2. See *Ruyijun zhuan*, 44 and 45; and JPM, 27.357, 50.645 and 649, 51.666, 73.1023, and 79.1142.

3. Quoted in Chen Hsiu-fen, "Visual Representation," 158, n. 41, my translation.

tender white legs . . . and wraps them around his waist" (把他兩隻白生生 . . . 嫩腿兒夾在兩邊腰眼間, 59.778).

To say what I have said here may be too obvious. But the question again occurs: what is the author doing, filling the pages with such graphically rendered depictions? He rounds every bend and captures every sight and sound, as if in the scene himself, bringing the reader to the immediacy of the sexual stage. I say "stage" because it is always a constructed scene, simply by the fact that it is written to be read and designed for particular effects that have to do with the sounds and sights of the sexual acts of a particular set of specifically defined characters.

Let us first examine the occurrences of the phrase "to feel an indescribable rush of pleasure," constructing a brief story of its appearance in the novel. It is neither particularly elegant in its expression, nor does it make explicit reference to the body or an action. It names utter pleasure as such, in simple terms. Anyone could experience it. Just after its first occurrence in chapter 27—that is, just after Ximen Qing reaches his height of pleasure—the sulfur ring breaks inside Pan Jinlian. She buckles up in pain and falls back onto the bed as if dead. In a later scene, the same expression is followed by Li Ping'er's appeal to Ximen Qing to slow down because he is hurting her (50.649). If readers were to think that the expression occurs only in descriptions of one-sided pleasure, or pleasure followed by pain, they would have to look at the scene of Ximen Qing and Wang Liu'er just before the one with Li Ping'er: "As he performed a series of shallow pulls and deep thrusts, he experienced an indescribable rush of pleasure" (淺抽深送, 覺翕翕然暢美不可言, 50.645). As for Wang Liu'er, "she was drunk with wanton desire and sank into the bed numb with pleasure, moaning and groaning with satisfaction, continuously calling out, 'You big Daddy prick! Your wanton bitch will die today!'" (婦人則淫心如醉, 酥癱于枕上, 口内呻吟不止. 口口聲聲只叫: "大雞巴達達, 淫婦今日可死也," 50.645). A slightly modified version of the expression occurs in a later chapter, in a similar scene of lengthy and unrestrained sex, in which Ximen Qing "feels utmost pleasure, more than words can describe," as Pan Jinlian cries out, "Dada, enough! You have fucked Little Fivey to death!" (心中翕翕然, 美快不可言; 親達達, 罷了, 五兒合死了, 51.665–666). Both scenes take place soon after Ximen Qing acquires the new aphrodisiac, which he tries with one woman after another in rapid succession.

A similar scene portraying extreme enjoyment in both partners is the one already mentioned that takes place in chapter 73, when Ximen Qing "feels an indescribable rush of pleasure" while Pan Jinlian faints and goes limp (73.1023). Similar states of the woman's semiconsciousness, with similar wording, occur elsewhere in *Jin Ping Mei*, *Ruyijun zhuan*, and across Ming and Qing fiction.[4] Ominously in this scene Ximen Qing "keeps staying rigid" (*gangjin rugu* 剛勁如故). The drug has granted him indescribable pleasure, but now it has brought him to the point where pleasure descends into the stagnation of an unquenchable erection. The same result occurs in chapter 79 in the last appearance of the phrase "to feel an indescribable rush of pleasure," when Pan Jinlian has him swallow three of the monk's pills. She swallows one herself—the only time a woman does so in the novel. In this case the pleasure is once more one-sided, but the side is the woman's. She ties on the white silk band and, as Ximen Qing still sleeps, straddles him, and applies the monk's cream to the opening of his penis, which she inserts as she begins to gyrate, "giving herself an indescribable rush of pleasure, so that her whole body felt numb with bliss" (覺翕翕然， 渾身酥麻， 暢美不可言). The graphic description continues: "The woman could not contain herself. Putting her tongue in Ximen Qing's mouth, she cradled his neck in her arms and rubbed and grinded herself around him with all the energy she had, massaging and kneading in whichever way it made her feel good" (婦人情不能當, 以舌親于西門慶口中, 兩手摟着他脖子項極力揉擦, 左右偎擦, 79.1142). By the time of the third watch, she had used five handkerchiefs to wipe up her fluids and "came" (*diu* 丟) twice in a row. But to her alarm, because of the overdose of aphrodisiac that she has given Ximen Qing, his penis begins to swell until it erupts in a long flow of semen followed by blood.

The novel contains no fuller rendition of the drastic collapse of pleasure. One might ask, is Pan Jinlian's demand for enjoyment no more than a portrayal of the woman as a relentless savage in her demands for satisfaction? To be sure, when she gives Ximen Qing the three pills, the Chongzhen commentator points out the similarity to her administering

4. In *Ruyijun zhuan*, the empress "goes out of her mind with bliss" (*shensi hunmi* 神思昏迷), 45; feels "dizzy, as if no longer knowing where she is" (我頭目森森然，莫知所之, 45; the latter quote also found in *Jin Ping Mei*, 27.357); and cries out, "the pleasure is killing me" (*kuaihuo sha wo ye* 快活殺我也, 45 and 51).

the poison to Wu Da (79.1142).[5] But the portrayal of her energetic enjoyment nevertheless recalls other portrayals of utmost pleasure in the novel, both before and after this scene. It resonates with the portrayal of female pleasure that anchors the ancient art of the bedchamber, though it takes a new leap in portraying an aggressive woman who hardly conforms to what by contrast is the idealized, passively enjoying partner of the male master of the art of the bedchamber. In this scene, mutuality is drastically out of kilter. The phrase "to feel an indescribable rush of pleasure" applies to the lone partner, who does what she knows will give her pleasure, though not necessarily with the intention of harming Ximen Qing. She simply takes what she can from him when she can and in the way that she can.

Graphic description, as I said above, is not used to refer to the main wife or a sublime lover. Only the rawest and least restrained sex—and the most passionate and frenzied—can be depicted this way. Such is the convention of sexually explicit portrayal in *Jin Ping Mei*. The tone of the graphic combines with that of the grotesque, also blending with the imagery of sexual bliss in a way that both enhances and detracts from the portrayal. Is the author looking on with a leer and expecting or leading the reader to do so as well? The arousal is awesome, fascinating, and uncanny. But are there also dissonant notes? Does the author care if he repels his reader? Is he trying to repel the reader? The answer is yes in a novel such as *Guwangyan*, but *Jin Ping Mei* is more ambiguous. However readers may react to such descriptions, and however skewed they may be toward the male perspective, the fact remains that the author creates a constructively contradictory effect, which denies the reader the simple choice between a morally skewed affirmative or negative portrayal. The graphic description can for moments exist independently of the characters and situations portrayed, leaving the energy of the sexual act to stand on its own—as also is the case in the modes of the high erotic and sex as battle. The following examples of the graphic mode are more concrete than the phrase "to feel an indescribable rush of pleasure," focusing on the sights and sounds of sex and allowing us to push further in asking how to read the tenor of such portrayals.

5. Zhang Zhupo makes the same point in JPMCH, Bu Jian, ed., 79.1913.

The first example is the boldly explicit scene of Ximen Qing's session with Ruyi in chapter 78. It is bold because of its direct, even if momentary, portrayal of the female genitals during sex. This is not the first such portrayal, but it is more graphic than the earlier ones of Zheng Aiyue and Pan Jinlian. Ximen Qing's affair with Zheng carries an air of high erotic artifice and formality, as I described above. In Ximen Qing's eyes, her body is like a goddess's. The brief description of her body is from the same eyes, which see her vagina as "immaculate and hairless, like a white steamed cake, soft and tender and delightful to behold" (59.778). The scene of the first view of Pan Jinlian's nakedness many chapters before is similar, when he finds her "woman's gate devoid of hair, pure and fragrant and plump to fullness, just like a risen bun" (牝户上並無毳毛，猶如白如馥馥，鼓蓬蓬發酵的饅頭, 4.60–61).[6] The scene then shifts to a high erotic description of their sex. In these two cases, the vision of the woman's sex is pure and unblemished, and in both instances it is compared to a delicious edible treat.

In contrast, the affair with wet nurse Ruyi is hotly sensuous from the beginning. In Ximen Qing's eyes, Ruyi is lusty and voluptuous, which is no accident in that by her calling and selection as a wet nurse, she is inherently fertile, robust, and sexually experienced. His affair with her is also distinct because it is deeply sentimental. He sees in her a double of Li Ping'er, as he is moved to tell her during an earlier meeting (67.911). Intimacy with her includes going to drink her breast milk, which he takes because his doctor prescribes breast milk for him as medicine for the newly arisen pain in his loins. It is as if Ximen Qing is taking refuge in a warm maternal nest, in which he hopes to find the love and care of an alternative to his deceased wife. On her part, like Ben the Fourth, Ruyi is eager to please her master, who could elevate her status in the household. As he does in the scene with Pan Jinlian in the grape arbor, Ximen Qing mixes pain with pleasure and, as he does with Ben the Fourth, adds an element of bondage and sadistic impulse in a way that he also does with Wang Liu'er and Lady Lin.

6. About a subsequent reference to the presence of hair, Hsia calls this a discrepancy that "mars the naturalistic texture" of the narrative (*Classic Chinese Novel*, 166; see also 173). Others would say that the novel cannot be taken as consistently naturalistic. See Ding, *Obscene Things*.

The pain derives from the three pieces of moxa left over from his session with Lady Lin that he burns on three parts of Ruyi's body, including just above her vagina. Burning moxa on the woman's body is like a rite that Ximen Qing carries out on the bodies of his victims. I say "rite" because the act is a kind of ceremony that establishes a type of symbolic certainty. These are his women, to whom he can deliver pleasure and pain. Burning moxa on her flesh causes the woman to writhe, which also presumably incites the man—though the novel leaves the effect it has on him implicit. As the scene continues, Ximen Qing puts a mirror beside them to enjoy the sight of his thrusting. Watching himself in such a way happens elsewhere in the novel, as we have seen, and this behavior also appears in *Ruyijun zhuan*, where it is the empress who likes to do so.[7] It is similar to the ritual of burning moxa in its effect of capturing or conserving a moment in the otherwise passing action. Ruyi winces and clenches her teeth, trying to endure the pain, and then softly cries, "You've done me in, you're hurting me so!" (罷了我了，好難忍也). He has her declare that she was once the wife of Xiong Wang (熊旺) but now belongs to him, which he follows with, "Am I a good fucker?" She replies, "'Dada, you are the best fucker of cunts.' And so they continued, uttering all manner of amorous and lustful words" ("我會合不會?" . . . , "達達會合毯"; 兩個淫聲豔語，無般言語不說出來). This is the second time in the same chapter that the word "*ri*" (fuck) occurs in a naming of the act during the act itself, thus again signaling the pointedly raw quality of Ximen Qing's sex with first Ben the Fourth and now Ruyi.[8] The word occurs approximately forty-nine times in *Jin Ping Mei* (the *cihua* version), but at the other times, as I have said, it occurs only as part of cursing someone or as a scathing reference to the act in a context removed from the act itself.

The scene reaches a descriptive climax in a portrayal that has no parallel in the novel, with the slight exception of the scene in the grape arbor. There likewise the narrative eye is on the vagina, but there Ximen Qing's goal is to titillate and tantalize Pan Jinlian, doing his best to expose the vagina and render her helplessly aroused. In the scene with Ruyi,

7. *Ruyijun zhuan*, 44 and 51.

8. See 78.1111 and 1121. The same word appears in reference to Ruyi's face turning red (75.1040).

however, the focus is on the sheer movement between the two aroused organs and the tightly embracing bodies:

> Ximen Qing's organ was so thick that it filled the woman's vagina completely. The action of its going in and out turned the color of her flower's heart rouge like the tongue of a parrot, dark like the wings of a bat, moving back and forth in a pleasing way. Ximen Qing then wrapped her two legs around his waist as the two hugged tightly and pressed against each other closely. His word plunged to the root, leaving not a hairsbreadth outside. The woman's eyes fell into a stare and she lost her voice, as her wanton waters flowed out in waves. His passions reached the height of ecstasy, and his semen erupted like the gush of a fountain. Little knowing that the tidings of spring had already arrived, all they felt was the melting sensation of body and bone.
>
> (西門慶那話粗大，撐的婦人牝户滿滿，往來出入，帶的花心紅如鸚鵡舌，黑似蝙蝠翅，翻覆可愛. 西門慶于是把他兩股扳抱在懷内，四體交匝，兩相迎湊. 那話盡沒至根，不容毫髮. 婦人瞪目失聲，淫水流下. 西門慶情濃樂極，精邀如湧泉. 正是: 不知已透春消息，但覺形骸骨節鎔, 78.1121).

Some of the words and images that appear in this scene appear verbatim elsewhere, such as "plung[ing] to the root, leaving not a hairsbreadth outside" and "semen erupt[ing] like the gush of a fountain."[9] The graphic outweighs the high erotic coda that appears at the end (with the poetry continuing for another few lines in the *cihua* edition).[10] The pain he causes her and the crude and blunt language that they use push the graphic quality of the scene to the extreme. Pain and pleasure overlap. As in high erotic passages, the description of extremes evokes the intensity of the drive. The focus is on the action of thrusting, especially as illustrated in the metaphors of the rouge of the parrot's tongue and the dark wings of the bat, which do not occur elsewhere in the novel. Such images are cases of aestheticizing the sexual act at its most climactic point, though in

9. "To the root, leaving not a hairsbreadth outside" and her "eyes falling into a stare" are from *Ruyijun zhuan*, 45. The eruption of semen appears elsewhere in JPM, as in the common expression that occurs eight times: "and he came in a great gush" (for example, *yi xie ru zhu* 一泄如注, 27.350 and 38.495). For the provenance of other lines, see Roy, 4.78.603–604 and 4.78.840, nn. 39–41.

10. JPMCH, 78.2469.

translation they may fail to convey the qualities that they have in Chinese. "Parrot's tongue" may stand for clitoris, but whether or not it can be read in such a precise sense, the words resemble others used elsewhere that do, such as "red hook" and "chicken tongue" in a scene discussed below. "Dark like wings of a bat" may refer to the labia, and in Chinese the phrase does not carry the ghoulish or grotesque sense that it has in English. Neither tongue nor wings should be considered unambiguously grotesque, though they belong to what I call graphic description—not to the realm of adumbrative elegance. But what qualifies as grotesque and to what degree are questions that need further examination.

The Monstrous Penis and the Woman's Flood

In terms of the sights and sounds of sex, the graphic mode especially favors two recurrent images: the penis bounding into erection and exerting its ferocity, and the woman's flooding waters. The first typically occurs under the influence of aphrodisiacs, while the second appears as the woman's increasingly aroused response to the man's act of thrusting. In the case of the first, a general feature of such descriptions is that when erect and in action, Ximen Qing's organ appears angry, ugly, and grotesque. Zheng Aiyue affirms its ugliness in her first bout with him. His erect penis is a monstrous, pulsating, bulging thing that works with a driving force, frightening her, and (because it is too large) slow and painful upon insertion. The author uses a common set of terms to portray such effects. After applying an aphrodisiac cream, for example, Ximen Qing's "word becomes proud and firm, its edges bulge forth, and it flies into violent rage" (那話昂健奢稜，暴怒起來, 27.357). It reacts similarly after Pan Jinlian gives him fellatio: "in no time his word flew into a violent rage. Like a melon bursting open, its sunken eye bulged wide, and from its surrounding whiskers it bounded straight up" (那話登時暴怒起來, 裂瓜頭凹眼睜圓, 落腮鬍挺身直豎, 28.360).

There are two key aspects of all remaining descriptions of the organ in this state: first, they occur after Ximen Qing begins taking the monk's aphrodisiac; and second, they begin to give the organ qualities that are suggestive of the little human already seen in the chapter on sex as battle.

The penis turns into a little being that controls and manipulates the woman. The first such scene says: "In no time the drug took effect, making his word fly into violent rage. Its edges swelled out, its head leapt up, its sunken eye bulged wide, all its capillaries sprang forth, and it turned purple like the color of liver" (50.645). A recurrent word in these descriptions, which also appears in the scene above in which he applies the aphrodisiac cream, is the one I translate as "edges"—namely, the character *leng* (稜), as in *angjian sheleng* (昂健奢稜), "it became proud and firm, with its edges bulging forth," and *lu leng tiao niao* (露稜跳腦), "it edges swelled out, its head leapt up." *Leng* means corner or edge, as well as protrusion.[11] It may also refer to the rim around the glans, which can be simply translated as the head or knob of the penis. The character occurs in other combinations as well, such as: "he had already completely submerged the head [*leng*] of his turtle" (*yi er jin mo gui leng* 已而僅沒龜稜, 50.645 and 51.665); "its edges [*leng*] bulged forth and its head leapt up" (*she leng tiao nao* 奢稜跳腦, 61.810); and "his turtle head stood proud and lofty, and needed much moistening before its edges [*leng*] could be fully submerged" (龜頭昂大，濡研半响，僅沒龜稜, 51.665). Another repeated image is the penis's movement in and out, as in the expression *mo leng lu nao* (沒稜露腦), which appears ten times in the novel, as in: "All he does is to make deep and shallow thrusts, burying and exposing the head [*leng*] without stopping" (只顧沒稜露腦，淺抽深送不已, 52.676).[12] Nothing in these descriptions suggests beauty or elegance, as striking as the imagery may be. The penis has head and eyes, like a little human; and it is "purple like liver," the same as the monk's head in the scene in which he gives Ximen Qing the new drug (*se ruo zi gan* 色若紫肝)—an image that occurs only after this event.

The other favored image, the woman's abundant sexual waters, carries its own share of grotesque qualities, but to a lesser degree. As a recurrent image it brings us to a delicate distinction between Chinese and English, or between how readers from different perspectives and different eras react to or evaluate a given image or word. In the scene above, Pan Jinlian uses "five handkerchiefs to wipe up her fluids," words that the

11. *Leng* appears twenty times in JPMCH.

12. For *mo leng lu nao*, Roy has "submerging and exposing the knob of his glans," 3.52.257. Elsewhere he translates *leng* as "protuberances," 4.61.15.

author takes from *Ruyijun zhuan*. In another example from *Jin Ping Mei*, the "wanton waters flood beneath her," referring to Ruyi (*yinshui yixia*, 淫水溢下, 67.911).[13] However readers may react to such descriptions, the woman's flood is a sign of the fullness and intensity of her arousal, and as such it is a recurrent part of descriptions in the art of the bedchamber of all periods (as it is in Indian texts such as the *Kamasutra*). In erotic poetry, such images appear as early as the rhapsodic portrayal of sex in the Tang *Dale fu*, where the wiping up of "abundantly flowing" (*yangyi* 洋溢) sexual waters likewise takes place during a pause before the couple resumes their passionate embraces.[14]

But other descriptions in *Jin Ping Mei* do impart a grotesque and bestial quality to the woman's arousal, as in the recurrent comparison of the waters to "a snail secreting its slime" (*ru wo zhi tu xian*, 如蜗之吐涎), an image that appears three times and that also comes from *Ruyijun zhuan*.[15] In all three cases, as in *Ruyijun zhuan*, the scene depicts a man intentionally tantalizing a woman. The word *xian* 涎 can primarily be translated as saliva, but also includes the senses of drool, slobber, or slime, all of which in English sound unmistakably grotesque and repugnant, though in Chinese that effect is not necessarily as strong. In Chinese, conventional imagery characterizing female beauty might refer to gems and flowers (such as jade, orchids, and roses), images that carry well into English. Other conventionally elegant imagery is disconcerting in English, such as the comparison of a woman's delicate fingers to scallion stalks (*congbai* 葱白) or, perhaps slightly less so, that of her eyebrows to moth wings (*emei* 蛾眉). Different aesthetic systems generate and result from different sets of expectations. *Xian* also occurs in the name of an expensive and highly sought after aphrodisiac, dragon incense (*longxian xiang* 龍涎香), which could be translated as something like "incense of dragon spray" to avoid the off-putting sense of saliva or slime. It appears, for

13. See *Ruyijun zhuan*, 51. Other references to sexual waters include "the wanton essence flowed out" (*yinjing liuchu*, 淫精流出, JPM, 27.355).

14. *Dale fu*, 95, where the couple takes a cloth "to wipe themselves dry, then the man inserts himself again" (方以帛子干拭，再内其中), and "the essential fluids flood copiously, the wanton waters flow abundantly" (*jingye liu si* 精液流澌, *yinshui yangyi* 淫水洋溢).

15. *Ruyijun zhuan*, 44 (若我蜗牛之吐涎; I used Roy's translation, 2.27.144). See also JPM, 27.355, 38.494, and 79.1140 (the first with Pan Jinlian, the second two with Wang Liu'er).

example, in a late Ming poem about a woman's boudoir, in which it contributes to the sensuous atmosphere of the room. In such a case, it is a sign of vital cosmic energy.[16]

However, there is also the case of *xian* as it appears in the common expressions for a "shameless" or "cheeky-faced" man (*xianzhe lian* 涎着臉, *xianpi* 涎皮), where the word carries an unmistakable tone of lewdness in its reference to lustful drooling. It appears as such in a description of one of the handsomest and most sensitive to women characters in Chinese literature, Jia Baoyu 賈寶玉, when he once "lusts" (literally, "salivates" or "drools") over the neck of the maid Yuanyang 鴛鴦.[17] Neither of these two cases of the use of *xian*—dragon incense and lustful drooling—qualifies as grotesque, though lustful drooling would be anathema in the context of the art of the bedchamber and erotic poetry. But when used to describe sexual waters and combined with snail, *xian* automatically enters the territory of the obscene and grotesque. *Ruyijun zhuan* uses the expression to describe the wanton Empress Wu. In *Jin Ping Mei* it appears in one scene with Pan Jinlian and two with Wang Liu'er, both of whom belong to the category of Ximen Qing's most wanton women (27.355–356, 38.494, and 79.1140). Snail combined with slime, as opposed to dragon combined with slime, connotes wantonness. If the author had wanted to create a more delicate image, he would have avoided such an expression and instead, for example, suggested some sort of sublime fragrance and richness, as a high erotic *xiangyan* poem cited below shows in its reference to the woman's sexual waters.

The element that most clearly indicates what direction to take with the image of the snail's slime is the fact just mentioned: it occurs in scenes in which the man tantalizes and goads the woman. While Ximen Qing has Pan Jinlian's legs suspended from the grape arbor, he "uses his toe to prod and poke her flower's heart, which after a while had the effect of causing her wanton essence to flood forth in a way that looked like slime secreted from a snail . . . It made her vulva gate swell so wide that the

16. Min Zhengzhong 閔正中, *Meiren shi* 美人詩, 5 from "Making fragrant the coverlets with incense" (Gouxiang xun xiuqin 篝香薰繡衾). Thanks to Li Xiaorong for this reference. See her *Poetics and Politics*, 120–121 (her translation of the poem, in which she renders *longxian xiang* as "Dragon-Saliva Incense"). For details about *longxian xiang*, see Su Yufen, *Mingdai chunyao yanjiu*, 31–34 and 73.

17. Cao Xueqin 曹雪芹, *Honglou meng*, 24.329.

red hook became engorged and the chicken tongue began to protrude" (先將腳指挑弄其花心, 挑的淫精流出, 如蝸之吐涎 . . . . 使牝户大張, 紅鉤赤露, 雞舌内吐, 27.355).[18]

A scene with Wang Liu'er resembles the one with Pan Jinlian. After rubbing aphrodisiac ointment on his turtle's head (*guitou* 龜頭), which "gives her unbearable stimulation" (*mayang buneng dang* 麻癢不能當), Ximen Qing "then plays and prods with her flower's heart, holding back and refusing to go deeper, making the woman become so desperate that her wanton river begins to flow, like a snail secreting its slime" (又挑弄其花心, 不肯深入. 急的婦人淫津流出, 如蝸之吐涎, 79.1140).[19] Another scene with Wang Liu'er resembles the one with Pan Jinlian in that Wang has Ximen Qing suspend one of her legs from above. "From her vagina rivers begin to flow like a snail secreting its slime, in one silky wave after another" (牝中之津如蝸之吐涎, 綿綿不絕). In this instance, the lushness of arousal suddenly takes an unsavory turn when a "white pasty liquid" (*baijiangzi* 白漿子) begins to appear. "What is this white stuff coming out of you?," he asks (你如何流這些白). Without identifying it, she insists on licking him clean. The sounds of this reignite his lust, making him turn her over and apply himself to her anus—into which it takes a while before he completely submerges himself, the author again using the word "*leng*." She pretends to welcome this, even though she winces in pain (38.494–3895). Wang Liu'er will do anything to please Ximen Qing, even when suffering pain or a gynecological disorder—the latter of which, unlike Meng Yulou in a scene discussed below, she pretends is not there.

Regardless of high or low tenor, the woman's flood is a recurrent feature of sexually explicit portrayal in the art of the bedchamber, sexual alchemy, erotic poetry, and pornographic fiction. It is a sign of richness and abundance, but also by implication it is a sign of excess verging on loss of control. The woman is by nature prone to such abundance, which is sometimes celebrated. However, it is also something that the man takes advantage of, whether to appropriate essence from her, as in sexual alchemy, or to goad and tantalize her, as in *Ruyijun zhuan*, *Jin Ping Mei*, and other fiction. Sexually explicit fiction tends to exploit such

18. For Roy's translation, see 2.27.144.

19. For Roy's translations, see 2.38.388 and 4.79.635. The expression *mo leng lu nao* (79.1142) again occurs here.

arousal for its sensationalism. Graphic and grotesque details are inherent in that effect.

The Sounds of Sex

Another realm that is subject to pornographic sensationalism is the sound of sex, which includes what others overhear or spy upon. The passage in *Jin Ping Mei* that takes the sound of a woman giving fellatio to a man and compares it to the sound of a flute stands at one end of the spectrum, creating a double entendre with the term for fellatio, "playing the flute" (17.208). With tongue in cheek, the author strives for a mock-sublime effect. At the other, more graphic end, he describes the woman's moaning, as in the early scene in which monks overhear Ximen Qing and Pan Jinlian having sex: "Her voice was trembling and soft; she sighed and moaned, panted and groaned" (顫聲柔氣，呻呻吟吟，哼哼唧唧, 8.104).[20] Nothing grotesque appears in this description except the background image of the bald monks listening lustfully. Her trembling voice and moans cannot but come off as a tender, sensual image. In the scene of Ximen Qing and Pan Jinlian having sex in the bath, "the sounds coming from her mouth were more wonderful than words can describe, like the twitter of swallows and murmurs of orioles" (口中燕語鶯聲，百般難述). In this case, the metaphors of bird sounds place her moans on a high erotic plane.[21] But *Jin Ping Mei* does not stay consistently at that level. The sound of orioles and swallows comes soon after the description of the sounds the partners make in the bath, which are "just like crabs mucking around in the mud" (其聲如泥中螃蟹一般, 29.380). In two other scenes, the sounds of thrusting are "like a school of loaches plunging through

20. Roy, 1.8.167, his translation (slightly modified).

21. The same reference to orioles appears in a late Ming *xiangyan* poem by Min Zhengzhong, who refers to "the murmur of the orioles" (*yingsheng* 鶯聲) that is heard from "deep within the covers" (*beidi* 被底), in "Quivering Breath behind Bed Curtains after the Lamp Is Turned off" ("Deng hun hou zhangzhong weichuan 燈昏後帳中微喘), in *Meiren shi*, 20. See the translation of the poem in Li Xiaorong, *Poetics and Politics*, 133–134. Elsewhere in *Jin Ping Mei*, oriole sounds appear in the midst of graphic description (52.676).

the mud" (如數鰍行泥淖中相似, 27.355), a variation of the image in *Ruyijun zhuan*, which has "bulls stampeding in the mud."[22] Crabs and loaches are variations on snails, evoking the intensity of arousal with a tinge of the grotesque.[23]

An unmistakably negative and grotesque tone emerges in a description of sexual waters in a scene about unwanted sex. When Meng Yulou sees Ximen Qing put on his clasp, she says, "Just as I thought! You think of nothing but this lowly act" (我說你行行就下道兒來了). He starts thrusting vigorously until her secretions begin to flow so loudly that it sounds like "a dog licking up slops" (如狗舔糨子一般, 75.1053).[24] She finally tells him that she has been unwell lately, suffering from a "white discharge"—using the same words that appeared in the scene with Wang Liu'er, who preferred not to reveal her disorder and insisted on maintaining the appearance of enjoyment.

Other descriptions of the sounds of sex have to do with what others nearby hear. Ximen Qing's affairs are for everyone to see, no matter how indecent. In fact, he expects his supposed indecency always to be permitted. His affair with Wang Liu'er is especially visible since it is an open adultery that the husband and wife manage for the sake of earning profit from Ximen Qing. The house on Lion Street where Wang Liu'er lives is in effect a one-customer brothel in which the wife is both madam and prostitute. Although Ximen Qing's wives do not at first know about the affair, the servants do who escort Ximen Qing to the house and help prepare the food and room for him and Wang Liu'er. Two scenes of people spying on the partners use the same seven characters: "he was banging away at her so hard that it shook the entire room" (搧打的連聲响喨). *Feida* (搧打) is a vulgar slang expression that is similar to the English words "bang" or "ram," and here it takes on a note of ribaldry. Especially with someone (in the first case, a child) looking on from a hidden position, sexual acts take on the air of an antic comedy. It is as if the actors are laboring at sex, noisily colliding, breathing heavily, and shaking the

22. That is, 其聲猶數牛行泥淖中 (*Ruyijun zhuan*, 45). The same expression containing crabs also occurs in the novel *Yiqing zhen* 怡情陣 (Jiangxi yeren 江西野人, *Yiqing zhen*, SWXHB, vol. 22, 2.23).

23. The same images appear in the *cihua* edition's description of Ximen Qing having sex with Lady Lin (JPMCH, 78.2456) but are omitted in the Chongzhen edition (78.1116).

24. Roy, 4.75.484, his translation.

bed and floor around them. The first of the two scenes is presented from the point of view of Little Iron Rod (Xiaotiegun'er 小鐵棍兒), the young son of Yizhangqing (一丈青), who looks through a crack in the wall to see Ximen Qing "banging away" and "lunging back and forth, for what had to be hundreds of times, ramming so hard that it shook the entire room. Their huffing and panting and bouncing around made it sound as if they were going to break the bed. The noise could be heard all over the house" (一進一退往來搧打，何止數百回,搧打的連聲响喨，其喘息之聲，往來之勢，猶賽折床一般，無處不聽見, 42.546). The boy is so absorbed that he does not notice the arrival of his mother, who grabs him by the tuft of his hair and drags him away. Similarly in the second scene, a young man, Hu Xiu 胡秀, spies on the same pair through a crack in the wall, when they are "right in the middle of it" (*zheng gande hao* 正干得好). They are in a well-lit room in which he can "see them clearly and distinctly" (*lingling lili kanjian* 伶伶俐俐看見) as Ximen Qing suspends Wang Liu'er's legs from the bed frame and "bangs away so hard that it shakes the entire room."[25] The vocal calls of lovers in the midst of sexual frenzy are another of the common sound effects. In this scene, "every word imaginable came out of her mouth" (口裡百般言語都叫將出來, 61.807). In another scene, Chunmei discovers the maid Qiuju peeking through a crack, listening to Ximen Qing and Pan Jinlian having sex and hearing "all their cries and calls, every possible sound that they made" (怎的作聲喚，口中呼叫甚麼, 78.1128).

In still other scenes, no actual listener is present, but the effect is similar, making it seem as if the partners are in public for everyone to witness their actions. The author recreates the cacophony of sex and the blunt sounds that come from skin slapping against skin. In a session between Ximen Qing and Pan Jinlian in which he insists on anal intercourse, she wants him to hurry and finish because of the burning pain that it causes her.[26] He asks her to "call out *dada* to me in your sexy way" (浪浪的叫着達達), which, he says, "will make your *dada* cum" (哄出你達達㞞兒來罷).[27] She complies with "all manner of tender and amorous words, impossible to describe" (口中艷聲柔語，百般難述), until "Ximen Qing feels himself on the verge. Grabbing her thighs he rams her with all his might, slapping

25. "Clearly and distinctly" are from Roy, 4.61.9.

26. The pain is such that, when he draws himself out, "a bloody red stain shows on his stalk" (*xinghong ran jing* 猩紅染莖, 52.676).

27. The word for "cum" (*song* 㞞) occurs in only one other passage, when Dai'an mocks the servant Huatong 畫童, Ximen Qing's catamite (50.644).

against her skin and making an endless racket. The woman lay beneath him moaning steadily, helpless to make him stop" (西門慶覺精來，兩手扳其股，極力而𢶍之，扣股之聲响之不絶．那婦人在下邊呻吟成一塊，不能禁止, 52.676). In a session between Ximen Qing and Ruyi, the sounds they make "in the quiet of the night could be heard many rooms away" (夜靜時分，其聲遠聆數室, 67.911). Again, Ximen Qing's affairs are for everyone to see and hear; no one would think of stopping him.

The Woman's Gate

The fact that the graphic mode is about the raw sights and sounds of sex goes along with the fact that the wanton woman is at the center of its portrayals and that her "woman's gate" is more exposed here than anywhere else. At the same time, the exposure goes only so far and occurs only rarely. Going only so far has to do with the words and images that the author employs, the most vulgar appearing only in Ximen Qing's little dialogue with Ruyi. Even there it is not part of the description of her body. Instead, it is the word Ximen Qing uses when he takes on the role of the master of another man's woman, as he does when with Ruyi (78.1121). Otherwise, as I have said, the author reserves such words for when characters swear and mock, as when Pan Jinlian refers disparagingly to other women. In short, the crudest word for vagina is for expressing crude truth and raw anger and passion, but not for referring to the organ in explicit descriptions of sexual pleasure and acts. Angry at Yueniang for favoring the baby Guange and treating him as if he were the "heir apparent" (*taizi* 太子), Pan Jinlian says to Meng Yulou, "whatever we do, she just opens those two cunt-hole eyes of hers and starts yelling at us" (行動就睁着兩個屄窟窿喓喝人, 31.403).[28] When a bracelet goes missing and Ximen Qing wants to have all the maidservants searched, Pan Jinlian says that it is ridiculous for him to do so and that "if they don't laugh at you with their mouths, they'll laugh at you through their cunts" (口裏不笑, 屄眼裏笑, 43.553).[29]

28. Roy, 2.31.229, his translation (slightly modified).

29. Roy, 3.43.46, his translation. Other cases include Pan Jinlian's cursing Yueniang ("she should stop talking through her cunt" [没的扯那屄淡, 75.1043; Roy, 4.75.468, his translation]). See also Pan Jinlian's swearing at Ximen Qing, using "fuck" and "cock"

It is an aesthetic choice for the author to refrain from using such words when describing sexual pleasure and acts. In doing so he roughly follows the tradition of the art of the bedchamber, which uses only the most elegant terms. In the art of the bedchamber, the woman's body comes under minute scrutiny, but it is for the sake of instruction and elucidation—though titillation is also part of the picture. The texts use terms such as "red pearl" for clitoris or "zither strings" for the first inch inside the vagina. *Jin Ping Mei* uses a narrower range of terms, but it nevertheless stays within the realm of euphemism and avoids the crudity of *bi* (cunt 屄). The novel's common term for vagina is "woman's gate" (*pinhu* 牝户). Sometimes it uses "the gate of yin" (*yinhu* 陰户) or the "woman's channel" (*pinkou* 牝口). As with the words for penis, both require an effort to translate into English. "Vagina" sounds too clinical, and "mons veneris" has become too rare; "vulva" and "mount of Venus" can sometimes suffice. The novel also uses the expression "flower's heart," which I take to stand for the so-called shallow (*qian*) part of the vagina, while "red hook" and "chicken tongue" stand for the clitoris. It calls the place deep inside the woman the "vagina chamber." But regardless of the terms or tones used, the narrative eye of *Jin Ping Mei* is on the woman's genitals in a more lurid way than anywhere in the art of the bedchamber or *xiangyan* poetry, as the scene above with Ruyi illustrates.

Besides the scenes with Ruyi and Zheng Aiyue, and the one with Pan Jinlian in the grape arbor, only two other instances describe the vagina, but both do so without naming it and without portraying it in a scene of sexual action. Instead, the description is of the way it appeals to the lustful male observer, who imagines in the first case what it is like under the woman's clothes, and who in the second case looks at her when she is naked beside him. In the first instance, the author uses a ribald set piece, a slight variant of which appears in the earlier *Shuihu zhuan*. This is the scene in which Ximen Qing meets Pan Jinlian for the first time, a meeting the author represents in a description that follows Ximen Qing's eyes as he looks at her from head to toe and finally arrives at her

(51.664), and insulting her mother: "You can hold on to that old cunt between your legs and get going" (你明日夹着那老屄走, 58.764; Roy, 3.58.442, his translation). It is similar in the case of the vulgar word for the male genitals, which Pan Jinlian once uses to curse Li Ping'er (18.228).

"voluptuous breasts and white lush thighs" (肉妳妳胸兒, 白生生腿兒). The author then says: "And there is yet something else, a place that is tight and firm, red and plush, white and fresh, dark and yielding, who can say what it might be?" (更有一件緊揪揪, 紅縐縐, 白鮮鮮, 黑裀裀, 正不知是甚麽東西).[30] In spite of the luridly onlooking eye, the tongue-in-cheek tone of the passage produces an overall tone that avoids being crude or degrading. The man is eagerly, but not rapaciously, aroused by what he sees.

The second instance occurs in their second sexual encounter and consists of a pair of doggerel verses about the genitals of first Ximen Qing then Pan Jinlian. In seven words per line, they are parodies of regulated verse, both evoking the same kind of ribaldry and satire as in the set piece above. Ximen Qing is first, who: "has a thing long in length, sometimes gentle and soft, sometimes hard and stiff. When soft it is like a fallen drunkard; when hard it is like a madly careening monk. It is a skilled traveler in the lands of Vulva and Venus; its home is in the Province of the Loins, just under the navel. He takes his two sons wherever he goes, wherever he fights with his gorgeous foes" (一物從來六寸長, 有時柔軟有時剛. 軟如醉漢東西倒, 硬似風僧上下狂. 出牝入陰爲本事, 腰州臍下作家鄉. 天生二子隨身便, 曾與佳人鬪幾場, 4.60).[31]

A sharper contrast with the bulging, engorged monster of the later descriptions cannot be imagined. The portrait of Pan Jinlian follows, when the partners are already naked in bed. While the first part of the passage echoes the set piece from the first time he sees her, the second part adopts the same style of regulated verse in seven words per line that described Ximen Qing, who:

> found her woman's gate completely devoid of hair, like a risen bun, fresh and fragrant and plump to fullness. Soft and yielding, it was red and full of folds, like a fruit-filled treat just out of the steamer. It was truly a thing of beauty, loved by thousands, craved by millions:

30. JPMCH, 2.53. The Chongzhen edition leaves out *hong zhouzhou* 紅縐縐 (2.35). See also *Shuihu quanzhuan*, 44.723 (更有一件窄湫湫, 緊搊搊, 紅鮮鮮, 黑稠稠, 正不知是甚麼東西). A similar set piece, but without passages on privates, can be found in Feng Menglong, *Gujin xiaoshuo* (36.6b).

31. "Province of the Loins" is from Roy, 1.4.90–91.

Warm and tight, fragrant and dry, as tasty as lotus root. Soft and supple, it never fails to delight.
When happy it sticks out its tongue and breaks into a joyful smile; when tired it takes a nap and snuggles by the thighs.
It performs its duties in the County of Crotch, making its home in a garden next to a grassy edge.
When chancing upon a handsome and romantic lad, it rushes to battle with no need for words.
(西門慶摸見牝户上並無毳毛, 猶如白馥馥, 鼓蓬蓬發酵的饅頭, 軟濃濃, 紅縐縐出籠的果餡, 眞個是千人愛萬人貪一件美物:
溫緊香乾口賽蓮, 能柔能軟最堪憐.
喜時吐舌開顏笑, 困便隨身貼股眠.
肉襠縣裡爲家業, 薄草涯邊是故園.
若遇風流輕俊子, 等閑戰鬪不開言, 4.60–61).[32]

Thus begins the affair of the two central characters, who are presented as if accompanied by two other characters in the form of a pair of retainers, their penis and vagina. If the tone of these passages were to predict the rest of the book, the reader could imagine that what follows are only rousing meetings between two partners who were fitly matched.

Comic doggerels such as these exemplify a mode that combines both high erotic and graphic, though it is closer to the latter. The tongue-in-cheek tone parodies the style of high literature, using seven-word verses to describe organs ever ready to join in charming battle. A late Ming poem by Min Zhengzhong in regulated verse, called "Her Private Place Rises Like a Mound" ("Sichu fen qi," 私處墳起), is a contrasting example of finely crafted high eroticism in the *xiangyan* style. It is a rare instance of explicit reference in a kind of poetry, regulated verse, that usually would never address such a topic.

To look at, soft and smooth, all free of blemish;
To go inside, lush with spring, and fragrant as orchid and musk.
Like a pearl, the fragile pistil rests against ribboned sides,
Like a piece of jade, the flowered terrace hides under silky skirt.
From afar he knows the River Wei's flow, fragrant and sweet;

32. The differences between the Chongzhen and *cihua* editions are minor. See JPMCH, 4.106–107. "Warm and tight, fragrant and dry" is from Roy, 1.2.91.

They meet at Mt. Wu where they make clouds and rain.
Do not wonder whether the peony has yet to bloom,
Wait for the midnight dew, which is for the asking, Lord of the East.
(看來柔滑淨無紋
就裏藏春蘭麝芬.
嬌蕊似珠低繡帶,
花臺如玉臥羅裙.
遙知渭水流香膩,
會見巫峰出雲雨.
莫怪牡丹猶未發,
三更垂露問東君).[33]

The descriptions of Ximen Qing and Pan Jinlian are also in regulated verse, but in the form of easy-to-read doggerel that resembles in tone the erotic folk songs that Feng Menglong collected later in the Ming. In contrast, Min's poem is reticent, refined, and reverent. "Fragile pistil" drastically contrasts with "red hook" and "chicken tongue" and is a degree finer than "flower's heart." "Ribboned sides" contrasts with "dark like the wings of a bat." The image of sexual waters hides inside the allusion to the River Wei's flow: the river is an image that was long associated with feminine beauty, though its association with sexual fluids is unique to this poem (legend says that the river is filled with the powder and rouge of palace women). Mt. Wu 巫 refers to the legend of the tryst between the king of Chu 楚 and the goddess of the mountain.[34] "Dew" is a gentle, suggestive reference to semen. The Lord of the East stands for the sun. Nothing quite like Min's poem appears in *Jin Ping Mei*, whose high erotic passages do not aspire to such elegance and refinement. Under the novel's pornographic eye, sexual love can never be so rarefied and ideal. The graphic mode wants ferocity and precipitousness, as does the mode of sex as battle. In the graphic mode, Ximen Qing's penis "slaps and splashes" (*shanpeng* 搧硼, 67.911), "leaps and gallops, beats and pounds" (*xian teng gu dao* 掀騰鼓擣, 78.1116), and "rubs and grinds" (*rouca* 揉擦, 79.1142). Such is the essence of the novel's graphic portrayal.

33. Min Zhengzhong, *Meiren shi*, 26–27; and Li Xiaorong, *Poetics and Politics*, 130–131, her translation (slightly modified). The Lord (or Master) of the East also appears in JPMCH, 78.2469.

34. See Li Xiaorong, *Poetics and Politics*, 131.

Conclusion: Going to Excess

Jin Ping Mei's moral and didactic position, especially as expressed in narrative asides and poetic interludes, is that the sexual adventures of Ximen Qing, Pan Jinlian, and others belong to the sphere of destructive, dissipating behavior in which the self wastes itself; violates the welfare of the family; and risks illness, injury, and even death. The novel delivers such judgments in both pronounced and unpronounced ways. Its use of the noises and sights of sex is a good example of how it passes judgment instead of—or in addition to—doing so through direct pronouncement. The noises and sights of Ximen Qing and his partners make it seem as if they are performing in public for everyone to witness, as I have said, and as if they expect those witnesses to accept and condone what they do. In other words, Ximen Qing assumes the privilege of having unrestrained sex without hindrance or punishment. He is the local powerful man, to cross whom can be dangerous and to please whom can be profitable.

But as with the other types of description, something else is going on. The author has his rules, but he also ignores them. The main rule, I think, is the same one that applies in the case of the high erotic: the author will not explicitly portray ideal lovers having sex. The use of the graphic mode proves this point most strongly. It is the mode for ramming and banging and for the extreme close-up, as the act unfolds before the reader's eyes. The engorged, drug-induced, and relentlessly thrusting man and the moaning, writhing, and richly flooding woman are the center of attention, along with her pain and discomfort. The sexual organs are more exposed than in any other type of description. The something else that is going on (the overflow of meaning that I have referred to) is the fact that the author in any case is still engaged in creating an aesthetics of the sexual act. The high erotic is not the only way to do so. As ugly and vulgar as the graphic mode may sometimes be, it is not only so. And the ugly and vulgar have something to contribute as well. The fact that the characters portrayed in this mode always include the wanton woman and the fact that graphic sex is raw and precipitous seem to contradict the sense of aestheticizing the sexual act, but the graphic mode can be said to have its own aesthetic—though it has to make do in the realm of what must be characterized as base excess. In that realm, the graphic and vulgar serve as ways of getting at the raw core of sexual sensuality. Making do in that realm has to do with the fact that the author will not or cannot portray ideal lovers in such an explicit way. Ideal lovers must reside somewhere else, where desire supposedly does not drive them to such extremes. As Mark Stevenson says, "Non-transgressive sexuality is, by definition, not to be seen or heard by other parties."[35] Once it is seen, it is transgressive. Although little trace of the art of the bedchamber can be found in *Jin Ping Mei*, the novel still follows its basic principle: ideal lovers do not go to excess. A parallel principle applies here as well, which has to do with the ancient trope of the ineffability of truth. High truth cannot be spoken about except in hidden ways. High pleasure cannot be described directly and graphically, and it does not go to extremes. This principle is also a moral one. As daring as the author is in his flaunting of obscenity, he still follows the rule that the lascivious person must be portrayed in a darker light. It is just that his darkness is not governed by as stern a god as that of his censors. While using the thematic framework that condemns Ximen Qing and his wanton women for their dissipation, the author will nevertheless explore and describe the world of desire in its state of overwhelming and even unbearable excitation, while at times lending such portrayals a degree of raw and provocative beauty.

35. Stevenson, "Sound, Space and Moral Soundscapes," 289.

CHAPTER 6

Different Sex with Different Women

Keeping Him Sexual, Keeping Him Listening

Jin Ping Mei portrays sex differently depending upon the woman Ximen Qing is with. So far I have made distinctions in types of portrayal in terms of language and imagery, but only partly in terms of the situational differences between the women.[1] Such differences have to do with a variety of distinguishing features, including social status; wealth; and personal traits such as looks, character, and talent. Each person takes advantage of the options available to her, whether her status is that of main wife, concubine, servant, or courtesan, for example—statuses that can be divided into subtypes, such as remarried widow and courtesan turned concubine. The different ways the women interact with the polygamous philanderer are affected by the specific situations and characters of each woman, including such things as whether she has a chance of bearing a son or has whiter skin than someone else, or how clever she is in speech. For instance, Pan Jinlian is a concubine who lives in Ximen Qing's compound, and thus she has the advantage of knowing more about his affairs than Wang Liu'er, an extramarital lover who lives separately and who relies on rawer sex than Pan Jinlian to retain Ximen Qing's attention (what "raw" means will become clear below). Lacking the advantages of

1. I referred to these in chapter 1 using the term "situational complexities" from Ding (*Obscene Things*, xx, xxi, and 137).

high status and wealth that Wu Yueniang, Meng Yulou, and Li Ping'er enjoy, Pan Jinlian and Wang Liu'er are more reliant on keeping Ximen Qing sexually interested than other women are. In short, they want to keep him sexual. In the language of the novel, they are among the most "wanton women," and as such are portrayed as most enjoying sex, most desiring it, and most willing to please Ximen Qing sexually, even if at times he makes them suffer. Their examples support the notion that, in simplest terms, the rawest sex in *Jin Ping Mei* involves the women who most rely on it to gain favor.

To make sense of the notion of keeping him sexual, consider the words of Dame Wang (Wang Po 王婆) when she says that Pan Jinlian "is like a dog who can't stop eating shit—she has no way to change" (只當狗改不了吃屎, 86.1231). She says this just after hearing about Pan Jinlian's affair with Chen Jingji. Reacting to Pan Jinlian's affair with Dame Wang's son, the Chongzhen commentator says, "whether old or young, rude or refined, high or low, there is no one she [Pan Jinlian] won't try" (老的少的, 村的俏的, 貴的賤的, 皆有所遇, 86.1233). Lest such characterizations be taken purely as assertions of the base insatiability of the "wanton woman," we should also think in terms of sexual opportunism, which consists of the tactics through which a woman such as Pan Jinlian seeks survival and gain by commanding a man's attention and affections, though she takes risks and suffers consequences in terms of both her individual destiny and the condemnation and suspicion that she receives from others. Moreover, sexual opportunism is far from being merely sexual. In Pan Jinlian's case, she also keeps Ximen Qing listening, which means engaging him with words. Clearly, the strongest user of words in the novel is Pan Jinlian. As reliant upon her sexual appeal as she may be, she excels all others in terms of her talents of speech.[2]

Both keeping the man sexual and keeping him listening are closely related to the fact that each woman, as I just said, has a range of particular options—which for convenience I call situational differences. Each can strive for gain or suffer loss depending on those differences. A bond servant or concubine can be summarily sold off, but it is harder to divorce a main wife, as the episode about Chen Jingji's trying to divorce

2. See Ding, *Obscene Things*, xx (on sexual opportunism) and 184 and 206 (on speaking talents).

Ximen Dajie 西門大姐 shows. Women gain from their liaisons with Ximen Qing, but not to the same degree. Sun Xue'e begins as a maid and rises to concubine. But she is from his earlier days, when he was not as wealthy or successful. Having once appealed to Ximen Qing because of the whiteness of her skin, she later sinks into the background, assumes the role of cook, and rarely receives his visits. During one of those visits, she hastily cleans up her humble quarters, which the reader sees for the first time. And the author says simply, "Of their night together, we give no details" (*yisu wuhua* 一宿無話, 58.751). Sex with her is not important in advancing the story; she is no longer able to keep him sexual. Others notice her happiness the next day, since it is an honor for the master to have visited her (58.757). But it is a brief moment with hardly any follow-up: Ximen Qing sees her two more times, the last when he is ailing and goes to her for a massage (78.1118).[3] Nevertheless, her lack of favor allows her a measure of distance. Resentment at her bad luck fuels her rivalry with Pan Jinlian and Chunmei and instills in her a sense of liberty, which allows her to involve herself in an adulterous relationship in the hope of starting a new life—though her plan fails miserably. Given her lot in the household, staying loyal to Ximen Qing has no practical use to her.

Sun Xue'e is one of many women who break the rules of elite morality. Depending upon the women's conditions, some are more likely than others to break the rules. According to that morality and its legal system, an adulterous woman is subject to divorce and even killing if she is caught in the act. Social custom further dictates that a widowed woman should not consider remarriage, though legally she is permitted to do so. But under certain circumstances, even women with higher status will decide to ignore such rules. This is the case for the rich neighbor's wife, Li Ping'er, who is not satisfied with her husband but who is wealthy from her current and former marriages, and whose wealth allows her to consider an advantageous adultery—even if it means descending from main wife to concubine. Another rich young wife, the newly widowed Meng Yulou, will decide for herself whether to remarry (and if so, who her husband will be), and she no longer listens to the demands of relatives. She too will descend from main wife to concubine, but she will gain a foothold in a wealthy, up-and-coming household, in which her status will allow her to

3. The narrative gives no details about the other visit (76.1080).

maintain a certain independence and stay out of harm. Pan Jinlian, the wife of a poor, runtish, and therefore easily cuckolded man, will stand at the door watching passersby, hoping to advance her lot by attracting a better-off man. The wife of a household retainer sees in the rich polygamist an opportunity for advancement and calculates with her husband the advantages of becoming the rich man's mistress: this is the case of Wang Liu'er, the wife who prostitutes herself to Ximen Qing. A servant's wife chances to meet Ximen Qing in a secluded spot, he immediately proposes sex to her, and she accepts, sure to gain in wealth and status because he never fails to reward his sexual partners generously: this is what happens with both Song Huilian and Ben the Fourth. The other rich young widow, Lady Lin (originally the main wife of a high official) remains a widow and does not compromise herself by getting remarried, but she will enjoy herself with the handsome and virile Ximen Qing (and other men she periodically selects), who will in addition do her the favor of protecting her son from unsavory friends. Finally, the family's wet nurse, Ruyi, reckons that Ximen Qing's attraction to her will give her a permanent foothold in the household, though like all the other women she must keep an eye on rivals—especially the most dangerous of them, Pan Jinlian.

The situational differences of each woman also translate into quantifiable terms such as numerical rank in the family and price in silver when she is bought into the household or sold out of it. Each concubine has a numerical rank, which with the exception of Sun Xue'e depends on the order of entry into the household. Such rank has bearing in terms of seating order at gatherings, for example, or order of greeting when guests arrive, but it has little to do with a woman's standing in terms of such things as wealth and favor with Ximen Qing. Li Ping'er, for instance, is last (number six) but is his sentimental favorite. The ones who enter the household with wealth, such as Meng Yulou and Li Ping'er, differ vastly from Pan Jinlian, the daughter of a commoner who had only a few sticks of furniture when she entered and who had been a bond servant. The courtesan is in yet another category: if she becomes a concubine, she has to be purchased from her brothel. This is the case of Li Jiao'er. She gathers wealth while in the household, all along retaining ties to her brothel, and she is readily sold to another man when Ximen Qing dies, achieving a higher price (the large sum of three hundred taels) than before because of having once belonged to a powerful rich man. She is the first to steal from Wu Yueniang after Ximen Qing dies, when it is clear that her stay in the household is ending. Her life with Ximen Qing, the man who pays a great sum to deflower her, is in effect a long-term rental. Had she not been murdered, Pan Jinlian would also have sold for a high price because of the advantage of having been Ximen Qing's concubine, which allows Dame Wang to drive a tough bargain when trying to sell her, though she can only get as high as a hundred taels—but then Wu Song murders both Pan Jinlian and Dame Wang.[4]

Some characters are more accepting of their lot than others. Pan Jinlian is an example of one who tries aggressively to make the most of the hand she has been dealt, if not even to evade her lot or radically change it. Although reality tells her that she cannot become a main wife, she will try to become one in a de facto sense by creating strife between Ximen Qing and Wu Yueniang and in general trying to increase her importance. As someone who comes from a poor commoner family and who was sold twice as a bond servant before becoming Ximen Qing's concubine, she knows she cannot compare with the concubines Meng Yulou and Li Ping'er, who brought great wealth with them when they entered Ximen Qing's household—making him a considerably richer man. In entering his house, Pan Jinlian turns from the main wife of a poor man into the concubine of a rich one. In contrast to Meng Yulou and Li Ping'er, she must rely entirely on her "looks and talent"—that is, she must rely on the master to "favor" her (*chong* 寵).[5] Meng Yulou and Li Ping'er are more accepting of the reality of their lives than Pan Jinlian, who strives to be the most emotionally and sexually intimate with Ximen Qing. She knows best how to read his mind, manipulate him, and defy and even mock him.

4. Other prices are as follows: In the beginning, Pan Jinlian is sold for thirty taels to Zhang, a merchant. To deflower Li Guijie, Ximen Qing pays fifty taels (11.138), and he later rents her for twenty taels per month (20.261). Chen Jingji buys Feng Jinbao 馮金寶 for a hundred taels (92.1303). In contrast, maids usually sell for under ten taels, as in the cases of Song Huilian (who sells for five taels; 22.284) and Sun Xue'e (whom the vengeful Chunmei buys for eight taels and sends directly to the kitchen; 90.1285).

5. Tian Xiaofei, *Qiushui tang*, 29 and 40, respectively.

The Lot of Pan Jinlian, Core Sexual Companion

The evidence for Pan Jinlian's wanting to be the most important wife comes from her attempts to control Ximen Qing, for example by getting him to visit her rather than someone else or by challenging his authority. An instance of the latter occurs when she disagrees with his lenient treatment of Song Huilian and persuades him to change his mind (25.325). Pan Jinlian has a dominating sense of self-possession that she expresses in open forms of irreverence, as when she scorns Ximen Qing for mourning Li Ping'er. "Who knows where people go after they die" (人也不知死到哪裡去), Pan Jinlian says, mocking him for putting on such a show of compassion and reverence (73.1018). She has little respect for filial piety—in particular in terms of her mother, who sold her twice as a bond servant. She once rudely dismisses her, saying: "You can hold on to that old cunt between your legs and get going."[6] It is the power of words that distinguishes her the most from the other women and allows her to survive: what Wu Yueniang calls her "strong tongue" (*zuiqiang* 嘴强) or "that mouth of yours" (*ni zheige zuitouzi* 你這個嘴頭子, 43.554). These comments come just after a remarkable argument with Ximen Qing, in which Pan Jinlian outtalks him to the point that he "just can't get the better of her" (*nai he ta buguo* 奈何他不過). Wu Yueniang warns Pan Jinlian that she just risked a severe beating: "Don't you know that the male of the species has dog's hair growing on his face?! Yet there you go as careless as could be, arguing ruthlessly with him as if nothing else mattered!" (漢子家臉上有狗毛，不知好歹，只顧下死手的和他纏起來了, 43.555).[7]

The argument occurs in a scene that contains a classic example of Pan Jinlian's unique manner of speaking, which makes her most stand out among all characters in the novel and which can be characterized by its rapidity and convolutedness. It is remarkable that the author can produce its splendid, tumbling effect. In this scene a bracelet goes missing, and Ximen Qing wants to have all the maidservants searched. He becomes

6. Roy, 3.58.442, his translation. Later Pan Jinlian refuses to help her mother pay for her sedan chair (78.1123).

7. "The male of the species . . . on his face" is from Roy, 3.43.49. On the kind of equality that exists between Pan Jinlian and Ximen Qing, see Tian Xiaofei, *Qiushui tang*, 40.

enraged when Pan Jinlian says that it is ridiculous for him to have them searched. As he holds her down and raises his fist to strike her, she cries out, "You always single me out for abuse" (只欺負的是我), and then she proceeds to taunt and insult him: "What is holding you back? Go ahead and beat me. No matter how hard you beat me, I'm sure you'd never leave me for dead. And if I died, you'd better worry about my frail mother siccing herself on you" (那箇攔着你手兒哩不成? 你打不是的. 我隨你怎麼打, 難得只打得有這口氣兒在着. 若沒了, 愁我家那病媽媽子不問你要人). No matter how powerful he is, she continues, her mother would fight him all the way. "So what if you are a battalion commander with his own yamen. You're nothing but a poor indebted official with a ratty old silk cap" (你說你是衙門裏千户便怎的? 無故只是個破紗帽債殼子窮官罷了). At this, Ximen Qing breaks out in laughter and calls her a "splay-legged whore" (*xiao wailagu'er* 小歪剌骨兒), which incites Pan Jinlian to utter a remark that perfectly captures her talent at repartee: "'How can you call me a splay-legged whore?' And, lifting up her leg, she said, 'Look at your little lady's leg, what's there crooked about it?!'" (你怎的叫我是歪剌骨來! 因蹺起一隻脚來. 你看老娘這脚, 那些兒放着歪?!).[8] Suddenly taking him literally, her riposte has the effect of hollowing out the meaning of his words. Seeing that he cannot get the better of her, he simply leaves and goes off to an engagement (43.553–554). The Chongzhen commentator provides a penetrating yet admiring analysis: "These few words of hers show a refusal to back down that bears just a hint of the coquette, but also a seriousness that still carries a bit of mockery. Combine a bit of crazy jealousy, another bit of guileless guts, and yet another bit of merciless harangue—without these she would never succeed in reacting so readily and slipping through like this. Jinlian is truly wonderful!" (數語倔強中實含軟媚. 認真處微帶戲謔, 非有二十分奇妒, 二十分呆膽, 二十分靈心利口, 不能當機圓活如此. 金蓮眞可人也, 43.553–554).

An ancient trope in China is the lament of the spurned official, who speaks the truth to the leader who refuses to listen and rejects him. Pan Jinlian has the same fearlessness in saying the truth, no matter what the consequences—though in terms of gender and station in life, she is far

8. "Splay-legged whore" is from Roy, 3.43.47. *Wailagu* is a slang insult referring to a lowly, shrewish, and disreputable woman. Pan Jinlian literalizes the word *wai*, meaning both "crooked" and "devious."

from having any resemblance to a Qu Yuan 屈原 or other such person. Her skill with words helps keep her afloat, especially when it comes to her sense of resentment, which compels her to refute Wu Yueniang when the latter once advises her: "We [wives] are just pieces of dumb goods, who can never suit his wishes. Just let him say whatever he will and forget about it" (你我本等是遲貨, 應不上他的心. 隨他說去罷了, 73.1016). Pan Jinlian replies: "That's impossible. If I don't go after him, what he says puts us down too much. I mean, we have no way of getting over our resentment" (不是, 咱不說他, 他說出來的話灰人的心. 只說人憤不過他).[9] She is reacting to his recent lament, which she overheard and now recalls to him: that since Li Ping'er's death, he has not had a single bite of decent food. Jinlian adds a reference to his affair with Ruyi, whom he might as well raise to concubine, she says sarcastically, and she concludes with a type of slang insult that is characteristic of her, calling him "a thieving piece of a shameless house wrecker" (賊沒廉恥撒根基的貨, 73.1017).[10] Hearing this, he jumps up and tries to kick her, but she runs away.

Pan Jinlian's lot is to live in a zone of dependence and forced abjection. As a master of a household, Ximen Qing is free to beat, whip, and kick her, though she can run away if possible and wait until his anger passes. Within this zone, she holds fast to her place as Ximen Qing's core sexual partner, a position that she retains by being the one with whom he has sex the most steadily, starting with the first scene of sexual description in the novel. A key sign of this position is the fact that she is the one with whom he stores his bag of sex tools (*yinqi bao* 淫器包). Though Wu Yueniang is the one who stores money and other treasures, Pan Jinlian is the keeper of that which, besides the monk's drug, supplies Ximen Qing with that without which he does not have sex. She resents his taking this bag to use with other women, as once when she discovers that he took it to Li Ping'er's. When he visits her later, Pan washes herself, applies rouge to her lips, and takes a breath sweetener, but after a little while of sex, she refers to the bag and uses the most vulgar words possible to remind him of her never-disappearing jealousy: "So we are to be fucked by the leftover prick?" (俺每是雌剩髢髢肏的?). Words such as these have their effect not only because Ximen Qing hates for women to be jealous, but also

9. Borrowing from Roy, including the punctuation after *bushi* (不是; 4.73.398).

10. *Sagenji* (撒根基) means to undermine and ruin the foundations of.

because of the words' vulgarity, which as I have said mainly occurs in settings such as these and rarely in the portrayal or act of sex. "And yet you claim not to have favorites," Pan continues (你還說不偏心哩), thus challenging him with the most solid fact that the wife of a polygamist can cite: the polygamist can never avoid the appearance of favoritism, an accusation that never fails to irritate Ximen Qing (51.663–664).

Keeping him aware of the accusation of favoritism is Pan Jinlian's mission, in which others occasionally join. Ximen Qing constantly does what he thinks he can do to quell its appearance, including hiding it whenever possible. Pan Jinlian never stops caring about it. Wu Yueniang, Meng Yulou, and Li Ping'er take it for granted, sometimes grumbling among themselves, as in Yueniang's remarks above. But Pan Jinlian wants to police Ximen Qing.[11] To such an end, she keeps a vigilant eye on all of Ximen Qing's sexual partners, male and female. Anyone who looks as though he or she will mount a challenge becomes a target. When Ximen Qing hints at treating Li Ping'er as if she were a main wife, even after her death, Pan Jinlian leaps at the opportunity to expose him for such a transgression.[12] When Li Ping'er gives birth to her son, Jinlian goes to her own room, closes the door, and weeps. That is a reality she cannot alter, unless she has a son herself—which she later attempts to do by means of a special drug. But she can nevertheless plot to destroy her co-wife, as she eventually succeeds in doing.

Two aspects of the relationship between Pan Jinlian and Ximen Qing most concisely summarize its depth: the fact that, as mentioned above, she can argue with him furiously and at length and get what she wants, and their strenuous and lengthy bouts of sex, which the author portrays in both high and low modes from the beginning to the end of their relationship. In short, of all women in *Jin Ping Mei*, Pan Jinlian enjoys the highest level of verbal and sexual intimacy with Ximen Qing, even if others may exceed her in specific ways. For example, the Chongzhen commentator writes that Wang Liu'er's skill at "hooking him in and leading him on" (*laolong qianwan* 牢籠牽挽) is superior to Pan Jinlian's. But this

11. See Hsia, *Classic Chinese Novel*, 197–198 (on attempted dominance over Ximen Qing).

12. A line from their wedding song refers to Li as if she were a main wife (20.258–259), prompting Yueniang to refer to Li as "that rich girl of his" (他的富貴的姐姐), not "a poor officer's daughter like myself" (窮官兒家丫頭; using Roy's translation for the latter, 1.20.417). A similar instance occurs at Li Ping'er's funeral (63.855–856).

is because she lives "farther away" (*di yuan* 地遠) and so has to use "softer" (*rou* 柔) methods. Pan Jinlian is "nearer" (*di qin* 地親) to Ximen Qing and so can be "more forceful" (*qiang* 強, 61.807). Meng Yulou and Li Ping'er do not have to try as hard, since they enjoy higher status because of their wealth and the social standing they had before their marriage to Ximen Qing. As for Wu Yueniang, besides her social standing as daughter of a battalion commander (*zuowei* 左衛), as main wife she can advise Ximen Qing, make him listen, and even scold and admonish him, as a main wife is expected to do. But she will hardly try to "hook him in," nor will she taunt and insult him, and she does not have the will or patience to argue with him at length. However, she can afford to stop speaking to him. If Pan Jinlian enjoys the highest level of verbal and sexual intimacy with Ximen Qing, it is because she has the will and need, not to mention the ability, to do so. On one occasion, Wu Yueniang refuses to tolerate Pan Jinlian's arguing and bandying with him in front of others and has them break it up (73.1010). As Tian Xiaofei points out, encounters such as this are precisely the sign of their greater intimacy, which Yueniang cannot stand.[13] However many relations with other women Ximen Qing may have, he never fails to come back to Pan Jinlian.

At the beginning of this chapter I used the word "raw" to refer to the type of sex that Ximen Qing has with his most so-called wanton women. Raw sex, in whatever mode it is portrayed, is the type he has with women other than his main wife, Wu Yueniang, or women who are like main wives, Meng Yulou and Li Ping'er after becoming a mother. Just what type of sex that is, and how that circle of women is defined, emerge from two episodes of oral sex. The episodes illustrate the particular nature of the familiarity and openness that exist between Ximen Qing and Pan Jinlian, as long as we avoid taking these words as canceling the status imbalances between them that otherwise exist. The two are constantly at war, but it is an intimate war. Furthermore, what she does to him with her mouth is an integral part of that war, including both the words she directs at him and the mouth that she uses to fellate him (she drinks not only his semen but also, on one occasion, his urine). In the latter episode, the narrator addresses the reader: "In general, the way of the concubine is to rouse and lure the master, using any method possible, and willingly submitting to degradation and humiliation, which she hardly

13. Tian Xiaofei, *Qiushui tang*, 217.

considers shameful" (大抵妾婦之道，鼓惑其夫，無所不至，雖屈身忍辱，殆不爲耻). "A main wife" (*zhengshi zhi qi* 正室之妻, 72.998) would never act in such ways.

Oral sex, as I have said before, is a special act that takes place only with what can be called Ximen Qing's special inner circle of concubines, servants, prostitutes, and illicit lovers (though not Lady Lin)—in other words, his wanton women. The circle begins with its first two members, Pan Jinlian and Li Ping'er, though with the latter it stops after she becomes a mother. Oral sex in the context of *Jin Ping Mei* is a case of the most wanton sex. It is an act between partners familiar with how it should go and for which Ximen Qing uses the familiar term, the duplicated compound "*pinpin*"—which when he asks it of them translates as "take a taste of it" or "taste it for me" ("suck" is not a good translation; that is used for the word *za* 咂, as I make clear below). *Pin*, of course, is a character that consists of a group of three mouths (品), which in regular usage means to taste and evaluate.

It is the aspect of mutual awareness (a kind of complicity) that I want to emphasize in the novel's presentations of oral sex—that is, the aspect in which the women know or are at least subliminally aware of the fact that in doing this with him they are acting as one of a special group of women. In the episode in chapter 61, Ximen Qing has Jinlian do it when she knows that he has just had Wang Liu'er do it. Pan Jinlian lets him know that she has guessed at his secret relationship with Wang Liu'er, which he denies. But she and others saw Wang Liu'er in possession of something that they know he gave her (61.809). Jinlian proceeds to disparage Wang Liu'er's looks, with her "lips daubed so red that they look like a bloody cunt. . . . She is nothing but a wanton bitch, the skin of her face and neck all dark and purple" (搽的那嘴唇鮮紅的—倒相人家那血毴 . . . 一個大紫腔色黑淫婦). The sight of his "yang thing" all soft, still wearing the clasp, spurs another of Jinlian's virtuoso outbursts: "There you go again, you're like a slice of cured duck that's been simmering in a pot, its meat all soft, but its beak as hard as ever" (可又來，你臘鴨子煮到鍋裏—身子兒爛了，嘴頭還硬). That is, though his penis is soft, in denying his relationship with Wang he is "as stiff-tongued as ever" (嘴頭兒還強哩, 61.809–810).[14]

14. "Its beak as hard as ever" is from Roy, 4.61.14–15.

A remark by the Chongzhen commentator captures the notion of complicity that I have just mentioned. They get into bed, he swallows a pill, and he tells her to "taste" him. She responds: "That filthy thing! You want me to suck it for you after it's been ramming the hole of that wanton bitch?! I'd die of disgust at the filth of it!" (好乾淨兒!你在那淫婦窟窿子裡鑽了來，教我替你咂，可不髒殺了我!). While he uses the word *pin* (to taste), she uses the rawer word, *za* (咂, to suck). She tells him to wash his penis, but he refuses. She then takes a piece of cloth to wipe it and begins to fellate him, at which point "its edges [*leng*] swell out, its head leaps up, and it flies into a violent rage" (奢稜跳腦，暴怒起來). The Chongzhen commentator remarks: "Jinlian knows that he's just come from Wang Liu'er's and so she has no choice but to suck him herself. As for Ximen Qing, he knows that Jinlian knows he has just come from Wang Liu'er's, and therefore that he can make it such that she won't dare not to suck him. How well it works! This is how he gets Jinlian to enter the scope of his control!" (金蓮明知其從六兒個中來，不得不咂; 西門慶亦知金蓮知其從六兒個中來，而使之不敢不咂．十分妙用，金蓮入其範圍矣, 61.810–811). She can speak brazenly to him, but it is mainly in the hope of attracting and fixing his attention. As for what the "scope of his control" (*qi fanwei* 其範圍) over her means, it begins with the privilege he enjoys as polygamist in the brute sense that he can openly and licitly have relations with numbers of women. In terms of his relation with Pan Jinlian in particular, it means that he can openly have a secret lover and then compel Jinlian to have sex with him just after he has had sex with that woman, when Jinlian knows that he has, and without washing himself. Such is the ultimate mark of the "scope" (or "sphere") of his control. After she arouses him, he begins thrusting furiously and painfully. She asks him to be easier with her, but he taunts her about being disrespectful. She will be good, she says, but she once more asks him to slow down because her hair is getting messy (61.811). She has no more leeway with him now, the excuse of her hair getting messy not being a powerful enough hook. She can only endure him until he finally tires.

To sum up before moving to Wu Yueniang, Li Ping'er, and others: The complicity between Ximen Qing and his most wanton group of women indicates a sense of both privilege and transgression—his privilege of being such a philanderer and the transgression of plundering other men's women (which also includes his wives' maids). The fact that he denies his relationships with such women (that is, women who are not his openly recognized wives, physically installed in his home) signals that the scope of his activities marks him as a triumphant transgressor, one who claims extra privilege. Another mark of transgression is the kind of sex he has with the wanton women. Oral sex, anal sex, the use of sex tools, burning moxa, and performing hundreds of thrusts in alternating positions all belong to that sphere. As for the women, they belong to the privileged group of Ximen Qing's inner circle of wanton women. They are transgressors in a different sense, trying to outmaneuver both each other and the more socially privileged women, whom they occasionally succeed in defeating.

Finally, another key aspect of this complicity is Ximen Qing's attempts to claim emotional authenticity—that is, genuineness of feeling, no matter for how many partners. At one point he has returned from a trip and asks Pan Jinlian whether she missed him. Yes, she did, she answers, adding that she wept many tears. And how did he feel, she asks. He says, "Even though there are the others in the house, who has any doubt but that my heart yearns for you the most" (這一家雖是有他們,誰不知我在你身上偏多). She scoffs and begins a long complaint, referring to how he abandoned her during his affair with Song Huilian, again after Li Ping'er had her child, and now during his affair with Ruyi (whom she wants him to stop seeing). How can he do that, he replies, noting that anyway Ruyi is nothing but "a lowly servant" (*shouxia ren* 手下人, 72.1002) and hardly a challenge to Jinlian. He will make her kowtow to Jinlian and thereby ensure that Ruyi knows her place. Besides, he confesses, he sleeps with Ruyi for no other reason than that "he can't get over his feelings for Sister Li" (越不過李大姐情, 72.1001–1002). With this last remark, he claims a depth of feeling for someone else besides the one for whom he just claimed depth of feeling. In other words, he automatically presumes that such sincerity should count as an acceptable feeling and (it goes without saying) that he need not hide such a feeling. It is a confession asking not for forgiveness, but instead for unquestioning acceptance and sympathy.

It is impossible for Pan Jinlian to have complete monopoly over Ximen Qing and become his only lover, though that is what she wants to happen. Short of that, she demands that Ximen Qing achieve a level of fairness, preferably a level that she can define. As Ding Naifei says, however, "There is no such thing as an equitable distribution of favor and attention in a polygamous household." Demanding fairness in such ways is what Pan Jinlian does openly. But she also resorts to "the art of maneuvering power," which besides open confrontation also works from beneath and around to exert its effects, beyond the control and awareness of the "host body" of the master.[15]

A Main Wife and Two Alternative Main Wives

By long tradition, the main wife in a polygamous marriage is in charge of the other wives and their children and is supposed to see that harmony exists among them, including dealing with daily affairs and settling any disputes. Though a concubine's status rises if she has a son, custom says that she must still defer to the main wife and avoid offending other wives. Being a conformist and not a disruptor, Li Ping'er exercises no voice when, for example, Wu Yueniang decides to betroth the baby Guange to the Qiao 喬 daughter (41.528–31). Deference to the main wife and other concubines is even more important for lower-status women, such as Pan Jinlian and Ruyi. As the Chongzhen commentator writes, if Yueniang and Pan Jinlian fight, Ximen Qing is bound to take Yueniang's side. Although he may "prefer" (*ai* 愛; literally, "love" or have a soft spot for) Jinlian, "in the end he will favor Yueniang" (終以月娘爲重). But if Jinlian and Ruyi fight, Ruyi "doesn't dare make an enemy of Jinlian" (不敢敵金蓮, 74.1027). Yueniang derives status because of her standing as daughter of a battalion commander, which also bestows status on Ximen Qing (though not as much as marrying the daughter of a civil official would, something he would not have been able to do because of his lack of education and status). As such and as his main wife, she deserves the ear of Ximen Qing. At the same time, as his main wife she stays above the kind of taunting, insulting, and cajoling that Pan Jinlian uses. The main wife should not have to stoop to lengthy tirades and arguments. If the husband does

15. Ding, *Obscene Things*, 204. "The art of maneuvering power" (*quanshu* 權術) is a term from Zhang Zhupo that Ding expands upon (*Obscene Things*, 175, on *quanshu*, and 184, "host body"). For Zhang Zhupo's use of *quanshu*, see Hou and Wang, eds., *Jin Ping Mei ziliao huibian*, 94.

not listen, she will not insist. Again, as I said above, she can even afford to stop speaking to him altogether. Her main goal is to have a son, which would give her additional privilege. Otherwise, she has no deep feelings for Ximen Qing, as is evident from her relatively low-key type of jealousy: cold and cynical, not fiery and driven.[16] She once says that he can buy all the women he wants and that "we are like a troop of soldiers, just here to fill the ranks" (俺們都是老婆當軍，充數兒罷了). To the Chongzhen commentator, this is her way of expressing jealousy, a kind of "nonjealous jealousy" (*bu du zhi du*, 不妒之妒, 40.521).

Nevertheless, Ximen Qing and Wu Yueniang have a solid partnership: he spends nights with her; he stores his money, important keys, and other treasures with her, which he must go to her chambers to get; and they regularly meet and discuss affairs. When he first wants to marry Li Ping'er, Yueniang opposes it. Li Ping'er's mourning period for her husband is not yet over, and there will be gossip about his "hanky-panky" with her (*guihun* 鬼渾, 16.201–202).[17] Ximen Qing listens, perhaps considering Hua Zixu's social status (which is much higher than the other men he cuckolds). When he agrees to do a favor for an important man and buy him a concubine, he thinks Yingchun 迎春, one of Li Ping'er's maids, will do. But Yueniang reminds him that he had sex with her already, and it is inappropriate to present such a woman to another man. It takes time and deliberation to buy a girl, she continues, advising him to tell his friend that he already has a woman in mind but still needs time to prepare a dowry for her (36.472). Women—especially go-betweens but also wives and concubines, who themselves are subject to such transactions—are the ones to know the ins and outs of the buying and selling of women.

To say that Ximen Qing has two main wives is technically false and, according to custom, impermissible. But he implies that he thinks of Li Ping'er as being like a main wife at times such as their marriage, after the birth of their son, and at her funeral (as in his improper designation of her in a Daoist ritual, 39.511). To the other wives, his weeping and other observances before her spirit tablet are excessive: they constitute misplaced

16. See Tian Xiaofei, *Qiushui tang*, 101.
17. For her reasons for opposing the marriage, see Ge, *Xueyin lusi*, 210–215.

sentiment. His favor toward her grows after she gives birth to their son, reflecting the sense of the ancient saying "the mother is prized who gives birth to a son" (*mu yi zi gui* 母以子貴). Descriptions of sex between her and Ximen Qing drastically drop off: there are only two such scenes after she enters his house, in both of which she is uncomfortable. Nevertheless, he spends more time with her than with Pan Jinlian, whose jealousy grows fiercer until she finally manages to cause the deaths of both the child and Li Ping'er.

Compared to Wu Yueniang and Pan Jinlian, Li Ping'er uses soft tactics to keep herself in good standing. She is scrupulous about not offending the other wives. After her reunion with Ximen Qing, Li Ping'er shows him jewelry that she brought with her from her first marriage to the Privy Councilor Liang (Liang Zhongshu 梁中書) and her second marriage to Hua Zixu, when she received precious items from the wealthy eunuch director who was Hua's uncle.[18] Among her jewelry is a precious "fret of gold filigree" (*jinsi diji* 金絲鬏髻), which she does not dare wear because it is fancier than anything that the other wives have. Instead, she wants Ximen Qing to have the metalsmith make the fret into something humbler—namely, a hairpin in the shape of "nine golden phoenixes, each holding a strand of pearls in its beak" (金九鳳墊根兒, 每個鳳嘴啣一溜珠兒, 20.252). When he finally hurries off, he runs into Pan Jinlian, who discovers the fret in his pocket and decides that she wants a nine-phoenix pin made for herself. As she feels she must do, she learns what other women own and wear, what each item is made of, and how much it weighs and is worth. As for Li Ping'er, for her to show Ximen Qing her treasures is an important step because, as she knows but does not make too obvious, the addition of her wealth to the household makes Ximen Qing more prosperous than ever. But wearing a fret of gold filigree would be too ostentatious. After all, when Pan Jinlian is still married to Wu Dalang 武大郎, she is wearing a fret made only of hair, the lowest grade for such a thing (called *toufa diji* 頭髮鬏髻, 2.35). As is fitting for the wives of a household such as Ximen Qing's, by chapter 11 she is wearing one like Meng Yulou's, made of "silver filigree" (*yinsi diji* 銀絲鬏髻, 11.130).

18. See Dauncey, "Illusions of Grandeur," 62–63 (on jewelry originally intended for imperial use).

But none of the wives in such a household would wear one made of gold filigree.[19]

In the society of *Jin Ping Mei*, it is common to tease or even taunt others about sex. But the straightforward and guileless Li Ping'er is not one to tease others about such things, nor is she is clever at being teased. The maids Yuxiao 玉簫 and Xiaoyu 小玉 ask her one day about the previous night, which she spent with Ximen Qing: "Is it true that yesterday the emperor dispatched four border agents [*yebushou*] to ask you to seek an alliance with the barbarians?" (昨日朝廷差四箇夜不收，請你往口外和番，端的有這話麼; *yebushou* being a Ming dynasty term for border agent or scout). Li Ping'er has no idea what they mean, and Xiaoyu says: "They say that you are good at saying 'dada'" (說你老人家會叫的好達達; *dada* being the wanton term of endearment during sex, but also a double entendre with the word for the "Tartar" barbarians).[20] Li Ping'er, the former adulteress who likes to have sex on all fours with Ximen Qing behind her, "reddens and blanches in utter embarrassment" (羞的臉上一塊紅，一塊白, 20.256).

As for Meng Yulou, in general she is not one of Ximen Qing's favored sexual partners. She is like another alternative main wife, who in the original negotiations was in fact told that she would be his main wife. Learning the truth, she nevertheless settles for being a concubine who does not rock the boat. But though a concubine in name, she has a main-wife-like air. Only one scene describes sex with her, and it is not the raucous and robust kind that Ximen Qing has with Pan Jinlian or Wang Liu'er. Unlike the novel's first description of Pan Jinlian, its first description of Meng Yulou contains no sexual innuendo (7.87). How she fits into the bevy of sexual partners can be seen from the occasion on which Ximen Qing sleeps with her as if by assignment. In general, he sleeps with whomever he likes when he likes. But at times the household has a subliminally recognized system of taking turns, a woman's birthday being an occasion for her having a turn. On Meng Yulou's birthday, Yueniang

19. To wear such a fret is the sign of a married woman. Note that when Sun Xue'e becomes a maid in Chunmei's household, Chunmei strips Sun Xue'e of her fret. See Yang Zhishui, *Wu se*, 46 and 51 (on types of frets); and Bai Weiguo, *Jin Ping Mei fengsu tan*, 298–301 (on gradations of frets, and on Sun Xue'e, 300).

20. The word *dada* is related to the word *die* (爹, father). Tartar is *dada* 韃靼, also written *tata* 塔塔. See Zhang Huiying, *Jin Ping Mei lisu*, 138.

assumes the role of main wife by announcing that Ximen Qing should stay with Yulou. At this point, Pan Jinlian suddenly plays the role of a sort of subordinate officer by escorting Meng Yulou to her room, where Ximen Qing will join her. In another instance of open sexual teasing, Jinlian then pretends to be Yulou's mother, saying: "Go to bed now, my child, be good and sleep tight. Mommy will come back to see you tomorrow. Don't be naughty!" (我兒，好好兒睡罷. 你娘明日來看你，休要淘氣, 21.279). No description follows. The one time the novel describes sex between Ximen Qing and Meng Yulou is when he arrives in her room to find her ill and vomiting. He says that he did not know she was ill, and he wants to send for a doctor. "It's no surprise that you didn't know," she says. "We here are hardly a wife of yours. You should go and be tender to the ones you truly love!" (可知你不曉的, 俺每不是你老婆, 你疼你那心愛的去罷, 75.1050–1051). She wants him to go away, but he stays, starts fondling her, and begins to have sex in the scene discussed previously that is chiefly marked by the detail of its unseemly sound (like "a dog licking up slops"), which is followed by the appearance of her white discharge (75.1053).[21]

Meng Yulou holds herself apart from Ximen Qing and the others and, like Wu Yueniang, refuses to show any regard for his supposed sexual charisma or the notion that he is a rewarding lover. On another occasion, Wu Yueniang is angry to see Ximen Qing going to Pan Jinlian's room when she thinks he should be going to Meng Yulou's. But Yulou says: "Sister, let him pester whomever he wants. If you act like this, it's as if we are competing for his favor . . . , when in fact whomever he lusts for is beyond our control" (姐姐, 隨他纏去! 這等說, 恰似咱每爭他的一般 . . . . 他爹心中所欲, 你我管的他, 74.1033). Overall, she exhibits a calm knowingness, especially as shown in her subtle tendency to add fuel to the flames of Pan Jinlian's fires. She does not spy as directly as Jinlian does, but Meng Yulou's maid, Lanxiang 蘭香, is often in the kitchen, where she hears things that she then repeats to Yulou. As Tian Xiaofei reminds us, Meng Yulou's air of being apart may be what led Zhang Zhupo to see her as a representation of the author.[22]

21. No details are given about another night when Ximen Qing goes to her room (58.764).

22. On these last two points, see Tian Xiaofei's excellent discussion (*Qiushui tang*, 34 and 80–81).

Song Huilian, Rival Opportunist

A dangerous sort of rival to the wives in a polygamous family is the kind of woman who will take advantage of the ever-ranging desire of the polygamist master. Whether or not she is already married, if there is a man around whom she can profitably seduce, she will do so. Song Huilian is such a person, a more dangerous and hateful rival to Pan Jinlian than Wu Yueniang, Meng Yulou, and even Li Ping'er.[23] Song Huilian is the type of woman who "is unwilling to let her cunt lie idle" (不肯把毴閑着), and she "is an old hand at taking illicit lovers" (他是會養漢兒, 78.1122–1123). Although Jinlian uses these words to describe Ben the Fourth, they could also apply to Song Huilian. Wang Liu'er, Ben the Fourth, Huiyuan (another married servant woman), and Ruyi are variants on this worst type of rival. As maid and bondservant, Song Huilian occupies a lower status than Pan Jinlian does but is also the daughter of an urban commoner. As others do once they have had sex with Ximen Qing, Huilian gains a new kind of foothold in the household and does not hesitate to show it, fancying up her hair and displaying her new clothing. It even looks as though she could become a concubine, which would require her to divorce her husband and find another woman for him in exchange—actions that would not be unheard of in the world of the novel. Pan Jinlian cannot tolerate such an eventuality and sets out to destroy Huilian, her husband, and her father.

According to the first description of Song Huilian, "she is a champion teaser of men, a queen of ruining households" (嘲漢子的班頭, 壞家風的領袖, 22.284). She has a quick, clever, and fearless tongue and is brazen in her willingness to ask for things from Ximen Qing and to challenge him when she cannot get what she wants. In her last effort to save her husband from Ximen Qing's aggression, she is stubborn and headstrong, as others remark, "battling with him back and forth as if she were an equal" (和他大爹白搽白折的平上).[24] "She is no average woman," one of

23. For Song Huilian as a "slightly farcical" double of Pan Jinlian, see Ding, *Obscene Things*, 168.

24. For *bai cha bai zhe* 白搽白折 (to be unyielding, caustic, and cutting), see Shanghai shi *Honglong meng* xuehui, *Jin Ping Mei jianshang cidian*, 551–552; and Zhang Huiying, *Jin Ping Mei lisu*, 138. For an example of Song Huilian's brazen talk, see 26.330.

them continues. "It's as if she's been pulled off the body of the master" (這個媳婦兒比別的媳婦兒不同，從公公身上拉下來的媳婦兒，26.340).[25] Ximen Qing regularly exerts his privilege to have sex with not only his wives but also other men's wives, especially wives of servants working in his household. Such women in particular welcome his advances, but in Song Huilian's case, when he displeases her, she no longer cooperates with him and ultimately hangs herself in despair and defiance, refusing to surrender her dignity in the form of her loyalty to her husband.

In terms of lot and status, Song Huilian began at the same level as Pan Jinlian as the daughter of a commoner sold as a servant. Huilian entered Ximen Qing's household when she was sold for the second time for five taels, a common price for a maid in *Jin Ping Mei*. Far less money changes hands over her than over Pan Jinlian, and she is in general less talented. But she still resembles Jinlian too closely: originally she was also named Jinlian, and her name had to be changed. Like Jinlian, she is "by nature clever and quick-witted, and knows how to take advantage of situations" (性明敏，善機變，22.284). She has special skills, including sewing, cooking pig's head, and playing board games (23.296), which match those of Pan Jinlian except that the latter excels at something that gives her far higher value: the combination of singing, playing the *pipa*, and being literate. Finally, Huilian knows how to make herself attractive, especially from observing Meng Yulou and Pan Jinlian—after which she begins to doll herself up to attract Ximen Qing's attention. Still, even though her feet are smaller than Pan Jinlian's (as she proves when she ostentatiously wears Pan's shoes over her own [24.308]), she lacks the training and savoir faire that Pan Jinlian gained from the instruction she received when she was a bond servant in the household of Lady Lin. Huilian can only trail behind, as she does symbolically when wearing Jinlian's shoes and flirting with Chen Jingji, which occurs shortly after she observes Chen Jingji and Jinlian flirting (24.308). She is a dangerous rival to Jinlian because she threatens to climb to the position of concubine, which Ximen Qing eventually promises her (26.335). Jinlian challenges her

25. I interpret this as saying that Huilian has become so bold with Ximen Qing because she has had the privilege of sleeping with him. Roy has "a daughter-in-law who can hardly be wrested from her father-in-law's embrace" (2.26.119). Lévy has "Décrochez-moi qui vous voulez, grandes ou petites, aucune ne saurait se prétendre son égale!" (1.26.533).

mockingly, "so after all you are the one who is the main wife, carried here in a sedan chair, all proper and ceremonious!" (只嫂子是正名正頂轎子娶將來的，是他的正頭老婆, 23.299). Jinlian is always ahead of her in terms of her mastery of knowledge about and communication with Ximen Qing. For example, she is the first to discover his affair with Huilian and forces him to confess it (22.286).[26]

Ximen Qing's sex with Song Huilian, Ben the Fourth, and Huiyuan is of a unique sort compared with sex with others in his circle of wanton women. It begins quickly, with no drinking and eating first, no singing or playing music, and little or no foreplay. He has already promised Huilian jewelry and clothing (22.285). When the maid Yuxiao signals to her that Ximen Qing is waiting, Song Huilian goes to where he is and, "walking up to him, plants herself right in his lap" (走向前，一屁股就坐在他懷裏). They kiss, she "grabs" (*zuan* 揝) his "word," and then immediately asks for money (23.294). "Grabbing" him is a primitive and artless gesture, later performed by Wang Liu'er as well and described with the same word, *zuan* (37.487). Once the affair begins, Huilian takes on new airs, as others observe to their annoyance, seeing her constantly at the front gate of the house buying things and talking in familiar tones with the male servants. She is gregarious and fond of "badinage and repartee with the crowd" (常和眾人打牙犯嘴, 23.300).[27] She is street savvy, as exemplified in a scene that is remarkable for its details about the methods of cutting and chiseling silver to use for payment. She asks one of the servants to buy something for her, gives him "half an ingot" (*bance yinzi* 半側銀子), and asks him to cut (*zao* 鑿) and chisel (*chui* 鎚) it into the precise amount she wants for the purchase. He recognizes the ingot as having recently been Ximen Qing's and takes it to begin the work of cutting, at which point Dai'an intervenes to cut it himself and then tries to take some of the remainder, thinking that she will not notice. But she takes the entire amount back, only giving him a fragment of "four or five *candareens*" as a tip (*qian* 錢, *siwu fen yikuai* 四五分一塊, 23.301).[28]

In terms of verbal wit, Song Huilian once makes a remark comparable in mastery to Pan Jinlian's riposte to Ximen Qing when he calls her

26. On Pan's "mastery of information," see Tian Xiaofei, *Qiushui tang*, 71.
27. Roy, 2.23.58, his translation.
28. Roy, 2.23.60, his translation.

a splay-legged whore. After Jinlian refuses to let Ximen Qing borrow her room for a tryst with Huilian, he chooses a grotto in the garden instead, even though the weather is cold. This stirs Huilian to say, "You're just the sort who would donate ice to a homeless shelter in the dead of winter!" (*lengpuzhong she bing* 冷舖中捨冰). "That you'd have us meet in such an icy hell! You might as well put a rope in my mouth and drag my frozen body out!" (走在這寒冰地獄裡來了，口裏啣着條繩子，凍死了往外拉，23.297).[29] She immediately continues asking for things—in particular, some "shoe uppers" (*xiemian'er* 鞋面兒), adding that when she tried on Pan Jinlian's shoes, she discovered that she could wear Pan Jinlian's over her own, which Jinlian overhears since she is nearby, spying on them. "Dragging my frozen body out" is a minor example of the kind of subtle wit and ironic density of Pan Jinlian's speech. Song Huilian expects large rewards, has no emotional attachment to Ximen Qing, and feels no need to speak delicately and respectfully to him as do others such as Zheng Aiyue, Wang Liu'er, and Ruyi.[30] Only Song Huilian and Pan Jinlian reach such heights of brazen acuity, though Song Huilian soon disappears from the narrative.

Wang Liu'er, Polyandrous Sexual Warrior Woman

Wang Liu'er belongs to the category of women who are not concubines, maidservants, or prostitutes. But what she is and does was well known in Ming and Qing society. She practices a form of polyandry known as marital prostitution, which means that she has a husband but openly rents herself out for profit to another man. To explain her particular situation, we can begin with a comment from Zhang Zhupo, who says that when Wang Liu'er is having sex with Ximen Qing, "she will inevitably talk business" (*bi jiang maimai* 必講買賣).[31] She is a steady, confident, and

29. "Donate ice . . . winter" comes from Roy, 2.23.53.

30. On her lack of feelings for Ximen Qing, see Tian Xiaofei, *Qiushui tang*, 80.

31. Zhang Zhupo, *Jin Ping Mei dufa*, in Hou and Wang, eds., *Jin Ping Mei ziliao huibian*, 29–30. See also Huang Lin, *Huang Lin jiang*, 99; and JPMCH, Bu Jian, ed., 50.1038 (Zhang Zhupo's interlinear comment). She also profits from assisting in the Miao Qing 苗青 case (47.603) and later skims money from Ximen Qing's household.

successful profiteer, which makes her sound like a prostitute or sex worker. But she does not belong to a brothel and has no pimp or madam. When two prostitutes look her up and down, they do not know what to make of her (42.541). At her own behest, and in cooperation with her husband, she has an affair with Ximen Qing, who puts them up in a new house in a good part of town.

As Matthew Sommer explains, polyandry was a common social practice in the Ming and Qing, though it appears in this case in fictionalized and embellished form. In poor rural communities, it was known as a strategy of survival that allowed a family to stay together rather than fragment because of poverty. A husband and wife would arrange to have an outside male have sex with the wife in return for compensation (in the form of labor, money, or both), an arrangement that would usually last for a set period of time with all parties understanding the conditions. Polyandry included a wide spectrum of practices, including wife selling and marital prostitution (which usually took place in cities and which best matches the situation in *Jin Ping Mei*). Whatever the specific practice, the occurrence of polyandry reflects the fact that the "sexual and reproductive labor of women" was a form of family labor. Though women commonly suffered abuse, it was not unusual for the wife to be the one who initiated the arrangement and decided upon the "particular strategy a couple chose to pursue."[32]

Jin Ping Mei hardly yields reliable social data about polyandry, and none of the sources that Sommer uses (mainly legal cases involving peasants) would have the level of explicit sexual detail that appears in the novel. Nor is survival so crucial in Wang Liu'er's case, since she and her husband have other ways of making a living. But they covet the rewards to be earned from the wealthy and powerful Ximen Qing. The key points in common between the novel and social reality are the practice of polyandry in the form of marital prostitution and the active involvement of the woman, however fantasized that may be in the novel. In other words, the practice of "open cuckoldry" (*ming wangba* 明王八, 78.1122), as Pan Jinlian disparagingly calls it in the case of Ben the Fourth, is not

32. Sommer, *Polyandry and Wife-Selling*, 4 and 32–33, respectively; see also 56–57, and 69 (on wife's initiative and wives as "active participants," 212), 12–13 and 92–93 (on polyandry for support of the family and as survival strategy).

purely an invention of the novelist. Nor are Wang Liu'er's interest in pursuing and maintaining the affair; her husband's open consent to it; and the knowledge of the situation by others, including neighbors and members of Ximen Qing's household. In the legal terms of the Ming, the three of them are committing the crime of "openly engaging in illicit sex" (*zong jian* 縱奸), which under Ming law was subject to a punishment of ninety "blows of the heavy bamboo."[33] But though the state did not approve of such behavior, in reality it did not necessarily intervene unless a serious crime occurred.

The fictionalized component of the situation comes from Wang Liu'er's ways of taking control of the sexual act, her knowledge about pleasing a man and her efforts to do so, and the assertion of her demand for pleasure (not that such things would be impossible in reality). Pan Jinlian and Song Huilian are also polyandrous, but neither of them colludes with her husband. Pan Jinlian hides her affair from her husband, Wu Dalang, a runt of a man who not only could never have considered having concubines but who also already had had to tolerate his wife being polyandrous when merchant Zhang 張 continued to sleep with Jinlian after she got married. As for Song Huilian, she tries to hide the affair from her husband, who in turn tries to hide his affair with Sun Xue'e. Furthermore, although Song Huilian profits from her relationship with Ximen Qing, she does not challenge him sexually. In contrast, the sex between Ximen Qing and Wang Liu'er is a full-tilt battle, in which he must use all his tools and drugs to prevail. In addition to Pan Jinlian and Lady Lin, she is one of his fiercest opponents (and the first with whom he tries his new aphrodisiac).[34] She engages in fellatio and anal intercourse, both ways of delighting and stimulating the man, in hopes of reward. As the novel portrays her, she welcomes and initiates the acts, in the case of anal intercourse "rubbing her heart spot below until she comes. If she didn't, no matter what she did, she wouldn't be able to reach orgasm" (在下邊揉着心子才過．不然隨問怎的不得丟身子, 37.488).

The sexually demanding woman whom the man can hardly please is a motif that goes back to the art of the bedchamber and appears across Chinese fiction, as I have mentioned. She is ravenous for pleasure, which

33. See Sommer, *Polyandry and Wife-Selling*, 278; see also 92, 341, and 360.

34. On her "fierceness" in sex, see Tian Xiaofei, *Qiushui tang*, 119–120.

she takes to extreme heights. In some cases, she outdoes and shames the man or forces him to use special means to fight back. Stories about Prince Hailing of the Jin dynasty are a good example: they satirize and condemn the hated ruler by pairing him with women who sexually shame him.[35] Showing what it takes to defeat such a woman, the late Ming novel *Xiuta yeshi* includes a character named Dongmen Sheng 東門生 (a take-off on Ximen Qing's name) who is so inadequate with his wife that he has to have his virile catamite take his place with her. The catamite obtains drugs and tools from a Daoist, drives the wife to heights of ecstasy, and ends by bruising and exhausting her. In *Jin Ping Mei*, Wang Liu'er is a practical enjoyer of sex who knows how to use it to entertain the man, please herself, and obtain profit for herself and her family. The author feels no need to have her die of excess or renounce sex and become a nun, as happens in other novels—though her daughter eventually does the renouncing for her, so to speak, disfiguring herself to avoid marriage and becoming a nun.

Wang Liu'er can also be given another label, though it is one that I remove from its original context. She is a sexual version of the warrior woman (*xianü* 俠女), the usual version of whom battles for a cause such as avenging injustice against her father. She fights men as an equal in terms of strength and skill. She either never marries or marries a male warrior whom she joins in a righteous cause. Their sex is not an object of description. Wang Liu'er's resemblance to such a type lies in the fact that, more capable than her husband, she is the one to ensure the family's well-being and decide how to ensure its survival. She does so in a way that makes use of her physical strength and skill, though in her case the strength is sexual, not martial. She fights the man in sexual battles and is a formidable opponent to whom he would lose if he did not resort to special tools and drugs. In this regard, she sounds like the female sexual master discussed in the chapter on sex as battle (who is also discussed in the next section). But Wang Liu'er's sexual formidability does not involve occult techniques or the motif of stealing vital essence. Instead, the novel portrays her as enjoying herself in sex while also involving herself in a form of sexual labor that allows her to secure great profit for her family (a hundred taels in the case of her mediation on behalf of Miao Qing

35. See McMahon, *Celestial Women*, 51–53.

苗青). After Ximen Qing dies, she is ready to reap even greater profit, persuading her initially hesitant husband to abscond with over a thousand taels of Ximen Qing's money (81.1176–1177). The usual warrior woman operates outside the law, correcting injustice by punishing wrongdoers when others, including the state, fail to do so. Wang Liu'er only distantly resembles her in this regard, profiting and stealing from the corrupt merchant who claims too many women and too much ill-gotten wealth.

Lady Lin, Wanton Bodhisattva

Lady Lin also escapes the conventional labels, not being a wife, concubine, maid, or courtesan. She is a rich man's widow who likes sex and hires a go-between to arrange to have men visit her in her house (a recent partner is the man who deflowered Zheng Aiyue, who in turn is the person who arranged Ximen Qing's meeting with Lin). She is self-sufficient, except for one problem that makes her beholden to a man like Ximen Qing: she has a son who is in trouble and whom Ximen Qing can rescue. The label "polyandrous" comes to mind, but her behavior does not fit the usual scope of polyandry in that she is married to no man and does not conduct her liaisons with men for the sake of profit. It is easier to describe her in terms of a couple of literary motifs, the first of which is the sexually insatiable widow, a type that is commonly (though not in the novel) a subject of vilification. The eighteenth-century *Guwangyan* describes another widow who invites men to have sex with her—in her case, charging them unless the sex is good. In *Guwangyan*, she is less an individual than an allegorical stereotype that appears across Ming and Qing fiction and is derived from the assumption that the lack of a husband leads to a woman to desperate insatiability. *Jin Ping Mei* refrains from such a reduction, though the stereotype hangs in the background. *Guwangyan* describes the widow luridly and in demeaning terms, portraying her as one of many such women whom the novel scorns and satirizes as signs of a world lacking in sexually competent men.[36] However, even

36. The phrases used to label her include "getting married in dribs and drabs" (*lingsui jia* 零碎嫁) and "putting out a half-opened door" (*bankai men* 半開門)—that is, not like a

if Lady Lin is a lustful widow, she hardly fits the image of ravenous insatiability portrayed elsewhere (in spite of Zhang Zhupo's labeling her a "dissolute" adulteress).[37]

The second motif that describes Lady Lin is that of the figure of the female sexual master, to which I referred in the chapter on sex as battle and just now in regard to Wang Liu'er, and which applies to Pan Jinlian as well. As mentioned in chapter 4, the description of Xiwangmu (Queen Mother of the West) in a medieval text of the art of the bedchamber is one of the early exemplars. She is a kind of patron goddess of sex (though never referred to as such) who strengthens her pure *yin* by intercourse with multiple men who become ill after sex with her. Xia Ji, Zhao Feiyan, and Wu Zetian, among others, are mortal versions of this figure, women who in some cases (but not all) resort to occult techniques. All have been part of Chinese sexual lore for centuries.[38] Lady Lin, Pan Jinlian, and Wang Liu'er are likewise mortal versions of the legendary goddess of sex, though they lack royal identity. The courtesan Zheng Aiyue is an alternative example, especially considering that Ximen Qing's visit to her is compared to "entering a goddess's den in a sacred grotto" (59.777). In legends and stories that romanticize such a figure, the man chances to meet a beautiful goddess or female immortal, who welcomes him to her presence, grants him sexual blessing, but ultimately retains her status as an independent woman. She sets limits on the extent and duration of their affair. In some instances, the affair leaves the man with a beautiful memory; in others, he suffers emotional or physical loss, as in the case of Xiwangmu or the fox fairy, sex with whom drains the man of life essence.

In real social terms, Lady Lin is the highest-status woman Ximen Qing meets: she is the widow of an imperial commissioner (*zhaoxuan* 招宣). Li Ping'er is also of high status—higher than Wu Yueniang—in terms of her previous marriages and of the huge sum of money (three thousand taels) and other treasures that she brings into the house. Lady Lin

fully opened brothel (*Guwangyan*, 1.159). The female protagonist of *Zui chun feng* (discussed in chapter 7) also pays men to have sex with her.

37. Zhang Zhupo, *Jin Ping Mei dufa*, in Hou and Wang, eds., *Jin Ping Mei ziliao huibian*, 30.

38. For relevant discussions of this figure, see Richard Wang, *Ming Erotic Novellas*, 165 and 177. For an example from the Han, see the story of Nü Wan in *Liexian zhuan*, 66 (also see chapter 4). Also see Kaltenmark, trans., *Le Lie-sien Tchouan*, 180–183.

comes with another kind of loftiness, deriving from the fact that she lives alone in a luxurious mansion, invites Ximen Qing to have a sexual affair, but unlike Li Ping'er has no interest in becoming his concubine or kept woman. She does not need his financial support.

In the end, however, the author does not give much space to the fantasy, though he leaves no doubt about the link between Lady Lin and the figure of the goddess. For example, he describes her as "a lustful beauty from the chambers of silk, a cunt-bestowing Bodhisattva from deep in the boudoir" (是個綺閣中好色的嬌娘, 深閨内的施毯 的菩薩, 69.948). The violent clash between "cunt-bestowing" and "Bodhisattva" is paralleled by the description of Ximen Qing as "a model of a man, of awe-inspiring build and elegant speech" (身材凜凜, 語話非俗, 一表人物), which is immediately followed by the description of him as "a rich cheat, con man, oppressor of the good, cheater of the virtuous, and a debauched libertine" (就是個: 富而多詐奸邪輩, 壓善欺良酒色徒, 69.948). When they first meet, they kowtow to each other, he being a local tycoon and influential official and she the widow of a deceased man of much higher rank. As Huang Lin writes, Ximen Qing cannot quite "shake off the sense of inferiority that he feels in the company of an upper-class woman."[39] She is formidable in sex, a fully challenging equal if not superior with whom, as quoted in chapter 4, he "exerts all his earthly talent" (69.950). As portrayed in that chapter, theirs is an even match between two mutually fulfilled lovers. To prepare himself, the narrator adds, Ximen Qing visits Li Jiao'er the night before, about which the Chongzhen commentator teases that if Ximen Qing had been with Pan Jinlian instead, "he would hardly have had enough energy left" to manage with Lady Lin (*zende jingshen peiyang* 怎得精神培养, 69.947).

Courtesan Zheng recalls the same motif in her goddess-like appearance to her client, Ximen Qing. The scenes with both Lady Lin and Zheng Aiyue have a grandiose, artificial air that reflects the general lack of passion. No arguments ever occur between these partners. The affairs should go smoothly. Still, as in all Ximen Qing's affairs, a transaction occurs. In this case, though there is no suggestion of Lady Lin's abandoning her status as an independent widow, by the second visit she becomes beholden to him because of his agreement to protect her son. Ximen Qing

39. Huang Lin, *Huang Lin jiang*, 103 (my translation); see also 245.

then does with her what he also does with Wang Liu'er, Pan Jinlian, and Ruyi: he burns moxa on her chest and vagina, which is a final sign of her inclusion in his circle of wanton women.

Ruyi, Wet Nurse and Surrogate Li Ping'er

The polygamous household has its rules, as I have said, though they may be unwritten and the master and his wives may break them. Although wives and concubines are the master's formally recognized sexual partners, according to the widely accepted practice, he can have virgin maids as well. Such a maid is a well-established character type. According to the pattern of *Jin Ping Mei* and other works, she is someone with whom the polygamous master sometimes sleeps besides his wife or concubine. In recurrent scenes in Ming and Qing fiction, she spies on him having sex and may become aroused and envious of the spied-upon lovers. She may be seduced as a prelude for sex with her as-yet-unattainable mistress. In some cases, she is knowledgeable about sex and thereby enlightens or encourages her virginal mistress. In others, she is seduced after the man establishes himself with the mistress. The maid who has had sex with the master is not as privileged as a wife or concubine, but she is nevertheless more distinguished than other maids. This is demonstrated in the case of Chunmei, who wears fancier clothing and whose temper is thereafter more indulged. Society frowns upon selling such a maid to another family, as Wu Yueniang says about Yingchun. However, again the rule can be bent—for example, if the master has died. Wu Yueniang sells Chunmei to a man who prizes her because of what he hears about her and because Ximen Qing's liaison with her has heightened her value. Her involvement with the still living Chen Jingji, however, is kept secret because it would damage her image.

But where do other servants fit, such as wet nurses and bond servants who serve in capacities other than as personal maids to wives and concubines? Ruyi is a wet nurse (*naizi* 奶子) and a married bond servant, bought for six taels at Guange's birth. As the woman who nurses Ximen Qing's child, should she be outside the commonly accepted range of women that Ximen Qing's wives would countenance him having sex with? Should she be in another category, even to the philandering polygamist? After Guange and Li Ping'er have died, her usefulness to the household would seem to have disappeared. In fact, even before Li Ping'er dies, Wu Yueniang is already pregnant, though she has not yet told any of the wives. Ruyi's continued presence causes the others (especially Pan Jinlian) to watch her in a way that they do not with the maids Ximen Qing has slept with. The danger is that, already sexually experienced and proven as a mother, Ruyi could lure Ximen Qing to have sex with her, become pregnant, and thereby upstage the others. Furthermore, her continued presence in the deceased Li Ping'er's chambers makes her available to Ximen Qing, who often visits there to make offerings before Li Ping'er's spirit tablet. Ruyi begins to serve him intimately, "purposely pressing and bumping against him, pawing and squeezing him" (挨挨搶搶，掐掐捏捏, 65.882). When she draws the covers over him one night, he pulls her over to kiss her and, without a word, she gets on the kang, where "they do the clouds and rain in the most ecstatic way" (不勝歡娛, 雲雨一處). No description follows. Instead, there is only the chapter illustration in the Chongzhen edition, with a picture of Ximen Qing in bed with an erection, and words such as: "There is nothing she wouldn't do for him as they tossed and tumbled like a couple of well-matched phoenixes" (無不奉承, 顛鸞倒鳳, 65.883).

Pan Jinlian's method of discouraging Ximen Qing's relationship with Ruyi is to allude to rules that he should follow—even if they include rules that he did not follow in seducing Jinlian herself. She evokes the law against adultery, for example, when she asks him how he can carry on with Ruyi, who already has a husband. He replies by downplaying the affair, saying that Ruyi is just a servant. Pan Jinlian then switches to saying that it is all right for him to sleep with her, but he should not engage in "idle talk" (閒話 *xianhua*, 75.1038), thus attempting to create a rule that limits their intimacy—especially the kind that comes from chatting and exchanging information. Pan Jinlian is the master of information in the Ximen Qing household, and she wants no one to surpass her. Finally, she uses a pointed set of words to refer to his taking a woman on a permanent basis. She tells him that she does not want him to have Ruyi as a "long-term sleeping partner" (在一鋪兒長遠睡, 75.1038). She thus pointedly names what he is doing and thereby tries to prohibit it. Putting Ruyi on such footing would embarrass the other maids, Jinlian insists: they would feel upstaged. She thereby calls forth a rule that separates women Ximen Qing can sleep with from women he should not sleep with.

This exchange comes after Ximen Qing asks Jinlian to give him the bag of sex tools so he can to take it to Ruyi's. Saying that Ruyi will pollute them, Jinlian gives him only the silver clasp, which she throws at him. When he then goes to Ruyi, who serves him in her usual enthusiastic way, he promises her that he will raise her to concubine if she happens to get pregnant (75.1040). He especially loves Ruyi's whiteness, which reminds him of Li Ping'er's, he tells her, and thus when he hugs Ruyi he feels as if he is hugging Li Ping'er. Then begins an energetic session of sex, which makes "her starry eyes go blurry" (*xingyan mengmeng* 星眼濛濛) as "he keeps banging away," while she "cries and moans ceaselessly" until he "ejaculates" (*zhi gu shanda* 只顧搧打; *hu jiao bujue* 呼叫不絕; *jing xie* 精泄; 75.1039–1041).

As a category of women, wet nurses have special privileges and gain a certain aura because of their intimacy with the nursing baby—in this case, the family's male heir. But *Jin Ping Mei* adds another aspect to the wet nurse in assigning her the role of someone who knows all about sex. That aspect also appears in the case of Ben the Fourth, who was not only originally a wet nurse but who was also involved in an illicit affair with her current husband (both of them had absconded from the household in which she once worked). She likewise responds immediately to Ximen Qing's seduction, moaning to show her pleasure and willingness to do whatever he likes. "There was nothing she did not know," says the narrator, echoing the words said about Ruyi (甚么事兒不知道, 78.1112). Ruyi and Ben the Fourth belong in the same group of ultrawanton women noted above, with whom sex begins immediately and excitedly and who well know what to do and expect.

Wang Liu'er, Ruyi, and Ben the Fourth are all married women, which points to Ximen Qing's general attraction to older, experienced women. He may prize virgins and pay great sums to deflower them if they are prostitutes, as he does with Li Guijie, or be fond of initiating them, as he does with some of the maids of his wives. Nevertheless, he is not especially attracted to virgins. They are like handsome young boys in that he will have sex with them because they are attractive, but mainly because they are available in between his other, more sensuously significant, liaisons. Whether virgin or not, all such characters are partners in reserve, whom he does not fail to reward. Just as he is about to arrange his first tryst with Ben the Fourth, he gives both Ruyi and Yingchun valuable jewelry, after which he gives Ben the Fourth the considerable gift of six taels and two pieces of gold jewelry (77.1102 and 1104).

Li Ping'er's dying words to Ruyi and her personal maids further clarify their situational differences by showing how her advice conforms to the situation of each. She tells Ruyi not to bind her breasts yet and thus to keep being a wet nurse in case Wu Yueniang becomes pregnant (62.835). Yueniang concurs, saying that she can marry Ruyi to someone in the household (and not letting on that she is already pregnant; 62.837). Li Ping'er tells the maid Xiuchun 綉春 that she will have her sold out, but in motherly fashion tells her not to be her "silly coquettish" self anymore (*sa jiao sa chi* 撒嬌撒癡, 62.835). Furthermore, if Wu Yueniang does not want to retain her, Li Ping'er would like her to join a "monogamous household" (*danfu duqi* 單夫獨妻, 62.836)—in which, presumably, she would no longer be subject to seduction by a polygamist master. As for Yingchun, she has "already been under the master's hand" (*shouyong-guode* 收用過的, 62.835 and 836). Li Ping'er's reward for her is in effect to elevate her to the honorable status of chaste widow. She will have her stay in the household and serve Yueniang (who, as the main wife, is the most respectable woman to serve).

Li Guijie, Courtesan and Always Sexual

Prostitutes are the type of woman with whom Ximen Qing is said to have first proven his sexual prowess (1.4 and 4.60). To ask a fundamental question, what does being a prostitute mean? Let me start with a doggerel that puts it succinctly: "To sleep with all the casual flowers, however many there may be, cannot compare to going back home to bed with your wife. Though there's no sensual appeal when you sleep next to her, at least when you wake in the morning you don't have to pay" (宿盡閒話萬萬千，不如歸家伴妻眠. 雖然枕上無情趣，睡到天明不要錢, 20.262).[40] The appeal includes both the atmosphere (the theatricality that I have referred to

40. See JPMCH, 20.530, for a longer version of the poem.

above) and the sensual stimulation. A key part of the appeal is the socializing that goes on in the brothel, as pushed and profited from by Ximen Qing's friends—especially Ying Bojue. They are hangers-on at the brothel who egg Ximen Qing on, live off tips, and grab women for hugs and kisses when they can.

A parallel note about the juxtaposition of wife and prostitute, and key to the novel's portrait of the latter, is that she is someone with whom the wives and especially the concubines must compete. In an early scene, Pan Jinlian's "bed love" is said to be "better than a prostitute's by far. She will do all that she can to curry his favor" (枕邊風月，比娼妓尤甚，百般奉承, 6.81). This follows a description of her playing the *pipa* for Ximen Qing, which leads him to exclaim that no singing girl of the "brothel quarters" (*goulan* 构欄, 6.81) can play as well. He takes off her shoe, fills it with wine, and drinks from it—a type of behavior that, though it occurs only once in the novel, is a classic gesture of brothel behavior and is well-known in the tradition of courtesan culture.[41] They then "take off their clothes, get into bed, and begin to play" (解衣上床頑耍, 6.81). No description follows, because the main focus of the scene is not how they have sex but the prelude leading up to it.

But a concubine must also distinguish herself from a courtesan. Pan Jinlian lifts the skirts of some visiting courtesans to look at their shoes, noting how the shoes of women who are of the "inside" (*libian* 裡邊; that is, the home) differ from those of women who are from "outside" (*waibian* 外邊, that is, the brothel, 58.756). Having thus distinguished herself from the courtesans, she is glad to find that her shoes are better than theirs. More important is the fact that, as a comment by Meng Yulou implies, the wife or concubine is freer to be herself. Li Guijie is traumatized after the fracas at the brothel in which authorities arrest Lady Lin's son. She is the courtesan whom Ximen Qing deflowers for a great sum and whom he rents on a long-term basis for twenty taels per month. Housed at Ximen Qing's until the affair calms down, she offers to sing for the wives, spurring Meng Yulou to remark that Li Guijie is truly of the brothel, for she can "put on a new face instantly" and be ready to sing as if nothing had happened (*zuo lian'er kuai* 做臉兒快, 51.662).

41. See Li Xiaorong, *Poetics and Politics*, 128–129.

The prostitute is a woman around whom men automatically like to presume that they can be lewd (unless she is the refined and sensitive woman from the "green tower" brothel, *qinglou* 青樓).[42] They assume that they can tell dirty jokes in her presence. Not long after singing for the wives, Li Guijie breaks down in tears while singing for Ximen Qing and his male friends because Ying Bojue unleashes relentless sarcasm in response to every verse of her song (52.684).[43] His badgering continues when he barges in on her and Ximen Qing shortly afterward, when they are having sex nearby. This is a scene that features sex as a dumb act, a thing that a client and courtesan do that is so mundane that anyone can even come in, watch it, and remark on it. Li Guijie has just told Ximen Qing to hurry because someone might come when Ying Bojue enters. He says, "Hurry and throw water on the two huggers! They are all stuck together!" (快取水來，潑潑兩箇摟心的，摟到一答里了, 52.686).[44] He plants a kiss on her and tells Ximen Qing to "bang her all you want! Bang the bottom out of her for all I care!" (兩箇儘著搗，儘著搗，搗吊底也不關我事, 52.687).[45] As he is about to leave, he turns back to ask for the breath lozenges that he had been promised, after which Ximen Qing and Li Guijie continue having sex for another few hours. When he is done, Ximen Qing is sweating and out of breath, and he goes aside to urinate in a bed of flowers, while Guijie takes out a mirror and fixes her hair. It is a scene of sex at its least lurid and sensational.

Conclusion: The Real Man

Jin Ping Mei presents a full range of polygamous sexual relations, though it probably considers superfluous some scenarios that had already appeared

42. Such a brothel appears in the late Qing novel *Huayue hen* 花月痕. See McMahon, *Polygamy and Sublime Passion*, 68–79.

43. On this scene, see Ge, *Xueyin lusi*, 262–266.

44. This probably refers to the custom of throwing water on two copulating dogs to get them to separate. See Anonymous, *Yipian qing* 一片情, SWXHB, vol. 14, 11.203–204.

45. "The bottom out of her for all I care" comes from Roy, 3.52.276. *Dao* 搗 (to pound or beat) is common vulgar slang that is a level above the crudest word, *ri* 㒷. The two commonly occur together as *ridao*.

in other fiction and would appear yet again—such as sex with more than one woman in the same bed; games that men and women in orgies play to see who can produce the most sexual fluids or who has the largest penis; and sex with a catamite whom the master will allow to sleep with his wife or concubine in return. Such scenes appear in what can be loosely thought of as the more purely pornographic books of the time. This is a category to which *Jin Ping Mei* does not belong, though it is both influenced by and influences these other works (as I discuss in chapter 7). The novel's overwhelming interest is in the social and domestic context of polygamous sexual relations, which in this chapter I have viewed through the women's situational differences.

A question that Wu Yueniang asks Chunmei returns us to the topic of how to be the wife of a polygamist. When Chunmei visits Yueniang near the end of the novel, Yueniang asks her about her husband's concubines, wondering "whether the Master often goes to sleep with them" (他爺也常往他身邊去不去). The Chongzhen commentator remarks: "Yueniang judges the men of the world only according to the standard that Ximen Qing sets, thus the stupidity of her words" (月娘只以西門慶行事作榜樣看天下人, 所以語語滯呆, 96.1359). In saying this, she pries into how Chunmei manages herself with such a supposed man. As it happens, Chunmei's husband is often away on onerous official missions, returns home exhausted, and sleeps with his wives infrequently.

When she compares herself with Chunmei, Wu Yueniang must also be measuring herself in terms of how much control Chunmei has over her husband and his other wives. From when they begin as co-wives, Wu Yueniang and Pan Jinlian compete to be the most important wife, a key part of which is being able to lead the man to the women and the women to the man. To be that wife, a woman must know about the man's possible movements and, when possible, influence his sleeping arrangements. On another of Meng Yulou's birthdays, Yueniang again tries to have him go to Meng Yulou, not Pan Jinlian (74.1033). Although he goes to Pan Jinlian's room, as in chapter 21, Yueniang's attempt is a sign of her wish to play that role, which is the role of the main wife who administers the domestic relations of the household. The situation distantly recalls that of empresses and other senior women of the imperial household, who throughout Chinese history arranged marriages and other liaisons for the heir apparent or emperor, hoping to avoid his excessive favoring of a woman he selects on his own.

Later, when Meng Yulou convinces Wu Yueniang and Pan Jinlian to reconcile after their terrible fight, Ximen Qing is relieved, while Yueniang expects a reward for having given in. It is as if a deal has been made, according to which she now has the right to tell him to sleep with Li Jiao'er instead of Ruyi (76.1073). Like Pan Jinlian, Yueniang wants him to pay less attention to Ruyi. Later Ximen Qing finds Pan Jinlian weeping in her room, still angry that Yueniang had accused her of trying to monopolize him. She rages that Yueniang takes herself as the "genuine article" (*zhencai shiliao* 眞材實料)—that is, the "legitimate main wife" (*zhengjing fuqi* 正經夫妻): "If you were a real man, if you had your wits about you, you could settle the matter with a single blow of your fist!" (你是個男子漢，若是有主張，一拳柱定, 76.1076).[46] His response is that the previous night when he wanted to come to her, Yueniang would not let him, so he went to Li Jiao'er instead. But "my heart was only with you." (一片心只想著你), he insists. The Chongzhen commentator remarks: "When husbands encounter such situations, it takes an enormous amount of energy to resolve. For those who wish to have concubines, take note" (丈夫處此，大費調停，欲娶妾者，看樣, 76.1076). The phrase "such situations" refers to the complexities of the polygamous household, a theme that has been passed down for generations. The Sui 隋 emperor Yang Jian (楊堅, 541–604) put it concisely when his wife, Empress Dugu Jialuo 獨孤伽羅 (544–602), had a pregnant concubine murdered. In a famous statement after the murder, he reportedly exclaimed in frustration: "Here I am an emperor, yet I cannot do as I please" (吾貴爲天子，不得自由).[47]

In saying "if you were a real man," Pan Jinlian aims for the same effect as when she once criticized Ximen Qing for his lenient treatment of Song Huilian, saying, "You don't have your boots on straight" (你的皮靴兒沒番正, 25.325).[48] She pretends to be the determiner of whether or not he is a man. She strives to be the one to reward him with that label, as

46. Roy, 4.76.520–521, his translation (slightly modified).

47. Li Yanshou 李延壽, *Beishi* 北史, 14.533–534; see also McMahon, *Women Shall Not Rule*, 182–184.

48. Roy, 2.25.95, his translation.

well as to take it away. She plays that role when she influences his decisions or when she gets information out of him, such as when he begins his affair with Li Ping'er. Similarly in the scene above in which she escorts Meng Yulou to her room on her birthday, she pretends to play the role of mommy—that is, in effect, the one who supervises the polygamist's nights with his wives. In short, she wants to become the enforcer of rules, which ultimately means the one who is more important than not only the main wife but also the polygamist himself. Until she achieves such an impossible goal, she will be as wanton as possible, which means being as sexually demanding as possible. In the scene in which she causes Ximen Qing's death from an overdose of aphrodisiac, this translates into maintaining his erection as long as possible for herself.

CHAPTER 7

Jin Ping Mei *and Ming and Qing Pornography*

The More Purely Pornographic Novel

Jin Ping Mei became a notorious book because of its explicit sexual content, which I have been labeling its pornography. An underlying question throughout this study has been how pornographic is *Jin Ping Mei*? That is, how *yin* 淫 (obscene or lascivious) is it, to use the term of its own era—the term by which it was condemned? I answer this question by placing the book in the context of other Ming and Qing fiction with explicit sexual content, to which I have regularly alluded above. What I ask here is: What does *Jin Ping Mei* do and not do in comparison with this body of works in terms of pornographic portrayal? The answer has to come in several layers, ranging from a sketch of what the goal and contents of the other works are to both their categorization into various subgenres and a consideration of the issues and conundrums that they approach in their own ways (sometimes more facilely and in some cases more provocatively than *Jin Ping Mei*)—in particular, the motif of the sexually independent woman. My answer before I start is to say that *Jin Ping Mei* stops short of what its author (or authors) would consider gratuitous and superfluous—such as, for example, the scene that appears in several works of the polygamist in bed with all his wives at once. *Jin Ping Mei* does not contain such an episode. Furthermore, some other works flout taboos and explore sexual pleasure with more enthusiasm and sensationalism than *Jin Ping Mei*, which tends to subordinate such portrayals to the complexities of the surrounding narrative and in general to undercut its characters in the midst of their enjoyment—though some passages are exceptions to this.

In his 1924 history of Chinese fiction, Lu Xun (1881–1936) referred to a body of works from the Ming and Qing as containing "purely lewd language, with no pretensions to the name of literature."[1] In a 1927 article, Mao Dun 矛盾 (1896–1981) used two ways of summing up what he called this "literature of sexual desire" (*xingyu wenxue* 性慾文學), thus using the neologism *xingyu*—an example of the new vocabulary of sex that came into fashion at the time.[2] As he saw it, what that literature portrays is "one, sexual pleasure at its mad extreme, and, two, the methods of sex, the so-called 'art of the bedchamber.'"[3] As distant as these remarks may seem to be, they provide a basic direction for contrasting *Jin Ping Mei* with what Lu, Mao, and many others characterize as the more purely "lewd" works. Thus, I begin with the question of how pornographic *Jin Ping Mei* is. These other works are important because of the unprecedented nature of their appearance in literary history in roughly the same period as *Jin Ping Mei*, though the latter stands out because of the enormous attention it pays to other realities besides those of sexual activity. All these works, including *Jin Ping Mei*, have common vocabularies and sets of imagery, and they sometimes copy from one another. They are full of energy and drive in their repeated staging of characters having sex, which they portray in entertaining, creative, and provocative ways. At times the works convey a sense of serious thematic purpose, though the more purely pornographic ones gain their so-called pureness because they do not necessarily feel obliged to be as thematically serious.

As for Lu and Mao's characterizations, lewdness and the lack of literary quality are still acceptable terms, though they need unfolding. "Sex-

1. Lu Xun, *Brief History*, 226 (using "lewd language" instead of "pornography" for *xieyu* 媟语); and Lu Xun, *Zhongguo xiaoshuo shilue*, 141 (意欲媟语，而未能文). Thanks to Mark Stevenson for his critique of this chapter in its early stages.

2. Mao Dun, "Zhongguo wenxueneide xingyu miaoxie," 160; see also Rocha, "*Xing*," 613 (on *xingyu* as neologism).

3. Mao Dun, "Zhongguo wenxueneide xingyu miaoxie," 161 (一是色情狂，二是性交方法，所謂房術).

ual pleasure at its mad extreme" is a correct summation of many of these works, including *Jin Ping Mei*. And how to have sex is another of the subjects that are commonly portrayed, whether in terms of techniques, sex tools, or sexual positions. Lu and Mao's remarks spur us to try to define what is in these works that sets them apart and makes them so daring and offensive. Of course, they are also creative in their portrayals of sexual activity, which make up the main narrative thread—that is, the key node through which the narrative threads its way. All that matters is this thing, around which all relations are centered. As Ka F. Wong says in his study of one of the best known of the novels, *Xiuta yeshi* 繡榻野史 (The history of the embroidered couch), "only the varied exchanges of bodies matter" as authors "make the human body a stage and assemble all the conceivable physical pleasures and pains that can be performed on it."[4] Characters pursue pleasure until there is no more, except for the next time and the time after that. As one character describes it, such pleasure feels like "the most ultimate thing that could be" (*zhi yi jin yi* 至矣盡矣).[5]

Before proceeding, I must note that, even though I characterize these works as more purely pornographic, such generalizations always blur certain distinctions. The works differ among themselves, as I show below, and historical changes occur in them from the Ming to the Qing. It can be difficult to decide what even qualifies as being in this group, though the presence of titles on lists of censored books throughout the Ming and Qing provides a convenient criterion, as does a work's inclusion in a recent reprint series.[6] What does a work have to do before it verges into what would be considered serious literature? How many so-called explicit and obscene words does a text have to have before it counts as pornographic? These are questions that I approached in discussions of *Jin Ping*

4. Wong, "Anatomy of Eroticism," 301 and 309. The novel takes readers "directly to the realm of the sexual," aiming "to tell it all" (301 and 302). I include characters and translations for titles of works in this chapter, even if I have alluded to them in previous chapters. For another discussion of this novel, see Idema, "'Blasé Literati,'" li–lvii.

5. Qingyang yeren 青陽野人, *Chundeng mishi* 春燈迷史, SWXHB, vol. 23, 4.61.

6. Such reprint series include Chen Qinghao and Wang Qiugui, *Siwuxie huibao* 思無邪匯寶 (SWXHB, Collectanea of correct thoughts); and *Zhongguo lidai jinhui xiaoshuo jicui* 中國歷代禁毀小說集萃 (Collection of censored fiction in China through the ages).

Mei's modes of describing sex. I would stretch the word "explicit" to include even accounts since pre-Han times of the lascivious acts of reviled and notorious historical figures—accounts that Ming and Qing authors expand upon to create the new level of explicitness characteristic of the period. Examples of such figures include Xia Ji and Empress Zhao Feiyan. Historical accounts from the Zhou and Han tell of a duke and two ministers sharing Xia Ji and sometimes appearing at court wearing bits of her undergarments inside their clothing.[7] Such is the extent of explicitness in their accounts. Stories written sometime between the Han and Tang invent episodes about Empress Zhao Feiyan and her sister having affairs in the palace while serving as consorts of the Han emperor Cheng (成, 51–7 BCE), who in a Tang version of the story dies of an overdose of an aphrodisiac that one of the sisters gives him—an event that *Jin Ping Mei* adopted.[8] Their level of explicitness goes as far as reporting the occurrence of these scandalous affairs, but without sexual detail. Pornographic expansions of these stories occur in two short novels, the Qing *Zhulin yeshi* 株林野史 (The scandalous story of the Zhulin Grove), which is about Xia Ji, and the late Ming *Zhaoyang qushi* 昭陽趣史 (The sensational history of Flying Swallow), about Zhao Feiyan and her sister.[9] In the case of the Zhao sisters, references to their sexual affairs do not appear in the Han dynastic histories, only in early pseudohistorical accounts and works of fiction. The latter already hint in the direction of what would become a core genre of classical and vernacular fiction in the Ming and Qing, in which authors write in the spirit of "tell[ing] it all," to repeat Wong's words, and luxuriate in the verbal description of unbridled acts of sex.

7. The duke was Ling of the Chen kingdom (陳靈公, reigned 613–599 BCE). See *Zuo zhuan* 左傳 (The Zuo tradition) (from year nine of Duke Xuan 宣), in Li Mengsheng, *Zuo zhuan yizhu*, 456; Liu Xiang 劉向, *Lienü zhuan* 列女傳, 7.16a–17a; Kinney, *Exemplary Women*, 147; and Yang Jiarong, "*Zuo zhuan* Xia Ji" (for a summary of *Zuo zhuan* accounts about Xia Ji).

8. See *Xijing zaji* 西京雜記 and the late Tang novella *Zhao Feiyan waizhuan* 趙飛燕外傳 (The untold story of Zhao Feiyan). Both, especially the latter, supply the basis for the late Ming pornographic novel *Zhaoyang qushi*. See Li Jianguo, "Chuanqi zhi shou"; and Milburn, "On *Zhao Feiyan waizhuan*," and *Empress*.

9. For a French translation of the former, see Barbier-Kontler, *Belles de candeur*.

Entertainment, Shock, and Titillation

Let me begin with a generalization in the spirit of Mao Dun: in the simplest terms, the goals of these authors are entertainment, shock, and titillation. They portray the heights of sexual pleasure, which they say is the greatest pleasure that can be had. They enjoy the extraordinary, the comic, and the bizarre. They relish the flouting of taboos. As in European pornography from around the same period and since, it is de rigueur for them to begin with a scene of sex at or near the beginning of the story, regularly followed by similar scenes throughout. The authors enjoy displaying an extensive knowledge of sex—that is, how to do it—as Mao Dun wrote. They describe its sensual qualities and physiological details, including its delicacies. They refer to techniques and methods, sometimes describing them in step-by-step fashion, and at times they portray the choreography of sexual movements, as in how a man goes about anally penetrating his virgin male partner or how a man manages sex with multiple women on a single bed. They use recurrent motifs, scenes, and character types, such as the stock scene of sex among a group of people, the catamite who sleeps with both husband and wife, the sex-starved widow who is aroused when she sees a well-endowed man, and the scrupulously proper woman who becomes lascivious once exposed to sexual lure. It is especially a love of transgression that links these works, which at its root amounts to transgression of society's ethical standards as spelled out in the classic "Five Cardinal Relationships" (*wulun* 五倫).

In terms of style and composition, the works are notable for being written in an "undemanding style," as Wong says about *Xiuta yeshi*.[10] However, some works (such as *Zhaoyang qushi*) include dense passages in classical language. Some are unusually focused on scene after scene and variation after variation of sex. These works include *Xiuta yeshi* and *Langshi qiguan* 浪史奇觀 (The wonders of the rake), both of which were written in the late Ming and thus are among the earliest of the works discussed here. Although entertainment and titillation are key, this literature is not above complexity of plot, as in the Qing *Zui chun feng* 醉春風 (Drunken on the spring breeze) or *Zhulin yeshi*. Sometimes a work poses

10. Wong, "Anatomy of Eroticism," 301.

conundrums and addresses serious issues, though typically only briefly and casually, as in this comment about the relentlessness of desire: "Matters of lust and desire are something that no one can escape" (淫慾之事，人人不免的).[11] Some authors engage the issue of the social imbalances between men and women or, in the case of male same-sex affairs, including with male prostitutes, the clash between the lustful rake and his entrapped boy. Both males and females suffer from sexual predators, whom these authors usually vilify—as *Jin Ping Mei* does the sodomist licentiate Wen (温, in chapter 76). A serious theme of *Zui chun feng* is the pressure women suffer under the chastity regime, which denies them the freedom and tolerance that libertine men enjoy.

Jin Ping Mei's difference is that it does all of these things in varying degrees, but it is of far greater length and linguistic complexity. It is the largest-scale work from the Ming to make the most of the complexities surrounding sexual scenes, which thread the narrative from beginning to end. In their admiration for *Jin Ping Mei*, Lu Xun and Mao Dun both draw a clear line between it and the so-called lewd works that they otherwise single out.[12] In this regard, *Jin Ping Mei* is in a separate category of sexually explicit literature of the late Ming, which includes stories from the collections of Feng Menglong (1574–1646) and Ling Mengchu (1580–1644), which themselves have been subject to censorship but in general are less narrowly focused on scenes of sexual activity. Lenny Hu provides a basic but useful distinction, arguing that Ling Mengchu's fiction functions on two planes: that of the "depiction of fleshly enjoyment" and that of the "commitment to the containment of that pleasure for ethical purposes."[13] Hu's characterization aligns with that of Lin Chen 林辰, who distinguishes the fiction designed for the sake of sensationalism and titillation from the fiction that contains explicit descriptions but also includes moral and critical commentary.[14] The distinction that these

11. See Anonymous, *Taohua yanshi* 桃花艷史, SWXHB, vol. 23, 4.29.

12. So does Li Mengsheng, whose *Zhongguo jinhui xiaoshuo baihua* gives plot summaries of censored fiction, including the works covered in this chapter.

13. Lenny Hu, *In the Inner Quarters*, 45.

14. Lin names six categories of works: (1) works about love and sexual relations that do not include explicit descriptions; (2) works making only occasional references to sex, such as *Guilian meng* 歸蓮夢; (3) works referring to sex in an allegorical way, like *Hou Xiyou ji* 後西遊記; (4) works about sex designed to warn against its excess, such as *Wutong*

critics make between what I call the more purely pornographic works, on the one hand, and *Jin Ping Mei* and the works of Feng Menglong and Ling Mengchu, on the other hand, is one that I follow. But such distinctions aside, *Jin Ping Mei* and the works of Feng Menglong, Ling Mengchu, and others cannot be considered without looking at their contemporary cousins—that is, the pornographic works that Lu, Mao, and others single out—not only simply to see what these works have to say and how in some cases they go further than *Jin Ping Mei*, but also to learn how they may eliminate and gloss over topics that *Jin Ping Mei* and the others cannot but consider.

As an instance of Hu and Lin's second category, *Jin Ping Mei* sums up the relentlessness of sexual desire in one twelve-word aphorism that comes at the gruesome end of Ximen Qing's life: "Though one's essence and spirit have their limits, sexual desire has no end" (一己精神有限，天下色慾無窮, 79.1143). Leave it to the other works to further foreground and exhaust the sense of that relentlessness, though not necessarily with such a dire ending. What I propose to use here as a representative sample of these works begins with the late Ming *Langshi qiguan* and *Xiuta yeshi*.[15] The same period also includes the story collections *Bie you xiang* 別有香 (Of another fragrance) and *Sengni niehai* 僧尼孽海 (Monks and nuns in a sea of sin). A group of six short novels appeared in the Qing that forms a convenient subcategory in which, as Giovanni Vitiello summarizes the plots, "a handsome youth from a well-to-do family . . . pursues a double enterprise: a scholarly bureaucratic career as well as a sensual one," his ultimate goal being the formation of an "ideal polygamous household." It is a "world of pure pornographic utopia, a place where there

ying 梧桐影; (5) works like *Jin Ping Mei*, which use explicit descriptions to make social commentary; and (6) works purely for the sake of sensationalism and titillation, like *Langshi qiguan* (*Mingmo Qingchu xiaoshuo shulu*, 400–401). See also Lin Chen, "Yanqing xiaoshuo," 38–39 (for a list of subjects described in this literature) and 39–41 (on the early stages of this fiction in classical language).

15. This list partly overlaps with the ones in McMahon, *Causality and Containment*, 69, and Vitiello, *The Libertine's Friend*, 93–131. In addition to the works I list (except *Zhaoyang qushi*, *Chundeng mishi*, and *Zui chun feng*), Vitiello also examines *Chundeng nao* 春燈鬧, *Longyang yishi* 龍陽逸史, *Wutong ying*, *Wumeng yuan* 巫夢緣, and *Yichun xiangzhi* 宜春香質. Experience tells us that there are surprises to be discovered in works not yet read. A comprehensive list of pornographic fiction appears in Si Xin, "Sheji xing miaoxiede gudai tongsu xiaoshuo shumu."

is no room for pain or demise."[16] The six novels are *Nao hua cong* 鬧花叢 (Revelry among the flowers), *Taohua ying* 桃花影 (Under the peach blossoms), *Chundeng mishi* 春燈迷史 (Enchantment under the spring lanterns), *Xinghua tian* 杏花天 (Heaven of apricot flowers), *Wushan yanshi* 巫山艷史 (The romance at Mt. Wu), and *Taohua yanshi* 桃花艷史 (The romance under the peach blossoms). In another category of their own are five works that focus on female protagonists and that as a rule do not end in anything like pure pornographic utopia: *Ruyijun zhuan* 如意君傳 (The lord of perfect satisfaction), *Chipozi zhuan* 癡婆子傳 (Tale of an infatuated woman), *Zhaoyang qushi*, *Zui chun feng*, and *Zhulin yeshi*. In only the last of these do the women emerge into paradise. In the context of Ming and Qing fiction, they are part of an underlying and ongoing narrative debate about the question of women's desire and how it should be governed.[17] Another subcategory is about the relations between a man and his adolescent male lover or prostitute. This subcategory includes three late-Ming works, *Bian er chai* 弁而釵 (Hairpins beneath his cap), *Yichun xiangzhi* 宜春香質 (Fragrant essences of spring), and *Longyang yishi* 龍陽逸史 (Forgotten tales of dragon boys). In addition to a focus on women's desire, same-sex relations between men appear in most of the works listed so far. Not all works fit so conveniently into the above categories. Some belong to multiple categories: for example, *Ruyijun zhuan* and *Zhaoyang qushi*, which are about notorious imperial figures and as such form a subcategory, though they are also works that center on female protagonists.[18] The late Qing *Pinhua baojian* 品花寶鑑 (Precious mirror of boy actresses) is a later example of a novel focused on male love, but it is longer and more complex than the works just listed and is similar to *Jin Ping Mei* in having both serious thematic purpose and sexually explicit content. A few works exist from the Ming

16. Vitiello, *The Libertine's Friend*, 97–98. See also Richard Wang, *Ming Erotic Novellas*, 147.

17. See Stevenson, "Sound, Space and Moral Soundscapes, 264–265.

18. Besides Xia Ji, Zhao Feiyan, and Wu Zetian, other royal figures are subjects of fictional works, including (among others) the Northern Qi 北齊 Empress Hu 胡, the Sui 隋 emperor Yang 隋煬帝, the Min 閩 Empress Chen Jinfeng 陳金鳳, and the Jin 金 Prince Hailing.

and Qing that dramatize sexual love between women, but without explicitly sexual descriptions.[19]

A brief and rough chronology of the works I have listed begins with *Ruyijun zhuan*, which may date from as early as the 1520s.[20] It was followed by *Chipozi zhuan*, *Langshi qiguan*, *Zhaoyang qushi*, and *Xiuta yeshi*, which are cited as key examples of this genre, are repeatedly mentioned in later literature, and appear in lists of censored obscene books. *Bie you xiang* and *Sengni niehai* are also of the late Ming, as are *Longyang yishi* (first published in 1632), *Bian er chai*, and *Yichun xiangzhi*, the latter two of which are from the same Chongzhen-era publishing house (late 1620s). The others that I cite are from the Qing, including three from the same publishing house of the Kangxi era (1661–1722): *Zui chun feng*, *Wushan yanshi*, and *Xinghua tian*.[21] *Taohua ying* and *Nao hua cong* are earlier, from the early Qing, while *Zhulin yeshi*, *Taohua yanshi*, and *Chundeng mishi* are likely post-Kangxi. Although not all these works that I call more purely pornographic fit as easily as others into the framework I am defining, they are similar at least in their approximate length and in the fact that they have been banned as "obscene" and "lascivious books" (*yinshu* 淫書)—and because of that have (in some cases) almost been lost forever.[22]

"Your Spirit Floats Away"

Evoking the heights of sexual pleasure is a central feature of *Jin Ping Mei* and the works I have just listed. As a character in *Chundeng mishi* puts it, "Your spirit floats away. Your souls are in a daze. It's as if you're about to become an immortal" (只覺着神情飄飄魂魄迷迷，有欲仙的光景一般), and

19. See Laura Wu, "Through the Prism of Male Writing"; and Wenjia Liu, "Virtuous Wives and Shrews."

20. See Stone, *Fountainhead*, 114; Martin Huang, *Desire*, 114 and 117–123; and Stevenson, "Sound, Space and Moral Soundscapes."

21. All are "probably" by a group of writers who wrote for the publisher, Xiaohua xuan 嘯花軒 (Li Mengsheng, *Zhongguo jinhui xiaoshuo baihua*, 345).

22. Except for *Zui chun feng*, all the ones I list, including the ones Vitiello discusses, appear in SWXHB.

"Your whole body goes as soft as floss" (*hunshen ruanmian* 渾身綿軟).[23] An intense session of sex leaves a woman's voice hoarse and her body weary.[24] Another woman faints and has to be resuscitated; yet another loses her senses; a man needs a whole day or longer to recuperate.[25] It is even possible to die of excess, though the staging of such a death is usually less trenchant than in *Jin Ping Mei*. In one case, a woman wakes to find a man dead beside her. He had become obsessed with the desire to sleep with her and paid a nun to arrange it so that he could secretly enter the woman's bed while she slept. But he dies of joy at the realization of his wish, an outcome that the story presents as a farce rather than as a dark ending.[26]

In portraying such joy and its extremes, the authors do their best to shock and amuse the reader. They thrive on exuberance and flamboyance of expression, as well as on flouting taboos and overturning norms. After the use of explicit and obscene language, the next most fundamental taboo that they flout is that of having characters join with normally prohibited partners under normally forbidden circumstances. Two unmarried youths meet secretly and have sex. The youths are open with each other about their desire, and they find easy ways to get together. An unmarried son cheekily asks his mother if he can sleep with his young widowed cousin. She tells him not to talk nonsense, but he is soon with the cousin anyway.[27] But besides these most common forms of prohibited liaisons, which occur in nonexplicit literature as well, these writers further push the upturning of norms by staging sex between even more prohibited partners, such as a woman and her young nephew, a woman and her brother-in-law and father-in-law, or a man with both a woman and

23. *Chundeng mishi*, SWXHB, vol. 23, 4.61; *Nao hua cong*, SWXHB, vol. 19, 2.49. See also *Ruyijun zhuan*, SWXHB, vol. 24, 42; and *Xinghua tian*, SWXHB, vol. 17, 4.82.

24. See *Langshi qiguan*, SWXHB, vol. 4, 10.80.

25. See *Langshi qiguan*, 13.98, 14.103, and 16.113; *Chundeng mishi*, 5.77 and 7.93; *Ruyijun zhuan*, 45–46; and *Xiuta yeshi*, 2.155–156 and 2.201–202.

26. See *Sengni niehai*, *Xihu an ni* 西湖庵尼, SWXHB, vol. 24, 185–186. The original version is in Hong Mai 洪邁 (1123–1202), *Yijian zhi* 夷堅志, "Zhijing" (支景), 3.902–903. For other instances of death or sickness from sexual excess, see *Langshi qiguan*, 16.113; and Jiangzuo shui'an 江左誰菴, *Zui chun feng*, 8.171–172.

27. See *Nao hua cong*, 5.88.

her daughter.[28] Pan Jinlian's affair with Chen Jingji, Ximen Qing's son-in-law, is not quite as brazen, though the affair was still considered incestuous. *Jin Ping Mei* is mild in comparison with these other works. Sex between multiple partners (usually a man and multiple women) is another favored scene, as is sex in the presence of others (which also occurs in *Jin Ping Mei*): both appear in Qing erotic illustrations. Sexual pleasure passes around, inevitably spreading to others, especially servants and other lower-class individuals who imitate their superiors. Complicity also spreads, as when Pan Jinlian has Ximen Qing sleep with maid Chunmei. Besides delighting her master, Jinlian turns Chunmei into a fellow wanton woman, thereby ensuring her loyalty. As if trying to distinguish themselves from others, a few works portray types of bizarreness that rarely if ever appear elsewhere. Examples include a man who has sex with a woman's corpse—a lascivious empress, whose body is cold but whose vagina is still warm.[29] Lust is diabolically immortal: the sexual drive pushes even beyond death.

As a rule, pornography ignores consequences such as extramarital pregnancy and bastard children, but when these do occur (in *Chundeng mishi*, for example), they do not cause a crisis. The parents accept the situation and have the daughters marry their impregnator, a young man whom they deem to be an ideal mate anyway. In *Chipozi zhuan* and *Zui chun feng*, the woman has a son but no idea who the father is. At first she gets away with the situation, though she eventually suffers the condemnation that she would normally receive. Still, the *Chipozi zhuan* protagonist lives to tell her story, with both its ups and downs. When her father-in-law forces her to have sex with him, she asks him whether people will regard the baby if she becomes pregnant as a son or grandson, though the story goes no further with her provocative question.[30] In general, if pregnancy takes place, it belongs to a desirable ending in which the polygynous family enjoys a wealth of offspring. The fact that pregnancy seldom occurs in *Jin Ping Mei*, in spite of the frequency of sexual activity, in part belongs to the same sort of suppression of reality. But it is also the case

28. See story 4 of *Bie you xiang*, *Chipozi zhuan*, *Zui chun feng*, *Langshi qiguan*, and *Taohua ying*.

29. The woman is Empress Hu of the Northern Qi. See *Sengni niehai*, 1.53; and McMahon, *Women Shall Not Rule*, 169–170.

30. See Martin Huang, *Desire*, 123–124; and *Chipozi zhuan*, 2.52.

that the novel has a message of moral consequence: profligate men and wanton women will fail to enjoy the success of plentiful offspring and in particular to bear a son who is worthy and who will continue the family line. Similarly, Pan Jinlian's pregnancy and abortion as a result of her affair with Chen Jingji is an example of the author delivering consequences, not just pleasure, to adulterous lovers.

A bodily function such as menstruation might seem to be a bad fit in a pornographic story, but it becomes something to make light of in *Langshi qiguan* and *Taohua yanshi*. The woman in *Langshi qiguan* tells the man that she is menstruating, afraid he will not want to have sex with her. But he does not care, and afterward they cheerfully wash themselves off (25.161–162). *Taohua yanshi* makes a flamboyant comedy of the situation. While the man is licking the woman's vagina, her menstrual flow suddenly commences and runs onto him. The maids looking on laugh and "congratulate" him, saying, "Look, master, your first child is a boy!" (大叔恭喜，頭生就是一個兒, 3.24). This is a case of an author striving for yet another way to defy a taboo and engage in yet another imaginative leap, as if trying to outdo other authors.

The menstrual splash is a case of staging the sensational, the bizarre, and the comic. The use of sexual tools is another such case. In *Langshi qiguan*, a woman enjoying a dildo has such a strong flow of "wanton waters" (*yinshui* 淫水) that the dildo comes flying out. The man reacts to this extraordinary sight by saying, "It's just like the firing of a cannon (*falangji*)!" (兀的不是發硠磯出来了, 13.95–96). Cannons called by this name came into China in the early to mid-sixteenth century and were also called *folangji* (佛郎機)—which dates the book to sometime in the sixteenth or early seventeenth century.[31] A double dildo appears in *Langshi qiguan*, as does a more complex type in *Zhulin yeshi*, which has first to be steeped in hot water to make it swell and then tied to the woman's foot so that she can use it on herself (7.47). Authors thrive on portraying the expansions of pleasure allowed by such technologies. A man in *Langshi qiguan* uses Burmese bells to satisfy one woman while he is with another (they are called "mercury bells," *shuiyin ling* 水銀鈴; 39.243–244). *Xinghua tian* goes so far as to have the man use the bell for all twelve of his wives, taking turns himself with one wife at a time

31. See Chen Qinghao and Wang Qiugui, introduction, 16.

(13.254–255). Here the Burmese bell stands in for the male protagonist's penis. Dildos in *Jin Ping Mei* do not have as much power to please, nor do they provide as much entertainment for the reader. Instead, they are but passing details as items in Ximen Qing's collection of sex tools, though they were well known and widely available at the time the novel was written.

Authors strive for humor and virtuoso effects in passages such as these. In a story in *Bie you xiang*, a monk shows off his expertise in sexual positions, of which he has a fully "sequenced set" (*taoshu* 套數; 4.38–39). He announces the name of each position as he performs it for the woman, who voices her reaction to each. In the first one, he kneels and licks her genitals, calling this "the ruddy dragon stirs the gully stream" (*chilong jiao jian* 赤龍攪澗). In another, he "thrusts and stabs all around, deliberately ignoring where he is going" (左右塞插，故意不看門路). This is called "the homeward-bound swallow heading for its nest. The woman takes hold of it and sets it on the right path, saying 'The nest is right here!'" (歸燕尋巢，婦握入道，巢在此). As his thrusts become wilder, she says, "Now that is really doing it!" (*ci cai shi shiji* 此才是實際). When another position does not quite satisfy her, he picks her up with his arms around her rear and enters more deeply. "Wonderful" (*miao* 妙), she says. This position is called "the foreign monk plays the cymbals" (*fanseng xi nao* 番僧戲鐃), to which she responds, "Yes, quite like it" (*xiang, xiang* 像像). A similar position has him walking five times around the room, which he calls, "going from door to door with begging bowl" (*yan men chi bo* 沿門持缽, 4.38–40).[32] She finally tires, and they stop. Pornographic entertainment is a goal in itself in these passages. A comparable form of entertainment in *Jin Ping Mei*'s would be, for example, its poetic passages of sex as battle. But it would be unlikely to have scenes such as those described above without adding more elements of tension and thematic significance relating to the surrounding narrative.

Besides the virtuoso effect of this scene in *Bie you xiang*, a contest is in fact going on between male and female. As mentioned in the chapter on sex as battle, the episode ends with the monk accidentally revealing the way to make him ejaculate and the woman taking advantage of that

32. A series of positions, called *gushi* 故事 (literally, stories), appears with yet different names in *Zhulin yeshi*, 11.102.

to tire him out. She cannot let him give her too much pleasure without consequences, for then he would have the upper hand. However, dramatic tension is minimal because, except for the fact that the monk refuses to see her again, she suffers no ill effects. The positions and their outlandish names reflect a bravado and fertility of imagination in a writer who has invested in a radically unconventional, but perhaps also lucrative, form of literary endeavor. Although we have no information about the sales of this or other similar books, it is likely that such publications had an eager audience.

Sensual qualities, physiological details, and the finer pleasures of intercourse are another focus of attention. How does the body work; what do parts if it or its effluvia look, taste, or smell like; and how do partners move together? Descriptions alternate between the particularistic detail, including the credible and realistic, and the fantastic and hyperbolic. It is as if writers are feeling their way into a newly opened field of expression. *Langshi qiguan* makes sure to portray the fact that a man can last longer—he is more "long-lasting" (*jianjiu* 堅久)—after he has already ejaculated once (8.83). The same novel also dramatizes the delicate moment that occurs when a man tries to hold back and when just the slightest movement can make him lose control: "The Profligate caught himself and made gentle efforts to keep himself in check, as if holding back urine. But suddenly it was as if something so light as a falling leaf had landed on his waist, sending him into a state of alarm, and, indeed, he could hold it in no longer and let it all come out" (浪子卻如忍小便的一般，擒住輕輕提放. 忽然間，一枝落葉，正飄在浪子腰間. 浪子猛然驚駭，矜持不定，便都洩了，13.96).[33]

As mentioned above, *Xinghua tian* recites a step-by-step method for delaying ejaculation, a form of which the man in *Langshi qiguan* must be trying (without success) to put into effect. In *Jin Ping Mei*, Ximen Qing knows innately how to delay ejaculation—or it is simply that the author does not bother to consider such a matter. Ximen Qing is not one to be meticulous in following such a method. Anyway, after he begins using the monk's drug, it does the job for him.

Depictions of naked bodies in *Jin Ping Mei* and other literature usually vary only minimally. Detailed, particularistic close-ups are brief, but

33. *Tifang* 提放 can also be read as *difang* 提防, meaning to take precautions against.

they can be as precise and explicit as any such descriptions throughout Ming and Qing fiction, especially beginning in the late Ming. Though not describing the body itself, *Chundeng mishi* entertains the reader with a close-up of what a splash of semen on a coverlet looks like. A young servant has had a nocturnal emission and his master discovers it, to the boy's embarrassment. The master at first thinks the boy has urinated in bed, but when he looks again: "He sees spread there on the coverlet something that looked like candlewax, white, shiny, and sticky, soaking across the surface" (只見被上似撒了上邊一些蠟燭油的一般，白光光的年[黏]答答的沾在上頭, 4.57).

Xiuta yeshi features close-up views of a bruised and swollen vagina, the effect being both to demonstrate the intensity of the woman's recent bout with a man and to dramatize the sympathy that a second man has for her in her pitiable state.[34] Elsewhere the same novel portrays a man for the first time taking a "careful" (*zixi* 仔细) look at the woman's naked body, considering first her breasts, which are "round and smooth, gently and loosely nestling from her chest" (又圓又光，滑滑的貼在胸膛上); then her stomach, which is smooth because she has not yet given birth; and finally her vagina, which is compared to a "little mound rising like a steamed bun, surrounded by a few tender strands of dark hair" (像個饅頭突起，上面生些軟細細的黑毛，稀稀幾根兒, an image echoed in other works).[35] In *Langshi qiguan*, the libertine's eye wanders lustfully over the catamite's naked body, first his "stem" (*bing'er* 柄兒) and then his "buttocks" (*tun'er* 臀兒), both of which are "white and fine as snow" (*xuebaiyanghao* 雪白樣好).[36] In *Taohua ying*, the main wife, at whom the man peeks before marrying her, has a hairless vagina, while a lustier woman he previously had sex with has a few "fine hairs" (*ximao* 細毛) around hers—though in both cases the description is otherwise minimal.[37]

What is deeper inside enters the picture when *Zui chun feng* describes what the "heart of the cunt" (*bixin* 毴心) feels like when a man suddenly

34. See *Xiuta yeshi*, 2.177; and Wong, "Anatomy of Eroticism," 313.

35. See *Xiuta yeshi*, 1.113–114; and Wong, "Anatomy of Eroticism," 312. Comparisons to a steamed bun or cake also occur in *Chundeng mishi*, 2.38; *Zhulin yeshi*, 2.27–28; and JPM, 59.778.

36. *Langshi qiguan*, 28.177.

37. *Taohua ying*, 2.35, 3.55–356 ("with not even a single hair," 毫無一根毛影), and 10.173–74. See also *Jin Ping Mei*, 4.60–61 (on Pan Jinlian) and 59.778 (on Zheng Aiyue).

senses it. The woman has just asked him to thrust harder and tells him what pleasure she feels upon his touching that spot, which the narrative then proceeds to describe. "Indeed, there was something there like a piece of flesh but also like a piece of bone, larger than a person's thumb" (果然有一似肉非肉似骨非骨的東西，比大拇指略大些).[38] The scene recalls the one in *Jin Ping Mei*, which gives a similar anatomical analysis of what that novel calls the "vagina chamber." It is as if these bits of knowledge about the unfathomable woman are what men must be sure to understand and tell one another.

The strength of the woman's arousal becomes particularly apparent in the form of her sexual flood. I discussed this topic in chapter 5 in terms of the image's potentially grotesque or bestial qualities, and how fiction, including *Jin Ping Mei*, exploits the image for its sensationalism. The woman's flood has been a focus of attention and exaltation since earliest times in the art of the bedchamber. In Daoist sexual alchemy, such fluids are material manifestations of *jing* and *qi*. Their prominence in the literature of sexual desire should be read against this background. But if the art of the bedchamber and Daoism emphasize the guarding and enrichment of *jing* and *qi* for the sake of energetic and spiritual balance, then Ming and Qing pornography instead secularizes these and other bodily fluids, setting aside their Daoist halo and viewing them primarily as signs of the intensity and richness of pleasure.[39] The tasting and imbibing of these fluids is an inherent part of their richness. Ming and Qing fiction, including *Jin Ping Mei*, generally refers to such fluids in terms of their copiousness. *Xiuta yeshi* is exceptional in breaking the fluids down into multiple consistencies—somewhat resembling the Mawangdui text *He yinyang*, which the author could not have read—and analyzing their consistency according to ten stages.[40] The *Xiuta yeshi* passage is another example of the informative aside, which briefly touches on the various shades and densities of a woman's sexual fluids: "At first, it comes like the spray of a sneeze, then it turns into a clear mucus, and in the end it

38. *Zui chun feng*, 1.52.

39. For the idea of "secularizing," see Wong, "Anatomy of Eroticism," 321.

40. The consistencies include "clear and cool" (*qingliang* 清凉), "smelling like burning bones" (*chou ru fangu* 臭如燔骨), "slippery" (*hua* 滑), "greasy" (*zhi* 脂), and "gluey" (*jiao* 膠). See *He yinyang* and *Sunü miaolun* (referring to "slippery fluid," *huaye* 滑液), in Li Ling, *Zhongguo fangshu gaiguan*, 38 and 195, respectively; and Harper, "Sexual Arts," 591.

flows as if gushing from a spring" (初來的時節，就像打噴嚏一般．後來清水鼻涕一般，又像泉水汩汩的沖出來). When the man goes to taste it, "It is delightful and sweet and gives off a delicate fragrance" (味極甜，又清香).[41] In *Zui chun feng*, the man excitedly praises the woman's fluids, called *saoshui* 騷水 (randy waters), which are "not at all smelly, merely a bit fishy," and "the most fragrant thing that could be!" (全沒臭，只有些腥；香得緊；5.116). In other cases the fluid is a delicacy, to be tasted directly or mixed with liquor.[42] Such passages are examples of the focus on particular moments and qualities of sexual pleasure, evoking its sheer presence in the now as if to capture it in a way that gives rise to marveling and awe.[43] *Jin Ping Mei*'s renditions refrain from such marveling, as if to say that focusing on such aspects would be to go too far in forgetting the complexities of life that surround the sexual act.

The woman's sexual essence is not the only fluid celebrated in these works. In *Taohua ying*, a man in the midst of thrusting pauses to swallow some of the woman's saliva—which, as noted above, is considered healthful in *daoyin* practices, though that aspect does not explicitly come across in this case (7.147). *Bian er chai* portrays a man's anus functioning like a vagina, as "waves of passion" (*qingbo* 情波) flow forth, completely wetting the mat below (5.174–175). In *Taohua yanshi*, a man puts his tongue in a boy's anus, which is "just like eating honey or sipping tasty oil" (如吃蜜喝油的一般, 2.19).[44] In *Langshi qiguan*, the man's essence has a supernatural effect. A woman who drinks the catamite's semen "becomes more charming by the day" (日漸嬌媚, 29.185–186). In the same novel, semen spills into a nearby pool, where a group of gold fish eagerly devour it and become beautifully colorful (31.198). These two cases evoke something of the Daoist lore of the transformative properties of *jing*. A darker, demonic side of the imbibing of fluids also exists. A villainous polygynist in *Yesou puyan* (野叟曝言, A country codger's words of exposure) traps and drugs the novel's hero, has his concubines arouse the hero and position his penis through a hole in a wall, at the other side of which the villain drinks his semen. The homoerotic semblance of this act is displaced

41. *Xiuta yeshi*, 2.151; see also 2.155–156 and 2.179. The translation is from Wong, "Anatomy of Eroticism," 317, slightly modified.

42. See *Langshi qiguan*, 36.226; *Zhulin yeshi*, 7.46; and *Xiuta yeshi*, 2.151.

43. On the sense of presence, see Ullén, "Pornography and Its Critical Reception."

44. "Oil" (*you* 油) flows from a woman's anus in *Langshi qiguan* (33.209).

by the fact that drinking a potent man's semen is part of the villain's regime to increase sexual vigor and longevity.[45]

Sexual bodies in motion—aroused, driven, or ecstatic—is one way of summing up what these authors write about. Repetitive descriptions of thrusting abound, the focus being on vigor and endurance: the number of thrusts can go into the hundreds or thousands. More nuanced is an instance in *Bian er chai*, which stands out in its particularistic description of the movements of one man as he positions himself over another. The Hanlin 翰林 academician is the penetrator, and the student Zhao 趙 his virgin partner. They love each other deeply, but since Zhao is still new to the notion of physical love, he tries at first to resist:

> Zhao had no choice but to endure his caresses, but when the other's hands came to that place of extreme joy, Zhao pushed him away. The Hanlin took that opportunity to cup his hands behind the student's neck, hug him closer, and kiss him on the lips. Zhao averted his face, but in doing so just happened to turn his rear toward the Hanlin, who put his right foot under Zhao's, flexing it a little, then with his left foot pressed onto Zhao's right calf, and, cupping Zhao's neck with his right hand, drew his left hand up to wet it with saliva to rub on Zhao's cleft. Then, taking his left hand to spread the cheeks apart, he closed in and entered. In such a position, Zhao had no way to escape. (趙生只得聽他摸. 摸得極樂處, 趙生把手便推. 翰林乘勢將手插入趙生勁, 掰定親嘴. 趙生掉臉向裡, 恰好屁股朝着翰林. 翰林以右腳插入趙生右腳底下, 略屈些. 以左腳踏住趙生右腳脛上. 以右手掰定頭頸, 扯其左手, 以左手潤唾沫於屁股眼. 即將左手推其屁旁骨, 側身而進. 趙生到此地位, 推脫不得 . . . .; 1.3.85–86).

This is one of only two such close-up scenes in the story, the other being a passage about how to contract the bowels during intercourse so that no feces come out (1.4.87).[46] The writer's main concern is to extol the depth of love between the men. Explicit details detract from the rendition of sublime passion.

45. Xia Jingqu, *Yesou puyan*, 65.5a–7b. See also Vitiello, *The Libertine's Friend*, 158–159.

46. Stevenson refers to a similar passage in a story from the late Ming *Shi dian tou* (石點頭), in "The Male Homoerotic Wanton Woman," 62–63.

Sex among multiple partners is a favored scene in these novels, especially in stories about libertines who form polygamous households. A common penultimate scene is the grand gathering (*shenghui* 勝會), in which the man and his multiple wives have a joint session of sex. The fact that *Jin Ping Mei* does not portray such a scene is a telling sign.[47] Ximen Qing—the owner of a magnificent array of sexual drugs and devices and someone who already has been shown with maids present while he has sex with another woman—might seem to be just the kind of man who would like to have all his women on the same bed. But the particular reality that *Jin Ping Mei* presents prohibits such a scene. In the novels I discuss next, such a scene is part of a kind of "pornographic utopia," as Vitiello calls it, in which the women are willing participants. Ximen Qing's polygamy is not so harmonious.

To show more precisely what this difference means, let me begin by saying that the main challenge to the writer portraying a grand gathering is how to manage the description of a multitude of movements. He cares less, if at all, about the complex alliances and rivalries among the women, which is the focus of *Jin Ping Mei*. In the three cases cited below, the authors grant the man complete success, with only a lightly comic hint of the difficulty in making such an event work to everyone's satisfaction. The scene of joint sex goes by a similar name in all three works. In *Nao hua cong* it is called "the grand meeting of love" (*hehuan dahui* 合歡大會), which begins as the wives all "compete to be the first to grab and play" with the man's penis (*zheng xian duonong*, 爭先奪弄). He "madly thrusts with one woman" (*yitou kuang chou* 一頭狂抽), while using his toe with another (11.190). Although two others cry out that he ignores them, such complaints never turn bitter. Like the other works below, *Nao hua cong* is an erotic romance written in the wake of a set of similar works in classical language from the 1500s, all of which featured the harmonious marriage of a man and multiple wives and in which none of them suffer punishment or death.[48]

Xinghua tian goes to greater lengths, but instead of the kind of description in straight prose that appears in the above scene from *Bian er chai* or

47. Chen Jingji together with Pan Jinlian and Chunmei is the closest *Jin Ping Mei* comes to such a scene, 83.1201–1202.

48. See Richard Wang, *Ming Erotic Novellas*, 139, 144, and 146.

the brief one from *Nao hua cong* just discussed, it renders the event in a sequence of rhythmic, mainly four-character phrases—that is, in the style of parallel prose. After constructing a grand "love bed" (*hehuan chuang* 合歡床, 13.239), which takes months to build, the husband (Yuesheng) prepares himself by first taking an aphrodisiac and then having each woman insert a Burmese bell, so that each can be satisfied while he tends to them one at a time. He begins with one woman while the others look on, and the description proceeds in four-character rhythm: "It was a torrential bout of clouds and rain, the pleasures of which were overwhelming" (雲狂雨驟, 美暢難禁, 13.254). With the third woman, "His tortoise drank of her jade juice, which made him nod in steady approval, it was of such extraordinary quality. Her fragrant secretions soaked below, she lost control of her limbs, the covers spread into disarray" (龜尋玉液而飲, 點首不住, 有無限其妙. 香涎漬漬, 四體難支, 早歪重裀, 13.254–255). The author resorts to military metaphors such as "she wasn't ready for Yuesheng's golden lance as it pierced her through, for her heavy armor failed to block it" (不防悅生金鎗穿透, 重鎧難遮, 13.255). With this woman defeated and now lying to one side, Yuesheng takes on two others, who likewise soon retreat. A third cries out: "You merciless man. You're a brute, dealing my sisters such cruel defeat. Don't you try to escape. I'll take you on now and pull you off your horse!" (好冤家, 心情忒狠, 把我姐姐苦敗. 不要走, 我來敵對, 那[拿]你下馬, 13.255). She challenges him with her crotch, which she spreads threateningly before him. But he brags that he has more than enough weapons and armor to defeat her. He is "like a fierce tiger just emerging from the mountain wilds, a dragon who has just given rise to a thunderstorm" (猶如出山猛虎, 初興雲雨的蛟龍, 13.256). They engage in a dire struggle, but he defeats her soundly before taking one final woman. Then, in more four-character sequences, he finishes "victorious, as he removes his helmet and armor, dismounts from his war horse, thrusts his spear into the ground, and reins in his mount" (得勝, 解冑卸甲, 下了征駒, 搠鎗拴馬, 13.257). The passage recalls the mock battles in *Jin Ping Mei*, except that in *Jin Ping Mei* the foes are for the moment evenly matched, though Ximen Qing is the master figure in other contexts. In the "grand meeting of love" in these three works, the polygamist hero is the gallant victor.

A more prosaic, yet still genteel, rendition of the polygynist's orgy appears in the earlier *Taohua ying*, which is from the late Ming or early

Qing. It resembles *Bian er chai* in resorting to plain prose, barely making use of the four-character formula of *Xinghua tian*. The "grand meeting of love" (*hehuan shenghui* 合歡勝會) takes place in the last chapter on a large bed in a flower garden, just before the hero withdraws with his wives to a peach blossom paradise. Yuqing 玉卿 (whose name is a pun on "jade stalk") joins with five of his wives. His main wife does not take part, and she later disapproves, thus displaying the token bit of moral censure that works like this commonly end with. There is also the implication that the orgy will be the last such event before withdrawal into paradise, since in traditional lore sex only occurs in the earthly realm. As in *Nao Hua Cong*, the man lies in the center, his "chowry handle" erect, which "a flurry of hands, fifty fingers like jade shoots of bamboo, all compete to fondle" (分不開五十隻尖尖玉筍, 爭來捧弄). He is like a polygynous god, whom the five women share and adore, and who grants all five equal levels of ecstasy. There is only one note of discord, and it is easily resolved, when one of the women cries out to the rest, "You're only having fun for your own good and completely forgetting about me! You're pressing against my chest so much that it hurts!" (你們只管快活, 卻忘記了我的胸膛, 壓得酸疼; 12.198–199). It is a comic scene that amounts to the author's attempt at a climaxing tour de force.

Pornography, including *Jin Ping Mei*, must have its wanton women, though the more purely pornographic works tend to create a more easily aroused woman than *Jin Ping Mei* does. Her quick, even instant, arousal is a motif that has existed since at least the Tang; once triggered, she becomes sexually voracious.[49] Ming and Qing works show her becoming desirous after spying on others having sex (in one case, two boys exchanging positions as they have sex with each other [*Taohua yanshi*, 1.14–15]) or when she sees a man bathing or urinating (*Langshi qiguan*, 3.44), a man masturbating while looking at erotic illustrations, a man exposing

49. Stevenson writes that she has an "inner . . . predilection to licentiousness" ("The Male Homoerotic Wanton Woman," 63–64). And Wong writes that she "instantly converts into a sex-crazed woman" ("Anatomy of Eroticism," 293). In the Tang story "Hejian zhuan" (河間傳, by Liu Zongyuan 柳宗元, 773–819), the trigger occurs because of a rape. See Stevenson, "Sound, Space and Moral Soundscapes," 280–281, and "The Male Homoerotic Wanton Woman," 58 (citing Carlitz, "Weeping," 236); and Nienhauser, "Female Sexuality."

himself to her, or animals or insects mating.[50] Such scenes serve as incitements to launch the pornographic action.

As for the largeness of male genitals, another widely shared motif, Ximen Qing's great size is a recurrent image in *Jin Ping Mei*, in which the organ looks ugly and frightening. It causes pain, though eventually he arouses some of the women—or they act as if they were aroused. Other works refer to pain as if by rote, following it with unproblematic arousal and pleasure. In some cases, the author seems to acknowledge the difficulty of a virgin's first sex but treats it as something easily overcome and titillating at the same time. The woman in *Chundeng mishi* wishes the man could make himself smaller, but he cannot, he explains, as he proceeds to tell her in the manner of one giving an elementary lesson about sex. Being older by a year, her maid is therefore larger, and he reassures the virgin that easier times will soon arrive (5.77).[51] In short, the man's prowess needs to be suffered at first so that it can finally deliver its benefits. Such a scenario appears across Ming and Qing pornography, though *Chundeng mishi* is a more juvenile example.

The Libertine and His "Dragon Boy"

A common character in these works is the man who enjoys sex with an adolescent male, the latter of whom goes by several names, such as "dragon boy" (*longyang* 龍陽), "junior official" (*xiaoguan* 小官), or "pretty boy" (*luantong* 孌童). As Vitiello writes, "a conspicuous homoerotic streak . . . runs through the narrative of the mostly 'heterosexual' libertine of late imperial pornographic fiction." In Ming and Qing society, sex with a young man in his teens was widely accepted as a choice for sexual satisfaction, as these books show repeatedly and without surprise.[52] It was a matter of

50. Such stock scenes occur throughout late Ming fiction. See *Langshi qiguan*, 18.122 (on pigs mating); and McMahon, *Causality and Containment*, 93 (for references to Ling Mengchu, Feng Menglong, and others).

51. See also *Bian er chai*, where anal rape is painful at first but finally arousing (4.1.270–271).

52. Vitiello, *The Libertine's Friend*, 102; see also 5 and 17. See also Wu Cuncun, *Homoerotic Sensibilities*, 24; and Hinsch, *Passions of the Cut Sleeve*. See also Vitiello, "The

both "natural propensity" (*pixing* 癖性 or *pi'ai* 癖愛) and "one's erotic expertise."[53] That is, in some cases homosexuality was a man's exclusive interest, an inherent predilection. But it was also the case that, as a true libertine, a man should indulge in love for boys. It was fashionable to do so. When Ximen Qing wants to impress his honored guests, he does so by having his handsome boy attendant and sometime sexual partner, Shutong 書童, perform music for them along with four sing-song boys (36.476). Shutong sings a female role in woman's dress. Famous literati of the times were known to keep such boys, some of whom were actors and singers. Their passionate affairs were subjects of fantasy and hearsay.[54] A darker side existed in which boys were kept as brothel slaves, with greedy go-betweens arranging contracts between a boy and his family, on the one hand, and brothel owners or lecherous patrons, on the other hand. Male brothels were a new phenomenon in the Ming urban scene.[55]

In most of the works I discuss, the boy, younger man, or catamite is either the man's preferred partner to the near exclusion of women, or he is a partner enjoyed as much as, or only somewhat less than, women.[56] In both cases, the younger man may also have sex with the man's wife, concubines, and maids. In *Langshi qiguan*, he is even referred to as an "attending concubine" (*shiqie* 侍妾, 27.173), a role that he plays for both husband and wife. In this work as in others (*Xiuta yeshi*, *Taohua ying*, *Chundeng nao*, and *Nao hua cong*), it is a stock situation for the husband to let the younger man have sex with his wife or concubines in return for the husband's having sex with him.[57] In a recurrent scene, the older man gets the younger one drunk and then takes advantage of him, later

Fantasy of an Ugly Boy," "Forgotten Tears," and "Exemplary Sodomites"; and Volpp, "The Discourse on Male Marriage," "Classifying Lust," and "The Literary Circulation of Actors."

53. Vitiello, *The Libertine's Friend*, 21; see also 16, 17, 90, and 93–94.

54. The poet Yuan Mei 袁枚 (1716–1798), for example, was said to be rarely without such company. On him and others, see Wu Cuncun, *Homoerotic Sensibilities*, 45, 65, 69, 86–91, 94, and 105.

55. See Wu Cuncun, *Homoerotic Sensibilities*, 76–78, and "The Plebification of Male-Love," 75–76 and 79–80.

56. For the stock situation of the man "exclusively interested in boys," see Vitiello, *The Libertine's Friend*, 19.

57. See Vitiello, *The Libertine's Friend*, 102–111; and Li Mengsheng, *Zhongguo jinhui xiaoshuo baihua*, 83.

arranging to reward him with his (the first man's) wife. Himself a woman-loving libertine, the younger man may at first be angry, but he then accepts his rape and forms a "profound alliance" with the older man, who will guide and protect him for the rest of the narrative.[58] The younger man serves as a replacement for the husband when he is away from home or because the husband does not like sex with women (*Xiuta yeshi*). In *Chipozi zhuan*, the wife seduces the catamite when her husband is away from home. Sometimes all three have sex at once (*Langshi qiguan*, *Xiuta yeshi*, and *Nao hua cong*). The young man is not always a sympathetic character and can instead be an intruder and conniver. In *Langshi qiguan*, the wife grows to dislike him and plots against him, eventually causing his death. In *Taohua yanshi*, the catamite dares to sleep with the wife, concubine, and two maids, leading the boy-loving husband to have him killed. Such characters recall the motif of the heartless prostitute, who takes advantage of her client to captivate him both sexually and sentimentally, while draining him of his wealth. Another recurrent situation is the catamite who fleeces the "big shot" (*dalao guan* 大老官) customer. His methods include thrilling his lover by moaning and acting as if aroused, as Chen Jingji does at the end of *Jin Ping Mei*.[59] In contrast, the handsome dragon boy can also become an object of pity when dominant men abuse and entrap him. In such a case, he is a lonely soul trapped in a world of greed, vulgarity, and lust (*Bian er chai*, *Yichun xiangzhi*, and *Pin hua baojian*).

As Vitiello writes, a remarkable change takes place in pornographic fiction in the Qing, during which the story of the positively portrayed, boy-loving libertine begins to disappear, while "homosexuality tends to be attributed to servants and villains."[60] In other words, sometime after the early Qing the trend is for only the roguish, villainous characters to be sodomists. The mid-nineteenth-century novel *Pinhua baojian* is a prime example, in which sexual affairs take place only among the villainous

58. Vitiello, *The Libertine's Friend*, 99; and see *Taohua ying*, *Chundeng nao*, and *Nao hua cong*.

59. Wu Cuncun, "The Plebification of Male-Love," 75. See also *Taohua ying*, 9.149; and Vitiello, *The Libertine's Friend*, 24.

60. Vitiello, *The Libertine's Friend*, 119; see also 119–126, on *Wu meng yuan* 巫夢緣, *Wutong ying*, and *Taohua yanshi*.

characters. Refined young men fall in love but do not have sex.[61] Some works (*Wutong ying* and *Yesou puyan*) even feature a "pronounced critical stance toward homosexuality."[62] The change is also visible in terms of portrayals, in that late Ming works describe anal sex as a scene of vivid, wanton pleasure. The act may begin in pain, but it soon turns to utter satisfaction.[63] In contrast, in a Qing work such as *Shenlou zhi* (蜃樓志 Mirage, ca. 1804), anal sex is purely painful and degrading. In short, the positive and explicit portrayal in fiction of same-sex affairs is a short-lived phenomenon, mainly confined to the late Ming and early Qing. The love affairs of the libertine and his same-sex partner will nevertheless continue throughout Qing history, both in real life and in descriptions of it (though not sexually explicit ones) in other forms of literature—including miscellaneous collections (*biji* 筆記), poetry, gazetteers, and especially the flower guides (*huapu* 花譜) written in the mid- and late Qing about boy actors (*dan* 旦) who were female impersonators.[64]

Issues and Conundrums

As noted above, five narratives focus particularly on female protagonists. Three are from the Ming: *Ruyijun zhuan*, *Chipozi zhuan*, and *Zhaoyang qushi*, all from the sixteenth or seventeenth century. Two are from the Qing: *Zui chun feng*, from the Kangxi period; and *Zhulin yeshi*, from the Qianlong 乾隆 (1735–1796) period or slightly after.[65] Though each is worthy of a lengthy study, I treat them as a group by first asking the following questions. Because of their particular focus on female protagonists,

61. See Vitiello, *The Libertine's Friend*, 180–199; McMahon, *Polygamy and Sublime Passion*, 58–67; and Wu Cuncun, *Xi wai zhi xi*.

62. Vitiello, *The Libertine's Friend*, 121.

63. See Stevenson, "The Male Homoerotic Wanton Woman," 64–68 (including translations from *Bian er chai* and *Yichun xiangzhi*).

64. See Wu Cuncun and Stevenson, "Notes on Flower Appreciation"; and Wu Cuncun, *Xi wai zhi xi*.

65. Other such stories exist, such as two late Ming or early Qing stories in classical language, *Zhao Feiyan waizhuan* and *Yang Taizhen waizhuan* 楊太眞外傳. See Wu Cuncun, "*Cong Jingyuan michuan dongfang chunyi ce* zhong." On *Chipozi zhuan*, *Ruyijun zhuan*, and *Dengcao heshang* 燈草和尚, see Martin Huang, *Desire*, 111–136.

do they have more nuanced portrayals of the character type of the wanton woman? How should we evaluate their portrayals of women acting in sexually independent ways? How do they make us rethink *Jin Ping Mei*, especially in terms of what I call a nuanced portrayal of the wanton woman?

Let me begin with *Chipozi zhuan*, which is unique in Chinese fiction for having a first-person female narrator—though that fact cannot be taken to indicate female authorship or perspective.[66] In Paola Zamperini's words, *Chipozi zhuan* portrays the woman experiencing sexual intercourse in primarily "two modes: pain and orgasmic bliss."[67] As elsewhere, whether or not she is a willing participant, her reaction after initial pain, even in the case of rape, is a shift into bottomless ecstasy. The lack of subtlety points to male authorship in this and the other works just mentioned, as does the combination of other factors such as the frequent references to and satires of a man's poor sexual performance—not to mention the correspondingly overcompensating portrayal of male fortitude and the recurrence of such common sayings as "A woman's desire will not desist until she is beneath the earth" (婦人慾念入土方休). The pornographic literature of the Ming and Qing in general can be said to be an exploration of this proverbially weighty point, with some works painting women in a more vilifying light and some portraying them more favorably. Nevertheless, the woman-centered works attract our attention because of the questions they raise about the woman's sexual agency and the threat to men and the social order that such agency potentially presents. As Mark Stevenson writes, at stake is the moral status and positioning of the woman's sexuality.[68]

All five works portray a character type that can be thought of in a composite way: the woman as an independent sexual agent. We saw versions of this type in *Jin Ping Mei*'s Pan Jinlian, Wang Liu'er, and Lady Lin (especially the latter two). Concisely defined, she is a woman who is sexually strong, luxuriates in sexual pleasure, and goes from man to man.

66. See Zamperini, "Canonizing Pornography," 135–136; Vitiello, "Family Affairs"; and Stevenson, "Sound, Space and Moral Soundscapes." For a translation of *Chipozi zhuan*, see Wu Cuncun and Stevenson, *A Tale of an Infatuated Woman*.

67. Zamperini, "Canonizing Pornography," 280; see also 284 and 286–287; and Vitiello, "Family Affairs," 250.

68. Stevenson, "Sound, Space and Moral Soundscapes."

I referred above to the ancient motifs of the legendary goddess of love and the female master of occult sexual arts and discussed how these figures inform the characterization of women such as the three in *Jin Ping Mei*. The woman as independent sexual agent defines a further aspect of this type, especially in the context of vernacular fiction in which the woman is neither a goddess nor a master of occult skills. As a literary motif, she serves multiple purposes, the most immediate of which is the opportunity she provides for the author to engage in explicit sexual description. But she also allows a storyteller to explore questions about the moral status and positioning of women's sexuality, as just mentioned. However, needless to say, no portrait goes so far as to promote or theorize some kind of social change. An example is the following passage from *Zui chun feng* about the power of sexual desire, in which the author throws into question the social convention that tolerates the profligate man but not the wanton woman.

> Alas that there is this matter among humans of that which lies beneath the woman's skirt. Just consider that men and women each have their *yin* and their *yang*. A man has a wife, and a woman has a husband, and they can enjoy all their pleasures together. But take the situation of a man all flushed with desire and spending his days thinking of seducing some other woman, or of a woman all flushed with desire and spending her nights dreaming of seducing some other man. But for a man, when people speak of him seducing someone else's wife, it is a matter of mirth. When they refer to his wife having such an affair, she is an object of outrage. As for a woman, when she is actually being wanton, she heartily loves it. But once people curse her for being wanton, she feels nothing but anger and fury.
>
> (大凡天地間的人，偏有裙帶下的這樁事. 再不明理，一様陰陽二物，夫有婦，婦有夫，儘可取樂. 男子波波急急，鎮日想偷婆娘；女人波波急急，鎮夜想偷漢子. 男子們，人説他淫人老婆，就歡喜了；人説他老婆淫人，就惱怒了. 女人們，眞實是做淫婦，便忻忻以爲樂；人罵聲淫婦，便悻悻以爲恨；1.38).

In articulating such a conundrum, *Zui chun feng* in effect addresses a serious social imbalance. As *Jin Ping Mei* and other works do, it uses explicit sexual descriptions to address what it poses as a serious question—in *Zui chun feng*'s case, the situation of womanizing men who abandon their wives at home while having affairs elsewhere. Why does a woman have to tolerate such behavior? Why can't she take lovers while the man is gone? What happens if she does? Although *Zui chun feng* ultimately limits its own questioning, the questioning is what makes it exceptional.

I return to *Zui chun feng* below, but first I need to expand upon the notion of the exceptionality of this group of works by noting how another of the five, *Zhulin yeshi*, stands out. It does so in its concluding destruction of the male profligates and rescue of the wanton women. Men and women enjoy nearly even sexual power, but the women have an edge. The novel grants the female protagonist, Xia Ji, and her two female allies not only the opportunity to enjoy sexual pleasure but also the ability to overcome the man when they wish. In the story's Zhou and Han sources, Xia Ji has no voice or subjectivity but is merely a ravishing woman, a "kingdom toppler" (*youwu* 尤物), desired by one man after another.[69] *Zhulin yeshi* keeps the same tangled plot as in the *Zuo zhuan* but turns the men into fools and adds sexual content that is all but absent in the early sources. I say "all but absent" because of two sensational bits of detail that appear in the ancient sources. The first is the detail touched on previously in the *Zuo zhuan* and *Lienü zhuan* about two men having affairs with Xia Ji and "both for amusement wearing her undergarments inside their clothing at court" (皆衷其衵服以戲於朝).[70] The second is the one that the Han dynasty's Liu Xiang added to the biography of Xia Ji in *Lienü zhuan*, also referred to above, but that does not appear in the *Zuo zhuan*. Liu writes that she mastered the "techniques of internal constriction that enabled her to conceal her age and replenish her youth" (内挾技術, 蓋老而復壯者), which does not appear in any other source from that time.[71] This is an early and euphemistic reference to what Ming and Qing fiction describes more explicitly: the woman's ability to control her vagina by constricting herself and causing the man to lose control. It is the kind of minimal detail that appears in an early source that the authors of Ming and Qing fiction seize and expand upon. For them it has

69. *Zuo zhuan*, in Li Mengsheng, *Zuo zhuan yizhu*, 1180 (year 28 of the reign of Duke Zhao 昭). The *Zuo zhuan* says that she caused the deaths of three husbands, one lord, and her son, as well as the demise of two kingdoms and two ministers.

70. Li Mengsheng, *Zuo zhuan yizhu*, 456 (year 9 of the reign of Duke Xuan).

71. I referred to this briefly in chapter 4. See also Kinney, *Exemplary Women*, 146 and 269, n. 107, her translation (slightly modified); and Liu Xiang, *Lienü zhuan*, 7.16a–17a. In *Zhulin yeshi*, see 14.123–124, where she is "fifty-four" but looks "sixteen or seventeen."

pornographic potential. In the process of expanding upon it, they give Xia Ji sexual power and agency, thus undoing the original portrayal of her as a flat and featureless "kingdom toppler."

As *Zhulin yeshi* presents her, Xia Ji consorts with two pairs of men, and in the first pair, one is the "buttocks boy" of the other (*pigu haizi* 屁股孩子).[72] This is also an element not found in the original sources, but one that a Ming or Qing author is likely to add. One man in the second pair is her most satisfying sexual partner, illustrating the rule in these five works that, among the multiple men the woman consorts with, she is sexually happiest with one in particular (a point I return to in chapter 8).[73] *Ruyijun zhuan*'s Empress Wu and her favorite, Xue Aocao 薛敖曹, are the most prominent example of such a couple. In *Zhulin yeshi*, the man and woman both possess special skills, with the woman having been taught them by an immortal who rescues her at the end of the story when calamity nearly does her in. Another remarkable feature is that the man and woman do not necessarily use their methods to try to defeat each other, but instead to enjoy what is portrayed as mutual pleasure (for example, 13.117). In the two final sexual battles between two separate couples, the woman wins one and the man the other—after which all are arrested for their wanton conduct, with the immortal helping the women escape.

The image of the woman overcoming the man, cuckolding him, and in general becoming a sort of independent sexual agent pervades Ming and Qing fiction—again, even if it is an ultimately contained independence. At her extreme, she uses special clamping techniques to control sex with the man, even (in *Zhaoyang qushi*) to the point of preventing him from entering (2.138). In the same work, the sister consorts maintain a steady stream of partners both before and after they enter the palace. The emperor never prevails.[74] Such examples demonstrate another role of the motif of the woman as independent sexual agent: her use as a vehicle for satire and belittlement of the male polygamist.

This last point relates to something that Zamperini shows in the case of *Chipozi zhuan*, which is that though male sexuality is "unstoppable and relentless," the woman can launch a counterassertion. She insists on

72. *Zhulin yeshi*, 6.57.

73. See Vitiello, "Family Affairs," 250.

74. The case is similar in *Zhao Feiyan waizhuan* and *Yang taizhen waizhuan*.

her ability to say "when she is satisfied," "she knows what to do to achieve her pleasure" and "how to articulate her lack of fulfillment and her need for more sex to achieve her satisfaction." As in other works, the wanton woman typically has to share herself among the numerous men who force themselves on her or feel obliged to share her with others.[75] But she is nevertheless the judge and ranker of men in terms of their sexual capacity. As more men learn about such a woman, more want to sleep with her, as if to prove themselves among other men. They recall the men in *Jin Ping Mei* who yearn to have for themselves one of the women whom the deceased Ximen Qing once had.

To return to *Zui chun feng*, it is a fictional tour de force in its portrayal of the wife who dares to be sexually independent. In *Jin Ping Mei*, Pan Jinlian demonstrates a similar daring, first in her illicit affair with Ximen Qing; then with the servant boy, Qintong 琴童; and followed by Chen Jingji and finally Dame Wang's son. Chunmei embarks on another such path. But *Zui chun feng*'s Gu Sanniang 顧三娘 extends the possibilities and does so in a most baldly articulated way, such baldness being one of the hallmarks of pornographic literature in general. She expands upon the conundrum posed in the novel's first chapter about the stigmatization of the wanton woman. She resents the unfairness that traps women between the pressures of conformity to models of chastity, on the one hand, and the condemnation they receive if they show indulgence in sexual pleasure or express a desire for it, on the other hand. Just before her marriage, her elder brother enters her bed one night, though he ejaculates before being able to penetrate. She screams and scratches his face, after which he flees and their mother reassures herself that her daughter is still a virgin. But something then happens that conforms to what I have referred to above: the unwelcome incident turns into a sexual awakening. Gu Sanniang "is no longer as good a girl as before. When she goes to bed at night, she now likes to play with her little cunt" (不比起先老實了. 夜裡睡了, 這小毯兒便想要弄, 2.57). She begins mumbling angrily to herself: "To live in this world, a woman has to be either willing to die for her chastity, or else she is a wanton whore. There is no room in between chaste purity or utter indulgence. In the end you neither get a chastity

75. Zamperini, "Canonizing," 280–81. See also Martin Huang, *Desire*, 119.

arch in your honor, nor do you get to truly enjoy yourself"(人生在世，不做貞烈之婦，使做淫樂之人．切不可不貞不淫，造不成節婦牌坊，又不得十分快活; 2.57–58).

With such a manifesto at the beginning, the story presents a sequence of episodes about female sexual profligacy that resembles *Chipozi zhuan*, except that the woman travels beyond the household into a career of prostitution and acting—two forms of work that allow her to survive apart from her family and the rigors of a respectable marriage. Such travel beyond the home is what most distinguishes her from the women in works such as *Chipozi zhuan* and *Jin Ping Mei*. Gu Sanniang begins by marrying a man with whom at first she has blissful sex. He is a *jiansheng* 監生, or "student by purchase": because of his poor performance in exams, his wealthy father purchases his title. He is also a poor husband, as he proves when he leaves Gu Sanniang alone at home while he plays with other women—which in turn leads her to defy him by saying that, unless he takes better care of her, she will find other men. "Shame on you," he says. "You may have a beautiful face, but you wouldn't know how to be seductive. I bet no man would like you!" (羞羞羞！你面龐雖好，又不會騷，只怕也沒人歡喜你，2.66). This remark so infuriates her that, after he leaves home, she begins luring men to her home and going out to find them. She becomes renowned throughout the entire city, sleeping with a different man every night and eventually doing a version of what the philandering polygamist does in his glorious gathering. To celebrate the new year, she has a special bed made and a special door to let men in, and she has sex with three actors at once—actors, it is noted, because they have no families and are therefore free at the Spring Festival. Because the third of them is the best, she gives him a large sum of money (4.104–107). She enacts a parodic reversal of the situation of the philandering polygamist, except that she does not keep the men as concubines. After her husband and son leave her, she becomes a prostitute and eventually joins with a man to make a living performing opera. She then does the same with a former servant of her husband's, whom she marries. Both men are former catamites and so, like her, used to maneuvering in the role of the passive partner of dominant men. The first man is a so-called *menzi* 門子, a yamen runner or doorman—a term that in the parlance of the time of the novel also commonly referred to a man who is or had been a catamite.[76] The second man, A Long 阿龍, was the catamite of her husband. Both men represent the lower classes, whom she joins to escape the frustration and degradation of being married to a wastrel husband of the supposedly educated class. Both men satisfy her sexually, and both ally with her to engage in a successful career of opera performance (for example, see 7.15). She finally dies of a pain in her belly because, it is said, "of having been done it to too many times" (*bei ren nongde duo* 被人弄得多, 8.171). Meanwhile, her husband regrets his past behavior, manages to become an official, marries a virtuous prostitute, and dies.

Two things stand out in the book's portrayal of the wanton woman. First is Gu Sanniang's self-invented survival, and second is her alliance with men of the underclass—who treat her fairly in contrast to men of the elite, who abuse and hate her for her wantonness. Survival has two meanings in this case: First is her survival in the sense of making a living outside the shelter of an established marital household. Second is her survival in the sense of continuing to enjoy sex, which would usually be denied a woman whose husband is disloyal and leaves her alone at home. The men of the elite, far from gentle types such as Jiang Xingge 蔣興哥 or Jia Baoyu 賈寶玉, include three men: her first husband, the *jiansheng*; a customer from her days of prostitution who is a county scholar, or *xiucai* 秀才, and whom she briefly marries in her forties; and a second *jiansheng* whom she meets while performing opera. After marrying the county scholar as his concubine, she discovers that he already has another concubine, an aggressive woman who forces her to live separately (6.141–143), whereupon Gu Sanniang begins an affair with yet another man, who has a kinder wife. In a case of open negotiation, she appeals to the county scholar that, as a woman past forty, she needs to marry a man who can give her a stable life (7.147–148). The county scholar pretends to agree to her transfer to the other man but then turns on her and sues her in court, which results in the judge having her stripped, beaten, and sold as a prostitute. Echoing the treatment she receives from her lower-class companions, the runners in charge of the whipping respond to her appeal and make sure that half the strokes land on the ground, not on her body

76. See Vitiello, *The Libertine's Friend*, 38–41, and Wu Cuncun, *Homoerotic Sensibilities*, 50. By the late Ming *menzi* commonly served as male favorites of other men.

(7.154). Later the second *jiansheng* beats her so severely that she takes months to recover. A Long (the "doorman," *menzi*) and other "friends" (*pengyou* 朋友) look after her during her recovery (7.160–161).

Gu Sanniang finally achieves a few years of happy coexistence with A Long, whom she marries at age forty-six, when she is said to be still attractive and full of desire. A final scene portrays them in an act of wanton bliss, though compared to scenes in *Jin Ping Mei*, the language is jagged and artless. One evening Gu Sanniang and A Long drink until they are drunk, "take off all their clothes, grab the reed mat from their bed, and spread it on the deck of the boat, where A Long grips the woman beneath him as he takes his drunken cock and drives it into her drunken cunt. He bores into her until the raucous waters flow out in a torrent, the one going all out as he bangs her, the other defying life and death. The woman moans and shouts, with not a care for anyone walking by. In all world history, no wife or wanton whore has ever been as wanton as she!" (兩個都脱的赤條條. 扯來床上席子攤在那船板上, 阿龍把婦人捺倒在地, 挺著醉𣰆 射那醉毴. 只頂進去, 就有騷水亂流. 一個不知高低價, 搗這個不知死活價去. 婦人口裡哼了叫, 叫了哼, 也不顧船旁百人行走. 從古來老婆淫娼, 没一個賽得他過; 8.171).[77] They finish late in the night, when everyone else is in bed and then, recovered from their drunkenness, they drink more wine to put themselves to sleep.

The author here awkwardly imitates the formulaic parallelism found in *Jin Ping Mei* and other more artfully written works when he writes, "*the one* going all out as he bangs her, *the other* defying life and death." The style is rough and clumsy. At the same time, the spreading of the mat on the deck of the boat and the blitheness about passersby are remarkable in their portrayal of unabashed sex. The pronouncement that she is the greatest wanton woman in history is hardly a vilifying use of the term. The author gives her one last glorious moment, shortly after which, it is true, she dies of her excesses—though the implication is that her death results from her having suffered physical abuse.

Nevertheless, having finished her off, the author still has to deal with a problem that he has posed for himself and that he finally tries to solve. As he presents it, people typically excoriate such a woman. The path she

77. The character for "cock" in this text is *luan* 𣰆 (Wu 吳 dialect slang).

takes must necessarily lead to her demise. He knows that there has to be a limit; and he finally creates a practical solution for where that limit should be. Before dying, Gu Sanniang's first husband undergoes a moral transformation and then marries a virtuous prostitute, with whom he spends his happy last days and whom he leaves as a widow who becomes known for her resolute chastity. One night the maid wonders why the widow stays alone in her room. She peeks in and sees her open a box and take out a "shiny cock-like-thing she doesn't know made of what" (光光亮亮的，不知什麼做的毬), which she plays with until "she closes her eyes, stops breathing, and faints away for a while before finally moaning and coming around, muttering, 'feels so good, feels so good.'" (只見眼也閉了，氣也沒了，昏見了一會兒，哼哼的醒來，道，"快活，快活"!, 8.178). The word of this soon gets out, making some people laugh, though those who "understand the true situation" (曉得事體的) sigh in admiration, for in doing what she does she proves that she can truly "endure the hardship" of widowhood (*kushou* 苦守, 8.178).[78]

In portraying such a perspective, *Zui chun feng* puts a twist on the common assumption of the woman's inherent licentiousness. The widow still appears to be such a woman, and it is still true that once a woman becomes unrespectable, men assume that she is free for the sexual taking. In line with that reality, when *Chipozi zhuan*'s protagonist, A'na 阿娜, tries to settle for the man she finally likes best, she is denied the choice.[79] In contrast, *Zui chun feng* allows Gu Sanniang to chose her lovers and, like *Jin Ping Mei*, refrains from vilifying her. In its twist, it grants both her and the prostitute widow the honor of being able to enjoy sexual pleasure in a self-willed way, as circumscribed as that way may be.

The use of the word "friends" to refer to the men who care for Gu Sanniang after her beating is key to understanding the book's particular approach. They are men of the theater world, in which it is common for actors of either sex to be taken as objects of pleasure, but in which it is also the case that actors take their sexual pleasure with each other when they can. The lower-class men Gu Sanniang associates with, including the

78. *Dengcao heshang* has a similar theme about the widow's desire. See Martin Huang, *Desire*, 131. According to classical medicine, illness can result from unfulfilled sexual desires. See Wang Ying, "Constructing Patients," chapter 5.

79. See Martin Huang, *Desire*, 117 (Huang renders her name as E'nuo).

yamen runners who soften their strokes when beating her, see her as one of themselves, as opposed to the wastrel men who abuse her. *Zui chun feng*'s focus on these marginal men and their relations with Gu Sanniang link the novel with other late Ming works of sexually explicit literature that depict the life of urban commoners, such as *Longyang yishi* and *Huanxi yuanjia* 歡喜冤家 (Enemies enamored). All have in common a world of men and women who ignore moral rules in favor of what they need to do to get by. As Wu Cuncun writes in regard to *Huanxi yuanjia*, the demands on a woman's chastity are lower for poor urban folk. Poor economic conditions turn women into money earners, which makes them less reliant on men than the women of elite families are, and for which reason they more commonly emerge in public than those women and are more likely to ignore moral rules to meet the demands of survival.[80] Although the women in *Jin Ping Mei* live in relative luxury and rarely emerge in public, those from the lower end of the economic spectrum are the least likely to observe the rules of elite morality, including Pan Jinlian, Sun Xue'e, Pang Chunmei, Wang Liu'er, and Song Huilian. But better-off ones such as Li Ping'er may also bend the rules. When she can better herself with an attractive marital arrangement, even if it means becoming a concubine or marrying before a mourning period is over, she makes her decision based on what she thinks is best for her, regardless of orthodox pressures and values. Lady Lin is the most independent of all because of her economic self-sufficiency, to gain which Gu Sanniang has to work and suffer abuse. But the more trenchant difference between the two lies in the way in which Gu Sanniang serves as a vehicle for the negative portrayal of the profligate husband. Lady Lin's portrayal includes few such extra notes, as defiant of norms as she may otherwise be.

Conclusion: The Wanton Woman and Her Friends

It is common in these works, as I just said, that when a promiscuous woman tries to settle on the lover she prefers, other men interfere and prohibit her from doing so.[81] Those men are not her "friends," to use *Zui chun feng*'s

80. See Wu Cuncun, "The Plebification of Male-Love," "Cong *Huanxi yuanjia* zhong," 72–73 and 76, and "Cong *Jingyuan michuan dongfang chunyi ce* zhong."

81. On *Chipozi zhuan*, see Martin Huang, *Desire*, 120.

term. The alliance between Gu Sanniang and her friends (A Long and others) suggests a relationship of parity in spite of the boundaries of class and gender. With such men, she is both a professional and a sexual partner, which would hardly be possible if she were a member of the family of a wealthy merchant or literatus. It is difficult to imagine the author of *Jin Ping Mei* applying the word "friend" to any of the men or women Pan Jinlian consorts with. Chunmei is her closest ally and Meng Yulou is next, perhaps the closest to what could be called a friend. Pan Jinlian has no male allies, and needless to say, she has no independent, self-sustaining life outside the household. The same point applies to the women in the other works discussed in this chapter. In the case of *Ruyijun zhuan*, the empress most likes Xue Aocao, and given that she is the supreme ruler, no one interferes with her choice. But he is not her friend: instead, he is a courtier and loyal subject, whose loyalty does not work in the usual way. In the pornographic context of *Ruyijun zhuan*, loyalty displays itself in the way he has sex with her, which he puts to the service of pleasing her but also of ultimately delivering the loyal truth, which is that she cannot continue her usurpation of the throne. He persuades her to summon the heir apparent back to court and in doing so paves the way for her to step down and the dynasty to return to the male line of descent. With his mission completed, Aocao disappears, and Wu Zetian, the shrewish and wanton woman, has finally been tamed.

Although Ming and Qing fiction in general assumes an intimate connection between sexual and social disorder, the degree and depth of emphasis on that connection differs. The novels discussed in this chapter, especially the ones that feature the sexual hero whose success with women parallels his success in the world of officialdom, do not burden themselves with such serious messages. They present the ideal libertine, a man of refined taste and talent whose women are comparably skilled in such things as poetry, calligraphy, and painting. At issue is how sex can be enjoyed in as many ways and for as long as possible. Again, as Vitiello says, it is a "world of pure pornographic utopia, a place where there is no room for pain or demise," and where villains who attempt to block such pleasure ultimately fail.

Although we are still a long way from being able to make detailed, credible statements about the historical development of this literature, a trend does appear: at some point after the early Qing, works begin to vilify homoerotic sex. In addition, with a few exceptions, the pleasures that formerly included oral and anal sex, whether heterosexual or homosexual, either disappear or are confined to villainous and intemperate characters. The trend is part of a desire on the part of authors to "redefine [and] rectify" the image of the literatus.[82] Chapter 8 makes further historical remarks through a discussion of the eighteenth- and nineteenth-century novels *Guwangyan*, *Yesou puyan*, and *Shenlou zhi*, the first two and the latter of which I use to represent two ends of a spectrum of pornographic fiction in the post–*Jin Ping Mei* era of the Ming and Qing.

82. Vitiello, *The Libertine's Friend*, 138.

CHAPTER 8

The Ways of Being Pornographic

Pornography without Being Pornographic

Let us finish the examination of *Jin Ping Mei* by looking at three post–*Jin Ping Mei* novels from the Qing, beginning with a pair of eighteenth-century novels that resemble *Jin Ping Mei* in length and scale and share the theme of social decline and its parallel with sexual disorder: *Yesou puyan* and *Guwangyan*.[1] Both novels advocate society's need for superior male potency, without which chaos will prevail. In linking dynastic catastrophe with sexual disorder, *Guwangyan* and *Yesou puyan* are not unusual. Nor are they unusual in limiting pornographic portrayals to vulgar or unheroic figures, which is common in literature from *Ruyijun zhuan* and *Jin Ping Mei* in the Ming to one of the last novels of the imperial era with sexually explicit contents, the 1849 *Pinhua baojian*. What makes *Guwangyan* and *Yesou puyan* stand out is the intensity and outlandishness of their pornographic portrayals, coupled with the intensity and strength of their condemnations of what they pornographically portray. They share the goal of making pornography part of an "anti-libertine" vision of

1. Other novels could be considered. They include *Xingshi yinyuan zhuan* 醒世姻緣傳 (on which, see Martin Huang, *Desire*, 144–175; and Epstein, *Competing Discourses*, 120–121 and 126–134) and the *Jin Ping Mei* sequel, *Xu Jin Ping Mei* 續金瓶梅 (on which, see Siao-chen Hu, "In the Name of Correctness").

social harmony based on rule by the potent male.[2] Both advance a portrait of civilizational health and recovery, which arrive only with the success of such men. Explicit sexual description is necessary to their mission: without it, they cannot get at the core of the truth that they wish to deliver. They touch that obscene core as luridly as possible but pretend to be devoid of any taint.

In fact, *Guwangyan* and *Yesou puyan* go to remarkably obsessive lengths to mark the divide between the purity in themselves and the obscenity in others. It is as if the world forces them to write pornography, and along with their potent phallic saviors, they will pornographically save the world from pornography. Another way of saying this is that they condemn the acts that pornography describes, while at the same time inciting and producing those very acts to rule against them. They exemplify a kind of pornographic morality that, as Ding Naifei says, "produces its pornographic others." They evade and disavow all taint and responsibility while compartmentalizing it somewhere else. In what follows, I mainly concentrate on *Yesou puyan*, having written about *Guwangyan* in a similar light elsewhere.[3]

Yesou puyan lacks the leering ribaldry and caustic edge of *Guwangyan* but exhibits the same repetition compulsion that stages scene after scene of lurid sensuality in which both author and hero are innocent of carnal lust and intention. Early in *Yesou puyan*'s 154 chapters (which vie in length with *Guwangyan*, about which the author could not have known), the novel announces its fundamental theory of sexual pleasure, which has two parts: that intercourse (defined as the man ejaculating inside the woman) is for procreation only, and that pleasure and passion can exist only in the "moments before intercourse" (未經交合以前). Once intercourse takes place (*jiaohe* 交合, or "coition," "joining"), passion dissipates and vanishes. In the end, intercourse is nothing but "feet added to the snake: superfluous" (不過畫蛇添去而已). The genitals are there only

2. Vitiello writes that *Guwangyan* is "a pure anti-libertine story within an overwhelmingly pornographic narrative" (*The Libertine's Friend*, 140; see also 135 and 143).

3. Ding, *Obscene Things*, 139. On *Guwangyan*, see McMahon, "Pornographic Doctrine"; Martin Huang, *Desire*, 251–270; and Vitiello, *The Libertine's Friend*, 133–138 and 142–153.

for continuing the ancestral line of descent, not for "carnal enjoyment" (*yinle* 淫樂).[4]

The same compartmentalization continues in descriptions that shock and titillate, reaching levels of virtuosity that vie with the two novels' pornographic cousins, but all in the name of moral correctness. Thus, we see a glowing close-up of the vagina: "a mound of tender flesh, loose and white like snow; a fine seam-like opening, pink and gleaming like pearl" (一堆嫩肉鬆白如雪，一絲細縫紅潤如珠, 67.4b). But we are looking at it through the self-purifying eyes of the hero, Wen Suchen 文素臣—who, in the scene mentioned above, has just been captured by a polygamous villain, who contrives to have his harem women excite the hero to make him emit semen, which the villain will imbibe as an aphrodisiac. Wen's goal in this scene is to steel himself against the tempting sight of a woman's vagina. As he says to himself, "though I see the whore with my eyes, I do not see her in my mind" (目中有妓，心中無妓, 67.4a). On the surface, his action makes him look like a man who is captivated by a tantalizing and luring sight. But instead he aims to resist the stain that would usually result from such a lascivious act. Though the women succeed in making him ejaculate, he is innocent of involvement because "in his mind" he is not there. Similarly, *Yesou puyan* commits the transgression of writing pornographically but does so while creating the same aura of correctness and authority as Wen in this scene. A blurring occurs in the gap between the law of authority and what the law prohibits. In other words, the law both rules as the law should do and simultaneously incites and produces what the law prohibits. It creates its own transgression in order to right it.[5]

It is the same kind of gap in the case of Wen Suchen's own superphallic body. He has the master penis that both these and other novels

4. Xia Jingqu 夏敬渠, *Yesou puyan*, 6.11ab; see also 68.8b. See also Martin Huang, *Desire*, 236–251, especially 239 (on the same passage) and 247 (on the novel's method of "aiming at maximum desexualization of *qing*"); Epstein, *Competing Discourses*, 199–248; and Vitiello, *The Libertine's Friend*, 132 (the male protagonist as "staunch defender of . . . Confucian values").

5. In Lacanian terms, such gestures are acts of perversion, in which the hero deliberately creates the harm or evil that he rules against, and makes people victims of that from which he saves them. See Žižek, *Tarrying with the Negative*, 193–199, and *The Plague of Fantasies*, 14; Evans, *An Introductory Dictionary*, 138–140; and McMahon, "Polygyny, Bound Feet, and Perversion."

exalt, but we know this only in the displaced and compartmentalized way that is standard to both novels, not through the kind of pornographic scene that would have him aroused and enjoying the act of sex. For example, we see his phallic potency in the displaced, metonymic form of his urine—the tonic properties of which appear in an early chapter when he mixes it with medicine to cure a young woman (18.11b). We see his actual penis when he urinates one day as the villain's concubine looks on in delight, unbeknown to Wen. His "*yang* thing is tall and mighty, beyond all ordinary size" (陽道魁偉, 等閒不得), and he takes many minutes to finish, melting an entire bucket of snow (65.4b–5a). The man of the house, the villain Li Youquan 李又全, has had the bucket planted in a spot by the road to spy on men passing by and kidnap them to absorb their *yang* energy. One of the women drinks Suchen's urine, which she exclaims is sweet and fragrant, and she later returns for more of it (68.8a–9a).[6] This is the same episode in which Li Youquan drinks Wen Suchen's semen, which acts as an aphrodisiac that enables him to conquer a multitude of women in one night.

Repeatedly involved in the most compromising situations, Wen Suchen is never compromised. In another scene, he looks as though he is about to rape a woman when he suddenly tears off her clothes, but he is only doing what is necessary: give her a sudden fright to save her from a deadly illness (17.4b). He looks as though he is having lustful sex with a woman, but she is infertile, a "stone-maiden" (*shinü* 石女), whose breasts and vagina he massages for the sake of channeling his *yang* energy into her and starting her menses.[7] She moans in a state of "numb ecstasy that courses through her entire body" (渾身快暢, 遍體酥麻, 94.9a). The same vocabulary appears that we have seen in *Jin Ping Mei* and other novels, except that in this case the man is detached, merely engaging in a curative act. In another stunning set of scenes, the novel describes one of the harem women playing music by blowing through her labia, but it is the

6. To another woman, it tastes better than mother's milk (69.8b). Wen also resuscitates a dead man by urinating on him (83). See Vitiello, *The Libertine's Friend*, 139 (on Suchen's "extraordinary sexual potency") and 159 (on the Li Youquan episode as a variation on the trope of a man using his wife "to attract a young man in order to take advantage of him sexually").

7. For an excellent survey of the *shinü*, see Vincent Durand-Dastès, "Corps impénétrables."

drugged and paralyzed Wen who is forced to watch as the harem women perform genital acrobatics (67.7a–9b). Soon after, in one of the most sexual nonsexual scenes of the novel, Wen lies paralyzed but erect as the harem women take turns putting him inside, each reaching heights of ecstasy (68.1ab).

In *Guwangyan*, the wanton woman symbolizes the extremity of society's sexual imbalance. According to the novel's logic, women are innately prone to excess, which worsens if they suffer the failure of male sexual potency. The same logic applies in *Yesou puyan*, though the wanton woman is less prominent in that work. Instead, disorder is a matter of infectious *yin* excess invading the realm, upsetting its equilibrium, and depleting its *yang* energies. Wen Suchen is the agent of *yang* purity who will repair the imbalance. *Yin* excess takes the form of degenerate forces mainly as characterized in the monks, eunuchs, and semihuman monsters that constitute the novel's villains.[8] At one point, the imperial court is crippled because of excess *yin* due to the emperor's licentiousness in his harem. Wen Suchen's advice is to have the emperor restore his *yang* energy by sleeping with two young boys on either side of him (85). As in the case of Li Youquan's imbibing Wen Suchen's semen, the act looks homoerotic, but it is a desexualized version of such an act. The occasional example of the wanton woman appears in the case of Li Youquan's wives, a *yaksha* who tries to rape Wen Suchen with her long tongue (63), a female demon who bares her breasts and vagina against him in an attempt to kill him with projectile *yin* force (80), and female pythons who rape human males (94–96). As a rule, it is women who desire Wen Suchen, not he them. The novel also foregrounds upright women who join him, his sons, and male allies as representatives of the positive forces of *yang* energy. As Maram Epstein writes, such women exemplify the qualities of "masculine moral self-discipline."[9] Three of Wen Suchen's wives are specialists in math, military science, and medicine; his mother is more strictly orthodox than Wen Suchen himself; and female acrobats and warriors, some participating in armies with equally martial husbands, aid him in battles against *yin* enemies.

Portraying a vastly different world nearly a century and a half later, the late Qing novel *Jiuwei gui* (Nine times cuckold, 九尾龜, published

8. For this point, see Epstein, *Competing Discourses*, 205.
9. See Epstein, *Competing Discourses*, 229–238, and "Rewriting Sexual Ideals," 66.

serially between 1906 and 1910) has none of the explicit pornography of *Guwangyan* and *Yesou puyan* but inherits their perverse genes nevertheless.[10] It shares their equation of male potency with the mastery of women and presents a situation that is new: it is a case not only of dynastic decline but also of civilizational crisis in the face of a radically alien other, the invading Western nations. The sexually voracious woman now takes the form of the Shanghai prostitute, a focal figure of fiction and journalistic writing beginning in about the 1890s.[11] The master of the world of whoring is an expert in prostitute psychology, the mastery of which is an inherent part of the supremacy that would engineer China's civilizational recovery. He is the new, modern man, who has replaced the sexually inept and boorish man of the past. As the "love genius" (*fengliu caizi* 風流才子, 1.1) of the new era, he sees through the tricks of the new Chinese woman in the form of the savvy Shanghai prostitute, whom he declares to be "incorrigibly dissolute" (*fangdangguanle* 放蕩慣了, 2.13). He announces the end of the era of male submission to women. His method in the sexual arts exemplifies the way in which he envisions male mastery. When he is with a woman in bed, he says, he makes sure to have twice as much power as she, but if that is not possible, he uses the special trick of "teasing" (*tiaodou* 挑逗) her until she begs for battle.[12] In short, sexual mastery is all that is necessary to control her and keep her content. The hero is both the master of the brothels and the man who can lead China into the modern age.

Shenlou zhi: *A Moderate Case*

Yesou puyan and *Guwangyan* are outlandish examples of literary production, in particular because of how they are so blatantly and obsessively pornographic yet make it seem as if the pornography takes place somewhere

10. Zhang Chunfan 張春帆 (died 1935), *Jiuwei gui*. For fuller discussions of this novel, see McMahon, *Polygamy and Sublime Passion*, 126–136; and David Wang, *Fin de Siècle Splendor*, 109–113.

11. For key studies of this topic, see Henriot, *Belles de Shanghai*; Hershatter, *Dangerous Pleasures*; Yeh, *Shanghai Love*; and Zamperini, *Lost Bodies*.

12. *Jiuwei gui*, 179.1165–66. See also McMahon, *Polygamy and Sublime Passion*, 128–131.

else. But as strange and unique as they may be, like many other post–*Jin Ping Mei* works they can be regarded as derivative in the sense of trying to rewrite and repair or improve upon the original novel. My last example of a work that fits this mode of rewrite and repair is a novel that I label as being moderately pornographic, the 1804 *Shenlou zhi*, which presents a form of hedonistic polygamy that keeps itself within temperate limits—if hedonism and pornography can for the moment be imagined as being capable of moderation and temperance.[13] By "repair," I refer to the job that *Shenlou zhi* can be said to have implicitly assigned itself: correcting the negative extremes of its Ming predecessor, *Jin Ping Mei*. Correction mainly arrives in two ways, by creating a male libertine who is a benevolent polygamist husband and by creating wives and concubines who combine talent, gentility, and wantonness without the taint that "wantonness" usually carries. In terms of sexual explicitness, compared to the works discussed so far, *Shenlou zhi* is tame and temperate. It contrasts with *Yesou puyan*, *Guwangyan*, and *Jin Ping Mei* in that it confirms and upholds its pornography, though it is not as explicit as the other three. It embodies what can be called high erotic brevity, a mode that compresses its explicitness into short, adumbrative images. Sexually explicit scenes are shorter, less intense, and less raw than those in *Jin Ping Mei* and the works discussed in chapter 7. A representative example of the fullest kind of description that *Shenlou zhi* allows itself is when the hero, Su Xiaoguan 蘇笑官, feels a woman's breasts, undoes her belt, and reveals "the mound rising magnificently, tender and delicate and free of hair" (隆隆墳起，柔嫩不毛, 7a–7b). No further description precedes or follows this.

In terms of the history of Ming and Qing pornography, *Shenlou zhi* most resembles the earlier novels about lucky libertines who meet a series of women with whom they eventually establish a harmonious, sexually fulfilled family with a main wife and multiple concubines. *Shenlou zhi* evokes a similar levity in its promotion of an art of life that such a gentleman should enjoy. But besides its tempering of explicit descriptions, it differs from works such as *Xiuta yeshi* and *Xinghua tian* in its greater

13. For a translation of the novel, see Hanan, *Mirage*. The edition I used is Yuling laoren 庾嶺勞人, *Shenlou zhi*. See also Wang Junnian, ed., *Shenlou zhi*. Sequels to *Jin Ping Mei* also fit in this category. See Siao-chen Hu, "In the Name of Correctness"; and Rolston, "Oral Performing Literature," 36–54.

inclusion of adverse realities, and hence in contrast to them, it bears a modest resemblance to *Jin Ping Mei*. In the more purely pornographic works, as I have said, the repeated staging of characters having sex makes up the main narrative thread, the key node through which the narrative threads its way. All that matters is this one thing, around which all relations center. *Shenlou zhi*'s libertine hero has a similar series of affairs, but they do not constitute a single key node through which the story wends its way. The novel frames his life within a larger historical context, featuring endemic corruption—a phenomenon that plagued China beginning in the second half of the eighteenth century and lasted through the end of the Qing dynasty and beyond.[14] In such troubled times, the libertine moderates his temperament and behavior. He restrains himself in all that regards the four vices of "drink, lust, wealth, and ire" (*jiu se cai qi* 酒色財氣), for which others praise him at the end of the novel (24.14ab). The earlier libertine hero experienced sexual success in parallel to success in the attainment of high office. Xiaoguan (whose name means "scoff at officialdom") instead avoids the pursuit of both mercantile wealth and official prestige, both spheres being riddled with corruption. He most wants to enjoy the pleasures of domestic life on his country estate, protected from the machinations of officialdom and the convolutions of his father's foreign trade in Canton. He is a hedonist, but a corrected version of the hedonist Ximen Qing. At the same time, he is a milder, more viable version of Jia Baoyu in terms of sensitivity and lack of ambition, though neither he nor any of his wives approach the depth of cultural refinement of the characters in *Honglou meng*. In one episode Xiaoguan manifests a key virtue of Confucian statesmanship by assisting in both the quelling of a rebellion led by a rapacious monk and the downfall of a notoriously corrupt official. But he does so in passing, with no desire to become a grand hero in the mode of *Yesou puyan*'s Wen Suchen. In short, *Shenlou zhi* creates a modestly complex narrative about political and moral corruption that repeatedly affects the lives of the polygamist libertine and his multiple wives. Although those complexities ultimately shrink in the face of the establishment of the happy polygamous family, a vague uncertainty remains in the air. Things are all right for now, but that

14. See Will, "Officials and Money," 62 (on the general "deterioration in official morals and conduct"); and McMahon, "Attendant's Lament."

may not last for long. The man and his wives manage to stay above the fray, enjoying both sexual pleasure and the refined, high-cultural activities of their privileged household. The hero refrains from excess, treats his lower-class compatriots fairly and sympathetically, and avoids ambition and greed.[15]

The author of *Shenlou zhi* presumably could not have seen either *Yesou puyan* or *Guwangyan*, but we can nevertheless place his piece in a dialogue with them, while also referring to *Jin Ping Mei* and the body of pornographic works discussed in chapter 7. The first step is to examine the author's version of polygamous sexual ethics, which in simplest terms amounts to what the novel presents as acceptable libertine polygamy. A key element of such an ethics is something that *Shenlou zhi* shares with *Yesou puyan* and other Qing novels, including sequels to *Honglou meng*—a trope that I have previously called passive polygamy and that also applies to the novels about the lucky libertine polygamist.[16] In this world, women present themselves to the man rather than he to them. They see him as an ideal mate, not caring that he has other wives, though they ultimately expect that he not keep taking endless numbers of women. He may at first decline the offer of a new woman, thus showing that he is not a sexually greedy man like Ximen Qing. Instead, he is a deserving man, like an emperor with the mandate of heaven. Except for the main wife, moreover, all of the women fall in the category of concubine, maid, prostitute, or illicit lover. The circumstances of social reality are such that some women must fall into those ranks, including women who originally would not have become concubines or prostitutes but whose adverse circumstances leave them with no other choice. Xiaoguan is the perfect man to seek asylum with. Futhermore, the main wife knows that things must be this way, understands her husband's nature, and forms harmonious bonds with her co-wives. *Shenlou zhi* is among the last Qing novels to present such a picture.

The other key feature of *Shenlou zhi*'s version of ideal polygamous sexuality is the presence of the talented woman who loves sex but is not

15. Some of these ideas are taken from McMahon, "Review of Patrick Hanan, *Mirage*," 158–159.

16. See McMahon, *Polygamy and Sublime Passion*, 42–44, 90–95, 97–98, 118–123, and 141–143.

wanton. Alternatively, we can say that she is wanton but without the taint that such behavior normally implies. Such a woman already appears in earlier fiction, such as *Zui chun feng*, which pointedly raises a problem that *Shenlou zhi* and other novels otherwise resolve: the problem of the condemnation that a woman receives if she shows pleasure in sex. The main wife in *Shenlou zhi*, Huiruo 蕙若, differs from the temperate main wife of earlier pornographic fiction by being sexually robust. In their first time in bed, she outlasts her new husband, whose "gold-hooped rod fails to defeat the Ageless Dame's jade-fire tongs" (金箍棒終敵不過不老婆婆的玉火鉗). Here *Shenlou zhi* borrows allegorical language from an earlier novel, *Hou Xiyou ji*, in which the gold-hooped rod and jade-fire tongs are weapons in a sexually allegorical battle between a monk and a nun.[17] This is an example of the kind of euphemistic portrayal common in *Shenlou zhi*. The name "Ageless Dame" suggests that the main wife, Huiruo (like Xia Ji in the Zhou dynasty), is ever youthful and virgin-like, no matter how many men she has consorted with. "Jade-fire tongs" suggests that she has a Daoist adept's capacity to clamp on the enemy's penis, though it is an otherwise incongruous image in that the novel creates no context for such imagery. Elsewhere Huiruo conforms to the established fictional model of the tolerant, unjealous, and well-educated main wife, as displayed in scenes in which she, Xiaoguan, and others compose poetry together.

Another example of the way in which *Shenlou zhi* defines the acceptably wanton woman likewise borrows from earlier fiction. In the stories of the lucky libertines who meet a steady series of women, one or more of the women suffer from excess desire and are thus excluded from the libertine's family. Xiaoguan's main wife's precociously wanton sister, Suxin 素馨, is an example: after an early affair with Xiaoguan, she abandons him for marriage with a man with a larger penis but later comes to hate the man and withdraws to become a nun. Xiaoguan has deeply sensual affairs with two other women, but because of their wantonness, he later gives them away to lesser men. First, however, he discovers novel types of pleasure with them. In the first case, enemies try to trap him in bed with one of the enemy's wives, Woman Ru (茹氏). Their goal is to catch him

17. *Shenlou zhi*, 8.22ab; see also Hanan, *Mirage*, 8.125; *Hou Xiyou ji*, 32.369; and chapter 4.

in the act, charge him with adultery, and extort money from him. But the woman likes him and refuses to follow the plan. Later abandoned by her husband, Woman Ru asks to become Xiaoguan's concubine, trying to win him over by introducing him to a new kind of pleasure he has never experienced before: "playing the flute" (19.4a–5a). She later forms an alliance with another woman who has also been forced to use sex as a means of survival. Yerong 冶容 is the daughter of a corrupt official who dies when bandits attack his home. After suffering rape and abuse by monks, she falls into the hands of a husband and wife who traffic in women, in the process learning the tricks of satisfying a man. She becomes Ru's maid and joins with her to introduce Xiaoguan to yet another "novel variation" (*xinxian huayang* 新鮮花樣, 20.8ab) when both have sex with him at once. It is "an instance of sheer, unbridled license" (可謂淫而無度者矣, 20.8b).[18] No other scene of sex is as "unbridled" as this one. Playing the flute and having sex with multiple partners are common in earlier fiction, but in *Shenlou zhi*'s version of polygamous sexuality, Ru and Yerong are deemed to be too wanton. A parallel but superior pair of women, Xiaoqiao 小喬 and Xiaoxia 小霞, suffer similar misfortunes, the best way out of which is likewise to offer themselves as concubines to Xiaoguan. But they do not go as low as Ru and Yerong because they have stronger and nobler characters.[19] For example, Xiaoqiao is once referred to as a woman of "valiant heroism" (*liexing* 烈性, 7.10b), a feature that she exemplifies when she tries to commit suicide after being given as concubine to a vulgar profligate. When her father requests that she act pleasantly when in that man's presence, she responds by telling her father to "have a few more smiling daughters whom you can give to all the governors-general and governors you want!" (何不再養幾個會笑的女兒，送給總督巡撫, 9.18a).

In short, *Shenlou zhi*'s model of sensuality falls within precisely defined limits. The novel begins with a scene of same-sex anal rape by the villainous He Guangda 赫廣大. In contrast, Xiaoguan, the good libertine, does not like sex with men, in accordance with the trend in novels since

18. Hanan, *Mirage*, 20.307, his translation.

19. Both women offer themselves to Xiaoguan as a form of self-sacrifice, to save their families from disaster.

the early Qing.[20] In addition, he will not have too many women, as the novel's last chapter shows when Xiaoguan refuses the offer of more concubines and gives two women to other men. In parallel fashion, *Shenlou zhi* refrains from staging the finale of the "grand meeting of love" (*hehuan dahui* 合歡大會) that takes place at the end of *Nao hua cong*, *Xinghua tian*, and *Taohua ying*. The novel instead ends with a grand session of poetry writing attended by Xiaoguan and his wives. As for playing the flute, it can after all be part of the model polygamous household, as long as it takes place in a properly defined way—which the novel specifies in Xiaoguan's relationship with the maid, Wuyun 巫雲. His mother forbids him to have relations with her before his marriage, but she later allows the maid to follow him to his marital home. Explaining why he has long wanted to sleep with her, he tells one of his concubines, Xiaoxia, that Wuyun is good at playing the flute. Xiaoxia at first takes this literally, not knowing what the expression means. She blushes when he tells her, after which she hurries him off to Wuyun, whose "wondrous gate (*miaohu* 妙户) is said to be "tight yet moist, warm and welcoming" (緊而能潤，暖而能和, 19.17a).[21] It is another case of high erotic brevity. The heightened sensuality with Wuyun recalls that of Ximen Qing's affairs with the servants Huiyuan and Ben the Fourth, except that *Shenlou zhi*'s libertine is someone of whom the reader is supposed to approve.

Conclusion: Three Types of Endings

The ending of *Shenlou zhi* brings us to the general question of how to end the sexually explicit story. I want to ask that question of pornographic fiction across the Ming and Qing to address *Jin Ping Mei*'s ending. Fictional endings commonly have a way of escaping what has gone before. The author has to finish the story and somehow wash his hands of it, which explains the unsubtle and often blatantly didactic endings in

20. He does not favor the "male way" but "solely favors women" (*nanfeng* 男風, *zhuan hao nüse* 專好女色, 16.6a).

21. The passage about the "wondrous gate" does not appear in Hanan's translation. Another missing passage is from Woman Ru's seduction of Xiaoguan (15.13ab; and Hanan, 15.229).

many works of Ming and Qing fiction—including *Shenlou zhi* and, to some degree, *Jin Ping Mei*. The *xiaoshuo* 小說 is a risk-taking genre to begin with, and the sexually explicit *xiaoshuo* is one of the riskiest categories of the genre. In particular, it must account for its excesses. Three types of endings come to mind, all of which make some kind of statement that qualifies the previous indulgence in obscenity. The first type of ending involves a calamity, in which the wanton and illicit lovers suffer punishment or die horribly. The second type involves a pious awakening and religious withdrawal, with the characters realizing the emptiness of desire and vowing to end their attachment to it. Both the first and second types amount to a blacking out of the obscenity and excess that came before. The third type of ending projects an indefinite future of blissful lovemaking.[22] The third type describes *Shenlou zhi*, whose protagonist, Xiaoguan, neither dies nor withdraws from the sensual world but instead will continue to enjoy the company of his wives into the indefinite future. The monk Mola exemplifies the ending of utter extinction, while Suxin (the sister of the main wife, Huiruo) demonstrates pious withdrawal. Stories that end in the third way are didactic in their own manner: they promote the notion that sexual pleasure is a worthy pastime that under proper conditions allows hedonists to enjoy themselves without calamity and condemnation.[23]

In its largeness, *Jin Ping Mei* provides some of each of these endings, though it invests mostly in the first two types and only weakly in the third. Dying horribly occurs in the cases of Ximen Qing, Pan Jinlian, Chen Jingji, and Pang Chunmei. Ximen Qing dies from the poisonous effects of the aphrodisiac he takes and the excesses to which it drives him. Pan Jinlian's death follows the preexisting ending of *Jin Ping Mei*'s parent novel, *Shuihu zhuan*, in which Wu Song 武松 avenges the murder of his brother, Wu Dalang 武大郎. Chen Jingji's death is that of a scoundrel who incurs the vengeance of another scoundrel—his enemy, Zhang Sheng 張勝. Something else about Chen Jingji indicates another kind of

22. I was inspired by Li Mengsheng, who lists three types of ending: "karmic retribution," *baoying* 報應; "enlightenment," *dianhua* 點化; and the lack of any "regret or guilt," *fanhuizhi xin* 翻悔之心 (*Zhongguo jinhui xiaoshuo baihua*, 337–338).

23. The tasteful "craftsmanship" of the sensual *xiangyan* poetry of the Ming and Qing projects a similarly acceptable sexual hedonism. See Li Xiaorong, *Poetics and Politics*, 146.

ending: that of the polygamist's wastrel son who spends all the family wealth, even stealing money and women from his still living or just dead father. The notion is that if a man like Ximen Qing has sons, his retribution will be that they are flagrant wastrels. Chen is a son-in-law and thus not quite the same as a son, but other novels and stories play out this plot more fully. Pang Chunmei's death is the tritest. In a manner that diverges from his usually more careful narrative construction, the author simply extinguishes her by having her suddenly collapse while having sex with an illicit lover, thus providing an end for the novel's final wanton woman.[24]

The ending of pious awakening takes two main forms, that of the surrender of Xiaoge, Ximen Qing's son, to the monk Pujing 普静 (100.1416 and 1421), and that of the former prostitute Han Aijie's assumption of chaste widowhood, followed by her disfiguring her face to avoid marriage and finally becoming a nun. In mythical terms, both endings are types of apotheosis, combining Confucian and Buddhist elements—in spite of their ironic notes.[25] Xiaoge is the "Filial Boy" (as his name translates), whose becoming a Buddhist monk is a form of repentance for his father's corruption and profligacy. Pujing has already recited spells for the salvation and reincarnation of a crowd of souls, including Ximen Qing and the three women whose names make up the title of the novel, Pan Jinlian, Li Ping'er, and Pang Chunmei.[26] Aijie becomes homeless after the deaths of Chen Jingji, Chunmei, and Chunmei's husband and goes on a filial quest to find her parents—the filial quest to find long-lost parents being a well-established motif in the fiction of the period.[27] On the way the narrative describes her with the well-known phrase "masterless dog," or "a dog that has lost its home" (*sang jia zhi quan* 喪家之犬, 100.1413),

24. Tina Lu writes that the novel's *chuanqi*-like ending (傳奇) is "quite alien" to the prior ninety-nine chapters (*Accidental Incest*, 191; see also 191–200, especially 189–190 on Chunmei's death).

25. Carlitz considers Pujing a "charlatan" and Aijie's widowhood "ironic" and does not read Xiaoge in a redemptive light ("Codes and Correspondences," 7–8, 10, and 16). See also Tina Lu, *Accidental Incest*, 195. But Tian Xiaofei sees the ending of the *xiuxiang* version as more complex than that of the *cihua* version and takes Xiaoge as a redemptive figure ("Preliminary Comparison," 355 and 388). Ge Fei sees Aijie as an exemplary figure (*Xueyin lusi*, 337–339).

26. Also included are Chen Jingji, Wu Dalang, Han Zixu, Song Huilian, Zhang Sheng, Sun Xue'e, Ximen Dajie, and Zhou Yi 周義.

27. See Sibau, *Reading for the Moral*, 27–48.

which Sima Qian originally used to describe Confucius.[28] Just as Confucius was unable to find a worthy ruler, so Aijie is unable to find a worthy object of chaste loyalty. Her assumption of the mantel of a chaste widow—in spite of being loyal to an unlikely man such as Chen Jingji—is an instance of Confucian redemption, which she extends by disfiguring herself when her uncle and others pressure her to remarry (after which she becomes a Buddhist nun and eventually dies of illness). A related form of pious awakening occurs in novels in which the male libertine enjoys a series of erotic adventures but in the end withdraws from the world to pursue Buddhist or Daoist self-cultivation, in some cases accompanied by his multiple wives. The author of *Rouputuan* twists this type of ending into a grotesque farce, having the hero forswear sexual desire by cutting off his penis.[29] Both the endings of calamity and religious awakening are bows to moral authority, versions of which appear throughout *Jin Ping Mei*. The fact that Xiaoge becomes a monk marks the second time Ximen Qing loses a son, both cases fulfilling the moral logic according to which the profligate philanderer will fail to have offspring who will enjoy respectable success. According to a similar logic, likewise widely adopted, the wanton woman will fail to be fertile, die of excess, or withdraw to become a nun.

Jin Ping Mei's version of a future of sexual bliss is less pronounced than in other works, and some might question that there is any such ending at all. But it is nevertheless evident in the fact that not all characters meet dire ends.[30] This includes the most prominent of the wanton women, Wang Liu'er, Ruyi, and Lady Lin. Wang Liu'er is portrayed as enjoying sex with both Ximen Qing and her husband (who colludes in her affair with Ximen Qing, which brings them great profit). The end of the novel has her abandoning marital prostitution and joining her dead husband's brother "to dedicate themselves to a life of farming" (*zhong tian guo ri* 種田過日, 100.1414). The reader can hardly be expected to believe that Wang Liu'er will suddenly cease enjoying sex, especially given that she has shown no signs of pious awakening. After Ximen Qing dies, Ruyi continues as

28. See Sima Qian, *Shiji*, 47.1921.

29. Tina Lu sees the ending as the protagonist's "transformation from a sexual participant to a permanently dispassionate observer" (*Accidental Incest*, 264; see also 240–65).

30. According to Tina Lu, an "open-ended model of punishment is the rule in the novel," and not everyone's "folly" is punished (*Accidental Incest*, 189–190).

a wet nurse, later involving herself in an illicit relationship with the servant Laixing 來興. Since Wu Yueniang does not want the news of the affair exposed, she has them marry (the same occurs when she discovers the affair between Dai'an and the maid Xiaoyu [95.1344]). Lady Lin disappears from the narrative but presumably continues her secret liaisons with the help of her skillful go-between. Wang Liu'er, Ruyi, and Lady Lin all have in common the fact that, unlike Pan Jinlian or Pang Chunmei, they do not commit the fault of causing someone else's harm (though Wang Liu'er profits from the framing of Miao Qing and so is something of an exception). Wang Liu'er's wantonness is constructive, providing for her family's continued survival. Ruyi's also works for her survival. In contrast, Pan Jinlian destroys both Wu Dalang and Li Ping'er, while Chunmei causes harm at a remove in her alliance with Pan Jinlian and more directly in her aggression against Sun Xue'e.

As further examples of the prospect of continued bliss, Chen Jingji's two male lovers deserve a brief examination. They appear in *Jin Ping Mei*'s last episodes of explicit sexual portrayal, which take place at the bottom of society among men who resort to no drugs or tools but enjoy only what their bodies can afford them. Moreover, they do not come from the world of elite "homoerotic sensibility," in which a polygamist philanderer like Ximen Qing enjoys handsome youths as catamites and in doing so affirms his role as a masculine master.[31] During his time as a pauper, Chen Jingji has affairs with the Daoist monk Jin Zongming 金宗明 and the beggar Hou Lin 侯林, both of whom, besides enjoying his body, act as his protector and helper. In the case of his affair with the monk, the narrator adds two ribald details: the fact that the beggar has already penetrated him in the poor house, making it easier for the Daoist to penetrate him; and that Chen's experience since youth in the "world of love and passion" (*fengyuezhong* 風月中) has taught him all that he needs to know about such pleasures (93.1325). This last reference in effect places Chen in the world of elite homoerotic sensibility, since given his original family background he could have been similar to a man like Ximen Qing, though now in his condition of poverty he takes on the role of the penetrated partner of a lowly, lustful Daoist monk. "The two of them toss and tumble for a

31. Vitiello (*The Libertine's Friend*, 93–94, and also: "penetrating boys confirms rather than weakens a man's masculinity").

long night of mad love" (當夜兩個顛來倒去, 整狂了半夜), Chen cleverly "swearing loyalty as solid as the mountains and deep as the seas, uttering wanton cries and amorous calls, and fingering and sucking him until Jinzong was utterly overcome with pleasure and delight" (當下被底山盟, 枕邊海誓, 淫聲艷語, 摳吮㖭品, 把金宗明哄得歡喜無盡, 93.1325). Chen has lost all means of support and now finds relief in the Daoist's care. He has only to serve him sexually and can thereby gain the freedom to come and go as he wants, even continuing to visit the prostitute Feng Jinbao 馮金寶—with whom he has eager, energetic sex and is "hardly willing to stop" (*wei ken ji xiu* 未肯即修, 93.1327). These last words are a set expression that also appears in descriptions of Ximen Qing.

Hou Lin is a brutish looking man, whom Chen first meets in the "pauper house" (*lengpu* 冷鋪, 93.1318 and 1324; 96.1364). Later, when a man who cheated Chen is about to pummel him, Hou Lin steps in to protect him, in return for which Chen becomes Hou's "lover brother" (*xiongdi* 兄弟). Soon after, "Hou Lin is plucking the flower in the rear with Chen Jingji for the whole night, lavishing tender words on him, 'dear brother,' 'dear *dada*,' 'my darling man,' 'dear father!' There was no word of passion that he failed to call out" (這候林兒晚夕幹敬濟後庭花, 足幹了一夜. 親哥, 親達達, 親漢子, 親爺, 口裡無般不叫將出來; 96.1365). When other workers notice that the handsome Chen has become Hou Lin's "lover brother," they "taunt" (*xiluo* 傒落) him until Hou Lin, now the foreman of a crew, tells them to stop and get to work (96.1366).

Soon Jin Zongming and Hou Lin drop out of the narrative, though like Lady Lin they presumably continue to find partners to satisfy their desires. The novel then ends with four major deaths, which involve two good people, Commissioner Zhou (Zhou Shoubei 周守備) and Han Aijie, and two bad people, Chen Jingji and Chunmei. The ends of all four are instances of the type of ending that amounts to the erasing of the obscenity and excess that came before. The latter two characters are extensions of Ximen Qing and Pan Jinlian, though both are lower-grade versions of their mighty counterparts. The story of the profligate philanderer continues with the far less wealthy Chen Jingji, until his death at the hands of a petty enemy. Likewise, the story of the wanton woman continues with Chunmei, newly risen to a social status that surpasses that of her former mistress, Pan Jinlian. Her wantonness defines itself in the same way as Pan's, about whom the go-between Dame Wang had once said that she was "like a dog who can't stop eating shit—she has no way to change" (只當狗改不了吃屎, 86.1231). She says this just after hearing about Pan's affair with Chen Jingji. Likewise, after Chen Jingji dies and while her husband (Commissioner Zhou) is away at war, Chunmei "still burns with lust" (*yuhuo shao xin* 慾火燒心) as she "lures" (*gouda* 抅搭) the son of a senior servant, on top of whom she suddenly expires one day in an abrupt end to the life of an incurably wanton woman (100.1408).

The other two deaths are instances of the motif of "moral exemplarity," cases of which typically appear at the ends of stories by way of delivering justice to villains.[32] Commissioner Zhou is a minor character, but he is notable because he dies a loyalist's death defending the Song in its hopeless battle against the invading Liao.[33] Han Aijie's story constitutes a major episode of the last chapter, with her death coming not long after a stunning scene of graphic detail—though one that is no longer tinged with sexual content. She arrives in a village one evening and asks for hospitality from an old woman cooking for a crew of workers who are dredging the riverbed. It is a scene of vulgar, plebian life that *Jin Ping Mei* only rarely portrays but that further reinforces the effect of the novel's ending of distancing itself from the previous scenes of profligate excess. Aijie observes the older woman "in no time finishing a large cauldron of dried rice, beans, and mixed grains, to which she adds two large plates of raw vegetables sprinkled with a bit of salt. Next to her is a group of men with matted hair, bare legs, and breech clothes around their waists, whose feet are covered in mud, and who enter, put down their spades and hoes, and ask the woman if the food is ready yet" (登時做出一大鍋稗稻插荳子乾飯, 又切了兩大盤生菜, 撮上一包鹽. 只見幾個漢子, 蓬頭精腿, 裩褌兜襠, 腳上黄泥, 進來放下鍬. 便問道, 老娘, 有飯也未, 100.1413).[34]

The climax of the scene arrives when Han Aijie and one of the workers recognize each other: he is Han Er 韓二, Wang Liu'er's brother-in-law and her former lover. He now joins Aijie to help her find her parents and later becomes Wang Liu'er's new husband after Han Daoguo dies. Compared to the meals that the people of Ximen Qing's household enjoy,

32. The term "moral exemplarity" comes from Sibau, *Reading for the Moral*, 161–162.

33. According to Tina Lu, his ending does not "escape being thoroughly tinged by the ironic," since he suffers from "blindness about the corruption in his own family" (*Accidental Incest*," 183).

34. "Breech cloths around their waists" and "covered in mud" are from Roy, 5.100.403.

the food that Han Er shares with Aijie is so crude that she cannot stomach it. Matted hair and bare legs, feet covered in mud, and plates of raw vegetables—these are the graphic details that anchor the episode of the moral exemplar, Aijie, replacing the graphic obscenity of the pornographic mode.

Chen Jingji's plunge into destitution presents a similar kind of explicit detail, though in his case it is tinged with graphic sexuality. He is a version of the inveterate wastrel, the one who is immune to pious awakening, though some authors reform such a character (as in the case of Gu Sanniang's first husband in *Zui chun feng*). The details that describe Chen's liaisons heighten the portrayal of his degeneracy. Men dredging rivers and beggars living in "pauper houses" are by implication people who have always coexisted with the members of the Ximen Qing household, the latter of whom have been the novel's main focus until now. The novel ends with a show of moral exemplarity and the salvation of souls, also accompanied by a scene set among laborers—a plebian phase of the myth of eternal return in which the story for the moment diverges from the cycle of profligate excess.

The *Jin Ping Mei* author never abandons the theme of moral exemplarity, but he riddles it with counterexamples that question and qualify its possibilities. The novel leaves no doubt that Ximen Qing is a shallow profligate, but the condemnation is nonetheless never too heavy and the presentation is entertaining. Pan Jinlian is a more interesting case in that the author leaves the impression that she behaves as she should be expected to and that she is the way she is whatever people may think. As Epstein says, she "refuse[s] the stigma of shame."[35] My final word along these lines is about the affair between Chen Jingji and Pan Jinlian, which is incestuous and adulterous on the surface but nevertheless exemplifies a sort of passion whose portrayal overflows that surface. Here is one of the passages describing it, which I have quoted above:

> The one gently rocks her willowy waist, the other eagerly thrusts with his jade stalk.
>
> They pour words of passion into each other's ears, and by their pillows promise loyalty as solid as the mountains and deep as the seas,

35. Epstein, "Turning the Authorial Table," 163. On the softening of Pan Jinlian's portrayal in the Chongzhen edition, see below.

> The oriole is unchecked, the butterfly teases, arousing the beautiful maiden in thousands of ways.
> The rain is relentless, the clouds are blushing, as the enchanting woman flaunts an infinite display.
> The one keeps calling for his darling, the other pulls him close crying "my *dada* lover!"
> Behold: the willow suddenly turns a fresh new green, while the hue of the flower loses none of its prior red. (80.1164)

As we recall, the line "the willow suddenly turns a fresh new green, while the hue of the flower loses none of its prior red" comes from a poem by the woman poet Zhu Shuzhen about the freshness and promise of new love. Above, I labeled this scene mock high erotic and called it high erotic parody. It is preceded by the two having a passionate kiss, as Jinlian sticks her tongue through the latticework to meet the irresistible mouth of Chen Jingji (80.1165). A later scene ends with the declaration that they "swear never to part in this life, and vow to continue their joy in the next" (83.1201–1202), which above I labeled farcically incongruous.[36]

The passion between Chen Jingji and Pan Jinlian is unmistakable—as unheroic and villainous as they may be, and in spite of her disadvantage in status (he is a privileged male, though soon to be déclassé, and she is a concubine who can be bought and sold). Take away their personal characteristics and their differing status, and you have a scene of unabashedly passionate sex. Why grant them such undiluted passion and give them such an exalted air? Is it a case of what Shang Wei calls the author's "predilection for . . . incorporating the languages of incongruous styles, contents, and sources"?[37] Is he simply inserting formulaic language and high-sounding tropes to create a kind of a standard mosaic of sexual passion? Or is he mocking them for being so passionate in spite of their being an utterly doomed couple? Is kissing through the latticework supposed to make the reader laugh at a ridiculous lack of control? Or is the author staging a scene of two impassioned lovers having ecstatic sex, thus predicting the more purely pornographic novels that will populate the late Ming and early to mid-Qing—though with more positively portrayed

36. Her love for Chen Jingji also comes through in songs in chapter 82, including ones they sing to each other. See Hanan, "Sources," 62, n. 86; and chapter 3.

37. Shang Wei, "*Jin Ping Mei* and Late Ming Print Culture," 199.

characters? There are no pure yes or no answers, though I still lean toward taking the scene as a case of mock high erotic because of the characters involved.

However we view the scene, one thing stands out: the difference in Pan Jinlian's relation to Chen Jingji versus her relation with Ximen Qing. Pan Jinlian lives in a world in which men like Ximen Qing command the sexual field, and she must compete with other women for his attention. Ximen Qing can always summon a woman, and one is always available. He can decide when to have sex and when to stop—except when he is semiconscious beneath Pan Jinlian, who has made his penis conform to her demands by means of an overdose of aphrodisiac. She distantly resembles the men and women in other pornographic novels who use drugs or special skills to overpower their sexual partners and gain as much pleasure as possible for themselves. She enjoys a kind of dominance both in that scene and in her relationship with Chen Jingji. Again, she behaves as she should be expected to, given the conditions under which she has to live. The novel may end with her murder, but it nevertheless treats her as a virtuoso performer of a range of talents that she has cultivated since her childhood training in the house of Lady Lin's husband. However stigmatized she may be in her status as bond maid and concubine and her labeling as a wanton woman, she demonstrates a self-expression and self-possession that, as with *Zui chun feng*'s Gu Sanniang, can be extinguished only by her death.

Jin Ping Mei is remarkable for the same kind of unbridled speech and its saying-it-all narrative mode. Inheriting its plot about the affair of Pan Jinlian and Ximen Qing from *Shuihu zhuan*, it turns her into more than simply a wanton, lascivious woman. As Tian Xiaofei writes, the Chongzhen *xiuxiang* edition goes further than the *cihua* edition in softening her portrayal and making her more complex and sympathetic.[38] Moreover, Pan Jinlian is more than just that character, in that she appears in parallel but contrasting versions in the form of other variously wanton women, especially Song Huilian, Wang Liu'er, Lady Lin, and Ruyi. None of the latter three meet Pan Jinlian's gruesome end, and in general the wanton women are more vividly rendered than the male characters of the novel.

38. See Tian Xiaofei, "Preliminary Comparison," 371–386, especially 371–372; and Hanan, "Sources," 49.

A similar logic works with the novel's pornography, or what I use that word to mean by including the sense of the artful way of describing sex. By this I refer to the way in which the novel makes pornography speak, which means making it compelling—and, if you want, at times titillating and sensational but also both provocative and aesthetically rendered, not to mention comical and satirical. Sex is never just sex, as if that were even possible.[39] Besides being related to the complexities of the characters, their identities, and their situations, sex is also a matter of how it is described, the extent to which it is described, and the finely forged types of language that the author uses, both inherited from the past and newly invented, as I said in chapter 1. There is rawness and ugliness in sex, as well as exuberance, virtuosity, and brilliance. The portrayals float between, on the one hand, the effects of the ineffable (as if to say that true pleasure was impossible to describe) and, on the other hand, the effects of rounding every bend of describing sexual acts in all their visible and audible forms.

The novel's explicit portrayals, as well as its discussions and characterizations of them, continue to be sensitive and controversial. Some will disagree with my use of the word "pornography" to characterize them, as I have said above. Some would way, for example, that the word is too directly linked to the formation of modernity to be worthy of use in the context of sixteenth-century China. According to that sense, pornography is a "definitively *modern* phenomenon," as Yvon Wang puts it, and as such it has to be linked with movements to promote personal liberties—in particular, the expression of individual desire, especially that of women and other marginalized groups.[40] It connotes material that is fundamentally subversive of traditionally established political and cultural systems. How can explicit portrayals of polygynous sex, however daring and taboo shattering they may be, be considered modern in such a sense? How can sexual battles between partners deploying occult Daoist skills fit into the context of promoting personal liberty? Such questions deserve lengthy answers and multiple rephrasing, but suffice it to say that China

39. To follow the distinction David Halperin made long ago, when sex is not "just sex," it is sexuality—that is, a "cultural production" ("Is There a History of Sexuality?," 416).

40. Yvon Wang, *Reinventing Licentiousness*, 13 (emphasis in the original).

did undergo changes in the early twentieth century that make for a better fit for the use of the word "pornography," especially the 1910s to the 1930s. That was a time when a new vocabulary and understanding of sex began to take shape, with the appearance of neologisms such as *xing* 性 (sex), *tongxingai* 同性爱 (same-sex love), *nüxing* 女性 (female sex), *shengzhiqi* 生殖器 (genitals), and *huangse* 黄色 (pornography).[41] It was a time of national rejuvenation. New ideas about sex were key to these changes. The exaltation and celebration of sex and sexual desire were meant to reverse the repressions of the imperial past.[42] The sixteenth century still enforced the hierarchical values of that past, especially in terms of the assumptions about whose desires and pleasures were deemed legitimate.[43] With hints of exceptions, the art of the bedchamber and *xiangyan* literature both represent and further the same assumptions, which belong to an elite, exclusionary regime.

Some works of Ming and Qing fiction do so as well, including *Jin Ping Mei*. But even *Jin Ping Mei*, as I have interpreted it through its sexual portrayals, has the beginnings of the kind of challenges that would unfold more fully in the late Qing and early Republican period. As Wang and others show, the existence of this body of works and the print culture that produced it and continued to do so throughout the Qing marks what can be called the early modern shift toward what would more firmly and broadly—that is, globally—take hold two centuries later.[44] How China was part of this shift is something that has only begun to be considered, especially in terms of bridging the history of sexuality from early modern to modern China. For that matter, it is only recently that global discussions of pornography have included Ming and Qing China, a discussion to which this volume is another contribution.[45]

41. See Rocha, "*Xing*"; and Chiang, *After Eunuchs*, 3–14 (on a new lexicon of sex).

42. See Yvon Wang, *Reinventing Licentiousness*, 95–96.

43. See Yvon Wang, *Reinventing Licentiousness*, 18. Wang writes of "*yin* ideology" and "the hierarchy of licentiousness," which have to do with the sociopolitical divisions that privilege "legitimate desiring subjects" who are deemed capable of desiring "properly" (30).

44. Yvon Wang uses the term "early modern" to refer to the shift that began to occur in the late Ming; see *Reinventing Licentiousness*, 14 (on shift), 16–17, 25, and 31–35 (on print culture and *xiaoshuo* fiction). See also, for example, Brokaw and Chow, *Printing and Book Culture*; and Hegel, "Niche Marketing."

45. Examples include Rocha, "*Xing*"; Yvon Wang, *Reinventing Licentiousness*; and Chiang, *After Eunuchs*, as well as discussions such as those conducted at the conference

The final point I would like to raise is about the language of sexual description, especially in the form of the challenges of translation. As I mentioned above, there is a relative poverty of vocabulary in contemporary English when translating *Jin Ping Mei* and other premodern Chinese narratives about sexual acts. The economies and repertoires of the language and imagery of sex differ between English and Chinese.[46] In China the linguistic repertoire appears to have failed to be renewed and to continue to evolve in a comparably virtuosic way—that is, in a way in which explicit and linguistically manifold renditions of sexual acts seamlessly interweave with a complex plot or, in short, appear as deeply inherent elements of the narrative.[47]

English translators can look to Ming and Qing Chinese both in admiration and for inspiration, though English and other languages ultimately have to rely on their own possibilities for creative invention. Several hypothetical questions nevertheless arise: Given *Jin Ping Mei*'s artful and deeply thematic presentation of its sexually explicit scenes, would it (and if so, why would it) still have to be censored and abridged if it was made into a movie that contained the full range of representations that appear in its abridged editions? Would it still be relegated to the stigmatized zone of pornography, with all its X ratings, and still be pressured and complicated by both conscious and subliminal standards of acceptability and propriety? Whatever the case may be, such portrayals will always test the zones of acceptability and will have to be repeatedly visited and challenged. *Jin Ping Mei* is unique in this regard, having begun as a kind of underground literary production passed around and copied among fascinated readers for years until it finally reached published form. In taking sex as a vehicle for reading the world, it refused to be policed and imprisoned within the boundaries of cleanly authoritative language and instead opted for an energy and depth of writing that still

---

"Comparative Pornographies: Transnational Approaches to Writing Sex, East and West," held on March 9, 2019, at the University of California at Los Angeles.

46. The best discussion of this topic is Qi Lintao, *Jin Ping Mei English Translations*.

47. Jia Pingwa 賈平娃 (b. 1952) marks sexual passages in his 1993 novel *Feidu* 廢都 with empty squares that function as a tongue-in-cheek indication of how many words are missing. In this way he evades censorship and also demonstrates that such expression is still impossible. The book was censored anyway, but it is available in an English translation. See Howard Goldblatt, *Ruined City* (Norman: Oklahoma University Press, 2016).

has the potential of stirring creative exploration. The possibilities developed in one era and one part of the world do not have to reach a dead end.

The comment in the Chongzhen edition that I have quoted above gets at what *Jin Ping Mei* means to accomplish in its work of creation: "Of what goes on in the privacy of the bedchamber, what is there not to be found? It is simply that no one dares to expose it" (18.227–228). The quote I began with in chapter 1 makes a similar point: "This book is about exposing all the affairs of the world, no matter how trivial or momentous, no matter what level of intensity. Whatever the world may hold, the author doesn't hesitate to penetrate its depths" (52.681). In short, the message is in the sheer impact of description, which in its presentation blares its dismissal of a view that would block and condemn the novel's contents because they are licentious. Always risking the suspicion of portraying the licentious for the sake of the licentious, the novel nevertheless adds to that mix by portraying sex as a form of sheer expenditure that inherently veers to excess (including deadly excess), but, again, it does so not to condemn something such as sex but simply to show that things go on in that realm that a *xiaoshuo* writer cannot afford to ignore.

Bibliography

Abbreviations

JPM = *Jin Ping Mei* (Hong Kong Sanlian edition, with Chongzhen edition comments)

JPMCH = *Jin Ping Mei cihua* (Taibei Liren edition)

JPMCH, Bu Jian, ed. = *Jin Ping Mei cihua* (with comments by Zhang Zhupo)

SWXHB = *Siwuxie huibao*

Novels from SWXHB are listed by title, followed by "SWXHB" and volume, chapter, and page numbers. I include the author (or say anonymous, if that applies) only in the first footnote reference. After the first reference, I include only title and chapter and page numbers.

Primary Sources (by Title)

Beishi 北史. Li Yanshou 李延壽. Beijing: Zhonghua shuju, 1974.

Bian er chai 弁而釵. Zuixihu xinyue zhuren 醉西湖心月主人. In Chen Qinghao 陳慶浩 and Wang Qiugui 王秋桂, eds., SWXHB. Taipei: Taiwan daying baike, 1995: vol. 6.

Bie you xiang 别有香. Taoyuan zuihua zhuren 桃源醉花主人. In Chen Qinghao and Wang Qiugui, eds., SWXHB. Taibei: Taiwan daying baike, 1994: vol. 8.

Chan Zhen houshi 禪眞后史. Fang Ruhao 方汝浩. Taipei: Tianyi chubanshe, 1975.

Chipozi zhuan 癡婆子傳. Furong zhuren 芙蓉主人. In Chen Qinghao and Wang Qiugui, eds., *Zhongguo nüxing sanda qishu*. Taibei: Taiwan daying baike, 1997: vol. 2.

Chundeng mishi 春燈迷史. Qingyang yeren 青陽野人. In Chen Qinghao and Wang Qiugui, eds., SWXHB. Taibei: Taiwan daying baike, 1995: vol. 23.

Daoyuan yiqi 道元一氣. Cao Heng 曹珩. Beijing: Beijing shifan daxue chubanshe, 1990.

Erke pai'an jingqi 二刻拍案驚奇. Ling Mengchu 凌濛初. Shangyou tang 商友堂, ed. In Princeton University Gest Library, microfilm of original in Naikako Bunko Library.

Gujin xiaoshuo 古今小說. Feng Menglong 馮夢龍, Li Tien-yi, ed. Taibei: Shijie shuju, 1958.
Guwangyan 姑妄言. Cao Qujing 曹去晶. In Chen Qinghao and Wang Qiugui, eds., SWXHB. Taibei: Taiwan daying baike, 1997: vols. 36–45.
Hanshu 漢書. Ban Gu 班固. Beijing: Zhonghua shuju, 1962.
Honglou meng. Cao Xueqin 曹雪芹. Beijing: Renmin wenxue chubanshe, 1982.
Hou Xiyou ji 後西遊記. Anonymous. Shenyang: Chunfeng wenyi chubanshe, 1982.
Jin Ping Mei 金瓶梅. Lanling xiaoxiao sheng 蘭陵笑笑生. *Xinke xiuxiang piping Jin Ping Mei* 新刻繡像批評金瓶梅. Hong Kong: Sanlian shudian, 1990.
Jin Ping Mei (Shuanggexie chongjiao ping pi) (雙舸榭重校評批金瓶梅). Bu Jian 卜鍵, ed. Beijing: Zuojia chubanshe, 2010.
Jin Ping Mei cihua 金瓶梅詞話. Lanling xiaoxiao sheng 蘭陵笑笑生. Taibei: Liren shuju 里仁書局, 1996.
Jin Ping Mei dufa 金瓶梅讀法. Zhang Zhupo 張竹坡. In Hou Zhongyi 侯忠義 and Wang Rumei 王汝梅, eds. *Jin Ping Mei ziliao huibian* 金瓶梅資料滙編. Beijing: Beijing daxue chubanshe, 1985: 24–46.
Jiuwei gui 九尾龜. Zhang Chunfan 張春帆. Nanchang: Baihua wenyi chubanshe, 1993.
Kaiyuan tianbao yishi 開元天寶遺事. Wang Renyu 王仁裕. Shanghai: Shanghai guji chubanshe, 1985.
Langshi qiguan 浪史奇觀. Fengyue xuan youxuanzi 風月軒又玄子. In Chen Qinghao and Wang Qiugui, eds., SWXHB. Taipei: Taiwan daying baike, 1995: vol. 4.
Lienü zhuan 列女傳. *Gu Lienü zhuan* 古列女傳. Liu Xiang 劉向. In Sibu congkan 四部叢刊, shibu 史部. Taibei: Shangwu yinshuguan, 1966, vols. 265–267.
Liexian zhuan 列仙傳. Liu Xiang 劉向. Shanghai: Shanghai guji chubanshe, 1990.
Meiren shi 美人詩. Min Zhengzhong 閔正中 and Zeng Rulu 曾汝魯. Shanghai: Zhongyang shudian, 1935.
Mudan ting 牡丹亭. Tang Xianzu 湯顯祖. Beijing: Renmin wenxue chubanshe, 1978.
Nao hua cong 鬧花叢. Gusu chiqingshi 姑蘇癡情士. In Chen Qinghao and Wang Qiugui, eds., SWXHB. Taipei: Taiwan daying baike, 1995: vol. 19.
Rouputuan 肉蒲團. Li Yu 李漁. In Chen Qinghao and Wang Qiugui, eds., SWXHB. Taipei: Taiwan daying baike, 1994: vol. 15.
Ruyijun zhuan 如意君傳. Xu Changling 吳門徐昌齡. In Chen Qinghao and Wang Qiugui, eds., SWXHB. Taipei: Taiwan daying baike, 1995: vol. 24.
Sengni niehai 僧尼孽海. Tang Bohu 唐伯虎. In Chen Qinghao and Wang Qiugui, eds., SWXHB. Taipei: Taiwan daying baike, 1995: vol. 24.
Shenlou zhi. Wang Junnian 王俊年, ed. Jinan: Qilu shushe, 1988.
Shenlou zhi 蜃樓志. Yuling laoren 庾嶺勞人. In Beijing University Library.
Shiji 史記. Sima Qian 司馬遷. Beijing: Zhonghua shuju, 1989.
Shuihu quanzhuan 水滸全傳. Shi Nai'an 施耐菴. Hong Kong: Zhonghua shuju, 1976.
Shuihu zhuan 水滸傳. Shi Nai'an. Beijing: Renmin wenxue chubanshe, 1973.
Siyou ji 四遊記. Yu Xiangdou 余象斗. Shanghai: Shanghai guji chubanshe, 1986.
Su'e pian 素娥篇. Ye Huasheng 鄴華生. In Chen Qinghao and Wang Qiugui, eds., *Yanqing xiaoshuo zhenben*. Taipei: Taiwan daying baike, 1997.
Sunü miaolun 素女妙論. In Li Ling. *Zhongguo fangshu gaiguan* 中國房術概觀. Beijing: Renmin Zhongguo chubanshe, 1993: 190–203.

Taohua yanshi 桃花艷史. Anonymous. In Chen Qinghao and Wang Qiugui, eds., SWXHB. Taipei: Taiwan daying baike, 1995: vol. 23.

Taohua ying 桃花影. Yanshui sanren 烟水散人. In Chen Qinghao and Wang Qiugui, eds., SWXHB. Taipei: Taiwan daying baike, 1995: vol. 18.

Tiandi yinyang jiaohuan dale fu 天地陰陽交歡大樂賦. Bai Xingjian 白行簡. In Li Ling 李零. *Zhongguo fangshu gaiguan* 中國房術概觀. Beijing: Renmin Zhongguo chubanshe, 1993: 93–99.

Wanli yehuo bian 萬曆野獲編. Shen Defu 沈德符. Beijing: Zhonghua shuju, 1980.

Wushan yanshi 巫山艷史. Anonymous. In Chen Qinghao and Wang Qiugui, eds., SWXHB. Taipei: Taiwan daying baike, 1995: vol. 20.

Wutong ying 梧桐影. Anonymous. In Chen Qinghao and Wang Qiugui, eds., SWXHB. Taipei: Taiwan daying baike, 1994: vol. 16.

Xinghua tian 杏花天. Tianfang daoren 天放道人. In Chen Qinghao and Wang Qiugui, eds., SWXHB. Taipei: Taiwan daying baike, 1995: vol. 17.

Xingshi hengyan 醒世恆言. Feng Menglong. Taibei: Shijie shuju, 1973.

Xiuta yeshi 繡榻野史. Lü Tiancheng 呂天成. Zuimian ge 醉眠閣 edition. In Chen Qinghao and Wang Qiugui, eds., SWXHB. Taipei: Taiwan daying baike, 1995: vol. 2.

Xiu zhen yanyi 修眞演義. Tao Xialing 陶遐齡. In Li Ling. *Zhongguo fangshu gaiguan*. Beijing: Renmin Zhongguo chubanshe, 1993: 208–219.

Xixiang ji 西廂記. Wang Shifu 王實甫. Wang Jisi 王季思, ed. Shanghai: Shanghai guji chubanshe, 1978.

Xu Jin Ping Mei 續金瓶梅. Ding Yaokang 丁耀康. In Chen Qinghao and Wang Qiugui, eds., SWXHB. Taipei: Taiwan daying baike, 1995: vols. 31–33.

Yangjiafu yanyi 楊家府演義. Anonymous. Shanghai: Shanghai guji chubanshe, 1980.

Yesou puyan 野叟曝言. Xia Jingqu 夏敬渠. Piling huizhen lou 毗陵慧珍樓 edition, 1881. In Beijing University Library.

Yijian zhi 夷堅志. Hong Mai 洪邁. Beijing: Zhonghua shuju, 1981.

Yinglie zhuan 英烈傳. Anonymous. Hong Kong: Xuelin youxian gongsi, 1978.

Yipian qing 一片情. Anonymous. In Chen Qinghao and Wang Qiugui, eds., SWXHB. Taibei: Taiwan daying baike, 1995: vol. 14.

Yiqing zhen 怡情陣. Jiangxi yeren 江西野人. In Chen Qinghao and Wang Qiugui, eds., SWXHB. Taipei: Taiwan daying baike, 1995: vol. 22.

Yixin fang 醫心方. Tamba Yasuyori 丹波康賴. In Li Ling. *Zhongguo fangshu gaiguan*. Beijing: Renmin Zhongguo chubanshe, 1993: 100–143.

Zhao Feiyan waizhuan 趙飛燕外傳. Ling Xuan 伶玄. In Chen Qinghao and Wang Qiugui, eds., SWXHB, *waibian*. Taibei: Taiwan daying baike, 1997: vol. 1, 55–79.

Zhaoming wenxuan yizhu 昭明文選譯注. Xiao Tong 蕭統. Yin Falu 陰法魯, ed. Changchun: Jilin wenshi chubanshe, 1988.

Zhaoyang qushi 昭陽趣史. Yanyan sheng 艷艷生. In Chen Qinghao and Wang Qiugui, eds., SWXHB. Taipei: Taiwan daying baike, 1995: vol. 3.

Zhulin yeshi 朱琳野史. Chidao ren 痴道人. In Chen Qinghao and Wang Qiugui, eds., SWXHB, Taipei: Taiwan daying baike, 1995: vol. 20.

Zui chun feng 醉春風. Jiangzuo shui'an 江左誰菴. Taipei: Shuangdi guoji chuban, 1996.

Zun sheng ba jian 遵生八箋. Gao Lian 高濂. Chengdu: Bashu shushe, 1992.

Zuo zhuan. *Zuo zhuan yizhu* 左傳譯注. Li Mengsheng 李夢生, ed. Shanghai: Shanghai guji chubanshe, 2004.

Secondary Sources (by Author, Editor, or Translator)

Bai Weiguo 白維國. *Jin Ping Mei fengsu tan* 金瓶梅風俗譚. Beijing: Shangwu yinshuguan, 2016.

Barbier-Kontler, Christine, trans. *Belles de candeur: Zhulin Yeshi ou Histoire non officielle de Zhulin*. Arles, France: Éditions Picquier, 1990.

Barthes, Roland. Richard Miller, trans. *S/Z: An Essay*. New York: Hill and Wang, 1974.

Bataille, George. Mary Dalwood, trans. *Eroticism, Death and Sensuality*. San Francisco: City Lights, 1986.

Bauer, Nancy. *How to Do Things with Pornography*. Cambridge, MA: Harvard University Press, 2015.

Birch, Cyril, trans. *The Peony Pavilion*. Bloomington: Indiana University Press, 2002.

Bossler, Beverly. *Courtesans, Concubines, and the Cult of Female Fidelity: Gender and Social Change in China, 1000–1400*. Cambridge, MA: Harvard University Press, 2013.

Brennan, Samantha. Review of Francis Ferguson, *Pornography, The Theory*. In *Victorian Studies* 49.1 (2006): 155–156.

Brokaw, Cynthia, and Kai-wing Chow, eds. *Printing and Book Culture in Late Imperial China*. Berkeley: University of California Press, 2005.

Cahill, James. Introduction to Robert van Gulik, *Erotic Colour Prints of the Late Ming Period*, ix–xxv.

Carlitz, Katherine. "Puns and Puzzles in the *Chin P'ing Mei*: A Look at Chapter 27." In *T'oung Pao* 67.3–5 (1981): 216–239.

———. "Codes and Correspondences in *Jin Ping Mei* Author(s)." In *CLEAR* 8.1–2 (1986): 7–18.

———. *The Rhetoric of Chin P'ing Mei*. Bloomington: Indiana University Press, 1986.

———. "Weeping, Blushing, and Giving Way to Desire in Ming Dynasty Fiction and Drama." In Paolo Santangelo and Ulrike Middendorf, eds. *From Skin to Heart: Perceptions of Emotions and Bodily Sensations in Traditional Chinese Culture*. Wiesbaden, Germany: Harrossowitz Verlag, 2006, 229–248.

Chang, Jolan. *The Tao of Love and Sex: The Ancient Chinese Way to Ecstasy*. New York: E. P. Dutton, 1977.

Chen Hai 陳海. "G-dian yu Xihan nüyong xingwanju kao" G 點與西漢女用性玩具考. In *Kaogu yu wenwu* 3 (2004): 62–67.

Chen Hsiu-fen 陳秀芬. "Nourishing Life, Cultivation and Material Culture in the Late Ming: Some Thoughts on *Zunsheng bajian* 遵生八箋 (Eight Discourses on Respecting Life, 1591)." In *Asian Medicine* 4 (2008): 29–45.

———. "Visual Representation and Oral Transmission of *Yangsheng* Techniques in Ming China." In *Asian Medicine* 7 (2012): 128–163.

Chen Qinghao and Wang Qiugui. Introduction to *Langshi qiguan* 浪史奇觀. Fengyue xuan youxuanzi 風月軒又玄子. In Chen Qinghao and Wang Qiugui, eds., SWXHB. Taipei: Taiwan daying baike, 1995: vol. 4, 15–21.

Cherniack, Susan. "Book Culture and Textual Transmission in Sung China." In *Harvard Journal of Asiatic Studies* 54.1 (1994): 5–125.

Chiang, Howard. *After Eunuchs: Science, Medicine, and the Transformations of Sex in Modern China*. New York: Columbia University Press, 2018.

Clunas, Craig. *Fruitful Sites: Garden Culture in Ming Dynasty China*. Durham, NC: Duke University Press, 1996.

Cullen, Christopher. "Patients and Healers in Late Imperial China: Evidence from the *Jinpingmei*." In *History of Science* 31.2 (1993): 99–150.

Darnton, Robert. *The Forbidden Best-Sellers of Pre-revolutionary France*. New York: Norton, 1995.

Dauncey, Sarah. "Illusions of Grandeur: Perceptions of Power and Wealth in Late Ming Female Clothing and Ornamentation." In *East Asian History* 25–26 (2003): 43–68.

De Villiers, Nicolas. *Sexography: Sex Work in Documentary*. Minneapolis: University of Minnesota Press, 2017.

DeJean, Joan. "The Politics of Pornography: *L'École des Filles*." In Lynn Hunt, ed., *The Invention of Pornography*, 109–123.

Despeux, Catherine, and Livia Kohn. *Women in Daoism*. Magdalena, NM: Three Pines Press, 2003.

Ding Naifei. *Obscene Things: Sexual Politics in* Jin Ping Mei. Durham, NC: Duke University Press, 2002.

Doniger, Wendy. *Redeeming the Kamasutra*. New York: Oxford University Press, 2016.

Doniger, Wendy, and Sudhir Kakar, trans. *Vatsyayana Mallanaga: Kamasutra*. Oxford: Oxford University Press, 2002.

Du Sansheng 杜三升. *Mixitu daguan* 秘戲圖大觀. Taipei: Jinfeng chuban youxian gongsi, 1993.

Dudgeon, John. "Kung-fu for the Four Seasons," and "The Eight Ornamental Sections." In William R. Berk, ed. *Chinese Healing Arts: Internal Kung-Fu*. Burbank, CA: Unique Publications, 1986: 19–56.

Durand-Dastès, Vincent. "Rencontres hérétiques dans les monastères de Kaifeng: Le Bouddhisme Tantrique vu par le roman en langue vulgaire des Ming et des Qing." In Vincent Durand-Dastès, ed., *Empreintes du tantrisme en Chine et en Asie Orientale: Imaginaires, rituals, influences*. Leuven, Belgium: Peeters, 2016: 27–62.

———. "Corps impénétrables et nonnes entremetteuses: Destins romanesques de la fille de pierre (*shinü* 石女)." In Gladys Chicharro, Stéphane Gros, Adeline Herrou, and Aurélie Névot, eds. *Le Féminin et le religieux: En hommage à Brigitte Baptandier*. Paris: l'Asiathèque, 2022: 95–133.

Epstein, Maram. *Competing Discourses: Orthodoxy, Authenticity and Engendered Meanings in Late Imperial Chinese Fiction*. Cambridge, MA: Harvard University Press, 2001.

———. "Rewriting Sexual Ideals in *Yesou puyan*." In Fran Martin and Larissa Heinrich, eds., *Embodied Modernities: Corporeality, Representation, and Chinese Cultures*. Honolulu: University of Hawaii Press, 2006: 60–78.

———. "Turning the Authorial Table: Women Writing Wanton Women, Shame, and Jealousy in Two Qing Tanci." In Mark Stevenson and Wu Cuncun, eds., *Wanton Women in Late-Imperial Chinese Literature*, 157–183.

Evans, Dylan. *An Introductory Dictionary of Lacanian Psychoanalysis.* London: Routledge, 1996.

Ferguson, Frances. *Pornography, the Theory: What Utilitarianism Did to Action*. Chicago: University of Chicago Press, 2003.

Furth, Charlotte. "Rethinking van Gulik: Sexuality and Reproduction in Traditional Chinese Medicine." In Christina K. Gilmartin, Gail Hershatter, Lisa Rofel, and Tyrene White, eds., *Engendering China: Women, Culture, and the States.* Cambridge, MA: Harvard University Press, 1994: 125–46.

Gautam, Sanjay K. *Foucault and the Kamasutra: The Courtesan, the Dandy, and the Birth of Ars Erotica as Theater in India*. Chicago: University of Chicago Press, 2016.

Ge Fei 格非. *Xueyin lusi: Jin Ping Mei de shengse yu xuwu* 雪隐鹭鸶:《金瓶梅》的声色与虚无. Nanjing: Yilin chubanshe, 2014.

Goldin, Paul R. *The Culture of Sex in Ancient China.* Honolulu: University of Hawaii Press, 2002.

———. Introduction to R. H. van Gulik. *Sexual Life in Ancient China: A Preliminary Survey of Chinese Sex and Society from c. 1500 B.C. till 1644.* Leiden, the Netherlands: Brill, 2003: xii–xxx.

———. "Copulating with One's Stepmother—or Birth Mother?" In N. Harry Rothschild and Leslie V. Wallace, eds., *Behaving Badly in Early and Medieval China*. Honolulu: University of Hawaii Press, 2017: 56–69.

Halperin, David. "Is There a History of Sexuality?" In Henry Abelove, Michele Barale, and David Halperin, eds., *The Lesbian and Gay Studies Reader*. New York: Routledge, 1993: 416–431.

Hanan, Patrick. "The Text of the *Chin P'ing Mei.*" In *Asia Major* 9.1 (1962): 1–57.

———. "The Sources of the *Chin P'ing Mei.*" In *Asia Major* 10.2 (1963): 23–67.

———. "The Erotic Novel: Some Early Reflections." Unpublished article, ca. 1980s.

———, trans. *Mirage*. Hong Kong: Chinese University Press, 2014.

Harper, Donald. "The Sexual Arts of Ancient China as Described in a Manuscript of the Second Century B.C." In *Harvard Journal of Asiatic Studies* 47.2 (1987): 539–593.

———. *Early Chinese Medical Literature: The Mawangdui Medical Manuscripts.* London: Kegan Paul International, 1998.

———. "Ancient and Medieval Chinese Recipes for Aphrodisiacs and Philters." In *Asian Medicine* 1.1 (2005): 91–100.

Hegel, Robert. "Niche Marketing for Late Imperial Fiction." In Brokaw and Chow, eds., *Printing and Book Culture in Late Imperial China*: 235–266.

Henriot, Christian. *Belles de Shanghai: Prostitution et sexualité en Chine aux XIXe–XXe siècles*. Paris: CNRS, 1997.

Hershatter, Gail. *Dangerous Pleasures: Prostitution and Modernity in Twentieth-Century Shanghai*. Berkeley: University of California Press, 1997.

Hinsch, Bret. *Passions of the Cut Sleeve. The Male Homosexual Tradition in China*. Berkeley: University of California Press, 1990.

Ho, Josephine Chuen-Juei. "Self-Empowerment and 'Professionalism': Conversations with Taiwanese Sex Workers." In *Inter-Asia Cultural Studies* 1.2 (2000): 283–299.

Hou Zhongyi 侯忠義 and Wang Rumei 王汝梅, eds. *Jin Ping Mei ziliao huibian* 金瓶梅資料滙編. Beijing: Beijing daxue chubanshe, 1985.

Hsia, C. T. *The Classic Chinese Novel: A Critical Introduction*. New York: Columbia University Press, 1968.

Hu, Lenny, trans. *The Embroidered Couch: An Erotic Novel of China*. Vancouver, BC: Arsenal Pulp Press, 2001.

———. *In the Inner Quarters: Erotic Stories from Ling Mengchu's Two Slaps*. Vancouver, BC: Arsenal Pulp Press, 2003.

Hu, Siao-chen. "In the Name of Correctness: Ding Yaokang's *Xu Jin Ping Mei* as a Reading of *Jin Ping Mei*." In Martin Huang, ed. *Snakes' Legs: Sequels, Continuations, Rewritings, and Chinese Fiction*. Honolulu: University of Hawaii Press, 2004: 75–97.

Huang Lin 黄霖. *Huang Lin Jiang Jin Ping Mei* 黄霖讲金瓶梅. Shanghai: Zhongguo chuban zhongxin, 2017.

Huang, Martin. *Desire and Fictional Narrative in Late Imperial China*. Cambridge, MA: Harvard University Press, 2001.

Hunt, Lynn. Introduction to Lynn Hunt, ed., *The Invention of Pornography*, 9–45.

———, ed. *The Invention of Pornography: Obscenity and the Origins of Modernity, 1500–1800*. New York: Zone Books, 1993.

———. "Pornography and the French Revolution." In Lynn Hunt, ed., *The Invention of Pornography*, 301–339.

Huntington, Rania. *Alien Kind: Foxes and Late Imperial Chinese Narrative*. Cambridge, MA: Harvard University Press, 2003.

Idema, Wilt L. "'Blasé Literati': Lü T'ien-ch'eng and the Lifestyle of the Chiang-Nan Elite in the Final Decades of the Wan-Li Period." In Robert van Gulik, *Erotic Colour Prints of the Late Ming Period*: xxix–lix.

Illouz, Eva. *Why Love Hurts: A Sociological Explanation*. London: Polity, 2012.

Kaltenmark, Max, trans. *Le Lie-sien Tchouan*. Paris: Collège de France, 1987.

Kelly, Thomas. "Riddles in *Jin Ping Mei*." In *The Journal of Chinese Literature and Culture*, 8.2 (Nov. 2021): 341–370.

Keulemans, Paize (Gu Bo 古柏). "*Jin Ping Mei* chongtan: Cong liuyan dao chouwen" (《金瓶梅》重探：从流言到丑闻). In *Beijing daxue Zhongguo guwenxian yanjiu zhongxin jikan* 北京大学中国古文献研究中心集刊, 11 (2012): 395–411.

Kinney, Anne B. *Exemplary Women of Early China: The Lienü zhuan of Liu Xiang*. New York: Columbia University Press, 2014.

Kipnis, Laura. *Bound and Gagged: Pornography and the Politics of Fantasy in America*. New York: Grove Press, 1996.

Kohn, Livia. *Chinese Healing Exercises: The Tradition of Daoyin*. Honolulu: University of Hawaii Press, 2008.

Kohn, Livia, and Robin R. Wang, eds. *Internal Alchemy: Self, Society, and the Quest for Immortality*. Magdalena, NM: Three Pines Press, 2009.

Korda, J. B., S. W. Goldstein, and F. Sommer. "The History of Female Ejaculation." In *Journal of Sexual Medicine*, 7 (2010): 1965–1975.

Lee, Haiyan. *Revolution of the Heart: A Genealogy of Love in China, 1900–1950*. Palo Alto, CA: Stanford University Press, 2007.

Levin, R. J. "Wet and Dry Sex—the Impact of Cultural Influence in Modifying Vaginal Function." In *Sexual and Relationship Therapy*, 20.4 (2005): 465–474.

———. "The Clitoral Activation Paradox—Claimed Outcomes from Different Methods of Its Stimulation." In *Clinical Anatomy*, 31.5 (2018): 650–660.

Lévy, André, trans. *Fleur en Fiole d'Or* (*Jin Ping Mei cihua*). 2 vols. Paris: Gallimard, 1985.

———. Introduction to *Fleur en Fiole d'Or* (*Jin Ping Mei cihua*). Paris: Gallimard, 1985, 1: xxxvii–lxxi.

———. Marc Martinez, trans. "Introduction to the French Translation of *Jin Ping Mei cihua*." In *Renditions* 24 (1985): 109–129.

Levy, Howard S. *The Dwelling of Playful Goddesses: China's First Novelette*. Tokyo: Dai Nippon Insatus, 1965.

Li Jianguo 李劍國. "Chuanqi zhi shou: *Zhao Feiyan waizhuan*" "傳奇之首 《趙飛燕外傳》." In *Wenxue shihua* 文學史話 1 (2004): 33–40.

Li Ling 李零. *Zhongguo fangshu gaiguan*, 中國方術概觀. Beijing: Renmin Zhongguo chubanshe, 1993.

———. *Zhongguo fangshu kao* 中國方術考. Beijing: Renmin Zhongguo chubanshe, 1993.

———. *Zhongguo fangshu xukao* 中國方術續考. Beijing: Dongfang chubanshe, 2000.

———. *Wanbian* 萬變. Beijing: Sanlian shudian, 2017.

Li Ling 李零 and Keith McMahon. "The Contents and Terminology of the Mawangdui Texts on the Arts of the Bedchamber." In *Early China* 17 (1992): 145–185.

Li Mengsheng 李夢生. *Zhongguo jinhui xiaoshuo baihua* 中國禁毀小說百話. Shanghai: Shanghai guji chubanshe, 1994.

Li Xiaorong. *The Poetics and Politics of Sensuality in China: The "Fragrant and Bedazzling" Movement (1600–1930)*. Amherst, MA: Cambria Press, 2019.

Lin Chen 林辰. *Mingmo Qingchu xiaoshuo shulu* 明末清初小說述錄. Shenyang: Chunfeng wenyi chubanshe, 1988.

———. "Yanqing xiaoshuo he xiaoshuozhongde xing miaoxie" 艷情小說和小說中的性描寫. In Zhang Guoxing, ed., *Zhongguo gudai xiaoshuozhongde xing miaoxie*, 31–52.

Liu, Wenjia. "Virtuous Wives and Shrews in *Feng Shuangfei*: Empowering Female Characters through a Revision of Stereotypes." In *Journal of Chinese Literature and Culture* 3.1 (2016): 57–84.

Liu Xun. "Numinous Father and Holy Mother: Late Ming Duo-Cultivation Practice." In Livia Kohn and Robin R. Wang, eds. *Internal Alchemy*, 121–140.

Liu Yongqiang 劉勇強. "*Jin Ping Mei* benwen yu jieshou fenxi" 《金瓶梅》本文與接收分析. In *Beijing daxue xuebao* 4 (1996): 68–76.

———. *Zhongguo gudai xiaoshuoshi xulun* 中國古代小說史敘論. Beijing: Beijing daxue chubanshe, 2007.

Lo, Vivienne. *How to Do the Gibbon Walk: A Translation of the Pulling Book (ca 186 B.C.)*. Cambridge: Needham Research Institute, 2014.

Lu, Tina. *Accidental Incest, Filial Cannibalism, and Other Peculiar Encounters in Late Imperial Chinese Literature*. Cambridge, MA: Harvard University Press, 2008.

Lu Xixing 陸錫興. *Zhongguo gudai qiwu dacidian* 中國古代器物大辭典. Shijiazhuang: Hebei jiaoyu chubanshe, 2004.

Lu Xun. Yang Hsien-yi and Gladys Yang, trans. *A Brief History of Chinese Fiction*. Peking: Foreign Languages Press, 1976.

Lu Xun 魯迅. *Zhongguo xiaoshuo shilue* 中國小說史略. Nanjing: Jiangsu wenyi chubanshe, 2007.

Mao Dun 矛盾 (pseudonym of Shen Yanbin 沈雁冰). "Zhongguo wenxueneide xingyu miaoxie" 中國文學內的性慾描寫. In Mao Dun. *Mao Dun gudian wenxue lunwenji* 矛盾古典文學論文集. Shanghai, Guji chubanshe, 1986: 160–173.

Marcus, Steven. *The Other Victorians: A Study of Sexuality and Pornography in Mid-Nineteenth-Century England*. New York: Basic Books, 1974.

McMahon, Keith. *Causality and Containment in Seventeenth-Century Chinese Fiction*. Leiden, the Netherlands: Brill 1988.

———. *Polygamy and Sublime Passion: Sexuality in China on the Vergy of Modernity*. Honolulu: University of Hawai'i Press, 2010.

———. "Polygyny, Bound Feet, and Perversion." In *Extrême-Orient Extrême-Occident, Hors-série* (2012): 159–187.

———. *Women Shall Not Rule: Imperial Wives and Concubines in China from Han to Liao*. Lanham, MD: Rowman and Littlefield, 2013.

———. Review of Patrick Hanan, trans., *Mirage*. In *Nannü* 17.2 (2015): 158–162.

———. *Celestial Women: Imperial Wives and Concubines from Song to Qing*. Lanham, MD: Rowman and Littlefield: 2016.

———. "The Attendant's Lament: Loansharking, Squeeze, and Extortion in the Yangzhou Novel *Fengyue meng* ("Seductive Dreams")." In *Journal of Chinese Literature and Culture* 5.1 (2018): 1–33.

———. "The Pornographic Doctrine of a Loyalist Ming Novel: Social Decline and Sexual Disorder in *Preposterous Words* (*Guwangyan*)." In Howard Chiang, ed., *Sexuality in China: Histories of Power and Pleasure*. Seattle: University of Washington Press, 2018: 50–75.

———. "The Art of the Bedchamber and *Jin Ping Mei* 金瓶梅." In *Nan Nü* 21.1 (2019): 1–37.

———. "Wives, Concubines, Prostitutes, and Other Men's Wives: The Portrayal of Sex in *Plum in the Golden Vase*." In Andrew Schonebaum, ed. *Approaches to Teaching The Plum in the Golden Vase (The Golden Lotus)*. New York: Modern Language Association of America, 2022: 253–262.

———. "The Language of Sex in *Jin Ping Mei*." In *Harvard Journal of Asiatic Studies* 82.2 (2023): forthcoming.

———. "Sexual Portrayal in *Jin Ping Mei*." In Vibeke Børdahl and Lintao Qi, eds. *Jin Ping Mei—A Wild Horse in Chinese Literature*. Copenhagen: NIAS Press, 2022: forthcoming.

Milburn, Olivia. "On *Zhao Feiyan waizhuan*, China's Earliest Erotic Fiction." In *Asia Major* 31.1 (2018): 91–117.

———. *The Empress in the Pepper Chamber: Zhao Feiyan in History and Fiction*. Seattle: Washington University Press, 2021.

Mote, Frederick W. "Yuan and Ming." In K. C. Chang, ed., *Food in Chinese Culture: Anthropological and Historical Perspectives*. New Haven, CT: Yale University Press, 1977: 195–257.

Moulton, Ian Frederick. *Before Pornography: Erotic Writing in Early Modern England*. New York: Oxford University Press, 2000.

Mudge, Bradford K. *The Whore's Story. Women, Pornography, and the British Novel, 1684–1830.* New York: Oxford University Press, 2000.

Nienhauser, William. "Female Sexuality and the Double Standard in Tang Narratives." In Eva Hung, ed., *Paradoxes of Traditional Chinese Literature.* Hong Kong: Chinese University Press, 1994: 1–20.

Ning Zongyi 寧宗一 and Luo Derong 羅德榮. *Jin Ping Mei dui xiaoshuo meixue de gongxian* 《金瓶梅》對小說美學的貢獻. Tianjin: Tianjin shehui kexueyuan chubanshe, 1992.

Norberg, Kathryn. "The Libertine Whore: Prostitution in French Pornography from Margot to Juliette." In Lynn Hunt, ed., *The Invention of Pornography*, 225–252.

Nylan, Michael. *The Chinese Pleasure Book.* New York: Zone Books, 2018.

O'Hara, Daniel. *Visions of Global America and the Future of Critical Reading.* Columbus: Ohio State University Press, 2009.

Orrells, Daniel. *Sex: Antiquity and Its Legacy.* Oxford: Oxford University Press, 2015.

Owen, Stephen. *An Anthology of Chinese Literature.* New York: Norton, 1996.

Pan Jianguo 潘建國. "Mianling xinkao" (勉鈴新考). In *Wenxian* 文獻 1 (1996): 265–69.

———. "Daojiao fangzhong wenhua yu Ming Qing xiaoshuo zhong de xing miaoxie" 道教房中文化與明清小說中的性描寫. *MingQing xiaoshuo yanjiu* 3 (1997): 57–70.

Pei Xirong 裴錫榮, Han Minghua 韓明華, and Jiang Songyou 江松友. *Zhonghua gujin bingxie tukao* 中華古今兵械圖考. Beijing: Renmin tiyu chubanshe, 1999.

Pfister, Rodo. "Gendering Sexual Pleasures in Early and Medieval China." In *Asian Medicine* 7 (2012): 34–64.

———. "The Sexual Body Techniques of Early and Medieval China—Underlying Emic Theories and Basic Methods of a Non-Reproductive Sexual Scenario for Non-Same-Sex Partners." In Vivienne Lo and Michael Stanley-Baker, eds. *Routledge Handbook of Chinese Medicine.* Milton Park: Routledge Publishers, 2022: 337–355.

Plaks, Andrew. "The Chongzhen Commentary on the *Jin Ping Mei*: Gems amidst the Dross." In *CLEAR* 8.1–2 (1986): 19–30.

———. *The Four Masterworks of the Ming Novel: Ssu ta ch'i-shu.* Princeton, NJ: Princeton University Press, 1987.

Qi Lintao. *Jin Ping Mei English Translations: Texts, Paratexts, and Contexts.* London: Routledge, 2018.

Qian Nanyang 錢南揚, ed. *Tang Xianzu xiqu ji* 湯顯祖戲曲集. Shanghai: Shanghai guji chubanshe, 1978.

Raz, Gil. "The Way of the Yellow and the Red: Re-Examining the Sexual Initiation Rite of Celestial Master Daoism." In *Nan Nü* 10.1 (2008): 86–120.

Reid, Daniel P. *The Tao of Health, Sex, and Longevity; A Modern Practical Guide to the Ancient Way.* New York: Fireside, 1989.

Rocha, Leon. "*Xing*: The Discourse of Sex and Human Nature in Modern China." In *Gender and History* 22.3 (2010): 603–628.

Rolston, David, ed. *How To Read the Chinese Novel.* Princeton, NJ: Princeton University Press, 1990.

———. "Oral Performing Literature in Traditional Chinese Fiction: Nonrealistic Usages in the *Jin Ping Mei Cihua* and Their Influence." In *Chinoperl Papers* 17 (1994): 1–110.

———. *Traditional Chinese Fiction and Fiction Commentary: Reading and Writing between the Lines.* Stanford, CA: Stanford University Press, 1997.

Roy, David T. "A Confucian Interpretation of the *Chin P'ing Mei.*" In *Proceedings of the International Conference on Sinology, Section on Literature.* Taipei: Academia Sinica, 1980: 39–61.

———. "Chang Chu-p'o on How to Read the *Chin P'ing Mei* (*The Plum in the Golden Vase*)." In David Rolston, ed., *How to Read the Chinese Novel,* 196–243.

———. Introduction to David Roy, trans., *The Plum in the Golden Vase, or Chin P'ing Mei. Volume One: The Gathering.* Princeton, NJ: Princeton University Press, 1993: xvii–xlvii.

———, trans. *The Plum in the Golden Vase, or Chin P'ing Mei.* 5 vols. Princeton, NJ: Princeton University Press, 1993–2013.

Satyendra, Indira. "Metaphors of the Body: The Sexual Economy of the *Chin P'ing Mei tz'u-hua.*" In *CLEAR,* 15 (1993): 85–97.

Schipper, Kristofer. *The Taoist Body.* Berkeley: University of California Press, 1993.

Schonebaum, Andrew. *Novel Medicine: Healing, Literature, and Popular Knowledge in Early Modern China.* Seattle: University of Washington Press, 2016.

Shang Wei. "*Jin Ping Mei* and Late Ming Print Culture." In Judith T. Zeitlin and Lydia H. Liu, with Ellen Widmer, eds., *Writing and Materiality in China: Essays in Honor of Patrick Hanan.* Cambridge, MA: Harvard University Press, 2003: 187–230.

———. "The Making of the Everyday World: *Jin Ping Mei cihua* and Encyclopedias for Daily Use." In David Der-wei Wang and Shang Wei, eds. *Dynastic Crisis and Cultural Innovation: From the Late Ming to the Late Qing and Beyond.* Cambridge, MA: Harvard University Press, 2005: 63–92.

Shanghai shi *Honglong meng* xuehui 上海市紅樓夢學會. *Jin Ping Mei jianshang cidian* 金瓶梅鑒賞詞典. Shanghai: Shanghai guji chuban she, 1990.

Si Xin 斯欣. "Sheji xing miaoxiede gudai tongsu xiaoshuo shumu" 涉及性描寫的古代通俗小說書目. In Zhang Guoxing, ed. *Zhongguo gudai xiaoshuozhongde xing miaoxie* 中國古代小說中的性描寫: 387–400.

Sibau, Maria Franca. *Reading for the Moral: Exemplarity and the Confucian Moral Imagination in Seventeenth-Century Chinese Short Fiction.* Albany: State University of New York Press, 2018.

Sommer, Matthew H. *Polyandry and Wife-Selling in Qing Dynasty China: Survival Strategies and Judicial Interventions.* Berkeley: University of California Press, 2015.

Son Suyoung. "Reading an Authorless Text: The Reception of *Jin Ping Mei* in Manuscript and Print." In *Journal of Chinese Language and Literature* [Chungguk ŏmunhak nonjip] 81.8 (2013): 439–455.

Stevenson, Mark. "Sound, Space and Moral Soundscapes in *Ruyijun zhuan* and *Chipozi zhuan.*" In *Nan Nü* 12.2 (2010): 255–310.

———. "The Male Homoerotic Wanton Woman in Late Ming Fiction." In Mark Stevenson and Wu Cuncun, eds., *Wanton Women in Late-Imperial Chinese Literature,* 54–77.

———. "*Guwangyan,* Pornography and Sensory Exchange." Paper presented at "Comparative Pornographies: Transnational Approaches to Writing Sex, East and West," March 9, 2019, University of California at Los Angeles.

Stevenson, Mark, and Wu Cuncun, eds. *Wanton Women in Late-Imperial Chinese Literature*. Leiden, the Netherlands: Brill, 2017.

Stone, Charles. *The Fountainhead of Chinese Erotica: The Lord of Perfect Satisfaction* (*Ruyijun zhuan*). Honolulu: University of Hawaii Press, 2003.

Su Yufen 蘇玉芬. *Mingdai chunyao yanjiu* 明代春藥研究. MA thesis, National Chengchi University, 2011.

Sullivan, Rebecca, and Alan McKee. *Pornography: Structures, Agency and Performance*. Cambridge: Polity Press, 2015.

Swatek, Catherine. "Popular Songs and Drama in *Plum in the Golden Vase*." In Andrew Schonebaum, ed., *Approaches to Teaching The Plum in the Golden Vase (The Golden Lotus)*. New York: Modern Language Association of America, 2022: 295–309.

Tian Bing'e 田秉锷. "*Jin Ping Mei* xing miaoxie sibian" 《金瓶梅》性描寫思辯. In Zhang Guoxing, ed., *Zhongguo gudai xiaoshuozhongde xing miaoxie*: 224–244.

Tian Xiaofei 田曉菲. "A Preliminary Comparison of the Two Recensions of '*Jinpingmei*.'" In *Harvard Journal of Asiatic Studies* 62.2 (2002): 347–388.

———. *Qiushui tang lun Jin Ping Mei* 秋水堂論金瓶梅. Tianjin: Tianjin renmin chubanshe, 2003.

Ullén, Magnus. "Pornography and Its Critical Reception: Toward a Theory of Masturbation." In *Jump Cut* 51 (2009): https://www.ejumpcut.org/archive/jc51.2009/UllenPorn/.

Umekawa, Sumiyo. "*Tiandi yinyang jiaohuan dalefu* and the Art of the Bedchamber." In Vivienne Lo and Christopher Cullen, eds. *Medieval Chinese Medicine. The Dunhuang Medical Manuscripts*. London: Routledge Curzon, 2005: 252–277,

Valussi, Elena. "Men and Women in He Longxiang's *Nüdan hebian*." In *Nan Nü* 10.2 (2008): 242–278.

———. "Female Alchemy." In Livia Kohn and Robin R. Wang, eds. *Internal Alchemy*, 141–162.

Van Gulik, Robert H. *Sexual Life in Ancient China*. Leiden, the Netherlands: Brill, 1974.

———. *Erotic Colour Prints of the Ming Period: With an Essay on Chinese Sex Life from Han to the Ch'ing Dynasty, B.C. 206–A. D. 1644*. 2 vols. Repr. ed. Leiden, the Netherlands: Brill, 2004.

Vitiello, Giovanni. "The Fantasy of an Ugly Boy: Homosexuality and Salvation in Late Ming Pornography." In *positions* 4.2 (1996): 291–320.

———. "Exemplary Sodomites: Chivalry and Love in Late Ming Culture." In *Nan Nü* 2.2 (2000): 207–258.

———. "The Forgotten Tears of the Lord of Longyang: Late Ming Stories of Male Prostitution and Connoisseurship." In Peter Engelfriet and Jan de Mejer, eds. *Linked Faiths: Essays on Chinese Religion and Traditional Culture in Honour of Kristofer Schipper*. Leiden, the Netherlands: Brill, 2000: 227–247.

———. "Family Affairs: A Crazed Woman and Late Ming Pornography." In Antonino Forte and Federico Masini, eds. *A Life Journey to the East: Sinological Studies in Memory of Giuliano Bertuccioli (1923–2001)*. Kyoto: Scuola Italiana de Studi sull'Asia Orientale, 2002: 245–262.

———. *The Libertine's Friend: Homosexuality and Masculinity in Late Imperial China*. Chicago: University of Chicago Press, 2011.

Volpp, Sophie. "The Discourse on Male Marriage: Li Yu's 'A Male Mencius's Mother.'" In *positions* 2.1 (1994): 113–132.

———. "Classifying Lust: The Seventeenth-Century Vogue for Male Love." In *Harvard Journal of Asiatic Studies* 61.1 (2001): 77–117.

———. "The Literary Circulation of Actors in Seventeenth-Century China." In *Journal of Asian Studies* 61.3 (2002): 949–984.

———. "The Gift of a Python Robe: The Circulation of Objects in *Jin Ping Mei.*" In *Harvard Journal of Asiatic Studies* 65.1 (June 2005): 133–158.

Wan Jingchuan 萬晴川. "Lun fangzhongshu dui Ming Qing xiaoshuode yingxiang" 論房中術對明清小說的影響. In *Jinyang xuekan* 晉陽學刊 1 (2000): 70–73.

Wang, David. *Fin de Siècle Splendor: Repressed Modernities of Late Qing Fiction, 1849–1911.* Palo Alto, CA: Stanford University Press, 1997.

Wang Qiang. *Les secrets de la puissance sexuelle: Plaisir, vigueur et longévité grâce à la médecine traditionnelle chinoise.* Paris: Dervy, 1994.

Wang, Richard. *Ming Erotic Novellas: Genre, Consumption, and Religiosity in Cultural Practice.* Hong Kong: Chinese University Press, 2011.

Wang Rumei 王汝梅. *Wang Rumei jiedu Jin Ping Mei* 王汝梅解讀《金瓶梅》. Changchun: Shidai wenyi chubanshe, 2014.

Wang Ying. "Constructing Patients: Medical Narratives in Late Imperial Vernacular Fiction." PhD diss., University of California at Los Angeles, 2020.

Wang, Yvon. *Reinventing Licentiousness: Pornography and Modern China.* Ithaca, NY: Cornell University Press, 2021.

Weil, Rachel. "Sometimes a Scepter Is Only a Scepter: Pornography and Politics in Restoration England." In Lynn Hunt, ed., *The Invention of Pornography*: 125–153.

West, Stephen H., and Wilt Idema. *The Moon and the Zither: The Story of the Western Wing.* Berkeley: University of California Press, 1990.

Wile, Douglas. *The Art of the Bedchamber: The Chinese Sexual Yoga Classics, Including Women's Solo Meditation Texts.* Albany: State University of New York Press, 1992.

Will, Pierre-Étienne. "Officials and Money in Late Imperial China: State Finances, Private Expectations, and the Problem of Corruption in a Changing Environment." In *Corrupt Histories*, ed. Emmanuel Kreike and William Chester Jordan. Rochester, NY: University of Rochester Press, 2004: 29–82.

Williams, Linda. *Hardcore: Power, Pleasure, and the "Frenzy of the Visible."* Berkeley: University of California Press, 1999.

———, ed. *Porn Studies.* Durham, NC: Duke University Press, 2004.

———. "Porn Studies: Proliferating Pornographies on/Scene: An Introduction." In Williams, ed., *Porn Studies*: 1–23.

Wong, Ka F. "The Anatomy of Eroticism: Reimagining Sex and Sexuality in the Late Ming Novel *Xiuta Yeshi.*" In *Nan Nü* 9.2 (2007): 284–389.

Wu Cuncun 吳存存. *Homoerotic Sensibilities in Late Imperial China.* London: Routledge, 2004.

———. "'It Was I Who Lured the Boy': Commoner Women, Intimacy and the Sensual Body in the Song Collections of Feng Menglong (1574–1646)." In *Nan Nü* 12.2 (2010): 311–343.

Wu Cuncun. "Cong *Huanxi yuanjia* zhong de tongjian gushi kan wanMing chengshi putongren de jiazhiguan he daodeguan" "從《歡喜冤家》中的通奸故事看晚明城市普通人的價值觀和道德觀." In *Zhongguo wenhua* 41 (2014): 69–79.

———. "The Plebification of Male-Love in Late Ming Fiction." In Kam Louie, ed., *Changing Chinese Masculinities: From Imperial Pillars of State to Global Real Men*. Hong Kong: Hong Kong University Press, 2016: 72–89.

———. *Xi wai zhi xi: Qing zhongwanqi jingcheng de xiyuan wenhua yu liyuan siyuzhi* 戲外之戲: 清中晚期京城的戲園文化與梨園私寓制. Hong Kong: Hong Kong University Press, 2017.

———. "Cong *Jingyuan michuan dongfang chunyi ce* zhong liangpian gaixiede wenyan seqing xiaoshuo kan wanMing pingmin seqing xiaofeipin tixiande jiazhiguan he tedian" 从《京院秘传洞房春意册》中兩篇改寫的文言色情小說看晚明平民色情消費品體現的價值觀和特點. Paper presented at International Conference on Premodern Chinese Fiction, October 19–20, 2019, Beijing University.

Wu Cuncun and Mark Stevenson, trans. *A Tale of an Infatuated Woman*. In *Renditions* 58 (Autumn 2002): 60–97.

———, trans. "Notes on Flower Appreciation in the Phoenix City." In *Renditions* 69 (Spring 2008): 34–61.

Wu, Laura. "Through the Prism of Male Writing: Representations of Lesbian Love in Ming–Qing Literature." In *Nan Nü* 4.1 (2002): 1–34.

Wu Xiaoling 吳曉鈴. "*Jin Ping Mei* 'mianling' shi" 金瓶梅勉鈴釋. In *Wenxian* 文獻 4 (1990): 62–63.

Wu Yen-na 吳燕娜. "Zhongguo seqing xiaoshuozhongde funü xingxiang yu xingjiaoyu" 中國色情小說中的婦女形象與性教育. In Wu Yen-na and Wei Lun 魏綸, eds. *Zhongguo funü wenxue lunwenji, diyiji* 中國婦女文學論文集第一集. Taipei: Taoxiang chubanshe, 1999: 47–56.

Xu Yuanchong and Frank Xu, trans. *Romance of the Western Bower*. Beijing: China Intercontinental Press, 2012.

Xu Yuanzhen 徐元貞. *Zhongyi cishi* 中醫詞釋. Zhengzhou: Henan kexue jishu chubanshe, 1985.

Xue Yingjie 薛英傑. "Wenren shenfen yu tazhe xiangxiang: WanMing he Qingchude 'yinseng' gushi" 文人身份與他者想象：晚明和清初的'淫僧'故事. PhD diss., University of Hong Kong, 2017.

Yang Jiarong 楊佳蓉. "*Zuo zhuan* Xia Ji shishi yu meixue tanxi" 《左轉》夏姬史事與美學探析. In *Yu Da Academic Journal* 36 (December 2013): 63–85.

Yang Zhishui 揚之水. *Wu se: Jin Ping Mei du "wu" ji* 物色:《金瓶梅》讀"物"記. Beijing: Zhonghua shuju, 2018.

Yao Lingxi 姚靈犀. *Pingwai zhiyan* 瓶外卮言. Tianjin: Tianjinshi guji shudian, 1989 [reprint of 1940 edition].

Yao Ping. "Historicizing Great Bliss: Erotica in Tang China (618–907)." In *Journal of the History of Sexuality*, 22.2 (2013): 207–229.

Yeh, Catherine. *Shanghai Love: Courtesans, Intellectuals, and Entertainment Culture, 1850–1911*. Seattle: University of Washington Press, 2006.

Zamperini, Paola. "Pornography." In Bonnie G. Smith, ed., *The Oxford Encyclopedia of Women in World History*. Oxford: Oxford University Press, 2008: 487–492.

———. "Canonizing Pornography. A (Foolish?) Woman's Sexual Education in *Chipozi zhuan*." In Zhou Jianyu 周建渝, Zhang Hongnian 張洪年, and Zhang Shuangqing 張雙慶, eds., *Chongdu jingdian: Zhongguo chuantong xiaoshuo yu xiqude duochong toushi* 重讀經典: 中國傳統小說與戲曲的多重透視. Hong Kong: Oxford University Press, 2009: 270–297.

———. *Lost Bodies: Prostitution and Masculinity in Chinese Fiction*. Leiden, the Netherlands: Brill, 2010.

Zhang Guoxing 張國星, ed. *Zhongguo gudai xiaoshuozhongde xing miaoxie* 中國古代小說中的性描寫. Tianjin: Baihua wenyi chubanshe, 1993.

Zhang Huiying 张惠英. *Jin Ping Mei lisu nanci jie* 金瓶梅俚俗难词解. Beijing: Shehui kexue wenxian chubanshe, 1992.

Zhang Youhe 張友鶴. *Tang Song chuanqi xuan* 唐宋傳奇選. Beijing: Renmin wenxue chubanshe, 1979.

Zhang Zhang 張璋 and Huang She 黄畬, eds. *Zhu Shuzhen ji* 朱淑真集. Shanghai: Shanghai guji, 1986.

Zheng Binyu 鄭賓于. "Lun yinshu" 論淫書. In *Xin wenhua* 1.2 (1927): 147–151.

Žižek, Slavoj. *Tarrying with the Negative: Kant, Hegel, and the Critique of Ideology*. Durham, NC: Duke University Press, 1993.

———. *The Plague of Fantasies*. London: Verso, 1997.

Zurndorfer, Harriet. "Silver, Piracy, Conspicuous Consumption, and the Transformation of Ming China in the Sixteenth Century." In *Oxford Research Encyclopedia of Asian History*. Oxford University Press, 2016—. Article published April 26, 2021. Doi: https://doi.org/10.1093/acrefore/9780190277727.013.620.

Index

Italic page numbers refer to figures.

Harvard-Yenching Institute Monograph Series
(most recent titles now in print)

24. *Population, Disease, and Land in Early Japan, 645–900*, by William Wayne Farris
25. *Shikitei Sanba and the Comic Tradition in Edo Fiction*, by Robert W. Leutner
26. *Washing Silk: The Life and Selected Poetry of Wei Chuang (834?–910)*, by Robin D. S. Yates
28. *Tang Transformation Texts: A Study of the Buddhist Contribution to the Rise of Vernacular Fiction and Drama in China*, by Victor H. Mair
30. *Readings in Chinese Literary Thought*, by Stephen Owen
31. *Remembering Paradise: Nativism and Nostalgia in Eighteenth-Century Japan*, by Peter Nosco
33. *Escape from the Wasteland: Romanticism and Realism in the Fiction of Mishima Yukio and Oe Kenzaburo*, by Susan Jolliffe Napier
34. *Inside a Service Trade: Studies in Contemporary Chinese Prose*, by Rudolf G. Wagner
35. *The Willow in Autumn: Ryutei Tanehiko, 1783–1842*, by Andrew Lawrence Markus
36. *The Confucian Transformation of Korea: A Study of Society and Ideology*, by Martina Deuchler
37. *The Korean Singer of Tales*, by Marshall R. Pihl
38. *Praying for Power: Buddhism and the Formation of Gentry Society in Late-Ming China*, by Timothy Brook
39. *Word, Image, and Deed in the Life of Su Shi*, by Ronald C. Egan
41. *Studies in the Comic Spirit in Modern Japanese Fiction*, by Joel R. Cohn
42. *Wind Against the Mountain: The Crisis of Politics and Culture in Thirteenth-Century China*, by Richard L. Davis
43. *Powerful Relations: Kinship, Status, and the State in Sung China (960–1279)*, by Beverly Bossler
44. *Limited Views: Essays on Ideas and Letters*, by Qian Zhongshu; selected and translated by Ronald Egan
45. *Sugar and Society in China: Peasants, Technology, and the World Market*, by Sucheta Mazumdar
49. *Precious Volumes: An Introduction to Chinese Sectarian Scriptures from the Sixteenth and Seventeenth Centuries*, by Daniel L. Overmyer
50. *Poetry and Painting in Song China: The Subtle Art of Dissent*, by Alfreda Murck
51. *Evil and/or/as the Good: Omnicentrism, Intersubjectivity, and Value Paradox in Tiantai Buddhist Thought*, by Brook Ziporyn
53. *Articulated Ladies: Gender and the Male Community in Early Chinese Texts*, by Paul Rouzer

55. *Allegories of Desire: Esoteric Literary Commentaries of Medieval Japan*, by Susan Blakeley Klein
56. *Printing for Profit: The Commercial Publishers of Jianyang, Fujian (11th–17th Centuries)*, by Lucille Chia
57. *To Become a God: Cosmology, Sacrifice, and Self-Divinization in Early China*, by Michael J. Puett
58. *Writing and Materiality in China: Essays in Honor of Patrick Hanan*, edited by Judith T. Zeitlin and Lydia H. Liu
59. Rulin waishi *and Cultural Transformation in Late Imperial China*, by Shang Wei
60. *Words Well Put: Visions of Poetic Competence in the Chinese Tradition*, by Graham Sanders
61. *Householders: The Reizei Family in Japanese History*, by Steven D. Carter
62. *The Divine Nature of Power: Chinese Ritual Architecture at the Sacred Site of Jinci*, by Tracy Miller
63. *Beacon Fire and Shooting Star: The Literary Culture of the Liang (502–557)*, by Xiaofei Tian
64. *Lost Soul: "Confucianism" in Contemporary Chinese Academic Discourse*, by John Makeham
65. *The Sage Learning of Liu Zhi: Islamic Thought in Confucian Terms*, by Sachiko Murata, William C. Chittick, and Tu Weiming
66. *Through a Forest of Chancellors: Fugitive Histories in Liu Yuan's* Lingyan ge, *an Illustrated Book from Seventeenth-Century Suzhou*, by Anne Burkus-Chasson
67. *Empire of Texts in Motion: Chinese, Korean, and Taiwanese Transculturations of Japanese Literature*, by Karen Laura Thornber
68. *Empire's Twilight: Northeast Asia Under the Mongols*, by David M. Robinson
69. *Ancestors, Virgins, and Friars: Christianity as a Local Religion in Late Imperial China*, by Eugenio Menegon
70. *Manifest in Words, Written on Paper: Producing and Circulating Poetry in Tang Dynasty China*, by Christopher M. B. Nugent
71. *The Poetics of Sovereignty: On Emperor Taizong of the Tang Dynasty*, by Jack W. Chen
72. *Ancestral Memory in Early China*, by K. E. Brashier
73. *'Dividing the Realm in Order to Govern': The Spatial Organization of the Song State*, by Ruth Mostern
74. *The Dynamics of Masters Literature: Early Chinese Thought from Confucius to Han Feizi*, by Wiebke Denecke
75. *Songs of Contentment and Transgression: Discharged Officials and Literati Communities in Sixteenth-Century North China*, by Tian Yuan Tan
76. *Ten Thousand Scrolls: Reading and Writing in the Poetics of Huang Tingjian and the Late Northern Song*, by Yugen Wang
77. *A Northern Alternative: Xue Xuan (1389–1464) and the Hedong School*, by Khee Heong Koh
78. *Visionary Journeys: Travel Writings from Early Medieval and Nineteenth-Century China*, by Xiaofei Tian
79. *Making Personas: Transnational Film Stardom in Modern Japan*, by Hideaki Fujiki
80. *Strange Eventful Histories: Identity, Performance, and Xu Wei's* Four Cries of a Gibbon, by Shiamin Kwa

81. *Critics and Commentators: The* Book of Poems *as Classic and Literature*, by Bruce Rusk
82. *Home and the World: Editing the Glorious Ming in Woodblock-Printed Books of the Sixteenth and Seventeenth Centuries*, by Yuming He
83. *Courtesans, Concubines, and the Cult of Female Fidelity*, by Beverly Bossler
84. *Chinese History: A New Manual, Third Edition*, by Endymion Wilkinson
85. *A Comprehensive Manchu-English Dictionary*, by Jerry Norman
86. *Drifting among Rivers and Lakes: Southern Song Dynasty Poetry and the Problem of Literary History*, by Michael Fuller
87. *Martial Spectacles of the Ming Court*, by David M. Robinson
88. *Modern Archaics: Continuity and Innovation in the Chinese Lyric Tradition, 1900–1937*, by Shengqing Wu
89. *Cherishing Antiquity: The Cultural Construction of an Ancient Chinese Kingdom*, by Olivia Milburn
90. *The Burden of Female Talent: The Poet Li Qingzhao and Her History in China*, by Ronald Egan
91. *Public Memory in Early China*, by K. E. Brashier
92. *Women and National Trauma in Late Imperial Chinese Literature*, by Wai-yee Li
93. *The Destruction of the Medieval Chinese Aristocracy*, by Nicolas Tackett
94. *Savage Exchange: Han Imperialism, Chinese Literary Style, and the Economic Imagination*, by Tamara T. Chin
95. *Shifting Stories: History, Gossip, and Lore in Narratives from Tang Dynasty China*, by Sarah M. Allen
96. *One Who Knows Me: Friendship and Literary Culture in Mid-Tang China*, by Anna Shields
97. *Materializing Magic Power: Chinese Popular Religion in Villages and Cities*, by Wei-Ping Lin
98. *Traces of Grand Peace: Classics and State Activism in Imperial China*, by Jaeyoon Song
99. *Fiction's Family: Zhan Xi, Zhan Kai, and the Business of Women in Late-Qing China*, by Ellen Widmer
100. *Chinese History: A New Manual, Fourth Edition*, by Endymion Wilkinson
101. *After the Prosperous Age: State and Elites in Early Nineteenth-Century Suzhou*, by Seunghyun Han
102. *Celestial Masters: History and Ritual in Early Daoist Communities*, by Terry F. Kleeman
103. *Transgressive Typologies: Constructions of Gender and Power in Early Tang China*, by Rebecca Doran
104. *Li Mengyang, the North-South Divide, and Literati Learning in Ming China*, by Chang Woei Ong
105. *Bannermen Tales (Zidishu): Manchu Storytelling and Cultural Hybridity in the Qing Dynasty*, by Elena Suet-Ying Chiu
106. *Upriver Journeys: Diaspora and Empire in Southern China, 1570–1850*, by Steven B. Miles
107. *Ancestors, Kings, and the Dao*, by Constance A. Cook
108. *The Halberd at Red Cliff: Jian'an and the Three Kingdoms*, by Xiaofei Tian
109. *Speaking of Profit: Bao Shichen and Reform in Nineteenth-Century China*, by William T. Rowe

110. *Building for Oil: Daqing and the Formation of the Chinese Socialist State,* by Hou Li
111. *Reading Philosophy, Writing Poetry: Intertextual Modes of Making Meaning in Early Medieval China,* by Wendy Swartz
112. *Writing for Print: Publishing and the Making of Textual Authority in Late Imperial China,* by Suyoung Son
113. *Shen Gua's Empiricism,* by Ya Zuo
114. *Just a Song: Chinese Lyrics from the Eleventh and Early Twelfth Centuries,* by Stephen Owen
115. *Shrines to Living Men in the Ming Political Cosmos,* by Sarah Schneewind
116. *In the Wake of the Mongols: The Making of a New Social Order in North China, 1200–1600,* by Jinping Wang
117. *Opera, Society, and Politics in Modern China,* by Hsiao-t'i Li
118. *Imperiled Destinies: The Daoist Quest for Deliverance in Medieval China,* by Franciscus Verellen
119. *Ethnic Chrysalis: China's Orochen People and the Legacy of Qing Borderland Administration,* by Loretta Kim
120. *The Paradox of Being: Truth, Identity, and Images in Daoism,* by Poul Andersen
121. *Feeling the Past in Seventeenth-Century China,* by Xiaoqiao Ling
122. *The Chinese Dreamscape, 300 BCE–800 CE,* by Robert Ford Campany
123. *Structures of the Earth: Metageographies of Early Medieval China,* by D. Jonathan Felt
124. *Anecdote, Network, Gossip, Performance: Essays on the* Shishuo xinyu, by Jack W. Chen
125. *Testing the Literary: Prose and the Aesthetic in Early Modern China,* by Alexander Des Forges
126. *Du Fu Transforms: Tradition and Ethics amid Societal Collapse,* by Lucas Rambo Bender
127. *Chinese History: A New Manual (Enlarged Sixth Edition),* Vol. 1, by Endymion Wilkinson
128. *Chinese History: A New Manual (Enlarged Sixth Edition),* Vol. 2, by Endymion Wilkinson
129. *Wang Anshi and Song Poetic Culture,* by Xiaoshan Yang
130. *Localizing Learning: The Literati Enterprise in Wuzhou, 1100–1600,* by Peter K. Bol
131. *Making the Gods Speak: The Ritual Production of Revelation in Chinese Religious History,* by Vincent Goossaert
132. *Lineages Embedded in Temple Networks: Daoism and Local Society in Ming China,* by Richard G. Wang
133. *Rival Partners: How Taiwanese Entrepreneurs and Guangdong Officials Forged the China Development Model,* by Wu Jieh-min; translated by Stacy Mosher
134. *Saying All That Can Be Said: The Art of Describing Sex in* Jin Ping Mei, by Keith McMahon